T·H·E
WORD
OF THE
CROSS

A ●◑◐◒◓◔
CONTEMPORARY
THEOLOGY OF
EVANGELISM

LEWIS A. DRUMMOND
FOREWORD BY J. I. PACKER

BROADMAN PRESS
NASHVILLE, TENNESSEE

© Copyright 1992 ● Broadman Press

All rights reserved

4262-55

ISBN: 0-8054-6255-4

Dewey Decimal Classification: 269

Subject Heading: EVANGELISTIC WORK

Library of Congress Catalog Card Number: 90-19769

Printed in the United States of America

Library of Congress Cataloging-in-Publication Data

Drummond, Lewis A.

The word of the cross : a contemporary theology of evangelism /

Lewis A. Drummond

   p. cm.

Includes bibliographical references and index.

ISBN 0-8054-6255-4

1. Evangelistic work—Philosophy.   I. Title.

BV3790.D76 1992

269'.2—dc20   90-19769

          CIP

Foreword

There is something badly wrong with a Christian who does not have a passion for evangelism. As a Puritan once put it, a child of God does not want to go to heaven without company. To wish to share one's knowledge of the Savior with others is natural, and to do so is felt as a privilege, just as it is seen to be a duty, a central element in neighbor love. My neighbor's deepest need is to know the love of God in Jesus Christ, and my claim to love him or her is hollow if I make no attempt to meet that need as best I can. The activity that this attempt involves is what is meant by evangelism.

Evangelism is in essence the communicating of a message—good news about Jesus Christ as the source of life and hope for lost sinners. Evangelism has been described as one beggar telling another beggar where to find bread. When Paul declared himself debtor to the world, owing the gospel to everyone because everyone needs it, he identified himself as an evangelist, a man committed to the ministry of sharing the good news as often and as widely as he could. Paul was in many ways unique, but not in this. Every Christian is called and, when in spiritual health, actually desires to be an evangelist in this sense.

However, there is confusion about evangelism in the modern church. The trouble comes from our habit of defining the activity institutionally and behaviorally rather than theocentrically and theologically. Some give the name of *evangelism* to any kind of meeting in which the leader works up to an altar call of some sort, never mind what has or has not been affirmed before the call comes. Others will equate evangelism with any and every activity that expresses goodwill to persons outside the church, but these behavioral definitions of evangelism are imprecise. Any adequate definition will be cognitive, formulated in terms of the message that is being conveyed by means of the teaching, modeling, and institutional structuring that takes place. So the first step in learning to practice evangelism is to master the message one is sent to deliver.

This is where Dr. Drummond's book will help many. Starting at the beginning and taking nothing for granted, he draws out a full-scale theology of evangelism for evangelism—a theology that centers upon and is constantly controlled by the gospel itself. He ranges widely—current confusions about the message made that necessary—but nothing here is irrelevant to the evangelistic task. Instruction for the head, inspiration for the heart, and incentives to practical action are blended throughout. The church has cause to be grateful to the author for what he has done.

Evangelism unifies: that those who work together to spread the gospel find themselves drawn together in other ways is a matter of constant experience. In recent years, theological and political tensions have rocked Dr. Drummond's own denomination. Evangelism has always been that denomination's secret of strength and solidarity and its major contribution to the rest of the Christian world. Is it too much to hope that togetherness in evangelism on Dr. Drummond's model will become a means of reducing tensions elsewhere, as it becomes clearer to all parties what the truth of the spiritual gospel really involves? I, at all events, find myself hoping and praying for this to happen as I commend this fine book to the people of God.

J. I. Packer

Introduction

The task of evangelism has captivated the contemporary church as have few other interests. Decline in membership of many mainline denominations in the West and the phenomenal growth of the churches in the emerging nations have catapulted world outreach to top priority on many church agendas. The church has never seriously questioned its duty to fulfill the Great Commission. It must do so to be worthy of its name as the church of Jesus Christ, for He came to seek and "to save that which was lost" (Matt. 18:11, KJV). The nature of the kingdom of God impels Christians to be about the work of fitting people to become citizens of that kingdom.

At the heart of the kingdom stands the biblical mandate to evangelize. The Great Commission (Matt. 28:19-20) still stands as the marching orders of God's people. A person becomes a member of God's kingdom by experiencing the full redemption Jesus Christ offers. Such personal experiences populate the kingdom. The kingdom demands evangelism.

What is evangelism? Is it a series of actions one person simply trains another to perform? Or does it have deeper roots? The thesis of this work is that true evangelism grows out of deep theological roots. Evangelization revolves around *being* and *doing* as well as *telling*. The Lord demonstrated this in His earthly ministry. From His example and teaching, evangelism can be defined as:

> A concerted effort in the power of the Holy Spirit to confront unbelievers with the truth about Jesus Christ and the claims of our Lord (Acts 2:22-24,31) with a view to leading unbelievers into repentance toward God and faith in our Lord Jesus Christ (Acts 20:21) and thus into the fellowship of His church so they may grow in the Spirit.

Some would broaden the definition; others would narrow it. Still, this understanding of evangelization will form the background of this study.

To evangelize means many things. Christ's evangelizers are to *be* something: Christlike in character. Effective evangelists *do* something: minister to the whole person in the multiplicity of their needs. Faithful evangelists must also *tell* something: good news, the gospel of Jesus

Christ, the "word of the cross" (1 Cor. 1:18). "Telling" is not in any sense opposed to or isolated from "being" and "doing." Rather, each complements the other in fulfilling the Great Commission. These various aspects of ministry ought to be done with excellence in the power of God. The sharing of the gospel, as well as the "doing" and "being" of the gospel, should be undertaken with knowledge, commitment, and zeal.

This *contemporary* theology of evangelism seeks to help Christ's twenty-first century church build a well-rounded, informed, solid foundation from which to proclaim the evangelistic message. When the church acquires a firm hold on the gospel, the ministry of evangelization will be undertaken with knowledge, commitment, and zeal. This evangelistic theology is called a *contemporary* theology because it attempts to come to grips with what contemporary theologians are saying about evangelization. The writer stands firmly based in the evangelical perspective. Still people learn from those with whom they differ. Thus, thinkers from various viewpoints are encountered, examined, thanked for positive contributions, and challenged at key points. Granted, a full, balanced presentation of the thought of each theologian quoted is not undertaken. Such would require several volumes. The work may appear quite traditional in many respects. This is expected. The church through the ages has not been all wrong. The contribution of this work is to bring time-honored evangelical thought to the contemporary scene, interact with differing viewpoints, and challenge the church with its task for the future. In so doing, hopefully, an evangelical theology is not a relic of the past but relevant and vital to meet current needs.

This contemporary work is a theology of *evangelism*. It is not a pure systematical theological treatise. It seeks to touch the heartbeat of the contemporary church. Theological concerns dominate, but it contains elements of pragmatic and devotional materials. A theology of evangelism demands such.

I must thank those whose contribution to the production of this work has been invaluable. Many have made suggestions and given input. In particular, Dr. J. I. Packer, who wrote the foreword, has been most helpful. Faithful secretaries spent many hours on the manuscript. My wife, Betty, did her usual excellent work of proofreading. Above all, I thank my students who through the years listened to, and helped shape, my lectures on the theology of evangelism. They are the unseen fountains who produced much of the material in this book. Simply put, this is the production of many hands, and I express my gratitude to all. My prayer is that God will use it to spur us on to sharing the gospel with knowledge and zeal, for people do need to hear of Jesus Christ and His love.

Lewis A. Drummond

Contents

Part I

The Basis of the Theological Enterprise:
The Question of Authority

Part II

The Trinitarian God of the Bible and Evangelism:
A Unity of Purpose

Part III

Key Biblical Words in Evangelism:
A Scriptural Survey

Part IV

The Ministry of Evangelism:
A Pragmatic Theological Study

The Word of the Cross is folly
to those who are perishing, but
to us who are being saved
it is the power of God.
1 Corinthians 1:18

Part I

The Basis of the Theological Enterprise:
The Question of Authority

Introduction

The fundamental issue of the theological hour is the question of authority. Upon what firm basis do we attempt to formulate our Christian thought structures and test our conclusions? The church has given a myriad of answers to this obvious, basic query.

Some segments of the professing Christian community place significant stress and reliance on *tradition*. This, they say, is a primary source of truth. The Roman Catholic Church has been especially noted for such an approach. It teaches that when the pope speaks on faith and morals ex cathedra, "from the chair of Peter," he speaks infallibly. His words on religious and ethical matters thus become an authoritative truth tradition. Likewise, when the official councils of the church lay down doctrines and precepts, they become binding. Hence, a vast store of authoritative traditions have arisen.

Segments of the Christian church are not alone in this philosophy of religious authority. The Jewish traditional system in Jesus' day was vast, complex, and binding. The result: *Midrash, Mishnah, Halakhah*, etc. The Pharisees, for example, exalted these traditions even above their Holy Scriptures. Jesus encountered that mind-set constantly and usually rebuked it. Other world religions often take a similar stance on traditions handed down through the ages, that is, the *Vedas* of Hinduism, the *Koran* of Islam, and similar writings.

Some religions center authority on inspired, authoritative personalities: Confucius, Buddha, Muhammad, and a host of others. Often their concepts are relied upon as absolute truth. Christian believers affirm the words of Jesus as authoritative and true.

Since the Enlightenment, however, a new source of authority has arisen, which has impacted secular and theological circles alike, particularly in the West. It has been called "the rise of rationalism." Rationalism, coupled with empiricism (the scientific method), has all but dominated the intellectual Western world over the past three hundred years. Moreover, it shows little signs of abating. Masses of people build their entire structures of truth, reality, and value on that basis. In its Christian theological expression, rationalism must be dealt with.

The list of truth "sources" could go on. The issue is, however, where should those who profess the Christian faith finally resort when an authoritative word is demanded? Let it be understood, an authoritative word of truth *is* demanded, especially in constructing theological claims. However, it is right there the situation often gets muddled. One would think something of a basic unanimity might prevail among Christian thinkers in the vital realm of seeking truth. However, they have obviously resorted to many approaches. The results have been disagreement, despair, disillusionment, even serious deviations from the faith "once for all delivered to the saints" (Jude 3).

So the question of authority stands in high profile as one of the basic problems to solve. Actually, this issue must be settled before one can even begin to think about the faith, let alone make pronouncements concerning it in formulating theological axioms. Part I of this work takes up the knotty problem of authority and what it means regarding the centrality of evangelism in the church's mission. One must be established on firm epistemological ground before even beginning to formulate postulates on Christian evangelization.

1

Seeking Authority in Theology:
The Starting Point

"By what authority"? (Matt. 21:23)

Introduction

Every endeavor in life demands a starting point. Moreover, how one starts largely determines direction and thus where one ultimately arrives. Constructing a theology of evangelism proves to be no exception. Therefore, the question that thrusts itself to the fore is: How and where does one begin?

In answer to the above foundational query, Professor Clark Pinnock said the following:

> The central problem for theology is *its own epistemological base*. From what fountainhead does theology acquire the information from which she forms her doctrinal models and tests her hypotheses? What is the *principium theologia* which measures and authenticates the subject matter for theology and preaching? No endeavor in theology can *begin* until some kind of answer is given. . . . All issues pale before this one. It is the continental divide in Christian theology. Everything hangs on our solution to it.[1]

Professor Pinnock is certainly correct in saying that the issue of finding authority for theological truth claims, as it emerges out of a comprehensive epistemological base, stands as the primary issue in fabricating a theology of evangelism.[2] The key question is: How does a person authenticate what he or she says about God? That constitutes the very starting point.

Constructing an epistemological base whereby one can form "doctrinal models and test . . . hypotheses," as Pinnock put it, is an individual's initial responsibility. The venture into the ambiguous world of epistemology is not without some fear and perhaps presumption. It is fearful because first of all it calls for some rather plodding, pedantic argumentation. Then, secondly, it is an attempt to discover where to find authoritative theological truth. That may be somewhat presumptuous, for such truth is in some respects quite difficult to uncover. However, fearful, presumptuous, or not, the student must forge ahead, for

Pinnock was absolutely right: "no endeavor in theology can *begin*" until this is accomplished.

The Epistemological Base for a Theology of Evangelism

Epistemology can be defined as "the branch of philosophy which investigates the origin, structure, methods, and validity of knowledge. . . . The term *theory of knowledge* is a common English equivalent of epistemology."[3] In simple terms, epistemology essentially seeks to discover the sources of reliable and authoritative truth and the way one thus comes into contact with reality. Everyone operates with some sort of epistemology. Everyone resorts to some basis of authority for one's truth claims. Thus, everyone does have an epistemology and needs to be aware of his epistemological methodologies, especially in theology.

The task of building an explicit epistemological base for an individual theology of evangelism can be launched by examining the interplay of the mind with reality as a person comes into contact with what he conceives to be sources of truth, that is, those "mechanisms"[4] whereby he thinks he comes into contact with truth and reality. Actually, there are several such "sources" to which the mind reacts.

Empirical Data

The first obvious source or contact with truth is through what philosophers call *empiricism*, that is, sense perception. Everyone comes into regular encounters with the real world through sense perception. For example, as I write these words, I feel the pen in my hand, see the words appearing on the page, and hear the subtle scratch of the pen point on paper. What a person sees, touches, smells, tastes, and hears enables him to become aware of the "facts" of the world out there and constitutes an empirical experience. Those "facts" are called empirical data, perceived by the mind's empirical faculties. Normally, a person relies on those empirical mechanisms to make what is considered to be truth claims about the real world. Hence, an individual daily makes statements like: "I was there, I saw it, I know it is true." Much of human awareness of the objective world comes through empirical data.

Rational Concepts

Another clear claim to truth is *rationalism*. This epistemological principle gets a hefty workout every day. For example, whenever two plus two is added correctly, the conclusion has been reached through the rationalistic, logical process. All mathematical reasoning is an extension of rational logic, even the complex labyrinths of higher mathematics, such as Einstein's $E=MC^2$. Another example of logical rationalism is the simple Aristotelian syllogism:

All people are mortal.
I am a person.
Therefore, I am mortal.

Everyone uses this epistemological principle constantly being quite confident that statements like "two plus two equal five" stand in error. They fail the rational criteria of truth. We regularly bring such a test to life's encounters to validate what claims to be true.

A Priori Truth

Then there is a little more obscure principle called *a priori* truth. *A priori* concepts are those innate realities we find "just there." One cannot rationally or empirically demonstrate them, at least not incontestably. Still, we sense they are there and are real. What are some of these *a priori* realities? A big debate rages as to whether they exist at all, let alone what they are. But most thinkers positive to the general idea list things like *self-consciousness* (Rene Descartes held to this.), *moral consciousness* (Immanuel Kant argued for this, calling it the "categorical imperative."), the *concept of God* (Many hold to this position.). They constitute the truth we assume in our cognitive (thinking) activities because, when we think, we discover them simply *there.* I find it rather difficult even to think without granting at least some *a priori* realities. Descartes had it right when he said, "I think, therefore I am." I assume my own self-consciousness when I think. Can anyone *really* think about *all* reality and deny there are at least some *a priori* principles? Too many vistas of truth and reality are barred from investigation if one refuses to accept the validity of *a priori* concepts, even if they are relatively few in number.

There may well be other epistemological principles (sources from which we discover truth and reality) such as *intuitionalism*; nonetheless, the above principles illustrate some general precepts of epistemology.

There is, however, another epistemological principle which Christians put forth as a source of truth. Great importance is placed on it. Believers in Jesus Christ hold to the epistemological principle called *revelation.*[5] Christians declare God has revealed Himself, and in such a self-disclosure one can arrive at authoritative truth concerning God's nature, actions, and expectations. This is an epistemological truth claim believers continually make. However, this principle seems to raise questions.

Revelational Truth

"Oh," retorts the critic concerning revelational truth claims, "One must have *faith* to accept as true the concepts Christians claim God *reveals* about Himself. One must *believe* to say any revelation is true." The clear implication of this quite common rejoinder to the Christian thinker is that empiricism, rationalism, and *a priori* concepts are on a different plane of authority than revelation, because a person has to *believe* to accept revelational realities. They seem to say (at least the more unsophisticated thinkers) that empiricism, rationalism, etc. need no "faith" to be accepted as valid sources of truth. They imply, and may well believe, their epistemological principles stand superior to revelation, because they feel they need no "faith" to authenticate their position. Are they right? If they are, believers do have a problem, for revelational truth claims certainly are a faith demanding presupposition.

An Important Principle

All epistemological principles are what philosophers call presuppositions. They are all assumptions upon which one operates in cognition. Very few, if any, epistemologists deny this central reality. In other words, empiricism, rationalism, *a priori* concepts, and intuitionalism, as well as revelation are all presuppositions. Their validity cannot be demonstrated uncontestably; hence, they are *presupposed* as valid sources of truth and reality. Why cannot their validity be incontestably established? The reason is quite obvious; one must assume these types of epistemological principles to use them. For example, we are forced to assume, or presuppose, the validity of empiricism to arrive at what one thinks is true from empirical input. We are compelled to believe that empiricism is a valid source of truth about reality to accept empirical data when it is encountered. Simply put, it begs the question; one has to use empiricism to "prove" empirical data. So we must *believe* our sense perception is bringing us in contact with reality. Thus it is a presupposition. All such epistemological principles are presuppositions.

The conclusion to this epistemological principle jumps right out at one. In light of the fact that all epistemological "sources" of truth are presuppositional in nature, it takes "faith," or "believing," to accept and assimilate any epistemological truth claims. All presuppositions are a "leap of faith." Therefore, empiricism, rationalism, *a priori* concepts, and intuitionalism rest on the same epistemological, presuppositional "leap of faith" plane as does revelation. They all demand "believing," in that cognitive sense. So revelation, at least in principle, stands as a valid claim to truth as well as any other epistemological claim. Revelational truth claims just cannot be *a priori* ruled out of court by implying they rest on another epistemological level because it takes a "leap of faith" to accept. All truth claims are on that plane in principle.

The Problem

Probably the reason revelation seems different to many is the fact that we live much of our daily life thinking about empirical and rational realities. Familiarity with these sorts of truth claims thus seems to elevate them above the claims of revelation. Moreover, the Western world's virtual worship of the scientific method, which is a purely rational-empirical method, has no doubt deepened the problem as well. Even enamorment with materialism has contributed to this attitude. But again, let it be stressed, all the epistemological principles we have been discussing are presuppositions, demanding faith to accept their claims, and thus, in principle, rest on the same basis.

Therefore, Christian believers need not take a back seat regarding revelational truth claims and feel they cannot "prove" their claims as can the materialists with their empirical-rational methodologies. They cannot "prove" their claims either. In a very real sense, all truth claims, because they are presuppositions, defy final, formal, utterly incontestable proof of reality. This may sound as if we do not really know anything for certain. I suppose, in a formal sense, we do not. But such is hardly a tenable, workable epistemology. All people live and act upon what they understand to be true. This quandary shall be approached later. Revelation is, in principle, as valid a source of truth as anything else, at least in the formal fashion we have been arguing.

Actually, a solid case can be made for accepting a revelational presupposition—a very wise cognitive move. Why? Because revelation provides data to develop a far more comprehensive, broader understanding of reality. It opens up realms of truth and reality otherwise closed if one rejects revelational data. Actually, the mature Christian believer is not a narrow-minded thinker as often accused; he or she is broader in epistemological scope because of the acceptance of another source of truth and reality: revelation. That presuppositional acceptance can display beautiful vistas of reality otherwise barred from one's cognitive life.

The more of reality one accepts, the more valid it makes one's worldview. The scientists and others who restrict themselves to empirical and rationalistic presuppositions alone are actually the narrow-minded people. Of course, they can reject revelation as a source of truth, such is their cognitive privilege; however, that is probably why the scientific method in isolation fails to explain *all* reality. A purely rational-empiricism epistemology simply cannot explain spiritual realities—not even realities like love or peace of mind, let alone God. Utopia, as is now clear, is not to be found in the laboratory alone. So revelational presuppositions are not only as valid as others in principle, but also they help create a more comprehensive, coherent worldview. But more of this line of argumentation in a moment. First, we must come to grips with a "game" we play in all cognitive activity.

An Epistemological Game

Everyday life is obviously filled with the cognitive, presuppositional exercises we have been discussing. That is how we arrive at what we consider true and real, and in such a cognitive setting we constantly play a little game.

When we were children, many of us played the game we called "king-of-the-hill." Remember how it went? You would climb to the top of a small hill, then your playmates would scramble up in an attempt to send you tumbling down so they might take their stand on the top as "king-of-the-hill." Epistemologically, we constantly play that sort of game. At one time we make empiricism "king," at other times rationalism. That is, on one occasion we rely primarily on our empirical experience to give us truth; on other occasions rationalism takes first place. There is some balance between the competing players, of course. This cognitive exercise is how we attempt to arrive at a coherent view of reality.

Persons normally play the cognitive game quite unconsciously. But if a conscious conflict between two or more epistemological presuppositions arises, the balance breaks, and then the game becomes very explicit—if not quite disturbing. For example, seeing a cow flying by the window causes a real cognitive dilemma. Rationally, people know cows do not fly, but one just sailed by. Suddenly rationalism and empiricism come into conflict with each other. So persons have to play "king-of-the-hill" to decide which presupposition, rationalism or empiricism, is going to be "king." Which will get top priority, or authority, rational awareness or empirical experience? A decision must be made to resolve the cognitive dilemma. Did experience show a cow flying, or not? This illustration is an extreme instance, but people play that game constantly.

Whenever or however an epistemological conflict arises, people try desperately to work out the solution because all demand that the world of cognitive experiences be internally *coherent*. The world must hold together and "make sense" on the basis of epistemological experiences. Humanity cannot live with major epistemological conflicts raging. Those who forsake demanding coherence in their thinking processes become psychotic. Coherence is the constant quest of the mind. Thus people play the "king-of-the-hill" game and decide which epistemological presupposition will rise as the top authority in given situations. This process resolves most dilemmas, even if a mystery is left on rare occasions.

The Relation of Revelation to Religious Truth Claims

How does all of this relate to Christian commitment to truth derived from revelation which is, in principle, as valid a presupposition as rationalism or any of the other epistemological presuppositions? What do people do with revelational presupposition as they cognitively build their system of truth—especially theological truth? Simply put, how is revelation relative to other epistemological presuppositions? Well, if there is no conflict between revelation and, for example, rationalism, no problem is raised. As a case of point, when the Bible (which many Christians say is revelational truth[6]) says that Jesus sat by the Sea of Galilee and taught, there is no rational or empirical conflict problem with revelation. Someone sitting by a seaside and teaching is not irrational or nonempirical. There should be no problem on such issues. However, when Jesus walked across the water to the other side of the Sea, that is a rational problem. Rationally, no one walks on water. We have a serious conflict between rationalism and revelation. What do we do? There is no alternative to playing "king-of-the-hill." Which epistemological presupposition will get one's vote for final truth and authority? Will it be the revelational claim that Jesus walked on water, or the rational claim that people cannot walk over the waves? This decision is necessary to have a coherent world. People cannot rest in a conflicting epistemological dualism and keep their sanity.

Evangelical Christians have usually opted for revelation as the *final* authority for truth and reality when such cognitive conflicts arise. They make revelation "king." Evangelicals (the term *Evangelical*, although generally understood, will be defined in detail in the next chapter) do not deny rationalism and empirical claims when there is no conflict; they simply place revelation as superior when and if a real conflict between competing principles surfaces. Obviously, all thinkers, even some who profess Christianity, have not done so. There are those who, when it comes to the crunch, put their stock in rationalism or intuitionalism or some other presuppositional approach. Consequently, they develop some explanation for subjugating an obvious revelational claim to another epistemological presupposition, for they, too, must have a coherent world to keep their own sanity.[7] One cannot just ignore a competing claim. Evangelicals traditionally choose revelation as the theological "king" of presuppositions. Is there a rationale for so doing?

The Primary Issue

Is it wise for Evangelicals to hold that revelation is the proper "king-of-the-hill" when epistemological presuppositions come in conflict with revelational claims? Perhaps there is a prior question: *Does this approach of most Evangelicals produce the most comprehensive worldview?* Is the evangelical-revelational epistemology, as over against a pure rational-empirical approach, theologically or otherwise, the most comprehensive view of reality? Is it internally *coherent*, does it *correspond* to the experience of reality, is it *noncontradictory*, and does it best encompass and explain one's apprehension of truth and reality?[8] Such is the key issue. The most comprehensive, noncontradicting, corresponding, coherent view is the best view. Thus, Evangelicals are forced to bring to their revelational superiority claims the test of things fitting together in a system that makes the best sense. If they are to make those claims stick, they must show that a revelational epistemology really does pass the test with the highest marks.[9] Can it be done? The conviction of many Evangelical thinkers is yes; revelational supremacy in truth claims concerning God does produce the best, inclusive epistemological approach to truth and reality. They hold it passes best the tests of internal coherence, noncontraction, and correspondence. It corresponds to reality in a better comprehensive fashion than any other approach.

I confess I take my epistemological stand with Evangelicals on the supremacy of revelation in truth about God. But can one argue convincingly for such an epistemological cause? Its importance is obvious; one's theology hangs in the balance.

The Argument

The defense of the superiority of revelational, presuppositional truth claims about God has its beginning with who and what most believers say God actually is.[10] The argument may seem rather long and pedantic; yet, it is vital to the building of a convincing case. Therefore, let the argument of looking at the evangelical claims concerning God's essential character begin.

God as a Worshipful Being

Evangelical Christians, most Christians for that matter, hold that there is an Ultimate Being who is the ground of all being and is deemed worthy of worship. It follows that if the object is genuinely deemed to be worshipful, certain attributes that can be cognitively expressed theologically *must* be true of that being.[11] First, true worship is directed towards:

A Supernatural Being.—All genuine religious thought and experience contains a certain element of *mystery* surrounding the worshipful object. This sense of mystery always surfaces in true worship. The mode of being and functioning of the worshipful object comes as essentially different from the familiar processes in things and persons that are experienced on a merely empirical and rational basis. The Worshipful comes to persons as transcending the limited time-space world. In a word, God possesses something of a *supernatural quality*. If this were not true, people would hardly *worship* Him, although they might *admire* Him.

A Being of Transcendent Value.—The object of genuine worship must further be one of profound worth or value. This follows because real worship implies *adoration*, and such a deep and significant emotion can only be evoked by that which is felt to possess transcendent value. This aspect of the Worshipful is important in that it excludes from the ranks of true religious experience that of the cults and perverted paganism. The reason is: the end purpose of these religious systems is merely to satisfy human temporal cravings or mollify the hostility of "demons." The objects of this kind of "worship" can hardly be seen as possessing transcendent worth. However, the worshipful Being in all *true* religious experience must be One who possesses a supernatural nature and has transcendent value. Real worship implies it, and this is intuitively grasped when persons actually adore God. Of course, in stressing the transcendence of God, it is easy to downplay or even ignore His imminence. We must avoid this danger . The rest of this book will attempt to keep these two aspects of God's nature in dynamic balance. However, for the momentary sake of the argument, His transcendence is emphasized.

A Being of Transcendent Power.—Genuine worship is permeated with a sense of *awe*; and the objective correlate of awe is power, that is, power that is mysterious and overwhelming. Of course, the power of the Worshipful is not *merely* mysterious. For power to inspire real awe, it must also be a transcendent power of ultimate worth. Few would worship the split atom, as powerful as that is. To be *religious* awe, the object of our awe must be an unlimited powerful object of transcendent worth, as seen above.

A Being of Perfection.—Moreover, the Worshipful, being endued with transcendent power and value, must be free from any imperfection. God must be *perfect*; and if God is perfect, He is infinite, for finitude implies limitation. Further, if God is perfect, He must also be one. This follows, for a plurality of ultimate beings is untenable: that would precipitate an ultimate metaphysical dualism. Not only that, a perfect being cannot have a mere transitory existence. He must be above time. He cannot exist fully *in* it. This follows because time as humanity knows it is incomplete, finite, and relative.[12] Every conceived time is part of a larger time, which is part of an even larger time, *ad infinitum*. Therefore, to conceive of God as existing in time is to conceive of Him as being conditioned. This is impossible for a perfect being. This does not mean that God *excludes* time. He is not *timeless*, that is, standing aloof from the temporal order and, consequently, from the world of persons as the old deists claimed. Actually, the time order depends upon Him. Thus God must somehow *include* time in His being while He somehow *transcends* it. This idea is the key to the real meaning of "eternity." Eternity is not just everlasting time or mere timelessness. It is a mode of being which at once transcends, but also includes, time. The same argument holds for space as well. This line of thought will be taken up in more detail in a later chapter.

Thus, the worshipful Being is endued with "Mystery, Power, and Value"—in all essentials, Rudolf Otto's *Mysterium Tremendum et Fascinans*.[13] This is the essence of genuine religious experience and its reasonable implications and conclusions. So it can be seen that the attributes of true worship demand of its "Object" that which are in line with what Evangelicals say of its "God."

What then is the conclusion of this line of reasoning? First, the basic tenets of mature evangelicalism relative to the ultimate nature of God are found in the very essence of worship. Theology and mature religious experience come together coherently. Secondly, genuine religious experience implies and points to a "suprarational"[14] strain in the conceptualization of God. Mature religion forces the understanding of God as ultimately "suprarational." Evangelicals are moved religiously to accept a suprarational God.[15] This is the only conclusion to draw to give the concept of God all that the word *God* means.

As has been implied earlier, philosopher-theologian Rudolf Otto is very sensitive to this central idea and its importance in all theology. His line of reasoning is most helpful. It will aid us to see even more clearly the argument concerning the centrality of the suprarational strain in apprehending God and what all this means in building our case for the supremacy of revelation in our epistemological base in formulating theology.

Suprarational Theology in the Thought of Rudolph Otto

Otto begins his argument by pointing out that most theologians are willing to acknowledge formally the suprarational in religious experience. But when it comes to formulating their *theological claims*, Otto contends they tend to lapse into a purely rationalistic, formal theology; ultraconservatives and ultraliberals alike often do this. Otto protested against this regress into Christian rationalism, and quite correctly so. In his classic work *Das Heilige*, he set out what he considered to be the proper propositional analysis of the Christian faith.

Otto took, as a starting point, the concept of God as "holy." He pointed out that it is commonly held that the distinctive character of the

Worshipful is "holiness," that is, moral and ethical perfection that sets Him apart as the "Holy Other." Few, if any, believers would have problems with such a claim; but surely, mere human rational concepts, and hence the verbalizing of those concepts, cannot exhaust the meaning of "Holy" when it is used to describe an aspect of God's perfect, ultimate nature. There is something more in the apprehension of any of the divine attributes than can be expressed in mere rational terms. No matter what characteristics we ascribe to God, for example, power, love, wisdom, all human descriptions fall short of giving these terms their *ultimate, perfect* meaning. There is something more in these terms than human cognition can ever verbalize or exhaust. Otto called this "something more" the "numinous." Apprehension of the numinous cannot be fully conceptually defined. If we could fully grasp the "something more," the theologian would be ultimate and perfect also. God's final, ultimate nature is obviously beyond finite, human cognition. Yet, the numinous can be religiously experienced. Therefore, one must "direct his mind to a moment of deeply-felt religious experience, as little as possible qualified by other forms of consciousness"[16] to grasp the significance and meaning of the idea of the numinous "Holy Other."

Such an analysis of the numinous experience throws light on the three aspects of one's religious life. Otto described it in the previously quoted phrase *mysterium tremendum et fascinans*. The *mysterium* aspect of the numinous experience indicates that one is in contact with something "other," that is, something "whose kind and character are incommensurable with our own, and before which we therefore recoil in a wonder that strikes us chill and numb."[17] The *tremendum et fascinans* gives content to this *mysterium* aspect of the experience. The *tremendum* has three elements: (1) the *numen* is grasped as awe inspiring, (2) as overwhelming in might and majesty, and (3) as superabounding in living energy and "urgency." The *fascinans* describes the *numen* as a mysterious, rapturous experience. That is the "numinous experience." But is the *numen* personal? This is a most important question for us who are persons. We would hardly be moved to worship any entity that is not "person," even if the *numen* does create within us something of a *mysterium tremendum et fascinous* reaction.

The answer to the above question can be found by looking at reality *as a whole*. Personhood is one thing that appears central to all reality. Intuition brings the recognition that "personality" is at the very heart of the real. In the final analysis of reality, personhood matters most. It is the belief that the person or entity is more than mere materialistic or crass behavioristic nature, and of far more worth. A rationalistic, naturalistic view of human personhood does not satisfy.[18] In their deepest moments human beings know they are having real experiences. Human beings are not the mere sum of them, as behaviorists claim.

It is also true that human beings are on a search for transcendence. They are constantly on a quest to grow, develop, and be more than they *capability of a person to transcend reality is reality's most important matter.* are at the moment. This seeking for transcendence presupposes true personhood, for only a Person can transcend a person. Naturalism, that is, pure empiricism and/or rationalism, precludes transcendence. A rock can hardly transcend a rock, or a dog a dog. Thus it seems most reasonable to conclude that transcendent personhood lies at the core of the thing called reality, even though empiricism and/or rationalism may fail to verify it. Not only is transcendent personhood at the center of all things, it is the most important entity of reality.

Now if personhood and transcendence rest at the center of reality, why does it seem strange to presuppose that the ultimate, suprarational transcendent Reality who calls mankind to worship is *Person*? It is not strange at all. Actually, the apprehension of reality virtually demands it. If God is perfect, that is, the highest concept the human mind can grasp, and if personhood is the most worthy entity perceived by cognitive life, then it follows that God must be Person. Any other conclusion would be quite absurd. Moreover, the Worshipful must be a Person who is the ultimate Source of all personhood. This is no doubt why Augustine said, "We are restless, O God, until we rest in thee." Our whole religious experience points to a *Person* whom we address as the *mysterium, tremendum et facunus*—the personal "Holy Other."

This description of God as "Holy Other" must not be given a purely rational, naturalistic meaning. The emotions, thoughts, and expressions excited by the *numen* are not like simple, natural, rational-empirical reactions. The glory of God is something that eye cannot behold, or tongue tell. Actually, the numinous consciousness is understood far more coherently as an *a priori* consciousness. As Otto argued:

> It issues from the deepest foundation of cognitive apprehension that the soul possesses, and, though it of course comes into being in and amid the sensory data and empirical material of the natural world and cannot anticipate or dispense with those, yet it does not arise *out of* them, but only *by their means*.[19]

And this *a priori* endowment of the capacity for the numinous experience is a gift that *all* possess. An objective investigation of all societies and peoples demonstrates this.

This is the suprarational strand in the idea of the Holy. Yet how can the religious consciousness, if the Holy transcends rational concepts, attribute conceptual characteristics to the numinous object? Otto's answer is found in what is conveyed by the word *schematism*.[20] What Otto meant by *schematism* is:

The emotions which the numinous object evokes in us, though qualitatively unique, have a *felt analogy* with certain emotions evoked in us by
attributes and objects in ordinary experiences of which we *can* form clear
conceptions. It is on the basis of these felt analogies that a 'conceptual
translation' or schematism of the pure numinous content becomes
possible.[21]

There is an "inward necessity of the mind," as Otto put it, to think of
deity as overwhelmingly possessing value and power even though those
terms do not exhaust the *numen*. Yet, the "felt analogy" does give those
terms meaning as far as we finite humans can grasp any truth.
It is clear that "analogy" implies difference as well as identity. In the
case of the numinous experience, the difference is of vital importance,
for the numinous experience comes to us in the aura of a supranatural,
suprahuman, suprarational occurrence. Still, one is tempted to rational-
ize the experience and say this is the sum and substance of it all. This is
probably due to the fact that it is most difficult to maintain the "white-
hot temperature" of the numinous experience and express that. At the
same time, however, a rational strand has its place. Some rational cognition is necessary to even think of the experience. But the rational concepts that grow out of the experience must be understood as finite,
limited expressions only. They are true as far as they go, but they do not
express *ultimate* truth. They simply cannot do so. They are analogies.
Therefore, as Otto has quite clearly shown, the only viable theology
must recognize that God goes beyond mere rational concepts and expressions. Thus we are once again led to the important postulate of a
suprarational, personal God.

A Problem

The primary problem, briefly mentioned above, for a suprarational
understanding of God centers in the criticism that the concept drains
religion and theology of all cognitive meaning. This is a problem, for
religion must have its human expressions, even if they are limited. Otherwise, there would be no theology at all, let alone a theology of evangelism. This criticism can be adequately met by realizing that rational concepts of God are valid statements of the divine nature *as far as they can
express the ultimate God*, even if they do not exhaust God as conceptually
apprehended.

Therefore, it seems there is reasonable justification for the claim that
statements made concerning God have objective validity. They are a
true but finite expression of the nature of the suprarational God. Theological claims are true as far as they can express truth regarding the suprarational God. They are necessitated by the very nature of the mind

when persons try to "think" God, even if they do not fully "explain" God.[22] To say "God is love," is true as far as the infinite "God" and His infinite love can be grasped and expressed by the human mind. It is certainly *not* true to say that "God is hate." Even if God is spoken of in human, limited, logical terms, let it again be stressed that His final nature remains suprarational. Paul said, "The love of Christ . . . surpasses knowledge" (Eph. 3:19). The Bible further states:

> "My thoughts are not your thoughts,
> neither are your ways my ways," says the Lord.
> "For as the heavens are higher than the earth,
> so are my ways higher than your ways
> and my thoughts than your thoughts" (Isa. 55:8-9).

This principle shall be alluded to regularly in this work.

What does all this mean to the general epistemological argument for an evangelical theology? It means that religious experience is just the beginning of the general argument for a suprarational God. There is a more formal argument from the very nature of intellectual thinking, that is, *cognition*.

The Self-Contradictory Nature of Cognition as an Argument for a Suprarational God

Most thinking people generally agree that theology attempts to gain a view of God which will satisfy the human spirit and intellect. What is the criterion of intellectual, theological satisfaction?[23] When all cognition is scrutinized, theological or otherwise, the criterion is found to be *noncontradiction.* The human intellect will not accept as "the real" a concept of any nature that essentially contradicts itself. People simply know it is wrong to say "black is white." The world must make sense, and that precludes basic contradictions, even if at times this leads to "mystery." The issue thus becomes: What is the essence of noncontradictory cognition, and how does it relate to theology?

I hold with many epistemologists when they say the essence of all thinking activity is the *cognitive judgment.* That is, all thinking is essentially a judgment on our experiences, for example, the rose is red, the candy is sweet, the room is cold, etc.[24] These sorts of judgments, most of which are relatively "unconscious," are what move thinking processes along. What if it can be shown that daily cognitive judgments are self-contradictory in a formal sense? Then the rational judgment can hardly express *ultimate* reality. Most would agree that *ultimate* reality must be noncontradictory, and there is the rub. Cognitive judgments do prove to be inherently self-contradictory; therefore, the purely cognitive, rational judgment cannot express the *ultimate* nature of reality. Can that be true?

Can rational cognition, in a formal sense, really be shown to be innately self-contradictory? Yes, as strange as it seems! The reasoning for this rather startling statement is as follows:

Everyone will acknowledge that the cognitive judgment, that is, the essence of thinking, is essentially the assertion of unity in diversity. Thinking unites differences. For example, in the predicative judgment, "The rose is red." Roses and redness are obviously different cognitive entities, yet, in cognition, they are united and thus verbalized: "The rose is red." This is necessary because neither unity nor diversity can be eliminated in predicative thinking. Unless there is a uniting, the terms *rose* and *red* simply "fall apart." Again, unless there is genuine diversity, there is no movement of thought at all. "Roses are roses" says nothing. Real thinking cannot be expressed in the tautological formula "A is A," as philosopher Immanuel Kant correctly pointed out. Therefore, all thinking must *unite differences*. This principle can be expressed as a formula. If *rose* is called "A" and *red* is called "B," the cognitive judgment formula "A is B" can thus express the true form of all thinking activity.

A Cognitive Problem

Do we find "A is B" any improvement over "A is A," however? To some extent, at least a judgment is made. Nevertheless, serious difficulties still assert themselves. The problem emerging centers in the fact that, strictly and formally speaking, B, as long as it is different from A, can be expressed as "not-A." So the cognitive judgment formula actually reads "A is not-A." Now it is evident this formula not only asserts, but it annuls at the same time. This is simple self-contradiction. Consequently, the uniting of differences, which is the goal of all cognition, cannot be expressed as "A is B" and save itself from inherent self-contradiction. Strictly interpreted, it becomes the very essence of self-contradiction which judgments about final reality abhor.

It may be objected, however, that in cognitive judgments it is not implied that A is identical with B. What we actually mean is "A has B," for example, the rose *has* redness, not *is* redness. Does this refinement of the judgment escape the reduction to formal self-contradiction? By no means! It merely disguises the contradiction. In thinking the assertion is made that "A has B." "A has B" is surely the same as saying "A is such-as-to-have-B." Now we dare not say that "such-as-to-have-B" is synonymous with A, for we will have our problem of the tautology again. There will be no movement of thought: for example, roses are roses, etc. "Such-as-to-have-B" must be different from A to have genuine movement of thought. Therefore, let "such-as-to-have-B" be called C. The new formula now reads: "A is C." One would hardly say that this restatement is any improvement over "A is B." Self-contradiction still prevails.

Therefore, *formally speaking*,[25] the uniting of differents produces constant self-contradiction. Still, the life of thought centers around uniting differences. It is done in every conscious, cognitive moment. Moreover, in so doing, valid, true assessments about reality are made. Surely, there must be some way in which the cognitive judgment can successfully accomplish its task of grasping reality without being plagued with constant formal self-contradiction.

Only one answer to this problem seems feasible: the differents in thinking (judgment making) must be seen as elements of a "system," where the overall system is conceived as a whole of mutually implicatory parts. Formal thought rebels at the uniting of bare, self-contained, different units; but if the differents are seen as diverse expressions of a unified, single system, thought is not repulsed. In such a system, let it be called "X," this system necessarily expresses itself as *A* and *B*. Thus, the diversity of the system is not a fact opposed to its unity, for there is nothing within the diversities that is external to the whole unified system. In other words, in this kind of system, identity and diversity are but obverse sides of the same fact. For example, the "heads" and "tails" of a coin are different, but they are merely different sides of the one coin, the coin being the system that unites them. Although *A* and *B* are differents, their very nature is derived from the identity of which they are but expressions. Therefore, the proper formula for cognitive judgments is neither "A is B," nor "A has B"; genuine cognitive judgments are expressed as "Xa is Xb" (*X* representing the system that expressing itself as *a* must also necessarily express itself as *b*). As the British epistemologist F. H. Bradley has said, the unity of "bare conjunctions" is the very essence of contradiction. We must find a system if we are to unite differents.

Common sense says, however, this implies that the bulk of everyday statements or thoughts are self-contradictory, for who in the world constantly looks for a system to unite differences in everyday thinking and/or language? Rarely do we do that. We constantly connect redness with the rose, coldness to the room, etc. To look for a ground or system to mediate these connections is far more the exception than the rule, at least in everyday life.

Furthermore, people rarely realize they are guilty of affirming something in cognitive judgments that is abhorrent to the very nature of noncontradictory thought. Is this really true? If the intellect does *not* shrink from these bare conjunctions, is it not possible there is a serious flaw in this epistemological analysis of the thinking process we call the judgment? That is a probing question. Yet, there is really no real flaw in the argument. It must be remembered that people generally think to live, not live to think. In the pragmatic affairs of everyday life, for rough and ready purposes, bare conjunctions work. Of course, intellectual falsity often results, for example, in stating the sun travels around the world. People speak of cognition when the intellect thinks pure; and when it does come to *pure* thinking, they are forced to conclude, formally speaking, there is an implied contradiction in *all* judgments, even if people rarely consider it *formally*. Furthermore, even in everyday affairs they implicitly demand at least some sort of coherence in their assertions. For example, a reasonable relevance between the subject and predicate of our assertions like "roses are red" is insisted upon. Roses and redness do in some sense connect. Statements like "roses are airplanes" are wrong. When one leaves pragmatic affairs and enters a field where the intellect is the prominent feature, the unmediated conjunction is most problematical as in the fields of science, philosophy, and theology.[26] Here thinkers almost invariably express a disrespect for a mere *de facto* connection, that is, roses are airplanes. They insist upon the thorough-going mediation of whatever lays claim to be believed.[27]

Yet, the original problem is still present: if real differences do not remain, there can be no genuine judgment, hence, no movement of thought. Thought demands differences, while at the same time abhors contradictions. What to do? *Here resides a vital and important conclusion.* The whole dilemma vividly points out there is an "insuperable barrier" which seemingly lies in the path of the mind's search for *ultimate truth.* Seeing the intellect is repulsed by uniting unmediated differences, a judgment can only be accepted as characterizing reality as long as it is in a form of unity which exhibits a perfect mutual implication of the differents. There must be a "system" that unites the differents of predication. This alone can satisfy the intellect.

The second serious rub in cognition surfaces right here. There is no system to make it formally correct in a noncontradictory fashion. As already clearly seen, the problem centers in the need and nature of a ground or a system to unite differences. Thought demands this ground to save itself from the self-contradictory act of uniting differences. Yet, in the actual cognitive process, this ground remains partially external to the differences it connects. Thus the intellect is faced with the further question as to how the ground itself is connected with the differences it attempts to combine. Consequently, a "deeper ground" that would unite the first ground to the differences is necessitated, and the problem goes on *ad infinitum.* The ground, or the *why*, can be continually pushed back until a more unified and coherent system is achieved. Yet a true, ultimate, and final "manifold in unity," wherein *perfect*, mutual implication reigns, forever eludes one's grasp. In other words, no matter what is cognized, and thus made a judgment concerning reality, the question *why* can always be raised.

This principle is true for all human thought in its endeavors to characterize the ultimately true and the real. The reason for it is clear: "Thought knows nothing of *intrinsic* connection of differents."[28] The intellect demands a self-consistency that can be found only in a system where the ground is *internal* to the differents it connects, but the only thing the mind can achieve is a complex of differences which must constantly refer beyond itself for its ground. The ground *always* remains at least partially external to the entities it unites. Furthermore, this defect is incurable. A "unity of differences" that would fully satisfy limited human intellect as characteristic of the real is unattainable at *any* level of thought.

This significant point and its important conclusion is well expressed in C. A. Campbell's words:

> Although such a unity is the inherent demand of the intellect, and thus needful for the assurance of apprehending *ultimate reality*, it is a unity that is *not attainable by the intellect*. And this failure, it will appear, is a failure not merely in degree. It is a failure *in principle*. For—and this is the central paradox of human experience—the route which the intellect takes, and must take, in its effort to realize its ideal, is one which never can, by reason of its intrinsic character, lead to the desired goal of mutually implicatory system or unity in difference which *never can, therefore, yield us apprehension of the real*.[29]

Summary and Conclusion of the Argument from Cognition

The route that human cognition *must* travel, a route that necessitates the assumption of relations, that is, the cognitive judgment, can never lead to its goal of a perfect, self-implied whole. It simply cannot come up with it. We cannot "think" on that track. It is a path, therefore, which can *never* lead to *Ultimate Reality*. Consequently, Ultimate Reality must be disparate from every mere rational thought product, and the term *disparate* is to be taken seriously. Finite thought and final reality are, in a formal ultimate sense, incommensurable. So it must be that:

> Reality owns a character which transcends thought—a character for which, since a label is convenient, we may term 'supra-rational'; and . . . there is no possibility of measuring the degree in which any particular content of thought manifests the character of Reality.[30]

Thus the very essence of the cognitive life demands a supra-rational Ultimate Reality. The term *Ultimate Reality* is simply the philosophers way of expressing God. Our God is the Ultimate Reality of all being. So it can be stated categorically that all cognitive activity demonstrates that God, the final Ultimate Reality, must be *suprarational*. This is also Otto's argument from religious worship. Now all this plodding argumentation comes together. Everything encountered in cognitive existence points to a suprarational final Reality, that is, a superrational God.[31]

Moreover, the epistemological and religious arguments for a suprarational Reality or God can be multiplied: for example, the argument from morality, the problem of error, etc. Space forbids that exercise here, but it should by now be very evident that an *exceedingly strong* case for a suprarational view of Ultimate Reality, that is, for God, can now be posited. Therefore, it appears quite safe to conclude that a thoroughly rational, empirical epistemology cannot explain reality in its final character. Thus it surely cannot express God. When it comes to thinking about God— and thus developing a theology about Him—limited human rationalistic cognition simply cannot plummet the depths of His *final* character. All cognitive activity and religious experience seems to demand this conclusion, but the issue begging for an answer is: What does all this have to do with what people say about God, and what does that have to do with our epistemological game—"king-of-the-hill"? The answer to this pertinent question has been hinted at often, but now must become explicit.

Beginning to Draw the Conclusion for Theology

The argument from cognition has shown Ultimate Reality to be suprarational. Moreover, in religious experience the God of Evangelicals possesses the same basic suprarational nature. These facts strongly suggest that the suprarational Ultimate Reality encountered in cognition and the personal suprarational God worshiped *are one and the same.* If the highest concept of Reality that we can grasp is personhood, the identification of the personal God of Evangelicals and Ultimate Reality of the philosophers surely follows.[32] Moreover, one could hardly have any *ultimate* suprarational dualism. It would be self-contradictory to say the *Ultimate* God and *Ultimate* Reality are different. So again, the identification of cognition's Ultimate Reality and the Evangelical's suprarational God follows. In other words, all human awareness— religious, ethical, rational, or what have you— points to an Ultimate, Infinite, Personal Reality who is the ground of all being, religiously expressed as "God" and beyond mere rational grasp alone. That suprarational aspect of God is most important, because it moves into an epistemological stance in formulating theology that is most vital to be understood.

The Point for Theology

Here is the central point: if God is truly an ultimate, transcendent, suprarational Person, He could hardly be known *personally* or understood in any redemptive in-depth sense by mere finite empirical, rational, intuitive grounds alone. Finitude can hardly claw its way up to Infinity. As the psalmist expressed it, "Such knowledge is too wonderful for me;/ it is high, I cannot attain it" (Ps. 139:6). Empiricism and rationalism are finite, presuppositional, cognitively formal, self-contracting principles, principles that simply cannot fully grasp or adequately express ultimacy. H. L. Martensen, Bishop of Denmark and university tutor of Soren Kierkegaard, saw this clearly as he emphasized the "invisible majesty of God, his sovereignty as creator, and his opacity in relation to man's ability to acquire knowledge."[33] He said this in his reaction to the Hegelian rationalism of the day.

Therefore, it follows an ultimate, infinite, personal God would in some sense be forced to *reveal* Himself to humanity in their finite, humanly inadequate level if they were to know Him in any depth at all. Even if intuition, or *a priori* knowledge, or even rationalism and empiricism, gave people some sort of indication of His existence and some veiled hints concerning aspects of His nature,[34] revelation would be absolutely necessary to know personally, and hence *redemptively*, the ultimate Person. Finitude simply cannot ascend the heights and cognize infinity fully and completely. That is why the Bible itself states: "A natural man does not accept the things of the Spirit . . . and he cannot understand them" (1 Cor. 2:14, NASB). That basic, central fact is one of the weaknesses of limiting oneself to just the finite, epistemological presuppositions of empiricism and/or rationalism, and of demanding such a verification for all one accepts as the Real. Human beings simply cannot rationally ascend to the infinite God. All cognition and religious experience militates against it. Persons can conceive of infinity but cannot cognize on an infinite level. As the Bible says, "He [God] has put eternity into man's mind, yet so that he cannot find out what God has done from the beginning to the end" (Eccl. 3:11). Therefore God must come to mankind for them to come to a deep knowledge of Him. Otherwise, people are shut up to His revelation of Himself.[35]

A revelation of God is not only what humanity desperately needs, but also exactly what the Christian religion claims has occurred. God has seen mankind's plight and has come to us in revelation. The Scriptures state: "It is written,

> 'What no eye has seen, nor ear heard [empiricism],
> nor the heart of man conceived [rationalism],
> what God has prepared for those who love him,'

God has *revealed* to us through the Spirit" (1 Cor. 2:9-10, author's italics). Evangelical Christians hold that God has graciously made Himself known, and has done it in many ways and manners. "In many and various ways God spoke," (Heb. 1:1), but there is *one supreme way* God has revealed Himself clearly and unmistakably. The Bible says, "The true light that enlightens every man was coming into the world. He [Jesus] was in the world, and the world was made through him, yet the world knew him not. He came to his own home, and his own people received him not. But to all who received him, who believed in his name, he gave power to become children of God" (John 1:9-12). As the passage quoted from John's Gospel implies, the infinite, suprarational God has finally and fully revealed Himself, even incarnated Himself, in Jesus of Nazareth. That virtually boggles the mind, but remember, God had to do some revelational thing if human beings were to come into personal, knowledgeable contact with Ultimacy. Cognition demands such.

Furthermore, if God as *Person* were to reveal Himself fully to *persons*, He could hardly have done it in any other fashion other than to do it as a *Person.* That is why the writer of Hebrews declared:

> God spoke of old to our fathers by the prophets; but in these last days he has spoken to us by a Son, whom he appointed the heir of all things, through whom also he created the world. He reflects the glory of God and bears the very stamp of his nature, upholding the universe by his word of power (Heb. 1:1-3).

Rudolf Otto has clearly seen this. Speaking of Jesus Christ, he stated:

> His firm, unfaltering hold upon God, His unwavering, unfailing righteousness, His certitude of conviction and assurance in action so mysterious and profound, His spiritual fervour and beatitude, the struggles and trustfulness, self-surrender and suffering, and finally the conqueror's death that were His—whoever goes on to consider all this must inevitably conclude: "That is godlike and divine; that is verily Holiness. If there is a God and if He chose to reveal Himself, He could do it no otherwise than thus."[36]

It thus seems very plausible and logical indeed that revelation is just what Jesus Christ came to perform.[37] Christians firmly believe He did much more, as shall be seen, but He did reveal God in a full and satisfying way. Jesus said, "He who has seen me has seen the Father" (John 14:9). We believe He uniquely revealed God as fully as human limitations can intellectually and experientially grasp God. Christians claim the suprarational God came to us in Jesus Christ.

Can Jesus Christ, however, be accepted as being a true revelation of God as Evangelical Christianity holds—as most any brand of Christianity claims? Was Jesus of Nazareth really that true revelation of God so desperately needed? Evangelicals say *yes* for many reasons, two of which are quite convincing. First, there is something unique about Jesus Christ. His exemplary life cannot be just thrust aside (see Otto above). No competent historian or thinker attempts to disparage Jesus anymore.[38] Jesus was so radically different there really is no other sensible answer except He truly was God's Son, as the Scriptures state. Secondly, Jesus Himself claimed that the suprarational God broke into human history in His own personhood. He said, "Have I been with you so long, and yet you do not know me, . . . I am in the Father and the Father in me" (John 14:9-10). Jesus Christ as *person* presented the very nature of Ultimate Reality, suprarational *Personhood*, on humanity's personal level. "The Word was God" (John 1:1).

The Final Summation and Vital Conclusion

Thus revelational Christianity scores on all points. First, it presents a valid, presuppositional epistemology. Secondly, an epistemological revelational principle "fits" coherently and corresponds in a more comprehensive way with what we recognize Reality is like in its deepest, ultimately, suprarational sense. In light of the fact that God is suprarational, the noncontradiction test is met. Thus the Christian revelational principle scores with a valid, presuppositional epistemology and meets the test of coherence, correspondence, and noncontradiction when tested by our grasp of Ultimate Reality.[39] It simply presents the most comprehensive grasp of truth. Its worldview is quite impeccable.

Moreover, if God is Absolute and suprarational Personhood, as all reality demonstrates, God revealing Himself is mandatory; and this He did in the only real fashion He could, in and through His Son, Jesus Christ. It all comes together making coherent sense.

Therefore, one can conclude that the Christian revelation principle as the key source of truth is not only as epistemologically respectable as any quest for truth, it answers best all the pressing cognitive questions of basic epistemology. The evangelical believer does not have to be intellectually embarrassed by any epistemological system. Furthermore, the Christian revelation gives answers concerning the personal, ultimate God that can be gotten no other way. That knowledge meets mankind's greatest need.

The Primary Point

Therefore, *Christian revelation, as over against any and all other epistemological systems, must be viewed as "king-of-the-hill" in formulating theology.* The epistemological experiences of Christians point to and *demand* this. Rationalism, as a case in point, must take a second seat to revelation when it

comes to making theological claims about a suprarational God. Rationalism can give us mathematical truths for example, but it cannot "reveal" a suprarational God. He is ultimate; humanity is finite. Therefore,
God must speak. Revelation is actually the only source of truth about
God that believers can finally rely upon. It is their only cognitive hope.
Such is the coherent, sensible conclusion to draw.[40] Revelation is "king"
when cognitive issues in theology arise.

Thus it is wise to take with utmost seriousness the revelational claims
of Christianity and exalt that epistemological principle above all others
in developing theology. Therefore, when epistemological, presuppositional conflicts surface, Christians will do well to choose revelation and
put the "king's" crown on its head, for there, and there alone, rests *the
final authority for Christian truth.* Moreover, believers must be consistent in
that exercise. The believer cannot be a pure "rationalist" one day and a
"revelationist" the next. Epistemology must never be whimsical; it must
remain consistent, especially when presuppositional conflicts arise.
That, and that alone, constitutes the *principium theologia* to do theology as
Clark Pinnock told us we must.

Conclusion

So the final conclusion is clearly a most vital and important conclusion in fabricating a theology of evangelism. Although rationalism and
empiricism can tell us much about reality, for there is an essential rationality in the universe, they can never fathom a *suprarational* God, even
though He is the basis of the essential rationality. Therefore, God must
"speak," if persons are to understand Him and His purposes for humankind.[41] This He has done supremely in His Son Jesus Christ. The revelation of Jesus Christ is the final test of all theological truth claims.[42]
When it thus comes to formulating theology, and one must opt between
choosing a rational-empirical conclusion about God or a clear revelational statement about Him, to play the epistemological game "king-of-
the-hill" properly, one must *always* choose presuppositional revelation
because of God's suprarational nature and mankind's cognitive finitude.
Revelation is the epistemological, presuppositional "king," and Jesus is
its Lord. There alone rests the final authority for theological claims. *God
has spoken.* Therefore, the ultimate religious issue is, in Kierkegaard's
words, "Will you obey? or will you not obey? Will you bow in faith [to
God's revelation] . . . or will you be offended?"[43] *The choice of revelation
becomes our starting point in all theology.*

One large question still remains, however, if God has *authoritatively and
finally* spoken, what did He say and where can we find out? To that vital
issue we turn.

Notes

1. Clark Pinnock, *Biblical Revelation* (Chicago: Moody Press, 1971), 11.

2. Certain aspects of Pinnock's position will be discussed in a later chapter.

3. Dagobert D. Runes, ed., *The Dictionary of Philosophy* (Patterson, N.J.: Littlefield, Adams and Co. 1961), 94.

4. The action of the mind as it is addressed by "sources" of input is assumed to be pointing to objective and subjective reality.

5. It can perhaps be argued that to accept the concept of revelation implies the Cartesian form of the ontological argument. But that tends to strengthen the case. Also, it is possible to contend that *all* cognition, at least in some sense, is a revelation, and as an object impinges upon awareness; however, the revelation of God still stands as a basic epistemological presupposition.

6. Whether or not the Bible is actually revelational of God is not the point here. That important issue shall be taken up later. At the moment it is for illustrative purposes alone.

7. Of course, Evangelicals must present a "rationale" for their subjugating rationalism, empiricism, etc. to the supremacy of revelational data. They, too, must keep their sanity. That "rationale" shall be presented shortly. Christians do have a very sensible argument for their epistemological stand on revelation.

8. It may be true that the correspondence test and comprehensive test are very similar, but there is an obvious nuance of difference, a difference worth making.

9. A case can be carried on from this point to set forth an apologetic to help the total unbeliever or agnostic. It can be pointed out that to put the concept of God into one's worldview develops the most valid worldview, but that is another line of development of the epistemological argument that must be reserved to other studies. The point here is that revelational presuppositions present not only the best worldview but also are the most authoritative presuppositions concerning God's truth. Evangelicals hardly need to be convinced of the superiority of a theistic worldview; what is being argued is that the evangelical, revelational, epistemological view is the most valid one.

10. Some professing believers, such as the so-called process theologians, will perhaps disagree with the time-honored claims concerning God's essential nature as set forth here. Their "process" approach will be discussed in a later chapter.

11. This line of reasoning is a phase of the so-called argument for God based on religious experience. Because religious experience is found universally in all cultures and peoples, it is a strong, valid line of argumentation. Moreover, granting that religious experience is true, the line of reasoning employed surely holds. Religious experience when genuine is not devoid of reason.

12. Even Einstein has shown us this in his book *Relativity* (New York: Henry, Holt and Co., 1920). See chapters 3, 8, 12, 13, 26, and 32.

13. This approach of Rudolph Otto, philosopher-theologian, will be developed in more detail in a moment.

14. "Suprarational" means *truth* that is above and beyond mere human comprehension or cognition. The meaning and importance of the expression "suprarational" regarding theology will be approached shortly.

15. Some may object to attributing a suprarational nature to God. This does

not mean God is irrational; He simply transcends finite, rational capabilities. Yet, He is *Logos*, and thus suprarationalism connects with human rationalism.

16. Rudolf Otto, *The Idea of the Holy* (London: Oxford University Press, 1923), 8. Modern sociologists and anthropologists tend to call the numinous "the sacred."

17. Ibid., 28.

18. This line of reasoning has been the basis of my argument earlier against crass rationalism in theology. See page 16.

19. Otto, *The Idea of the Holy,* 113.

20. Otto borrowed this term from Kant. He has been accused of turning Kant upside down. H. J. Paton stated that "with a strange perversity, Otto reverses the meaning of the terms he has borrowed. The pure rational concepts belonging to the category of the holy are described as the schemata of the non-rational instead of *vice versa*" (*The Modern Predicament* [London: Geo. Allen & Unwin, Ltd., 1957], 337). Yet this does not seem to invalidate Otto's position. Moreover, it appears that Paton has somewhat exaggerated this criticism. A clearer understanding of this critique may be found by reading "Otto and Kant" in Paton, 137-39.

21. C. A. Campbell, *On Selfhood and Godhood* (London: George Allen and Unwin, Limited, 1957), 337, author's italics.

22. This argument shall be approached in more detail later when the so-called Logos Concept is discussed.

23. In the argument that follows, I take my lead from C. A. Campbell, the Scottish epistemologist.

24. This position I am prepared to defend, but space precludes it here. It must be reserved for other studies. Moreover, a wealth of material has been produced by epistemologists to substantiate the position that all real thinking is essentially a judgment on our experience of reality. A bit of serious introspective evaluation of our thinking process makes it patent, it seems to me. (See the book *Skepticism and Construction* by C. A. Campbell [London: George Allen and Unwin, Limited, n.d.]).

25. It is important to note this is *formally* speaking. Persons rarely sit down in this fashion and scrutinize their thinking processes and thus realize they are uniting differents in their judgments. Yet, it is a fact and has an important point to make which the reader shall see shortly.

26. At this stage, it may be asked, what has all this formal epistemological argumentation have to do with theology? Hopefully, it will be evident in a moment, and then it should be clear why all of this is so essential to building a theology that is epistemologically sound.

27. This is why the intellect has such a difficult time resting in a metaphysical dualism, that is, a dualism of *ultimate* principles. As long as two or more principles fail to be connected in *one* ultimate principle, people are somehow conscious of failure.

28. C. A. Campbell, *Skepticism and Construction* (London: George Allen and Unwin, Limited, n.d.), 18, author's italics .

29. Ibid., 14-15.

30. Ibid., 20.

31. C. A. Campbell, *Skepticism and Construction*, 37. Critics of suprarationalism

say, "You hold Ultimate Reality to be unknowable. But if it is, what exactly is the basis of your judgment that the world of experience is not ultimately real? Surely that judgment implies that you are already in possession of the standard of the ultimately real? And if so, reality cannot be beyond knowledge."

C. A. Campbell answered this criticism in the following manner: "To condemn the world of experience . . . it is not necessary that we should know what reality is. It is enough if we know what reality is not" (*Skepticism and Construction*, 76). For example, to know that ultimate reality cannot have characteristic *A*, and that the experienced world does contain *A*, then the world of experience is obviously not the ultimately real. This is just the situation that metaphysical suprarationalism claims to find. Although we do not positively know what reality is like, we do know that it cannot be self-contradictory, and the world of human experience is. Consequently, the experienced world cannot be the *final* reality; therefore, our mere human experience (that is, rationalism and empiricism) surely cannot exhaust our statements about God.

32. Professor Campbell in his Gifford Lectures has argued that the highest human conception is personhood. Therefore, *Ultimate* Reality of necessity must be personal. See *On Selfhood and Godhood* (London: Allen and Unwin, Limited, 1960).

33. J. H. Schjorring, "Martensen," *Bibliotheca Kierkegaardiana*, (1982), 185.

34. The psalmist does tell us, "The heavens are telling the glory of God; / and the firmament proclaims his handiwork" (19:1). Rationally and empirically we can know some things about God. This so-called natural revelation is real and important, but to know God *personally* and *redemptively*, "special revelation" is demanded, that is, God coming to human beings personally and speaking. This is what is being argued. An exhaustive treatment of this principle is found in: Stuart C. Hackett, *The Reconstruction of the Christian Revelational Claim* (Grand Rapids: Baker Book House, 1984).

35. In speaking of God in masculine terms, no sexist language is implied. I am simply using biblical terminology.

36. Rudolf Otto, *The Idea of the Holy*, 170.

37. Remember, first of all, that revelation is as legitimate as any epistemological presupposition. Moreover, God *must* reveal Himself if people are to know Him meaningfully—which in turn constructs the most coherent world view and epistemological system.

38. The argument can be made that perhaps others came to reveal God uniquely, for example, Muhammad, Confucius, etc. Here the discipline of comparative religious studies plays an important role. This is a most important principle to grasp, for many of the world religions (such as the Moslems) do claim to be the final revelation of God just as Christians do. But when we make a *serious* study of the major religions of the world, it soon becomes clear that no religious leader will be found to come close to the life and teaching of Jesus. Everything He did and said testifies to His divinity, as Otto argued. Space precludes a long argument here, but it can be done. Few Christians doubt these realities.

39. These tests are, in some sense, pragmatic tests, a necessity when working with cognition.

40. This view does not decry or downgrade empirical, rational, intuitional,

etc. truth *as far as it can go.* It embraces *all* truth, provided it fits a coherent episte-mological system. And again, let it be said, this view does not deny the essential rationality of the universe. It simply declares God is above the finite rationalism of humanity, and thus to know Him, God must reveal Himself.

41. To make the case as to why God has chosen to reveal Himself is some-what redundant here. That apologetic may be helpful for the unbeliever, but that is not the purpose of this book, for all Christians of all persuasions accept at least the principle of revelation.

42. This revelational principle of God in Jesus Christ is what establishes and maintains the dynamic balance between God's transcendence and imminence.

43. Sören Kierkegaard, *Authority and Revelation,* trans. W. Lowrie (Princeton: Princeton University, 1955), 24-26.

2

The Authoritative Word in Theology:
The Holy Scriptures

"Thy word is truth" (John 17:17).

Introduction

We have learned in the previous chapter that unless God addresses us personally, we cannot come to know Him dynamically and redemptively; but God has spoken—and done so in a quite marvelous manner. To quote Rudolph Otto again, "If God were to speak, he could do it in no other way" than as He has done in His redeeming Son, the Lord Jesus Christ. Jesus of Nazareth is the heart, the final culmination, of God's revelation.[1] That is the final arbitrating principle in developing Christian truth, but the proposition raises another very fundamental and serious question for our theology of evangelism: *How do we know anything authoritatively about Jesus Christ, God's supreme revelation of Himself?* Actually, the real pragmatic issue in theology rests here.

Learning About the Revealed Christ

The answer to the above question is central to all thought about God. Although the answer bristles with implications and nuances of interpretations, many that go far beyond what can be discussed in this limited space, the essential answer is: God Himself has given us a Book that tells us about His redeeming Son. It dramatically and powerfully relates realities about Christ's life, His teachings, His ministry, His death, His victory over the grave, and the implications and meaning of His life and ministry. The Book? The Bible! Actually, there is no other source in which to discover anything of *objective* substance about Jesus and the meaning of it all other than in the Holy Scriptures? The few scant objective references to Jesus of Nazareth in Josephus and other contemporaries is so minimal, the life and ministry of the Lord and all that it means would probably have gained little, if any, notoriety at all were it not for the Bible. The verbal traditions and second generation references would probably have been long lost in the dust of history. Where then can people turn but to the Word of God, the Holy Spirit-inspired Scriptures? Thus the assumption at the outset is that *God has spoken in and through the Holy Bible*. There rests the primary source of authority in propositional theology. Granted, that is quite a categorical statement, but cogent arguments are available to substantiate it.

The *written* Word is not the *living* Word of God. Jesus and the Bible are certainly not one and the same, although some seem to talk in that tone. So the question naturally arises: Is the Bible then, in its propositional statements, a genuine, authoritative revelation of God and His truth? Jesus personally revealed God; but does the Bible reveal truth about Him, or is it a mere human record of personal revelations of God, not revelational in itself? Or to remove the question one step backward: Can revelation ever be be given in *propositions* (given in sensible statements) rather than *personal* encounter? Through the years, many have answered in the affirmative to that pressing question; today many others disagree. This foundational issue needs some comment.

Is Propositional Revelation Possible?

The general consensus of theological history up until the last two or three hundred years was virtually unanimous in the opinion that revelation, a Word from God, could be propositional as well as personal encounter. Few challenged the contention that revelation could be propositional as well as personal encounter, not only *could be* but actually was.

Today, however, many theologians insist on something of an antithesis between "personal" and "propositional" revelation, implying if revelation were one it could not be the other. They tend to reject the status of any sort of propositional revelation in their stress on personal, existential revelation. One of the earliest thinkers to do so was the existentialist theologian Friedrich Schleiermacher (1768-1839). Archbishop William Temple also expressed this basic attitude, saying, "There is no such thing as revealed truth. There are truths of revelation, that is to say propositions . . . which are not themselves directly revealed."[2]

Why should one sort of revelation preclude the other? Nothing in principle demands it. Actually, one implies the other. People relate to and learn from one another in that dualistic manner. If a man I have never seen walks up to me and just stands there in silence, I can learn a few things about him: his height, the color of his suit, and the look on his face; but that is not very much. I certainly do not know if I would like to become his friend; he may even be a threat to me, for all I know. Of course, I may get some hints if he smiles or hands me something. Still, I hardly learn enough to establish a deep and profound relationship with him. To understand him fully, he must communicate. He must truthfully tell me who he is, what he is like, and what he wants.

Then, and only then, can I make an intelligent decision as to how I will relate to him. All human encounters that possess any real meaning are like that. How could it possibly be different with God, at least in principle?

Of course, God's revelation of Himself is far more than dry theological statements. Since people want to face God person to person, how can they divorce the personal *and* propositional aspects of a full revelation? Why would they even wish to do so? The attempt to emphasize the personal aspects of revelation at the cost of God speaking, as some opponents seemingly want to do, is too dear a price to pay. As Charles Haddon Spurgeon stated in a sermon delivered May 17, 1887, "What God has joined together these [existential] . . . thinkers willfully put asunder, and separate the Revealer from his own revelation . . . Christ and his Word must go together." Actually, it does not make coherent sense to strike the aforementioned antithesis. J. I. Packer had it correct when he said:

> To deny that revelation is propositional in order to emphasize its personal character is like trying to safeguard the truth that cricket is played with a bat by denying that it is played with a ball. The denial undercuts the assertion.[3]

Or to put it another way, it is nice to have my wife actually stand before me and smile; it is nicer to hear her say, "I love you."

Why some contemporary scholars take a total nonpropositional line concerning revelation remains something of a mystery. Perhaps they are fearful of falling into the trap of building a wooden, inflexible view of revelation as did the scholastics of the middle ages (as did the post-Reformation Lutherans) and thus becoming too rational. What they do with passages like "The Lord said to David" (1 Sam. 23:2) is puzzling, however. The biblical records declare that God spoke in words and propositions that people could understand. How can that not be revelational? Apparently, as Packer feels, the existentially oriented theologians wish to keep the personal aspects of revelation vividly alive, but so do most theologians. Who wants *just* a letter from a friend when a personal visit is possible? Still, when the friend does come, it is better if that friend speaks and enters into dialogue. Such is real encounter that deepens relationships. So it is with God. Thus, propositional revelation is not only possible, it is inevitable and most desirable. The very nature of revelation virtually requires it.

Where, however, is that propositional revelation found? The answer seems quite straightforward: in the Bible! The church has historically held that view. For example, the *Thirty Nine Articles* of the Church of England stated the Bible is "God's Word written" (Article XX). The

Scots Confession of 1560 called the Bible "The written Word of God" (XVIII). The famous Westminster Confession of 1647 declared the Scriptures are "to be received, because it is the Word of God" (I,i,iv). The "Short Confession of Faith" of 1610 by the early Baptists said, "This only God in the Holy Scriptures is manifested and revealed."[4] The Baptist London Confession of 1644 stated: "In this written Word God hath plainly revealed whatsoever he hath thought needful for us to know."[5] Go back as far as the church fathers and trace the question through church history, and the question is answered virtually the same everywhere. Revelation is *both* personal (subjective) *and* propositional (objective), and the objective revelation of God is found in the Holy Scriptures.

That is exactly what the Bible is all about. It is God personally speaking in objective, propositional form. He comes to me in the Word and communicates; that is, God speaks.[6] Speaking is propositional; that is what speaking is: propositional utterance that makes sense, has meaning, and informs. Why cannot revelation be *truth* as well as *person*? There is no reason whatever, in principle, why it cannot be both. Furthermore such an approach to revelation makes far more coherent sense than to sacrifice one for the other. To say God cannot come to us in a personal *and* cognitive fashion, or does not do so, is quite absurd. That is what revelation is: the suprarational God putting His truth in our limited human language so we can grasp of Him what we are able. Actually, God is encountered personally in the context of truth, the Word. Hence the Bible states concerning itself: "The word of God is living and active, sharper than any two-edged sword, piercing to the division of soul and spirit, of joints and marrow, and discerning the thoughts and intentions of the heart. And before him no creature is hidden, but all are open and laid bare to the eyes of him with whom we have to do" (Heb. 4:12-13).

If all that is not true, what does one do with the prophets' insistence, "Thus saith the Lord."? If God does not speak and thus reveal some of His realities propositionally as He personally encounters His people, Old Testament prophecy is extremely weak at best. Above all, Jesus Himself, God's final personal revelation, certainly spoke as He stood before people. He prayed, "I have given them thy word" (John 17:14). His statements, words from God, were hung on to as tenaciously, as was His gracious presence and inspired miracles, as they are to this day. The Bible gives us these words.

Further, as Packer correctly pointed out, every significant event in salvation history has God's cognitive, propositional, interpretive revelation put on it. How could human beings have understood those events making up that history otherwise? For example, thousands of people were crucified in Jesus' day. Why should His death have any particular significance? The reason is obvious, because God spoke in propositional language, and the Bible reveals that Jesus died for humanity's sins.

There are a multitude of reasons that could be given for the empty tomb, even His "appearances," but God *stated* in the Scriptures that the tomb was empty because Jesus was resurrected and is alive. The same principle holds in the entire Christ event, not to mention the whole scope of salvation history.[7]

Yet, persons want more than mere bare-bone words in the biblical revelation: "The written code kills" (2 Cor. 3:6). No true believer can ever be truly satisfied by "worshiping" the Bible or "worshiping" bare propositional truth. Such an approach constitutes bibliolatry. There is as much danger of becoming too rational from a conservative, rightest position as from the liberal left. Jesus is Lord, and the most profound seeking is in longing to meet and personally encounter the true and living Christ. By the same token, however, believers do not want to be bound to a revelation of God that projects us into a mystical, existential, non-communication, never-never land where there is no objective criterion to evaluate Christian experience. Believers do not want to have to wonder what in the world happened or how to interpret the experience or how to react or even what God was trying to convey to them. Both approaches are wrong. The need is to strive to maintain a dynamic balance between propositional and personal revelation.

How can the personal and propositional aspects of revelation be combined in a satisfying way that believers can come through it all and say, "I know God"? It is not presumptuous to say that. Our Lord stated, "This is eternal life, that they know thee the only true God, and Jesus Christ whom thou hast sent" (John 17:3). How can all this be effected? Sinful humanity simply cannot do it. It lies beyond sinners. This was what Paul meant when he said, "The unspiritual man does not receive the gifts of the Spirit of God, . . . and he is not able to understand them because they are spiritually discerned" (1 Cor. 2:14). Actually, sinful humankind suppresses the truth of God, rather than seeking it or understanding it (Rom. 1:18). Is there then any hope? Yes. The Holy Spirit of God, the third Person of the Trinity, comes to the sinner's aid personally and declares to them personally the Word of the gospel (1 Cor. 1:21). After all, if the Spirit is the ultimate Author of Scripture, as the Bible claims, He alone can make it live: "All Scripture is inspired by God and profitable for teaching, for reproof, for correction, and for training in righteousness" (2 Tim. 3:16). In other words, the Holy Spirit, in a very personal encounter, addresses people face-to-face and enables them to hear, understand, and obey the objective, written Word of God. In that dynamic encounter, sinful humanity meets God personally and hears Him speak propositionally through His Word. That combination is the essence of true revelation, and it proves to be a beautiful system of checks and balances (subjective and objective).

The Pragmatics

Moreover, believers are to be doers of the Word, as they positively respond to the inner witness and work of the Spirit (Jas. 1:22). Sinners cannot do that, but the Spirit again comes to their aid and imparts His own presence to enable them to respond to the Word in commitment. That is how personal and propositional revelation is pragmatically realized. For example, Paul pointed out that the Holy Spirit enabled the Thessalonian believers to come to know God. He then said, "And we also thank God constantly for this, that when you received the word of God which you heard from us, you accepted it not as the word of men but as what it really is, the word of God, which is at work in you believers" (1 Thess. 2:13). Therein is the balance found. Openness to the Holy Spirit is the key to dynamic revelation as He encounters people personally and propositionally, speaking through Scriptural truth.

Whom does the Holy Spirit reveal in these dynamic moments? The Bible answers that forthrightly. Jesus said, "When the Spirit of truth comes, he will guide you into all the truth; for he will not speak on his own authority, but whatever he hears he will speak, and he will declare to you the things that are to come. He will glorify me, for he will take what is mine and declare it to you. All that the Father has is mine; therefore I said that he will take what is mine and declare it to you" (John 16:13-15). The Holy Spirit essentially reveals the person of Christ and the truths of Jesus that cluster around the entire Christ event. Moreover, He does that through the propositional truth of the gospel. As Paul said, "I am not ashamed of the gospel: it is the power of God for salvation to every one who has faith" (Rom. 1:16); and again, "It pleased God through the folly of what we preach [kerygma] to save those who believe" (1 Cor. 1:21).

It is important to realize that the above principle of the Holy Spirit revealing Christ by the gospel is true of His work throughout the entire written Word of God, all which in some sense speaks of Christ (Luke 24:27). The Holy Spirit addresses open people through every page of the Bible. He makes the Word powerful, alive, and relevant. No one desires a mere cold, "letter of the law" understanding of the Scriptures. The great, historic traditions of evangelicalism stood against that and contended for the dynamic balance between personal and objective revelation. Let it be stressed again, that the divine-human encounter becomes a pragmatic combination of personal and propositional revelation by the Holy Spirit through the written Word of God. They go together. That quality of revelational experience gives birth to dynamic Christianity.

Biblical Inspiration and Truthfulness

Of course, all that has been said concerning the Holy Scriptures up to this point has tacitly assumed the Bible is the totally inspired, truthful, trustworthy, authoritative Word of God.[8] Can that contention be sustained?

There is little question as to what the Bible says about itself in this regard:

> He gave to Moses, when he had made an end of speaking with him upon Mount Sinai, the two tables of the testimony, tables of stone, written with the finger of God (Ex. 31:18).
> "The Lord took me from following the flock, and the Lord said to me, 'Go, prophesy to my people Israel.' / Now therefore hear the word of the Lord" (Amos 7:15-16).
> Then the Lord put forth his hand and touched my mouth; and the Lord said to me, / "Behold, I have put my words in your mouth" (Jer. 1:9).
> He said to me, "Son of man, stand upon your feet, and I will speak with you." And when he spoke to me, the Spirit entered into me and set me upon my feet; and I heard him speaking to me (Ezek. 2:1-2).
> All scripture is inspired by God and profitable for teaching, for reproof, for correction, and for training in righteousness (2 Tim. 3:16).
> First of all you must understand this, that no prophecy of scripture is a matter of one's own interpretation, because no prophecy ever came by the impulse of man, but men moved by the Holy Spirit spoke from God (2 Pet. 1:20-21).

Even if all these passages are self-assertions, it is still important what the Bible declares about itself. The biblical personalities and/or writers certainly thought God moved them and and gave them revealed truth to record. Moreover, they were obviously convinced that the Word was absolutely truthful and authoritative, as did subsequent generations. For example, on the day of Pentecost, Peter quoted the prophet Joel and the Psalms as his authority to interpret the revelational events of the day. In Acts 4:25 we read: "Who by the mouth of our father David, thy servant, didst say by the Holy Spirit, / 'Why did the Gentiles rage, / and the peoples imagine vain things?'" That attitude and approach to the Scriptures runs throughout the entire New Testament. Not only that, Jesus Himself clearly held that view of the Scriptures. He said, "For truly, I say to you, till heaven and earth pass away, not an iota, not a dot, will pass from the law until all is accomplished" (Matt. 5:18). The list of citations concerning Jesus' attitude towards the Scripture is quite extensive (see John 3:14; 7:16-24; 8:26).

Historic Christianity has rarely seriously questioned the total inspiration of the Bible, including its unequivocal authority and truthfulness.

The church fathers, with few exceptions, agreed to that. For example, Irenaeus said:

> Since the writings [*literae*] of Moses are the words of Christ, He does Himself declare to the Jews, as John has recorded in the Gospel: If ye had believed Moses, ye would have believed Me: for he wrote of Me. But if ye believe not his writings, neither will he believe My words. He thus indicated in the clearest manner that the writings of Moses are His words. If then to Moses so also, beyond a doubt, the words of the other prophets are His. (*Moysi literas suos esse sermones . . . et reliquorum sine dubio prophetarum sermones pisius sunt,* IV:2,3 [3,1; ii:148], John 5:46-47).

Augustine of Hippo in a letter to Jerome wrote:

> For I confess to your charity that I have learned to defer this respect and honor to those Scriptural books only which are now called canonical, that I believe most firmly that no one of those authors has erred in any respect in writing (*Epistolae*, 82,i,3.).

Those sorts of quotations are more numerous than can be presented here. The overwhelming majority of the fathers agreed to the authority and trustworthiness of the Bible. Nor were the middle ages an exception. Although that period saw the exalting of tradition alongside the Scriptures as a source of truth and authority, the Roman Catholic Church still held to the total inspiration of Scriptures.

The attitude of the sixteenth-century reformers is well known. For Luther, Calvin, and others it was *sola scriptura*, the Scriptures only.

For the next two or three hundred years the reformation attitude essentially prevailed. Theological giants like William Perkins, William Ames, John Owen, Richard Sibs, Thomas Goodwin, John Gill, John Arndt, August Hermann Francke, Jonathan Edwards, and more than can be listed, all accepted the total inspiration, absolute authority, and unequivocal truthfulness of the Bible. They all testified that it is the very Word of God, hence revelational.

Not only that, the creeds and statements of faith produced by church bodies normally give a similar testimony. We have already seen some early British confessions. Other examples are numerous; for instance, the "Midland Confession" of 1655 (British) stated: "We profess and believe the Holy Scriptures, the Old and New Testament, to be the word and revealed mind of God."[9] The "Second London Confession" of 1677 called the Bible the "Word of God written," describing it as "the only sufficient, certain, and infallible rule of all saving Knowledge."[10] The "Orthodox Creed" of 1679 declared that in the Bible "the authority of God, . . . hath delivered and revealed his mind therein unto us."[11] The Sandy Creek Association (American Baptist) stated, "The Scriptures of the Old and New Testament are the Word of God."[12] The Elkhorn and South Kentucky Associations declared, "The Scriptures of the Old and New Testament are the infallible word of God."[13] The French Evangelical Association (1879, 1924), holds "The canonical writings of the Old and the New Testaments are the Word of God and constitute the only and infallible rule of faith."[14] The Baptist *Faith and Message* statement of 1963 (American Southern Baptist) tells us the Bible is "truth, without any mixture of error."[15]

Commentators have also made their contributions to this general evangelical consensus. Concerning God's Word, Lutheran commentator, R. C. H. Lenski stated: "They are inerrant in every word unless we intend to charge the Lord and his Spirit with errancy, fallibility."[16] Matthew Henry said: "It [the Bible] is a divine revelation, which we may depend upon as infallibly true."[17] The great reformer and biblical commentator John Calvin declared, "Moses and the prophets did not utter at random what we have received from their hand, but, speaking at the suggestion of God, they boldly and fearlessly testified, what was actually true, that it was the mouth of the Lord that spake."[18] In something of a summary, the well-known Westminster Confession reads: "It pleased the Lord . . . to reveal himself, . . . to commit the same wholly unto writing."[19]

Great preachers also agree to this testimony. Charles H. Spurgeon said, "This is the book untainted by any error; but is pure, unalloyed, perfect truth. Why? Because God wrote it" (Sermon preached March 18, 1855, on the text Hosea 8:12). Scholars like Professor A. T. Robertson— one of the greatest Greek scholars of this century—attests to the Bible's total truth and trustworthiness. In an address entitled *The Relative Authority of Scripture and Reason*, given at Philadelphia to The Tenth Baptist Congress (May 21, 1892), Robertson stated that in the Bible, God "gave a revelation to make it free from errors. I believe he first made it inerrant as he made nature so. Hence, I boldly maintain that the analogy of nature is in favor of the inerrancy of God's original Scriptures" (p. 6).[20]

From the Bible itself, history, personal experience, and coherent reason, it seems very acceptable to assume the total inspiration and truthfulness of the Bible. Some even argue for "inerrancy" in Scripture. However, that raises an important question: Is it truthful in *all* its assertions?

Are There Errors?

Now it must be granted that the inspired biblical revelation came through human beings, people subject to error, prejudice, limitations, and sin. Moreover, the various books of the Bible obviously reflect the vocabulary, grammatical and writing ability, sociological and historical conditions, theological viewpoints, and intent of the various writers. The authors of Scripture were certainly not passive "typewriters" in the Spirit's hands. They were people of their day and wrote like that. Further, no original autographs are available to display. Thus, to say the Bible is the Word *of God* is not the whole story; it is also the word *of human beings*. Does not all that open the door for error, and thus diminish scriptural authority and truthfulness? More than one says it does today.

The answer to the above question centers in what is meant by inspiration. Although God used limited, even sinful people to pen the Scriptures, why in principle could not the Holy Spirit keep them from error, even if He did let them express divine truth in their own way? After all, God is sovereign and always speaks truth. Freedom of thought and action and at the same time subjection to God's sovereign control are by no means incompatible. It is extremely difficult to say the God of all truth inspired the writers in the way the Bible says He inspired them, but then let them make mistakes. Of course, many contemporary scholars say such is exactly what happened. Yet, paradoxically, many of them declare very earnestly that the Bible is trustworthy and authoritative. There are obviously problems with that stance. It is extremely difficult to charge God with allowing error and then say the Bible is God's authoritative, trustworthy Word. How can error be authoritative? And to say there are no errors in what really matters (as some contend) raises another specter: Who decides that? That line sounds close to exalting rationalism over revelation. We saw earlier the weakness and error of that stance. To avoid that bind, some argue that the Scriptures are inerrant, but only in their Christological *purpose*. Yet that approach is tantamount to saying, for example, that Charles Wesley was infallible in one of his hymns because it achieved his poetic Christological purpose. Purpose alone is not the only consideration, the way that purpose is expressed is just as vital in establishing truth.

The whole issue of a fully truthful Bible is not easily sidestepped. Critical arguments, as stated above, come exceedingly close to the positivist's approach in exalting rational-empiricism presuppositions above revelation. That mind-set places the responsibility of deciding what is true on one's own rational faculties, which is a very dubious epistemological move as we discovered earlier. It amounts to playing the "king-of-the-hill" epistemological game with little wisdom. Regardless of how those who see errors in the Bible say this is not what they are doing, they just cannot extricate themselves out of the dilemma regardless of intellectual gymnastics.[21] The God of truth has either totally inspired the Bible or He has not, and that decides its truthfulness and consequential authority. There is really no other epistemological way out, at least not one that satisfies in any feasible fashion. To attempt to avoid that conclusion puts one on very shaky epistemological grounds—rationalism's supremacy in the things of God.

All that is not to say the biblical writers were mere automats in God's hands.[22] That we have readily conceded. They obviously expressed themselves in their cultural context. They spoke phenomenologically. They could not have communicated to their contemporaries had they not done so. Jesus did not express His teaching on life by talking about protons, electrons, neutrons, and quarks. He did not say He was the H_2O of life; He said He was the *water* of life. People would never have understood otherwise. What would $E=MC^2$ have meant to Galilean fishermen in the first century? John Calvin, who held a very high view of the Scriptures, was sensitive to this and expressed aspects of it in his so-called "Theory of Accommodation." Moreover, Calvin held no wooden view of the Bible that would cause one to quibble over words. The great reformer said:

> They [the apostles] were not overscrupulous in quoting words provided that they did not misuse scripture for their convenience. We must always look at the purpose for which quotations are made . . . but as far as the words are concerned, as in other things which are not relevant to the present purpose, they allow themselves some indulgence.[23]

Calvin probably took his lead from Augustine, who in like spirit, said:

> In any man's words the thing which we ought narrowly to regard is only the writers thoughts which was meant to be expressed, and to which the words ought to be subservient. . . . And we ought not to let the wretched cavillers at words fancy that truth must be tied somehow or other to the jots and tittles of letters.[24]

Still, Augustine prayed, "What thy Scriptures doth say, thou dost say."

Let it be asked again, why could not God in His sovereignty keep the writers from any real error while still using them as they were and for all they were culturally? Even I can keep myself from error by adding two plus two and coming up constantly with four. Surely, if utterances are "God breathed" truth, the writers can consistently say without error "Christ died for our sins." God is God. Packer has summed it up well by stating:

> The Holy Spirit so overruled all their subsequent mental activity in giving the message poetic and literary form that each resultant oracle was as truly a divine utterance as a human, as direct a disclosure of what was in God's mind as of what was in the prophet's.[25]

Although this is an acknowledged presuppositional view of what took place in inspiration, it certainly corresponds to what the Bible (as

well as evangelical historical theology) says about inspiration. Moreover, it seems to be the most coherent approach. The Word did not find
its basic inception in the psychology of the writer; rather, it came from
the God of truth Himself. As Peter expressed it, "No prophecy ever
came by the impulse of man, but men moved by the Holy Spirit spoke
from God" (2 Pet. 1:21). Thus it appears that the contrary presupposition that the sovereign God of truth allowed error in His own revelation
of himself is very dubious indeed. The traditional evangelical presupposition seems the wisest leap.

Dealing with Problems

What about the alleged errors and contradictions in the Bible? What
are we to do with them? It seems to me it is wise to be humble and
suspend judgment, and that is not playing the ostrich role of sticking
one's head in the Evangelical sand. We must face the issues, but many
supposed problems have been and are being solved. For example, for
years some historical critics contended the four Gospels were in error
because there was no external corroboration for the existence of Pontius
Pilate. Then a few years ago, archeologists discovered a stone at Caesa-
rea with Pilate's name inscribed on it. That solved the Pilate problem.
Another such incident occurred in the problem of the various biblical
references to the Hittites. For years, no archeological evidence could be
found for their existence. Some, therefore, held the Scriptures were in
error, but in 1906 a dig ninety miles east of Ankara revealed the capital
of the Hittite Empire. These sorts of illustrations can be repeated scores
and scores of times. Further, as the cultures, language, etc., of Bible
times are better understood, many supposed errors evaporate. As competent archeologists, linguists, grammarians, and historians do their
work, more and more problems are resolved. In his important work *Riv-
ers with Desert: History of Neteg*, Jewish archaeologist Nelson Glueck declared: "It may be stated categorically that no archeological discovery
has ever controverted a biblical reference" (p. 31). That is just a fact,
regardless how some may downplay the reality by stating there are still
many unresolved problems. It is true; there *are* still several problems, but
the general trend of solution is moving, fortunately for Bible believers,
in the right direction. To take the alternative route by saying the Bible
actually errs is a much more serious stance and simply bristles with
problems. It seems wise to be intellectually humble and wait to see the
outcome of continuing scholarship and investigations. To submit oneself in awe and humility to the Scriptures, rather than to superimpose
rational presuppositions on top of the Bible, is surely the best stance. As
Proverbs put it, "The fear of the Lord is the beginning of knowledge"
(Prov. 1:7).

Why do some insist on, and even seemingly emphasize, the so-called errors in the Bible? Professor A. T. Robertson asked the same question and then gave his answer: "Why in the world is it that there is such a terrible contention by the destructive higher critics? . . . I think I can tell; the school wants to change the whole order . . . they wish to get an entering wedge by having it admitted that there were inaccuracies in the original autographs, in order to shift and change the order of the Word, to suit themselves."[26] That may well be true, at least for the more radical school. A rationalistic epistemology is difficult for some to surrender it seems.

Like virtually all issues in this general arena, the real problem centers in epistemology. Ever since the Enlightenment, there has been a decided tendency to presuppose the supremacy of a rational-empiricism presuppositional base and then work from there. No doubt some rationalistic theologians have meant well in that move; they desired to make the gospel appealing to the more scientific age, but the price of assuming that epistemological line is high. It opens up the barn door that may let the horse be stolen. Moreover, this approach often imposes a Western rationalistic demand on all ancient Eastern views of science, history, psychology, and judges truth and error on that basis. This is hardly fair. How could the ancients have communicated if they did not speak in the categories of their day, as we have already stressed. Moreover, the biblical writers obviously spoke in phenomenological language, as we usually do. Not only that, more than likely, two thousand years from now our twentieth-century views and language, which we think are so accurate, will seem quite strange and erroneous to the people of A.D. 4000, that is, if they impose their contemporary categories on our statements.[27]

The Place of Rationalism and the Logos Concept

That does not mean, of course, we do not use rational categories as far as they can carry us. I confess my arguments above have been quite dependent on reasoning. Human beings are forced into that stance because they are limited, rationally cognitive creatures; they are not suprarational creatures, and they do not wish to be irrational. A suprarational God addressing us revelationally, although He is above mere rationalism, is certainly not irrational. Some have expressed it as "transrational." Thus there is nothing wrong in using rationalism *as far as it goes*. We have to be rational to think at all. All that has been said up to this point is certainly not meant to be construed as laying aside one's faculties and refusing to think critically. Faith in a suprarational God never means that. So when God addresses people cognitively in revelation on a limited level, they realize their finitude and confess that in revelation God has not shown them *everything* about Himself. That is not to say human beings do not think analytically and critically about that revelation; but at the same time, there is always an element of mystery about God. The ultimate suprarational nature of God demands mystery.

Still, there is no unbridgeable gap on God's part between suprarationalism and limited human cognition. Crossing that bridge is what God's revelation of Himself is all about. Granted, rational creatures cannot cross over and cognize fully the suprarational God, but He can certainly cross over and come to them. He did cross over in revelation. Rationally, believers are capable of grasping the connection between the ultimate Word and His finite Word of revelation. That connection or crossing is often termed the "Logos Concept." There is a definite connection or "oneness" between God as the ultimate "Logos" (Word) and the revealed Logos as we rationally grasp and apprehend it in the person and words of Jesus Christ. That is what John was talking about in the fourth Gospel when he wrote: "In the beginning was the Word, and the Word was with God, and the Word was God. . . . The light shines in the darkness, and the darkness has not overcome it. . . . And the Word became flesh and dwelt among us, full of grace and truth; we have beheld his glory, glory as of the only Son from the Father" (1:1,5,14). Since God is Logos, and human beings can comprehend logos (words), the two connect and are grasped in revelation. There is something of an "affinity" between the Mind (Word) of God and the mind of humankind. After all, human beings are created in His image.

So as long as our rational-empirical, critical awareness does not conflict with our apprehension of revelation, all is well. When pure rationalism does conflict, and on occasion it does, such as the resurrection of Jesus, then revelation must take precedence. Furthermore, to bring limited rationalism up against the suprarational God and critically approve or disapprove God's revelation by pure human rationalism is rather arrogant. Christians must learn to humble their minds as well as their hearts before the mystery of God. Believers are not called to a noncritical, anti-intellectualism but are called to be Christian in mind as well as heart.

Problem Words

It must be admitted, however, that often the problem of inspiration has been bedeviled by the use of words like *inerrancy, infallibility,* and *verbal inspiration.* In some groups, these terms have even taken ecclesiastical political connotations. They can become flag words for all sorts of weird and/or false ideas. Historically, such terms were not a problem. The idea of full truthfulness in the biblical revelation was largely assumed before the Enlightenment and the advent of higher criticism;

thus words like *inerrancy* and *infallibility* were not used consistently, although they were usually tacitly assumed. However, in the relatively recent theological battles, these particular words have acquired a high profile. The more rigid, elaborate statements concerning the nature of the Scriptures were formulated to oppose theologians who seemed to question the Bible's full truthfulness. Of course, high views of inspiration have been constructed through the course of the history of theology. Yet, if certain terms or expressions concerning the nature of the Bible are problematic in some circles, then they should certainly be clearly defined, if they are to be used at all. For example, the Chicago Statement on Inerrancy has attempted to do just that.[28] (See Appendix A.)

In some settings it may be best simply to lay the emotive terms aside and say the most coherent view of inspiration is that God has revealed Himself and given an absolutely truthful, trustworthy, authoritative, totally inspired Word of revelation.[29] One can hardly go beyond that with any words. Not only that, one does not wish to fall into a wooden, inflexible approach to the Scriptures. Still, it is extremely difficult to sidestep at least some sort of statement regarding inspiration, which reflects the absolute truthfulness and authority of the Bible, unless one wishes to be a committed rational-empiricist. Pure rationalism is a far cry from the Bible itself, and certainly is not traditional evangelicalism in any historic sense—not to mention its epistemological weakness.

Now, if the Holy Spirit takes the inspired, trustworthy Word of God and uses the truth to reveal God, the principles of hermeneutics (principles of interpretation) become vitally important. What interpreters do with the Bible when they pick it up is most significant in meeting God and learning of Him.

Bible Hermeneutics

To have a grasp of the nature of the Bible is not sufficient in itself to formulate theology. One must know how to interpret the text with a measure of skill and understanding. As J. I. Packer rightly pointed out, "Biblical authority is an empty notion unless we know how to determine what the Bible means."[30] Robert Jackson put his finger on it when he stated: "We who are evangelicals want Scripture to stand over us and judge us, not *visa versa* [author's italics]. The Bible is our soul [sic] and final authority. But for Scripture to function thusly, we must be able to read it properly. We must be able to interpret what it says."[31] That proper reading and interpretation involves certain principles called hermeneutics.

Biblical hermeneutics simply mean "principles of interpretations," but today the word *hermeneutics* has taken on a connotation in some circles to mean more than simple principles. For some it denotes a whole approach to Christian reality; for example, see theologians like Werner Georg Kümmel and Eduard Schillebeeckx. Here, however, we must restrict ourselves to the simple definition of hermeneutics and discuss the principles of how to interpret the Scriptures.

Probably the most pervasive, contemporary hermeneutical approach, at least in more sophisticated circles, is the so-called historical-critical method. Aspects of it have precipitated what is called the "new hermeneutic." There has been a quite interesting development of such hermeneutics over the past years.

Much modern thought on critical biblical interpretation really began with men like Schleiermacher. For him, the Bible must be approached from the viewpoint of the various authors of the various books. Barth and Brunner shifted the emphasis to the encounter motif: in the Scriptures one encounters the living God. Bultmann proposed his demythologizing methodology along with a radical existentialism.

The "new hermeneutic" *per se* began with Gadamer who saw the Bible properly interpreted as a "fusion of horizons," people encountering the text. Then came "structuralism." This view sought to find the deep meaning of a text. This school felt they had to "decode" the surface meaning of the Bible. "Deconstructuralism," next on the scene, came with the idea that one must deconstruct the historical elements of Scripture and "plan with meanings." Also, the reader of the text is to be "deconstructed" as well. Finally, came the "response" approach. The text is to transform the reader and *vice versa*. There seems to be constant development and shifts in the principles of interpretation, hopefully with helpful concepts arising in each shift.

Helpful insight to the meaning of Scripture has been derived by the scholarly, critical method of biblical interpretation. Understanding the historical-cultural setting, the type and structure of literature employed, the grammar of the biblical languages, the theological intent of the author, and the sources of the information used by the writers of Scripture all provide a rich source of help in understanding what God has said in the Bible. That is the goal of this method, and it has proved useful in certain aspects of understanding the Scriptures. Moreover, most Bible readers use it, or some phase of it, to a greater or lesser degree. Even the average layperson does so, implicitly or explicitly. Virtually all who seriously take up the Bible to hear God speak usually take into account the historical setting and what the authors were attempting to say, even if in an unsophisticated, limited fashion.

Any method or instrument, however, is good only to the extent it is used properly and wisely. For example, I can pick up an ax and wield it to clear out the underbrush blocking my view of a lovely vista so as to see the beauties of nature more clearly. I can also pick up the same ax and cut off someone's head. How I use the ax determines its helpful or destructive qualities. The ax itself is neutral. By the same token, how one uses the historical-critical method of interpretation determines its helpful or destructive qualities. The method in principle is neutral in itself, but it seems quite clear that it has been used both ways. What determines one's use of the critical, hermeneutical method for good or bad? It is the interpreter's epistemological presuppositions. That is the issue. If one exalts, for example, rational-empirical presupposition *above* revelation, it is going to eventuate in the use of the historical-critical method in a destructive fashion, even though the method in itself may be all right.[32]

That the critical approach has often been used quite destructively in some contemporary circles is obvious. Perhaps the primary reason for the negative use of the method is that it can quite easily lend itself to purely rationalistic presuppositions. As a case in point, the school of thinkers like Rudolph Bultmann, with their use of the critical method, thrust themselves into a serious position. Their presuppositional commitment to a rational, empirical view of history forces them to use form-criticism to "demythologize" elements of the suprarational, supernatural revelational truths of the Bible, such as the bodily resurrection of Jesus. Thus, they give an existential, nonhistorical interpretation that is compatible with their presuppositional categories. Although this criticism may be a bit of an oversimplification of the Bultmannian school, it is basically true, and such an approach is ultimately destructive. In so doing, they find a refuge in the rational aspects of the historical-critical method and thus use it to the hilt.[33]

However, that is not primarily the general critical method's fault; the problem is the interpreter's epistemology. As illustrated earlier, when the Bible makes the plain and clear revelational statement that Jesus walked on the water, we accept it and do not retreat into the rationalizing process using the historical-critical method to justify that rationalization. After all, what is so difficult in believing that God can and does perform miracles? To deny such is to be boxed into a pragmatic rationalism which denies the supernatural, and that is virtually tantamount to denying God's essential nature, let alone bad epistemology and dubious critical thought.

This sort of problem is widespread today in some educated circles and has produced a serious fallout. Wrong use of critical methods has so weakened confidence in the truth of Scripture for some students that it has undermined preaching, undercut teaching, weakened faith, discouraged lay Bible reading and study, and developed a skepticism that has hidden Christ from view.

There is a further danger in an inordinate commitment to a critical method with extreme rational emphasis. It metaphorically does to the Bible what the church did in the middle ages; chain it to the pulpit. If it is believed that only the trained critical scholar can *really* interpret the Word of God, that attitude in essence takes the Scriptures out of the hands of the average layperson, "chaining" it intellectually to the educated pulpit. For example, Professor D. E. Nineham, while teaching at the University of London when I was engaged there in doctoral studies, wrote: "The proposed new Anglican catechism appears to regard the private reading of the Bible as mandatory for every literate member of the Church. *Is that realistic?*"[34] That seems rather arrogant as well as poor epistemology, not to mention what the Bible says about the Holy Spirit as the Guide to scriptural understanding.

When Jesus said of the Spirit, "He will guide you into all truth" (John 16:13), Jesus was talking to common, unsophisticated people—fishermen and tax collectors. To wrest the Bible out of the hand of the average believer on "intellectual grounds" is nothing less than tragic. That is why reformers like John Wycliffe and a host of others were willing to die to put the Scriptures back into the hands of the laity. Why do missionaries strive today to translate the Bible into the vernacular and give it to the world's peoples? The answer is plain. When Paul, for example, wrote his epistles, he really thought those ordinary people in Corinth or Ephesus would actually understand what he was talking about and thus arrive at God's truth. It is truly amazing how some have seemingly overlooked that obvious fact. Moreover, it is very questionable to say the contemporary problem is that the first-century believers were so culturally removed from us today that the average, sincere Christian cannot now understand the Bible. After all, the Bible itself states the law of the Lord makes "wise the simple" (Ps. 19:7). We should make no mistake about it, the Word of God is for *all* the people of God of all times.

Moreover, it is quite refreshing to see how everyday believers who love God and walk in the Spirit can actually grasp the real heart of the biblical message. If the Holy Spirit "breathed" the Scriptures, He can surely communicate its truths to those who know Him. The idea that one must have an arsenal of critical tools and extensive education to understand God's Word simply is not true. The Bible is a book of the people for the people. Of course, all serious biblical students should avail themselves of all the help they can get. Yet, the Holy Spirit can and does reveal truth to all sincere, disciplined seekers.

Now all this is not by any means to disparage scholarship or scrap the historical-critical method out of hand. Scholarship is most important and helpful. The plea is to put it in proper perspective, use it with proper presuppositions, be genuinely humble before God, and let Him speak. The best scholarship apart from the Spirit's control will soon go astray. No one, scholar or otherwise, truly understands the revelation of God apart from a contrite heart and utter dependence on the Holy Spirit. Since the Spirit of God is the ultimate Author of the Scriptures, He alone is the final interpreter; and He speaks to all people of an open, humble, believing heart. As Professor A. T. Robertson pointed out, the Bible is "a supernatural revelation above reason which reason never could have obtained unless it had come in this way."[35] So we do well to remember that "God opposes the proud, but gives grace to the humble" (1 Pet. 5:5). Thus we humbly depend on the Spirit, in study and labor, and seek God's revealed truth in the Scriptures.

The Proper Approach

What hermeneutical principles do we then employ, as a scholar or an average Bible reader? The answer to that question calls for a book in itself. Only a skeletal outline can be presented here; yet it is the time-honored approach. Actually, it seems to be the biblical approach itself. Four issues in biblical interpretation must be addressed to get at the truth of the Scriptures. First, careful and extensive *exegesis* must be done. To understand the Bible we need to know what the writer actually said and what he meant to communicate. This demands contextualization. Six steps are helpful here:

1. Grasp the surface, simple message.
2. Get at the deeper, structural principles.
3. Understand the historical-cultural situation addressed.
4. Ask: how would the first hearers understand the passage?
5. Ask: Is the passage relevant today?
6. Ask: What is the general and specific application?

This calls for the use of the critical tools as much as possible according to the capability of the reader, but handled with real care and employing proper presuppositions. That means we take language seriously. We treat history as history, poetry as poetry, and figurative language as just that.

Second, putting the text in the coherent whole of the entire Bible is essential. This is the "analogy of faith" principle, as the reformers put it. It compares Scripture with Scripture, recognizing the coherent, noncontradictory nature of the entire Bible.

Then, we relate the text to general and specific contemporary situations. Relevancy must be sought. The question to ask is: What does this mean to my life?

Third, *application* is vital. We are to discover how to work out the truth in daily life *and do it.*

Finally, the *Christ-centeredness* of all Scripture must be constantly kept in the foreground. Jesus said of the Scriptures, "It is they that bear witness to me" (John 5:39). Christ is the final Word, the final authority. "I am . . . the truth," Jesus said (John 14:6).

Commentaries and writings are often quite helpful. To get an understanding of the history and culture of the times is a positive asset; but in it all, we utterly rely on the wisdom, guidance, and moving of the Holy Spirit. We utilize the best our minds can produce, but always we are finally dependent on the Spirit of God, and there is no antithesis between these two principles. Above all, we humbly submit, mind and heart, to God's Word.

Granted, these principles of interpretation call for much more elaboration, but much has been written on these themes elsewhere. Two excellent works on hermeneutics are: *A Guide to Contemporary Hermeneutics* (Eerdmans, 1986) by Donald K. McKinnon, and *New Testament Interpretation* (Eerdmans, 1977) by J. H. Marshall.[36] Still, the principles outlined above are the hermeneutical approaches that shall be used in formulating our theology of evangelism, and the employment of these principles in the practical theologizing that shall follow will hopefully explain and illustrate in more detail their meaning and use.[37]

The Final Conclusion

So there it stands: in the Holy Scriptures God has delivered an authoritative, trustworthy, true, propositional revelation of Himself that stands the epistemological test of comprehensiveness, coherence, correspondence, noncontradiction, and experience. Therefore, we build our theological structures on that solid, authoritative epistemological base. So we construct our theology of evangelism on scriptural propositions, led by the indwelling Holy Spirit. This will form the foundation of the entire doctrinal superstructure, and such an approach is not being a shallow, superficial "Bible thumper." All the previous argumentation has hopefully made that clear. As J. I. Packer correctly put it:

> The mental discipline of systematically submitting our thoughts, views, and purposes to the judgment of Scripture as it interprets itself to us in regard to our relationship with God, is more than one Christian tradition among many; it is a discipline intrinsic to Christianity itself.[38]

Perhaps the simple cliche is not quite as simplistic as may at first be thought:

> God said it,
> I believe it, and
> That settles it.

Using the Scriptures, under God, with proper epistemological presuppositions and good hermeneutics, should enable one to fabricate the sort of theology of evangelism that will be internally satisfying, true, and useful in pointing others to the "Lamb of God, who takes away the sin of the world!" (John 1:29). After all, that is the final goal of all theology. These principles have guided the people of God through the ages. The story is significant, as the next chapter shall demonstrate.

Notes

1. That revelation is progressive, or cumulative (which is probably a better way to express it), is hardly argued in any knowledgeable Evangelical circles today. This does not mean "later" revelations contradict "earlier" ones. It means essentially that God continually revealed "more" of Himself as people were ready for a deeper insight, culminating it all in Jesus Christ. God does speak to His people where they are in spiritual maturity and discernment.

2. William Temple, in J. I. Packer, *God Has Spoken* (Downers Grove, Ill.: Inter-Varsity Press, 1979), 77.

3. Packer, *God Has Spoken*, 52. Much of the argumentation is found in Packer's discussion of these issues. His work is most helpful and should be read in full.

4. William L. Lumpkin, *Baptist Confessions of Faith* (Valley Forge: Judson Press, 1959), 103.

5. Ibid., 158.

6. The dynamics and practicality of personal and propositional revelation, and how they combine in the reading of the Scriptures, will be discussed shortly.

7. Packer, *God Has Spoken*, 79. Some may retort that this line of reasoning is to characterize the situation. The critics may argue God's dynamic presence enabled the biblical writers to understand the meaning of the events, then they merely recorded their grasp of salvation history, but that tends to muffle God. Must God "explain" everything by mere encounter apart from propositional truth when He Himself has said the Word of God has come to believers in the Scriptures? Hardly!

8. It is probably presumptuous to even approach the concept of biblical inspiration in so few words. The subject demands volumes—and volumes have been written which should be diligently studied. What follows is no more than an outline; yet, one that can be well substantiated by cogent argument, even if space precludes it here.

9. Lumpkin, *Baptist Confessions of Faith*, 198.

10. Ibid., 248-49. The use of such words as *inerrancy* and *infallibility* are not the point here. That thorny issue will be taken up later. These creeds of statements of faith are quoted to demonstrate the high view of Scripture held by traditional Evangelicals.

11. Ibid., 325.

12. Ibid., 358.

13. Ibid., 359.

14. Ibid., 411.

15. *The Baptist Faith and Message* (Nashville: Baptist Sunday School Board, 1963), 3.

16. R. C. H. Lenski, *The Interpretation of St. Paul's Epistle to the Colossians, to the Thessalonians, to Timothy, to Titus and to Philemon.* (Minneapolis: Augsburg Publishing House, 1937), 845.

17. Matthew Henry, *Commentary on the Whole Bible* (New York: Fleming H. Revell Company, 1911), 6:846-47.

18. John Calvin, *Commentaries on the Epistles to Timothy, Titus and Philemon* (Edinburgh: Calvin Translation Society, 1854), 249.

19. Westminster Confession I.1.

20. An address given in Philadelphia to The Baptist Congress, May 21, 1892. It is printed in a pamphlet housed in the library at The Southern Baptist Theological Seminary, Louisville, Kentucky, under the title: *The Relative Authority of Scripture and Reason*, 6. The pamphlet is taken from the proceedings of the Congress. The Baptist Congress no longer meets. It is displaced by other general Baptist meetings.

21. Another issue which surfaces here is the "method" of inspiration, that is, did God inspire the actual words or just the thoughts of the writers. This problem is often called the battle between "dynamic" and "verbal" inspiration, but this seems a rather redundant argument. How can thoughts be expressed except by words? In taking "total inspiration" seriously, it must be maintained there is no word in the Scriptures God is not pleased with, regardless of how God inspired the writers: dynamically or verbally. To delve deeper is to get into the psychology of inspiration about which nothing is known.

22. Parallels or analogies have even been drawn between the human and divine in the productions of the Bible and the humanity and divinity of Jesus. One would not want to press that too far, for, although Jesus was human, He was also sinless.

23. Quoted by Jack B. Rogers and Donald K. McKim in *The Authority and Interpretation of the Bible*, (New York: Harper and Row, 1979), 109.

24. Ibid., 30.

25. Packer, *God Has Spoken*, 97.

26. A. T. Robertson, *The Relative Authority of Scripture and Reason*, 6. That may seem rather judgmental, but it may well be true in some cases.

27. That is assuming the Lord delays His second advent.

28. Some have contended that such statements and approaches qualify the term *inerrancy* so much it gives it all away and really is not "inerrancy" at all, but that does not refute the real point being made.

29. For a full, scholarly treatment of the authority and nature of the Bible, see J. I. Packer, *Fundamentalism and the Word of God* (Grand Rapids: Eerdmans Publishing Co., 1988); Also see R. V. G. Tasker, *Our Lord's Use of the Old Testament*, (Westminster Chapel, 1953).

30. Robert Jackson, "How We Interpret the Bible: Biblical Interpretation and Literary Criticism," *The Proceedings of the Conference on Biblical Interpretation* (Nashville: Broadman Press, 1988), 51.

31. Ibid., 51.

32. New Testament scholars like George Eldon Ladd and George Beasley-Murray have seen this clearly. Ladd's work *Criticism and the New Testament* bears a

careful reading. Also, for an excellent article on how to use the critical method from an evangelical perspective see Walter Kaiser, "Interpreting the Old Testament," *The Proceedings of the Conference on Biblical Interpretation,* 65 *ff.*

33. J. I. Packer, *God Has Spoken,* 28-32. Packer presents some very disturbing—and convincing—facts on this score. It deserves a careful study.

34. D. E. Nineham, *The Church's Use of the Bible Past and Present* (London: S.P.C.K., 1963), 162, author's italics.

35. A. T. Robertson, *The Relative Authority of Scripture and Reason,* 4.

36. Another worthy approach is found in John W. R. Stott's work: *Understanding the Bible* (Grand Rapids: Zondervan Publishing Company, 1979). He states there are three essential elements to be considered in biblical interpretation: (1) the inner witness of the Holy Spirit, (2) reason, (3) and tradition. These are to be kept in dynamic balance.

37. See addendum to Appendix A, *The Chicago Statement on Biblical Hermeneutics.*

38. J. I. Packer, *Keep in Step with the Spirit* (Old Tappan, N.J.: Fleming H. Revell Co., 1984), 238.

3

The Authority for Evangelism: A Biblical-Historical Survey

"All authority in heaven and on earth has been given to me.
Go therefore and make disciples of all nations"
(Matt. 28:18-19).

Introduction

Here is a parable: there was once a man who felt a certain uneasiness about his life. He found little real satisfaction and meaning, though he sought it in many ways. He did have a rather vague idea about God that he deduced from seeing the beauty and order of creation surrounding him. Moreover, he experienced a constant inner compulsion to do right. Thus he concluded there must be a "higher power" behind it all. There was also a subtle idea lurking in his mind that perhaps this God could give the satisfaction he so craved, but he was not sure at all. So he just muddled through life, hoping sometime things would be better. Then, one day, a man with serenity and peace deeply etched on his face came up to the plodding pilgrim and handed him a book. The title of the volume was the *Holy Bible.* The man of peace said to the troubled traveler, "Read through this Book carefully and fully. Then come back and tell me in *one sentence* what this Book is saying." The man agreed to do so. Several days later the traveler came back and with a glow on his face said, "I've read this wonderful Book, and here is what it says: God loves me and is out to redeem me and has told me all about how He does it in this blessed Book." Somehow the pilgrim knew he had found the answers he sought.

The parable hardly needs interpretation. The Book, the sacred Scriptures, is an authoritative, true *Book of redemption.* If it is anything, or does anything, it reveals the fundamental incontestable truth of how God has, and continues, to redeem all that is estranged from Himself—people and the entire creation. The troubled traveler read the Book correctly. That's good news.

In the light of our parable, one would fully expect the Bible and subsequent church history to abound in redemptive, evangelistic truth and activity. As one searches the record, biblically and historically, no disappointment will be experienced. World evangelization and redemption rests at the center of the biblical revelation and the church's continuing ministry. Redemptive truth and activity reign at the very core. The biblical-historical sweep this chapter undertakes should validate the contention that evangelism is foundational, and, if this is proved to be true, it should move one into a profound commitment to worldwide evangelization. If redemption truly is the heartbeat of the Bible, the church's responsibility of sharing the salvation message rests right at the center of her ministry.

A Biblical Survey

Redemption in the Old Testament

"Adam, . . . where art thou?" (Gen. 3:9, KJV). That plaintive cry, first uttered by a redeeming God in Eden, has echoed down through every age of human history. It becomes the central motif of the entire Word of God. The *misseio Dei* is set in order. God is after an estranged creation.

Interesting and relevant to the evangelistic redemptive spirit of the Scriptures is how and when the Bible was born. It had its inception in the context of one of God's marvelous redemptive acts, the exodus of Israel from Egyptian bondage. This fact is important in grasping the very nature and purpose of the Scriptures. The Bible was birthed in redemption.

The importance of the Pentateuch, Genesis in particular, in the entire sweep of God's historical revelation is difficult to overestimate. Genesis presents the beginning of God's great salvation plan. The very first chapters of the Bible tell us God moved to redeem the erring first family. At the very inception of the human need of forgiveness and salvation, God acted in grace. The Lord promised the sinning couple that one day a Redeemer would come:

> The Lord God said to the serpent,
> "Because you have done this,
> cursed are you above all cattle,
> and above all wild animals;
> upon your belly you shall go,
> and dust you shall eat
> all the days of your life.
> I will put enmity between you and the woman,
> and between your seed and her seed;
> he shall bruise your head,
> and you shall bruise his heel" (Gen. 3:14-15).

From the beginning, in a sort of "protoevangelism," the drama of God's gracious redemption deepens and broadens through the biblical revelation.

Some commentators find difficulties in the early Genesis account, however. The critical issue surrounding early Genesis centers in the historicity of the first eleven chapters. There is considerable feeling today that what we have is "saga" or "myth" or "parable," hence not real historical narrative; but that seems a rather weak supposition for several important reasons. First, it is obvious the New Testament writers assume an essential historicity in Genesis 1—11, as did Jesus Himself. That is important, regardless of critics who argue that the biblical personalities and writers of the first century were people of their day and did not have the sophisticated view of history we have currently acquired. Perhaps they did not record history as we do, and perhaps Jesus did in some sense accept the beliefs of the people of His day, but that does not mean they did not explore history, nor was Jesus wrong; neither does it drain the essential historicity from Genesis 1—11.

Further, just because considerable figurative language and obvious large gaps in the narrative exists, its basic historicity is not destroyed. We even do history today in that fashion when our goal is more than just a repeating of facts, and the goal of Genesis 1—11 was to portray God in His early redemptive role, not just lay out mere historical data.

Moreover, and of single importance, the whole redemptive theology of Paul is to some degree predicated on the historicity of Adam and the fall. Paul told the Romans:

> If, because of one man's trespass, death reigned through that one man, much more will those who receive the abundance of grace and the free gift of righteousness reign in life through the one man Jesus Christ.
>
> Then as one man's trespass led to condemnation for all men, so one man's act of righteousness leads to acquittal and life for all men. For as by one man's disobedience many were made sinners, so by one man's obedience many will be made righteous (Rom. 5:17-19).

Professor Wayne E. Ward had seen clearly the importance of this principle of Adam's historicity when he wrote:

> If there is not a headship of the old humanity in Adam, there cannot be a headship of the new humanity in Jesus Christ. If the fall of man is not a historical fact, then it is nonsense to talk about a historical act of redemption in Christ.
>
> Most modern mythologists are consistent enough to see this. They talk about the *myth* of Adam and the *myth* of the cross. But some who follow them only want to go half-way. These talk about the *mythical* fall and the *historical* redemption. If there is not a historical fall, there cannot be a historical redemption from the fall. Genesis is telling us about actual events. It is dealing with fact, not fiction.[1]

Ward is correct; Paul's concept of redemption rests on the historicity of Adam, just as it does on Christ. It seems very questionable to say Paul was speaking figuratively or parabolically about Adam and then literally and historically about Jesus Christ. Careful exegesis of Romans 5 hardly allows it. Moreover, it is well to remember that God is a God of history. He has constantly broken into the course of human history, even fashioned human history for redemptive ends. If the Bible is anything, it is a record of those historical dynamics. This principle is central to the entire biblical narrative.

Now, if the above argumentation on the historicity of Genesis chapter 3 is true, it seems to follow that the same must be basically true of the eleven chapters under consideration. There is no essential literary break in the entire eleven chapters. The author (redactor) wove it all together as a whole. And what do all the stories in this important passage declare? Redemption! Historical redemption! After the fall, the promise of salvation, and the death of Abel, God gave to Adam and Eve a son called Seth to carry on the godly line so the Redeemer would one day come (Gen. 5:4). The Lord saved Noah and his family, thus keeping the promise of redemption alive (Gen. 6—10). There was even salvation history in God's judgment at Babel (Gen. 11:1-9). There can be but one conclusion: God works dramatically in human history to redeem sinful people. The *misseo Dei* is enacted in the dynamics of history. As Paul put it, "Where sin abounded, grace did much more abound" (Rom. 5:20, KJV). Sharing that redemptive truth is evangelism; hence, the centrality of worldwide witnessing to a God who saves.

Genesis 12 ascends to a new level of God's historical revelation, however. It should be noted that beginning with Genesis 12, few Old Testament scholars doubt the basic historicity of what follows. As John Bright put it, "Although we cannot undertake to reconstruct the lives of Abraham, Isaac, and Jacob, we may confidently believe that they were actual historical individuals,"[2] and we have "confidence that the Bible's picture of the patriarchs is rooted in history."[3]

The Genesis 12 passage is a watershed. It tells of God's call to Abraham that initiated the godly line which would one day produce the "Seed" who would "bruise the serpent's heel." The call ushers in the Abrahamic Covenant. How important are God's words here:

Now the Lord said to Abram, "Go from your country and your kindred and your father's house to the land that I will show you. And I will make of you a great nation, and I will bless you, and make your name great, so that you will be a blessing. I will bless those who bless you, and him who curses you I will curse; and by you all the families of the earth shall bless themselves" (Gen. 12:1-3).

Concerning these important covenant verses with their wonderful promise, Harrelson said:

> The initiative lies entirely with Yahweh: He speaks and Abraham obeys. The picture of the call of Abraham is of decisive importance . . . , as Gerhard von Rad has shown. This *word of promise* dominates the entire Abraham narrative.[4]

The concept of *covenant* permeates the rest of the Old Testament—and the New for that matter. Covenant can be defined as "a gracious undertaking entered into by God for the benefit and blessing of man, and specifically of those men who by faith receive the promise and commit themselves to the obligations which this undertaking involves."[5] The significance of the Abrahamic covenant can only be grasped by tracing what God did as a result of the divine institution of the new relationship, and the response of those called into that dynamic fellowship.

Included in that covenant relationship is the unusual birth of Isaac, the divine choosing of Jacob over Esau, the providential journey of the family to Egypt, and the growth of the nation. All these dramatic events stand as symbolic of what God does in delivering His people. What words characterize these monumental moments? Redemption, deliverance, and salvation! God's covenant is a salvation covenant. God committed Himself that through Abraham's seed all the families of the earth would be blessed. God fully kept that covenant promise. Moreover, He constantly reminded His people of His redemptive acts in history and the subsequent responsibility that such deliverance entailed.

The promise was carried on in the Sinai covenant when God amidst thunder and lightning gave His people the Law. It then continued into the victorious conquest of Canaan. The establishment of the great Davidic kingdom was for those same gracious redemptive ends. Even the exile possessed profound redemptive purposes. It ended idolatry in Israel. And why were the powerful prophets sent? To interpret the covenant afresh and thus call the covenant people back to the obligations of the redemptive relationship. It is not incidental that the "old serpent" constantly strove to pervert God's people and thus break the covenant, but God, in sovereign grace, established the covenant and graciously preserved it intact. So the challenge was always before Israel: "If my people who are called by my name humble themselves, and pray and seek my face, and turn from their wicked ways, then I will hear from heaven, and will forgive their sin and heal their land" (2 Chron. 7:14).

Ward brought it together when he said, "The entire Bible is the account of God's call and preparation of a people, in order that through them the nations of the earth might be blessed. For this purpose God called the patriarchs and from their children called the nation of Israel into being."[6] *Redemption radiates from every page of the Old Testament.* So the nation was prepared for the "fullness of the time" (Gal. 4:4). That glorious day dawned and heralded the arrival of the world's Redeemer. God fully and finally revealed His great redemption plan. The good news, the evangel, the message of the evangelist, emerged full bloom. The New Covenant was introduced.

Redemption in the New Testament

Far from incidental is the fact that the first four books of the New Testament are called Gospels: *Euaggelion,* the root of the English word *evangelism.* Further, the authors of these Gospels are rightly known as the four "evangelists." That is because the church clearly recognized they wrote for redemptive purposes. The fourth Gospel expresses it perfectly: "These are written that you may believe that Jesus is the Christ, the Son of God, and that believing you may have life in his name" (John 20:30-31).

What is true of John's purpose is essentially true of the other three canonical Gospels. Gerald R. Borchert's *Dynamics of Evangelism* tells us: "The purpose of a Gospel, then, is to present the 'good news' or the gospel about new life through Jesus. As such, it is a kind of early evangelistic tract which was written to instruct people concerning the implications of the coming of Christ."[7] This truth is very obvious in the third Gospel. Luke was writing so that the receiver, Theophilus, might "receive the truth (1:4) about Jesus in order that he could make an adequate decision about the Lord," as Borchert expressed it.[8] The whole point of the four Gospels, written from different perspectives and to different audiences, is to convince readers that Jesus of Nazareth is the Messiah, that He lived, died, and rose again to purchase eternal redemption for all who will repent and believe. Evangelization is their message and goal. The Lord's last recorded words were the Commission to world evangelization. The four Gospels are essentially books on God's worldwide redemptive plan.

The Acts of the Apostles also falls in this general framework. Being the second volume of Luke's message to Theophilus, the beloved physician was still seeking the conversion of the "most excellent Theophilus." The entire rationale behind Acts, as Professor Frank Stagg contended, is to explain how a small, pietistic Jewish sect in obscure Galilee had, in a few years, become a worldwide evangelistic movement that had "turned the world upside down" (Acts 17:6).

The Book of Acts actually outlines itself on the basis of major breakthroughs in the progress of the gospel. The first victory came in Jerusalem on the Day of Pentecost when 3,000 were converted (Acts 2:41). That opened the door to the evangelization of the Jews. The Jerusalem church had grown to several thousand by Acts 4:5.

The next major move occurred in the ministry of Philip. The Samaritans, half Jews, came to Christ by the veritable multitudes (Acts 8:4-8). Next, Philip led a pure Gentile proselyte to Christ; the Ethiopian eunuch was saved (Acts 8:26-40).

Then we see Peter in Joppa. The event was most significant in the progress of the gospel. After Peter's disturbing vision (Acts 10:9-16), he went to the home of a Gentile, Cornelius, and preached Christ with great effect. The entire household was converted. A sort of Gentile Pentecost occurred. Jewish elitism received a death blow. The door to the Gentile mission was opened.

Paul subsequently came on the scene, and the great Gentile Antioch church thrived under the preaching of the gospel. In that setting, Paul's missionary ministry to the whole world was inaugurated (13:1-3). That ministry broadened and deepened until the Book of Acts ends with a dramatic adverb: unhindered. The book is open ended; the gospel goes on as it still does, unhindered. All obstacles—racial, cultural, economic, sexual, and political—fell before the power of the evangel (Rom. 1:16-17). The world truly was being turned upside down.

What does all of that mean? It means that the New Testament church was vitally interested in, and committed to, world evangelization. Acts is a chronicle of the heartbeat of first-century Christians to win others to faith in Jesus Christ. The early days of the church scintillated with evangelistic fervor. Despite all the problems and persecution the world hurled at them, they courageously took the good news everywhere. At last, the Great Commission (Acts 1:8) was set into action. Gerald Borchert summarized it well when he stated: "The Book of Acts . . . is an intriguing dramatic story concerning the evangelistic vitality of an initially small but genuinely transformed and determined group of human beings who dared to face death rather than reject the evangelistic imperative from God."[9]

The Pauline corpus likewise reveals the evangelistic motif of the New Testament. A. Skevington Woods, in his book *Evangelism, Its Theology and Practice,* called Paul's Letters the "incidental literature of evangelism." That is true. Paul wrote most of his epistles to churches he had founded for the purpose of solving problems in those congregations to the end that they might be God's effective agents in world evangelization. Paul himself became the archetype of the evangelistic model, and he led the churches along those basic lines.

The same is obviously true of the rest of the so-called General Epistles in the New Testament, and it seems most important that the last book of the Bible ends with a wide-open evangelistic appeal from our glorified Lord Himself: "The Spirit and the Bride say, 'Come.' And let him who hears say, 'Come.' And let him who is thirsty come, let him who desires take the water of life without price" (Rev. 22:17).

The Point of the Biblical Survey

The Bible is a Book of redemptive evangelism. It seems abundantly clear that no one can objectively approach the Scriptures and draw any other conclusion. The Bible vibrates with evangelistic truth and action. Even in the admittedly very scanty survey of the Word of God given above, the fact of the centrality of evangelism in the Scriptures is unarguable. Therefore, those who take the Bible seriously and view it as authoritative must take evangelism seriously. Biblical believers are compelled by the very content of Scripture to be evangelistic believers. There is really no other option. Thus, the role for a biblical theology of evangelism is seen. However, church history has something to say to us in this whole arena as well, something of quite important significance.

Lessons from a Survey of Church History

This book contends for a high view of the Scriptures, claiming them to be the totally inspired, fully truthful, propositional revelation of God. Thus, the Scriptures become the arbitrator in all theological truth claims. Moreover, it has been argued that evangelism holds a central place residing at the very core of the biblical revelation. Now if all that is true, it would seem to follow that history should demonstrate that, whenever a high view of the Scriptures was sincerely held, fervent evangelism ensued; and the church was thereby enhanced. Does history tell us such? Before launching into the actual construction of a theology of evangelism, we must answer that final question.

The First Centuries

In a previous chapter, it was quite conclusively shown that the early church held the Scriptures in high esteem. For example, concerning Augustine, Dewey M. Beegle stated, "Augustine's formulation comes the closest to expressing the doctrine of inerrancy."[10] By *inerrancy* the church fathers simply meant that the Bible is wholly truthful and absolutely trustworthy, true in all it states. Generally speaking, practically all the fathers and sincere believers adhered to such a view of the Bible. Although some argumentation and exceptions may be given, the general contention holds.

However, were these early years of the church evangelistic and missionary in impetus? Did these high views of the Bible give the believers a significant missionary commitment?

Evangelism and Missionary Endeavors in the Early Centuries

A few examples of evangelistic zeal may suffice to demonstrate the spirit that pervaded the early centuries of church life. As a case in point, by A.D. 250 Barbarian tribes from northern and eastern Europe were moving south and establishing settlements along the Danube River, which formed something of a natural northern boundary for the Roman Empire. In this fluid situation the nomadic marauders often took Roman captives as slaves. Christians were regularly taken. These believers had a vibrant testimony for Jesus Christ. As a consequence, many of the barbarians came to Christian faith, one of whom was a certain Ulfilas. After his conversion, Ulfilas was immediately moved by a deep desire to win his people to faith in Jesus Christ. He became something of a self-appointed missionary. Then, ordained as bishop of the Goths in 348, his work proved to be tremendously successful. One of the outstanding achievements of Ulfilas' ministry was his translation of a large part of the Bible into the Gothic tongue. Through his endeavors, many barbarians turned to the Christian faith.

During those dynamic days, Patrick of Ireland came on the scene. Saint Patrick was certainly more than a man who traditionally drove the snakes from that country and eulogized the shamrock. Patrick (390?-460?) was a true apostle of Jesus Christ. A native of Scotland, in the providence of God he was kidnapped by pirates and hauled off to Northern Ireland. This led to a genuine salvation experience of Jesus Christ. After his conversion, Patrick developed a deep love and burden for the conversion of the Irish. Through a series of unusual circumstances, the king came to believe that Patrick was sent by God and that the gospel was true. From this dramatic beginning, the influence of Patrick reached gigantic proportions. During his ensuing ministry, Patrick established no less than 365 churches and saw 120,000 converts come to faith in Jesus Christ. The Irish honor him as their patron saint.

The sixth-century epitome of evangelistic Christianity in pagan Scotland was Columba (A.D. 521-597). He was a very gifted young man and displayed unusual talent and aptitude. At the age of twenty-one, he dedicated himself to Jesus Christ to become a fearless proclaimer of the gospel. In 562, Columba and twelve brothers started their well-known venture for the Lord. They sailed to the small island of Iona off the coast of Scotland. There the center of the operation was established. Although Columba experienced much opposition from the Druids (the pagan priests), the king of the area came to realize the power of the gospel, and through a miraculous healing in his own life embraced the Christian faith. This opened the door for the evangel, and people by the thousands began to be converted. The doctrines Columba proclaimed were based on the Bible. God's Word was the cornerstone of his faith and life.

Through his vast evangelistic activities, many came to faith in Christ. He labored in the Iona community for thirty-four years. In June of 597, he went to his reward, dying as he had lived, sharing God's gospel with others.

In the dynamic years of the sixth century, the great Augustine of Canterbury burst on the horizon. Augustine was commissioned by Gregory the Great to pick forty companions to assist him in the evangelization of the Britons. In 596, Augustine and his band headed for the British Isles. They landed on the south shore of England in 597, not far from Dover.

Augustine immediately made contact with Ethelbert, the ruling personality of that general area, and Ethelbert was won to faith in Jesus Christ. Augustine established a base of operations which became known as Canterbury. From this new location, the missionaries began an itinerant evangelistic ministry. They demonstrated such love for the natives that soon many came to faith in Jesus Christ. The majority of the people of Kent, as the surrounding area was known, were brought into a vital relationship with Christ. Augustine became the first archbishop of Canterbury. By 605, the year of Augustine's death, the majority of the savage Angles and Saxons had been brought into subjection to Jesus Christ.

In these early centuries of the Christian mission, the Continent was not without its important personalities. The eighth-century embodiment of evangelistic endeavor was personified in Boniface (680-754). Boniface, a Britisher, became known as the "Apostle of the Germans." Boniface devoted himself to the propagation of the good news. He journeyed from England and began ministering first in Friesland and next in Gaul. However, he was eager to penetrate areas that had never been touched by the gospel. Consequently, he moved into the pagan portions of the Frankish Empire. Boniface gave himself recklessly to the challenge and faithfully preached the simple gospel of Jesus Christ based on a typical high view of the Scriptures. Many were won.

Space does not allow for recounting the tremendous experiences of a multitude of others who made similar contributions to the evangelization of the world in those dramatic early centuries of the church. The entire course of early church evangelism vibrated with life and power. With few exceptions, these great evangelistic endeavors were undertaken in the context of a commitment to the Bible and what it declared concerning world evangelization. Beginning in the first century itself, there is little question that along with the traditional high view of the Scriptures held by the Lord,[11] the apostles, and the church fathers, there was an ardent missionary-evangelism born that lived for centuries. This does not necessarily mean one dictates the other, but the implication seems evident.

Michael Green, in his classic work *Evangelism in the Early Church*, put it all together in the following statement:

> The writings that really evoked an abiding interest [in the early church] were the Scriptures. There is abundant evidence, : . . to show that Christians, unlike Jews, did use the Scriptures evangelistically. From the Acts of the Apostles down to Gregory and Origen we find the same story repeated time and again.[12]

Thus, a historical pattern seems to have developed that a high view of the Scriptures, interpreted with good hermeneutical principles, normally precipitates fervent evangelism and missionary activity. Now, we must look briefly at the next one thousand years.

The Middle "Dark" Ages

The fact that the church slowly slipped into what is commonly called the "Middle" or "Dark Ages" constitutes one of the tragedies in the history of Christianity. Although some fervent evangelistic activity took place during those bleak years, it required the Reformation to break the syndrome of the stagnant church and once again release the simple gospel. The problem of Rome was that tradition had ascended to a place of equal authority with the Bible. The consequences were that the gospel became shrouded in a host of church traditions, and few people grasped the simplicity of the salvation message.

One of the paradoxes of the Middle Ages, however, is that even during those rather dismal days, there were isolated individuals who came to grasp the kernel of the gospel and launched into fervent evangelistic endeavors. Almost without exception, it occurred when they rediscovered the sole authority of the Bible. That is most noteworthy.

One of the best known personalities in that context was Bernard of Clairvaux (1091-1153). Although Bernard had been preceded by earlier evangelistic missionaries, for example, Anskar of France (800-865) and Olaf Tryggvason of Norway (964-1000), it was the mighty ministry of Bernard that became one of the bright spots before the Reformation. Through a spiritual crisis, he was brought to an all-out surrender to the will of God. Immediately, he set out as a preacher and minister of the simple gospel. He was a man of devout love for God with a zeal to introduce others to Jesus Christ. One of his hymns is still sung in our churches today:

> Jesus, the very thought of Thee
> With sweetness fills my breast;
> But sweeter far Thy face to see,
> And in Thy presence rest.

Multitudes came to faith in our Lord by the simple proclamation that Bernard had gleaned from his scriptural knowledge.

No doubt the most singular personality of the whole period was the great Saint Francis of Assisi, Italy (1182-1226). In early manhood he searched for thrills and sensual pleasures; but after the disillusionment of an illness and a subsequent crisis that crossed his path, he came to vital faith in Jesus Christ. Immediately, he began a ministry of preaching. A mystic of the first order, he preached Christ in purity. Disciples soon began to gather about Francis, and an order was established. The disciples fanned out all over Italy and into other parts of the Roman Empire to preach Christ.

The secret of Francis's effective ministry centered in the fact that he got a grip on the essence of the gospel from the Word of God. Consequently, thousands came to genuine faith in the Lord Jesus Christ. The spirit of evangelism had so gripped all the disciples of the early Franciscan order that they learned the languages of the nations and traveled throughout the empire sharing Christ, singing the glad songs of the faith. It was a glorious movement as the good news once again was brought to the common people.

Another outstanding personality of this general period was the thundering Girolamo Savonarola (1452-1498) of Florence. Savonarola will stand as one of the great proclaimers of the gospel. A native of Ferrara, Italy, he was born in the year 1452. He was the antithesis of Francis. Being a dour young man, Savonarola spent many hours in fasting and prayer, even as a teenager. In 1475 he left home and made his way to a Dominican monastery in Bologna and presented himself for holy orders. The years of his monkish pilgrimage were devoted primarily to an intensive study of the Bible. Through saturating himself in the Scriptures, particularly the Book of Revelation, Savonarola came to the conclusion as historian Taylor put it, "The messages of this book, [Revelation] with their startling images, their awful denunciations of sin, their exalted and throbbing pity, could alone break up the corruption which abounded, and bring back to earth the peace of God and the recognition of the sovereignty of Jesus Christ."[13]

While serving as prior of Saint Mark's monastery in Florence, Savonarola was asked to give a series of Lenten sermons in the Church of San Lorenzo. He began to preach from the Revelation about the judgment of God which was certainly coming upon the church and the infidels because of their sin and corruption. He preached some three hundred sermons from that last book of the Bible. Soon the entire city of Florence was in the grips of a mighty spiritual awakening. Thousands upon thousands came to new vibrant faith in Jesus Christ as a consequence of Savonarola's discovery of the Bible and the principle of salvation by grace through faith. He is often called a "prereformer" Reformer. Such is certainly an apt description of the man, as was also true of John Hus of Prague. Through Savonarola's preaching, so many came to faith in Jesus Christ that it was said of Florence "the Carnival was like Lent." Great was the revival, great were the number of converts, and it came about essentially by a rediscovery of the Scriptures. Savonarola sealed his ministry with his blood. Yet, he will stand as one of the giants of the Middle Ages before the breaking in of the great Reformation era.

Lack of space precludes the accounting of the evangelistic and missionary ministries of men like Tauler of Strassburg (1300-1361), the Waldenses, the Lollards, and others, who in coming to grips with the Scriptures found the heart of the gospel and began to preach Christ. The whole period can be summed up in the words of George Duncan Barry. He himself was no believer in a high view of the Scriptures, nonetheless he readily admitted, "The fact that for 15 centuries no attempt was made to formulate a definition of the doctrine of inspiration of the Bible, testifies to the universal belief of the Church that the Scriptures were the handiwork of the Holy Ghost."[14] That commitment to the Word of God almost without exception bred fervent evangelization.

Again, a pattern seemingly emerges: a high view of the rediscovered Word of God precipitates evangelistic-missionary zeal. This now leads to the Reformation era.

The Reformation Era

Little needs to be said concerning the views of the Bible held by the great Reformers. Allusions to these dynamic days were made in the previous chapter. Moreover, so much has been written in this particular vein that it would be redundant to retrace in detail those steps again. The authority of the Bible was rediscovered through the lives and ministries and influence of the Reformers. With the high view of the Scriptures as formulated by Calvin, Luther, Zwingli, and others, evangelism soon followed. It is quite incontestable that the Reformation "tool" in the new commitment to evangelization was the Bible. Johnston contends that the major Reformation truth was a trustworthy Bible: "The judge and critique of experiences was not subjective but in subject to the Holy Scriptures. . . . Voltzel says that the Reformed Church of the 17th Century recognized the authority of Scriptures: they alone possess an absolute and infallible character."[15] It seems that, generally speaking, the Reformation doctrine of the authority and inspiration of the Scriptures was basically a continuation of the teaching of the early church fathers. The Reformers saw the Holy Spirit alone as the original Author of the Bible and that He gave us a totally true rule of faith. John Calvin, in his *Commentary* on 2 Timothy 3:16 stated:

Whoever then wishes to profit in the Scriptures, let him first of all lay down as a settled point this—that the Law and prophesies are not teaching (*doctrinarm*) delivered by the will of men, but dictated (*dictatum*) by the Holy Ghost . . . It was the mouth of the Lord that spoke . . . We owe to the Scriptures the same reverence which we owe to God, because it has proceeded from Him above, and has nothing of man mixed with it. (See also *Institutes,* VII. 1.)

Martin Luther held a very similar view, as we saw in chapter 2. Martin Bucer (1491-1551) built his entire theology upon the Scriptures, which he considered infallible. Along with Luther, Zwingli, Calvin, and others, Bucer did not consider his exegesis to be infallible, but he saw the Bible in that light.

When it was concluded that Roman Catholic traditions were not infallible, and a high view of the Bible was established, the Reformers built their entire theological structures on the principle of *sola scriptura.* That approach gave us the Reformation doctrines of grace, and moved the church into the fervent proclamation of the gospel. Consequently, multitudes came to faith in Christ. All historians of all theological persuasions attest to this fact. Granted, there has been some dispute as to whether or not Calvin and Luther believed in the actual inerrancy of the Scriptures; but in the light of all they said concerning God's Word, it seems evident that the burden of proof rests heavily upon those who would argue otherwise. The strongest case by far, it seems, can be made that these Reformers held a very high view of the Scriptures, so high that they did not hesitate to say the Bible is the infallible Word of God.

A high view of the Scriptures does not *necessarily* bring about great evangelistic fervor. It is seemingly quite easy to slip into a scholasticism that maintains proper doctrine and high views of the Bible but stultifies in a rationalistic quest for orthodoxy. That sort of trap can ensnare the most earnest "conservative." The latter part of the Reformation era is certainly a classic example of this problem. When Protestant scholasticism invaded the reformed church, it gave itself to an inordinate search for orthodoxy. Creeds became so rigid that one could not bend either to the right or to the left. The Bible was approached in a wooden, rationalistic manner that allowed for no deviation or freedom. Faith became essentially "intellectual" with little emphasis on personal experience. What Rome had done in stultifying the Christian faith by the rigid views of the "school men," segments of the Reformation church repeated in essence with a "scholastic" approach to their views of the Scriptures and their ensuing theologies. A rather dismal scene began to develop.

Just as the Reformation was seemingly bogging down, God suddenly did one of His marvelous acts of grace. A movement began that broke the rigidity of the Protestant "school men" and brought a new influx of spiritual life and vitality. With this, there came a somewhat more relaxed view of the Bible, although it was held in highest authority. This touch of God brought a fresh breeze of evangelistic fervor and missionary advance to the church. It became known as the Puritan-Pietistic movement. A fascinating history lies back of this thrust, and actually brings us up to our modern contemporary scene.

The Significant Puritan-Pietistic Movement

The English Puritan movement and the continental Pietistic movement should be grasped in the singular. Many modern historians contend this seventeenth/eighteenth-century movement is separated only by the geography of the English channel and the temperament and politics of two different peoples. For example, Ernest Stoeffler of Temple University states emphatically in his book *The Rise of Evangelical Pietism:*

> The fact is that essential differences between continental Pietism and what we have called Pietistic Puritanism cannot be established because they are non-existent. The pressure towards a certain pattern of piety within the Calvinistic tradition (regarded broadly), whether in England, the Low Countries, the Rineland, or elsewhere are basically the same.[16]

Having something of its early center at Cambridge University under influential professors like William Perkins, the Puritan-Pietistic movement made a tremendous impact, first in Britain and then later on the Continent. The prime point of the movement is projected in the German word *herzenreligion,* that is, "religion of the heart." The essential emphasis of the entire thrust became total *personal* involvement in the faith. For the Puritan-Pietist, faith was essentially inward, experiential, and all-consuming. This was clearly quite different from the "Protestant Scholasticism" of the day. Still, at the same time, heavy weight was laid on the objective Scriptures as the source of faith and as a balance to the existential elements of Christian experience. But creeds, mere intellectual assent, and theology were not seen as the sole essence of Christianity. William Ames, one of the first systematic theologians of reformed Pietism, stated, "Faith is the resting of the heart in God." Jonathan Edwards, who must be included in this noble train, clearly distinguished between what he termed a "speculative" and a "saving" faith. The former centers in the "assent of the understanding," but saving faith demands "the consent of the heart." He said, "True religion consists so much in the affections that there can be no true religion without them."[17]

The New Testament was of vital importance to the Puritan-Pietists.

Because of this biblicism, the movement never degenerated into religious humanism or mere mysticism. Pietists insisted on the absolute authority of the Word of God, and that held the movement in balance. Further, they believed the Holy Spirit is able to communicate the truth of the Scriptures to all sincere souls without the necessity of biblical professionals. The Puritan-Pietistic tradition would trust the opinions of theologically untrained but dedicated laypersons. This was tremendously important in rescuing the doctrine of the priesthood of believers from being no more than a reformed dogma. Moreover, it released a wave of evangelistic fervor not seen for many years. Again, the pattern of high views of the Bible precipitating evangelistic zeal surfaces.

By such an approach to the Bible, the foundation for the great evangelism which flowed from the Puritan-Pietistic movement was laid. As Johnston stated, "It was this type of Pietism . . . that must be considered the dominant spirit of the missionary movement. . . . The whole roots of Pietism are to be discovered in the Reformation doctrine of the Scriptures."[18] Being fully convinced God had spoken by His Son, the Lord Jesus Christ, as revealed through the Scriptures, this doctrinal and biblical firmness brought about the Pietists' quest for personal conversion and the responsibility of witnessing on the part of all God's people. It was this trust that eventually precipitated the great revivalism and evangelism of early America and eighteenth-century Europe. It gave birth to the significant missionary impetus of men like William Carey (1761-1834). Virtually every church historian recognizes the prominent place of Puritan-Pietism in this phenomenal missionary-evangelism movement. Johnston again made the point very emphatically: "This evangelistic zeal seems to be intimately related to the evangelical doctrine of the scriptures and the conversion and welfare of the individual."[19] Johnston finally went so far as to state in *World Evangelism and the Word of God*: "Pietistic evangelism was only possible because of the doctrine of infallibility as defined by the Reformation. This one divinely given Book was the only source of saving revelation, it was the Judge of man and the world in which he lived."[20] If Pietism was anything, it was a deep and profound spiritual awakening of worldwide missionary-evangelism. The Puritan-Pietists had it right, and that deep concern and burden grew out of and was controlled by their biblicism.

It is only correct—and fair—to point out one deviation to the pattern that emerged in Pietism. Count Zinzendorf of the Moravian pietistic movement had a somewhat lower view of the Bible than most of his pietistic counterparts. He believed the Scriptures contained errors. This is somewhat remarkable in light of the fact he was a Lutheran. Perhaps Zinzendorf was reacting to the scholasticism that had diminished the existential, evangelistic, spiritual elements of the faith in some Lutheran circles. Not only that, the strong emphasis on the inner work of the

Spirit gave a very decided emotional flavor to the Moravian work, even moving them to attempt to find God's will by "casting lots" and letting the Bible fall open at random to get God's message. That approach no doubt diminished the importance of the Bible, at least to a degree, in their practical theology. At any rate, Zinzendorf had a lower view of the Bible than many reformed Pietists; at the same time he and the Moravians had a great and fervent missionary-evangelistic commitment.

So one cannot say *invariably* that a person must be an inerrantist to be zealously evangelistic and mission minded; Zinzendorf puts the lie to that. Yet, it must still be admitted the count had quite a high view of Scripture and saw it as the only final authority in faith and practice. Zinzendorf used the Bible pragmatically as many "inerrantists" do. Further, he is more of the exception than the rule among mature Pietists. Moreover, the early Moravians later changed their stance on the Scriptures. George Whitfield wrote *An Expostulatory Letter to Nicholas Louis, Count Zinzendorf* in which he refuted the Moravian's view of Scripture. It proved to be the jolt that moved the Moravians to depend less on inner experience and revelations, giving more stress on the objective Scriptures.

Out of the great Puritan-pietistic awakening a noble history has flowed, biblically and evangelistically. Spiritual giants rose in that setting, but space precludes the telling of the marvelous ministry of the Continental Pietists personified in men like John Arndt, Philipp Spener (1635-1705), his protege, August Hermann Francke (1663-1727), and a host of others. Of course, the British counterparts were John Wesley and George Whitefield along with other great personalities like William McCulloch (1700-1771) and Howell Harris (1714-1773). The tremendous eighteenth-century British Great Awakening occurred in and through their ministries, but these stories are well known. All these men held high views of the Bible and, consequently, strove to maintain the purity of the gospel. As they preached Christ, literally hundreds of thousands came to faith in our Lord. America had its counterpart in the first Great Awakening of the eighteenth century. Most are conversant with the ministry of Jonathan Edwards, William Tennent (1673-1746), Gilbert Tennent (1703-1764), Theodore Freylinghausen (1691-1747), and the multitudes who became God's instruments in the first Great Awakening in America. All these revival leaders strongly argued for very high concepts of the holy Scriptures.

Spiritual life in America deteriorated in the wake of the Revolutionary War, and then the second Great Awakening dawned. That movement saw thousands converted. Heroes of the faith emerged in the setting of the second Great Awakening, for example, Lyman Beecher, Ashel Nettleton, and the great Charles G. Finney. Concerning the Bible,

Finney stated it was "infallibly secured from all error."[21] In this statement, Finney spoke for virtually all early nineteenth-century American Evangelicals.

The brief historical survey above has hopefully established a pattern that high views of the Bible generally develop strong commitment to missions and evangelism, but what about the more recent scene? Does the pattern still hold? This is the next subject, beginning with the last half of the nineteenth century.

Recent Years

An important nineteenth century educator and theologian was James P. Boyce. One of the founders of The Southern Baptist Theological Seminary and also professor of Systematic and Polemic Theology at Furman University, he made a very significant impact on the later part of nineteenth-century American Christianity. He represented the general approach of the influential Princetonian school. Boyce's biblical position reflects the views of much dynamic evangelism in the nineteenth century, such as D. L. Moody. His statements on the inspiration of the Scriptures can be found in an inaugural address delivered to Furman University on July 31, 1856, at the Annual Commencement. In his sermon he said, "The Bible as a book [is] not to be interpreted in any way fancy may direct." Why? Because of "the verbal inspiration of its writers."[22] Boyce wrote a rather extensive systematic theology. In it he said many important things concerning the Scriptures. Some of his statements are as follows:

> With reverence for truth, and especially for the truth taught in the Word of God . . . [We] are brought face to face with the fact that our knowledge is bounded by God's revelation, and are led to acknowledge it [the Bible] as its source. . . . We are consequently warned not to omit any of the truths assigned from any source, nor to add to it anything not properly ascertained [embraced] therein. A departure from this rule will lead to inevitable error.[23]

Boyce considered the Bible to be revelational in itself. This is evident by the following statement: "By revelation, we mean the knowledge which God conveys by direct supernatural instruction, preeminently that given in the book known as the Bible."[24] In the latter part of Boyce's theological presentation, he raised several questions concerning the Bible and then answered the queries. He forthrightly stated:

> How came it to be written? God inspired Holy men to write it; did they write it exactly as God wished: Yes; as much as if He had written every

word Himself. Ought it, therefore, to be believed and obeyed? Yes; as
much as though God had spoken directly to us.[25]

All this leaves little doubt in the mind of any objective reader what
James Boyce, an early and significant systematic theologian, felt concerning the Word of God.

Furthermore, Boyce clearly recognized the fact that interpretation of
Scripture is as vital to orthodoxy as giving high marks to believing the
Scriptures. He knew to state glibly "The Bible is our only creed" was not
sufficient. He was well aware of the fact that all sorts of weird sects
believe in an infallible Bible. He said, "It is not whether they believe the
Bible, but whether believing it they deduce from it such doctrine as
shows, according to the judgment of the Christian, that they have been
so taught by the Spirit of God as should be guided into the knowledge of
all truths." Did Boyce believe in evangelism? Absolutely; his whole life
and ministry attested to the reality of his evangelistic missionary
commitment.

Actually, the Evangelical world of the past century, especially the last
fifty years of that period, became an evangelistic epoch. The century
saw the advent of missionary and evangelistic activity unprecedented in
the history of the church, save in its early years. The dynamic nineteenth century became known, in the words of church historian
Kenneth Scott Latourette, as "the Great Century." The giants of evangelistic and missionary grandeur that century produced is quite fantastic. Gracing the scene were men and women like Charles Haddon Spurgeon, Mary Slessor, Charles Finney, D. L. Moody, Lottie Moon,
Alexander McClaren, Joseph Parker, Hudson Taylor, Ruth Paxon, C. T.
Studd, Amy Carmichael, and a host of other evangelists, pastors, and
missionary leaders. It looked like a parade of God's best through the
ages. The "Great Century" culminated in the renowned Edinburgh
Conference of 1910.[26] That missionary conference, spearheaded by John
Mott and other missionary statesmen, stood as the high-water mark in
commitment to world evangelization. Many leaders at the conference
held the Bible high in their theology.

Does all of this, however, really establish a contemporary pattern between a high view of Scripture and evangelistic fervency in missionary
involvement? In answering it may prove helpful to spend a moment
looking at this question from the negative perspective. Has a low view
of Scripture tended, especially in recent years, to diminish evangelistic
commitment and missionary involvement? That is the next question.

A Negative Approach

It has been made quite evident that most nineteenth-century Evangelicals by and large held a very high view of the Bible, but by the turn of the twentieth century, new thought, given rise by the earlier Enlightenment, precipitated a degree of Germanic rationalistic epistemologies in some Evangelical circles. It emanated essentially in something of the Hegelian tradition. Hegel's basic approach had already taken root in various continental theological thinkers as early as the late eighteenth century. Prior to this invasion of crass rationalism, traditional Evangelicals built their epistomological theological base on four essential presuppositions:

1. God has revealed Himself primarily in the life, ministry, death, resurrection, ascension, and continuing intercession of Jesus Christ, God's Son and the world's Savior.
2. God addresses us in propositional language about Jesus as well as in personal encounter with the person of Christ.
3. The propositional revelation of God is contained in the truthful, totally inspired Word of God: the Holy Scriptures.
4. Revelation is the supreme epistemological principle in formulating all Christian beliefs, that is, reason is subject to revelation.

The entire evangelical concept of revelation and subsequent theology and missionary understanding was predicated upon these epistemological and theological presuppositions.

The advent of the rationalistic, epistemological system, however, virtually eliminated all the above evangelical presuppositions save one, that is, Christ Jesus as God's supreme revelation. Even that idea was severely diluted by some, resulting in a low Christology. Human reason, based on a rational-empirical critical basis, was crowned "king-of-the-hill" in the epistemological game of attempting to derive truth and reality. For all practical purposes, the Scriptures lost their supreme position, even if that significant shift in authority was denied. As Berkhof pointed out:

> When the chill winds of Rationalism swept over Europe, natural revelation was exalted at the expense of supernatural revelation. Man became intoxicated with a sense of his own ability and goodness, refused to listen and submit to the voice of authority that spoke to him in Scripture, and reposed complete trust in the ability of human reason to lead him out of the labyrinth of ignorance and error into the clear atmosphere of true knowledge.[27]

Such an approach opened the door to all sorts of theological deviations; it even developed some rather strange concepts of the religious experience itself. The end result for evangelism was often either a universalism or a syncretism or both. The "exclusiveness" of the Christian faith was lost, as was some of the essential doctrines of Christ's work. Obviously, that was quite destructive to missionary-evangelism as Evangelicals have understood it.

These basic ideas, based on a nonevangelical set of presuppositions, had covered Europe and segments of American Christianity by the end of the nineteenth century. The theological battles that transpired are legendary. As an instance, it made its frontal attack in British Baptist life as manifested in the well-known "Downgrade Controversy" in which Charles Haddon Spurgeon was involved. As a consequence of the tragic Downgrade Controversy, Spurgeon withdrew from the British Baptist Union. He died a broken and crushed man. The devastating effect all this had on British religious life is quite obvious; many of the churches of Britain were severely reduced in evangelism and outreach. Of course, there were also significant revolutionally cultural elements that contributed to the demise of many congregations. There are yet today some significant exceptions to this rather depressed scene. Those exceptions are normally churches that hold a high Evangelical view of Scripture, fervently preach the gospel, and address the message and ministry of Christ in relevant cultural terms.

The same basic controversy swept through several of the major denominations of North America in what was termed the 'modernist-fundamentalist battles." All are aware of what happened to several mainline Protestant denominations in the early decades of the twentieth century as a consequence of that particular warfare. Many are still losing members at a disturbing rate.

Therefore, it does seem quite correct to surmise that as the traditional high Evangelical view of the Bible deteriorates, so does missionary-evangelism, and the loser is the local church. Johnston put it quite succinctly when he stated, "Rationalism did not leave a heritage of evangelism. To the contrary, to the extent which the supernatural elements were stripped from the scriptures, the same extent the force of Protestantism seems to have been diverted from evangelism to activities of public utility."[28] There are exceptions to be sure, but the general conclusion holds. Thus it seems the pattern sought between the high views of the Bible and fervent evangelism is demonstrated even from a negative perspective.

All this is clearly seen in the Edinburgh Conference of 1910. That particular conference was not only a high-water mark for Evangelical missionary-evangelism, it also saw the beginning of a new trend. Johnston understood this phenomenon as epitomized in the development of the International Missionary Council (IMC) that grew out of the Edinburgh

Conference. The conference still exalted the great missionary Watchword: "the evangelization of the world in our generation," but even at the conference, in a rather incipient form, Johnston told us, "A more liberal theological position influenced the evangelistic foundations by questioning the Watchword."[29] As early as 1908, Johnston contended, "A commission chaired by [J. H.] Oldham expressed concern that 'other activities' were crowding out evangelistic work."[30] Through the International Missionary Council, which in turn finally led to the well-known ecumenical movement, there developed a softening of high views of the Bible.

The Edinburgh Conference of 1910 was a watershed. New directions began there. Johnston is correct when he states, "The missionary movement of the nineteenth century left its pietist moorings at Edinburgh in 1910."[31] For example, there was considerable debate and disagreement concerning the idea of "verbal" inspiration. The theologies of Schleiermacher, Ritschl, Darwin, and Harnack began to infiltrate the general scene. The theological presuppositions at Edinburgh, therefore, were mixed. It was decided unanimity could be found around the "person of Christ." Both the "evangelical" and the "social" gospel could unite for world evangelization around the cross. It sounded like a solution, but Edinburgh admitted the higher critical theologians into the missionary movement and the deterioration of missionary-evangelism, as Evangelicals understood it, began. The New York Conference of 1900 had been thoroughly Evangelical, but Edinburgh represented the beginning of a significant theological shift. For this reason, Edinburgh was unable to come to a satisfactory and final decision on the nature of the Christian message to the non-Christian world, obviously a subject of great importance to evangelism.

The next worldwide missionary conference was held in Jerusalem in 1928, followed by a third significant conference in Madras, India, in 1938. They were indicative of the fact that a shift was rapidly developing towards a very broad based, nontheological stance in evangelism and missions. Johnston stated:

> The eighteen years between Edinburgh in 1910 and Jerusalem 1928 brought new developments in the theological scene. Although they were more apparent at Madras 1938 meeting, these changes were first apparent at Jerusalem. What was often implied at Edinburgh became evident at Jerusalem. The theological positions of Edinburgh influenced evangelism, and the practical work of the IMC [International Missionary Council].[32]

A multitude of things can, and perhaps should, be said regarding the biblical shift begun in Edinburgh in 1910, but obviously, space precludes it. Let it all be simply summarized by stating that the twentieth-century missionary conferences demonstrate that a critical rationalism with its inevitably lower view of the Bible decidedly tends to diminish evangelistic activity, at least as Evangelicals traditionally understand it. Moreover, since Edinburgh, the "shift" has continued and deepened in many older Evangelical circles. The exception is the Far East and southern nations in Africa and South America.

Where are we today? Segments of Western Christianity are, at the contemporary moment, in a quiet fluid state as the church in the East and southern hemisphere grows rapidly. What the future holds, only our Lord knows with certainty. Nevertheless, some things can be said concerning the basic thrust of this chapter. There are lessons to learn from history and the contemporary scene.

Final Historical Conclusions

The historical pattern is quite well established. Whenever a high view of the Scriptures emerges, interpreted properly from a solid epistemological base as traditional Evangelicalism has espoused, a commensurate commitment to evangelism and missionary activity usually follows. A low view of the Bible tends to arrest it. No matter how one approaches history, negatively or positively, the patterns generally hold, but such an observation could be expected. If the Bible revolves around redemptive truths and the obvious evangelistic implications, then a high view of the Scriptures should develop a deep commitment to world evangelism. Granted, there have been some exceptions to this rule. Further, there is the danger of a rigid rationalism invading one's approach to the Bible and stultifying evangelistic fervor. Such is true for Evangelicals and nonevangelicals alike. For Evangelicals it happened in the Protestant scholasticism of the later Reformation days; for nonevangelicals it occurred in the crass rationalism of the Germanic school. We must beware and keep to our Evangelical moorings. Nonetheless, the pattern basically holds.

With the variety of contemporary views of the Bible seeking acceptance, it seems wise to contend for a high concept of the Scriptures in order to propagate the Christian faith in a lost and dying world. If believers take the Scriptures with earnestness, they will not only build a viable theology of evangelism, but also the burden to evangelize will be hard upon them. That is a broad conclusion, but history seems clearly to establish it. The contemporary church in the Orient confirms it. Therefore, Christian faith must be properly built. To fail in missionary-evangelism is eventually to see Christian work become a relic of the past. Significant are the words of philosopher Santayana: "They who do not understand history are doomed to relive it." Therefore, may God move His people by His grace to undertake great exploits in missions and evangelism in the power of the Holy Spirit based on God's own authoritative, truthful Word.

Conclusion

Perhaps you are asking, why all this tedious epistemological argumentation and historical searching for three long chapters? The answer should be clear: because of the obvious theologically fluid state in Western Christianity. Old Evangelical denominations have dramatically changed. Triumphant evangelicalism is waning in many instances. Controversy has now raged for over two hundred years. In the light of all these dynamics, the construction of a viable, contemporary theology of evangelism demands such a background study as has been undertaken. Sensible biblical moorings must be recovered today to have any workable theology of evangelism and to refuse to just parrot the old dogmas. With this general, dynamic situation in mind, armed with God's unfailing truth as set forth in the Holy Scriptures as a criteria, and deeply committed to evangelistic responsibility, it is time to develop our theology of evangelism.

Notes

1. Wayne E. Ward, *The Drama of Redemption* (Nashville: Broadman Press, 1966), 26. It is also important to note that Genesis 1—11 has no real breaks within itself. The text itself flows into Genesis 12 and follows like a historical narrative. The geneologies of the Synoptic Gospels reinforces that reality.

2. John Bright, *The History of Israel* (Philadelphia: The Westminster Press, 1959), 92.

3. Ibid., 103.

4. Walter Harrelson, *Interpreting the Old Testament* (New York: Holt, Rinehart and Winston, 1964), 60, author's italics.

5. *Bakers Dictionary of Theology* (Grand Rapids: Baker Book House, 1960), 142.

6. Ward, *The Drama of Redemption,* 38.

7. Gerald L. Borchert, *Dynamics of Evangelism* (Waco: Word Books, 1976), 49. George Beasley-Murray in his significant work *Preaching the Gospel from the Gospels* makes the same point. He contends the four Gospels are actually the preaching of the early church written to win converts. This theory, incidentally, would explain why the strict laws of recording pure history are ignored in the Gospels. The authors were preaching to win people to Christ, not just to present a *rigid* chronological account of the life of Jesus.

8. Ibid.

9. Ibid., 88.

10. Dewey M. Beegle, *Scripture, Tradition, and Infallibility* (Grand Rapids: William B. Eerdmans Publishing Co., 1973), 138.

11. That Jesus held a high view of the Scriptures is acknowledged by most scholars. As Kenneth Kantzer has pointed out: J. J. Cadbury, Harvard professor

and hardly a conservative Evangelical, once declared that he was far more sure, as a mere historical fact, that Jesus held to the common Jewish view of an infallible Bible than that Jesus believed in His own messiahship. Adolf Harnack, one of the great church historians of modern times, insisted that Christ was one with His apostles, the Jews, and the entire early church in complete commitment to the infallible authority of the Bible. John Knox, author of what is perhaps the most highly regarded recent view of Christ, stated that there can be no question that this view of the Bible was taught by our Lord Himself. See Harold Lindsell, *God's Incomparable Word, Conclusion of the Early Church Period* (Minneapolis, Minn.: Worldwide Publications, 1977), 53.

12. Michael Green, *Evangelism in the Early Church* (London: Hodder and Stoughton, 1970), 233-34.

13. Mendell Taylor, *Exploring Evangelism* (Kansas City, Mo.: Beacon Hill Press, 1964), 124. The reference here is essentially to the Book of Revelation. Yet, the principle for Savonarola was true for all the Bible.

14. Harold Lindsell, *God's Incomparable Word, Conclusions of the Early Church Period,* 53.

15. Arthur Johnston, *World Evangelism and the Word of God* (Minneapolis: Bethany Fellowship, Inc., 1974), 29.

16. Ernest F. Stoeffler, *The Rise of Evangelical Pietism* (Leiden, Netherlands: E. J. Brill, 1971), 29.

17. Donald Bloesch, *The Evangelical Renaissance* (Grand Rapids: William B. Eerdmans Publishing Co., 1973), 106.

18. Johnston, *World Evangelism and the Word of God,* 32.

19. Ibid., 37.

20. Ibid., 16.

21. Charles G. Finney. *The Heart of Truth* (Minneapolis, Minn.: Bethany Fellowship, Inc., 1976), 19-20. All the leading personalities of the second Great Awakening would have agreed—and all were utterly committed to evangelism.

22. James Boyce, "Inaugural Address Delivered Before the Board of Trustees of Furman University," The Annual Commencement, July 31, 1856, 27.

23. James P. Boyce, *Abstract of Systematic Theology* 1887, pp. 6-7.

24. Ibid., 47.

25. Ibid., "Appendix: A Brief Catechism of Bible Doctrine," 1.

26. The significance and new shift of Edinburgh 1910 will be discussed momentarily.

27. L. Berkhof, *Systematic Theology* (Grand Rapids: William B. Eerdmans Publishing Co., 1939), 38.

28. Arthur Johnston, *World Evangelism and the Word of God,* 45.

29. Ibid., 78.

30. Ibid., 79.

31. Ibid., 127.

32. Ibid., 130.

Part II

The Trinitarian God of the Bible and Evangelism:
A Unity of Purpose

Introduction

The catholic faith is this,
That we worship one God in Trinity
And Trinity in unity
Neither confounding the persons
Nor dividing the substance . . .
The Father and the Son and the Holy Spirit
Have one divinity, equal glory and co-eternal majesty.

Any serious study of the nature of the Godhead makes one fact crystal clear: the scriptural presentation of God comes to us in a Trinitarian motif. When God speaks, He reveals Himself as Father, Son, and Holy Spirit, the divine "Three-in-One." God is assuredly One, yet we grasp Him as Three Persons.

God is *One*. The Bible declares that reality constantly and consistently. The great *shema* of the Jewish people proclaimed: "Hear, O Israel: The Lord our God is one Lord" (Deut. 6:4; Mark 12:29). The Israelites knew there was no other God besides the one Lord. The prophets despised the multiplicity of heathen deities (Isa. 45:20). The Israelites mocked the surrounding nation's idols and poured scorn on those who worshiped them (Isa. 44:9-20; Jer. 10:1-5). Yahweh is the "only true God" (John 17:3). There is no other god besides Him (Deut. 4:35,39). Philosophical reasons demand this position, as well, for we have learned there simply cannot be a dualistic or pluralistic *ultimate* principle.

The Scriptures also reveal God to be in "three persons." Immediately, this thrusts us into a rational quandary. How can three be one? Yet we cannot evade the clear biblical teaching; the one God is revealed as "Three-in-One."

Even the Old Testament, which is so insistent on the *oneness* of God, hints at Yahweh's Triune nature. In several passages God speaks of Himself in plural form: Genesis 1:26; 3:22; 11:7; and Isaiah 6:8. One of the key Hebrew names for God, *Elohim*, is a plural form. The significance of this, as Alan Richardson pointed out, rests in the concept that the use of the plural "represents a deep biblical insight: God is not, and never was, a lonely God. There is personality in God, and person could not exist alone . . . [as] 'unitarian'. " It is well known, of course, that many Old Testament commentators see the plural form of God's name as essentially a "plural of majesty." There is certainly truth in that contention; still, it appears Richardson has a valid point to make. At least the hint of a "plurality" strain flows through God's nature in these early documents.

Furthermore, there seems to be an embryonic presentation of the Holy Spirit in the Old Testament. The Spirit (*ruach*) comes from God and is known as the "Spirit of the Lord" (Judg. 13:25). The personality of the Spirit is emphasized in several significant passages. For example, He empowers God's people for service (Judg. 14:6; 15:14), directs the lives of individuals (Ps. 143:10), and teaches them (Neh. 9:20). Not only that, He "came mightily upon" some people (Judg. 14:19; 1 Sam. 11:6) and could be grieved (Isa. 63:10). In certain messianic passages, the Spirit of God was seen descending upon God's Servant (Isa. 42:1). If we maintain our Lord Jesus Christ was the Suffering Servant (Matt. 12:17-21), there is a Trinitarian reference in Isaiah 42:1, not to mention the "son of man" motif of Daniel (Dan. 7:13).

The concept of *wisdom* in the Old Testament is often found in a highly personalized setting. "Wisdom" expresses emotional reactions (Prov. 8:1-2) and is a participant in creation (Prov. 8:22-31). New Testament writers used this title and function to describe the person and work of Christ (1 Cor. 1:24,30; Col. 1:15-17; 2:2; and Heb. 1:1-3). Therefore, the Old Testament is not devoid of Trinitarian implications despite its insistence on God's *oneness.*

The New Testament, however, ushers in an unmistakable vision of the one God in three Persons. In many passages, Trinitarian doctrine becomes quite explicit, even if the word *Trinity* never appears in the actual text. In several passages in the Gospels, it appears mandatory to ascribe to God such a nature. For example, when the angel made the announcement of Jesus' birth to Joseph, he told the puzzled man that the child born to Mary would be called *Emmanuel,* "God with us," and this miraculous birth would be possible because her conception came about by the Holy Spirit (Matt. 1:20-23). Thus all three Persons are involved in the great incarnation event.

The same dynamic can be observed in the words of the angel to Mary. The angel declared that she had found favor with *God* (Luke 1:30). The One who would be born was to be "called the *Son* of the Most High;/ and the Lord God will give to him/ the throne of his father David,/ . . ./ and of his kingdom there will be no end" (Luke 1:32-33, author's italics). When Mary asked how this could possibly happen to a woman without a husband (Luke 1:34), she was told that the *Holy Spirit* would come upon her (Luke 1:35). Trinitarian thought pervades the entire scenario.

Further, when Jesus was taken into the temple for the rite of circumcision, Simeon held Jesus in his arms (Luke 2:25), blessed God (Luke 2:28), and the evangelist told us the Holy Spirit was upon the old man (Luke 2:25). Trinitarianism again surfaces.

Jesus' baptism at the hands of John presents another similar scene. The narrative declares "when Jesus also had been baptized and was praying, the heaven was opened, and the Holy Spirit descended upon him in bodily form, as a dove, and a voice came from heaven, 'Thou art my beloved Son; with thee I am well pleased' " (Luke 3:21-22; compare Matt. 3:16-17). Obviously, a Trinitarian formula is presented. One of the most striking Gospel passages, of course, is the Great Commission of Jesus (Matt. 28:19).

The idea of the Trinity in the Gospels comes to its climax in John's Gospel, particularly as it centers in the person and work of the Holy Spirit. Our Lord refers to the Spirit as the Counselor (*paracletos*) "whom the Father will send in my name" (14:26). The "Spirit of truth" proceeds from the Father and bears witness to Christ (15:26). Again, the Lord Jesus says the Spirit will assume a convicting ministry because Christ is going to His Father (16:8-10). In the upper room the risen Christ said, "As the Father has sent me, even so I send you. . . . Receive the Holy Spirit" (20:21-22). All these passages are clearly and explicitly Trinitarian.

Throughout the rest of the New Testament, Trinitarian statements abound. The reference to Christ's ministry in Acts clearly emerges in that context. The benediction used by the apostle Paul (2 Cor. 13:14) is Trinitarian. Moreover, these are not isolated or solitary verses. The list of such passages is impressive: Acts 2:33,38-39; Romans 14:17-18; 15:16,30; 1 Corinthians 12:4-6; 2 Corinthians 1:21-22; 3:3; Galatians 3:11-14; 4:6; Ephesians 2:18,22; 3:14-16: Colossians 1:6-8; 2 Thessalonians 2:13-14; Titus 3:4-6; 1 Peter 1:2; Jude 20-21; Revelation 1:4-5.

Many New Testament scholars are convinced the very form of the New Testament is predicated on Trinitarian presuppositions. Arthur W. Wainwright, for example, observes that the first eight chapters of Romans are dominated by this important biblical area. He points out that in the concluding section of Romans 8, the Spirit helps believers in their weaknesses and intercedes for them (v. 26), and they rejoice in the fact that God predestined them to be conformed to the image of His Son (v. 29).

Paul argued in a similar fashion in 1 Corinthians. The apostle declared Christ as the power and wisdom of God (1:18—2:9), and the indwelling Holy Spirit makes this known (2:10-16; 3:16-17).

The Galatian letter also presents the same thrust. In Galatians 1:1, Paul exulted in that his Spirit-empowered apostleship was not of human origin but "through Jesus Christ and God the Father."

Further, in the Galatian letter, the Father is the One who "sent forth his Son" (4:4) and who "raised him from the dead" (1:1). He also sent the Spirit of His Son into our hearts (4:6). Believers walk by the Spirit (5:16,25); they belong to Christ Jesus (5:24), knowing that by God's grace (2:21) they are part of the church of God (1:13). They are, therefore, sons and daughters of God (3:26). There is little question where Paul stood on the issue.

These and many other passages confirm the biblical presentation that in all Christian experiences of the one God; they encounter him as Father, as Son, and as Holy Spirit.

Through the years the theologians have not been dilatory in addressing this issue. The very earliest Christian writings dealt with and affirmed the doctrine of the Trinity, for example, *The Epistle of Barnabas* and *The Didache.* The same is true of the early church councils. As a case in point, the heart of the Nicene Creed reads:

> We believe in one God, the Father almighty . . . ; and in one Lord Jesus Christ, the only-begotten Son of God, begotten from the Father before all ages, light from light, true God from true God, begotten not made, of one substance [*homoousios*] with the Father . . . And in the Holy Spirit, the Lord and life-giver, who proceeds from the Father. Together with the Father and the Son He is worshiped and glorified.

The bastion of orthodoxy, Athanasius, declared: "He [the Son] and the Father are one . . . in the unity of the Godhead," and the Holy Spirit "is one with the Son as the Son is one with the Father." Basil, Gregory of Nysia, and other early fathers tenaciously held to the Trinitarian doctrine as did the great Augustine in his essay *The Trinity.* Something of an early benchmark in Trinitarian creeds was expressed in the well-known Chalcedonian formulation in A.D. 451.

The dynamic sixteenth century saw the doctrine of the Trinity fully expounded. That theological giant of the Reformation, John Calvin, said, "Under the name of God is understood a single, simple essence, in which we comprehend three persons, or hypostases. Therefore, whenever the name of God is mentioned without particularization, there are designated no less the Son and the Spirit than the Father; but where the Son is joined to the Father, then the relation of the two enters in; and so we distinguish among the persons." This same understanding is reflected in the Lutheran Augsburg Confessions (1530), the Thirty-nine Articles (1563) of the Anglican Church, and the Westminister Confession (1646). Right up to the present moment, orthodox Christianity has insisted the Godhead is the divine "Three-in-One."

One must beware, however, of what has been termed "tri-theism" in Trinitarian concepts of God, that is, seeing the Godhead as three totally separate "Gods." That is virtually tantamount to polytheism. Many rationalistic attempts to avoid this error have been made in the course of the history of theology. For example, Karl Barth maneuvered to sidestep tri-theism by ascribing "personality" to the undivided essence of the Godhead rather than projecting a threefold differentiation of the persons. Barth said the Father, Son, and Holy Spirit are "three modes of being of the *one* God substituting in their relationships with one another." Whether or not this is adequate to the full biblical teaching of the Trinity is doubtful. Actually, probably all rational explanations will in some sense fall short. To Barth's credit, however, he did recognize this fact in that he held the Trinity is always an inscrutable mystery.

Of course, it is well known that many contemporary religionists reject any and all concepts of a Triune God. Islam, Judaism, and other world religions take such a stance. Modern cultic groups like Christian Science, Jehovah's Witnesses, Latter Day Saints, and the Unitarians likewise reject the idea; but orthodoxy has always contended for the concept of the Triune God, mystery though it be.

Yet, how does one square the Trinitarian nature of God with the scriptural insistence that He is One? Merely to say the Old Testament presents Him as *One* and the New Testament as *Three* will not suffice because Jesus affirmed strongly the Jewish *shema* (Mark 12:29). What are we to do with this rational quandary, if anything?

First, notice that the concept is a *revelational* issue, and surely, enough has been said to demonstrate the supremacy of revelation above rational-empirical presuppositions in deciding theological truth, especially truth about God Himself. But where does this leave us? There seems to be no alternative other than to confess that a trinity is a revealed divine mystery for which no purely rational explanation exists. Trinity deals with a suprarational God who is wrapped in mystery. If God truly is God, mystery is inevitable.

This epistemological stance, however, does not preclude saying all that can be said about God. It does not give believers license to retreat into "mystery" and become a Christian "agnostic," refusing to face knotty issues. Yet, when all is said and done, God remains the infinite Lord of the universe and will always be shrouded with mystery; and for what He has done in revealing Himself, the faithful are grateful and rest upon the knowledge.

Furthermore, the biblical doctrine of the Trinity is not a mere metaphysical abstract concept. God pragmatically meets His people in such a fashion. As Torrey put it:

> It [the Trinity] involves our whole spiritual life, and it is of the highest importance in the very practical matter of praying. We need God the Father to pray *to*; we need Jesus Christ the Son to pray *through*; and we need

the Holy Spirit to pray *in*. It is the prayer that is to God the Father, through Jesus Christ the Son, under the guidance and in the power of the Holy Spirit, that God the Father answers.

Therefore, we conclude with Thomas C. Oden, "The source and end of all things is One." So when the one God reveals that He is Father, Son, and Holy Spirit, "Three-in-One," this truth can make persons thank Him as far as they can grasp it in their journey of theological pursuits. John Newport put it, "The *ultimate* source of all theology is the Triune God in self-revelation."

The earnest theological journey will immediately show that the Triune God comes to persons in *redemptive garb*. The very term *Godhead* declares that He is for humanity and wants to redeem persons by reconciling them to Himself. As Father, as Son, as Holy Spirit, He profoundly desires to save all persons. Such is the Lord's entire purpose in revealing Himself. The believers' task is now to attempt to see how the evangelistic motif in the three Persons of the Triune God unfolds in the Scriptures.

4

God as Father:
Author and Creator of Evangelism

"My Father is working" (John 5:17).

Introduction

True evangelism is rooted in the eternal Triune Godhead. Before the world was created, God as Father, Son, and Holy Spirit in "consultation" unitedly conceived and planned the redemption of fallen people. As Kuiper put it:

> In that plan God the Father was to send His Son into the world to redeem it, God the Son was voluntarily to come into the world in order to merit salvation by His obedience unto death, God the Holy Spirit was to apply salvation to sinners by the instilling of renewing grace within them.[1]

All this beautifully came to pass. The Father became the "Sender," the Son the "Sent," and the Holy Spirit the "Applier."[2] "Before the foundation of the world" (Eph. 1:4), salvation was set. Evangelism begins and ends in God.

It thus follows that a grasp of the essential nature of the Triune God in His redemptive covenant of grace, the *pactum salutis*, is essential to understand what evangelism is all about.[3] If evangelism is born in the heart of God, to know His revealed heart is where authentic evangelization has its inception. To attain that grasp we begin by looking at God the Father as the eternal Author and Creator of world redemption.

In the light of the above principle, it is obvious the plan of salvation is to be understood as *God-centered*, not human-centered, despite the fact it reaches all humanity. In other words, evangelism begins in theology, not anthropology. Failure to come to grips with this foundational fact can easily result in some sort of "evangelical humanism" that exalts human activity to the point of virtually leaving God's actions in evangelism out of the redemptive picture. This in turn precipitates evangelistic gimmicks, emotionalism, and even manipulation. That syndrome fills churches with those whose commitment is shallow at best, or superficial and spurious at worse. In evangelism we must see God for all He is, and that should profoundly affect our evangelism concepts and activity. To understand the redeeming Triune God is vital if evangelism is to have substance and stability. Also, to know God, "We shall have to deal with the *Godhead* of God, the qualities of Deity which set God apart,"[4] as Packer so well put it.

The Attributes of God and Evangelism: God Is a Father

The fundamental theological truth to be addressed first is the Fatherhood of God.[5] This staggering truth, staggering to think He actually is the Christian's Father in the light of who He is and who believers are, is presented in a twofold sense in the Scriptures. Initially, God is the universal Father of all humankind by virtue of His mighty creative act. "In the beginning God created the heavens and the earth. . . . Then God said, 'Let us make man in our image' " (Gen. 1:1,26). Because all humanity is fashioned in the likeness of God, He is in that sense the Father of all. For example, His fatherhood is clearly declared in the so-called parable of the prodigal son (Luke 15:11-24).

There is a second vital aspect of the fatherhood of God: it centers in redemption. The creating Father becomes the redeeming "Abba!" (Rom. 8:15-17). God reveals Himself as a personal, intimate, saving, forgiving Father. The Father of creation is also the Father of redemption for all who receive Jesus Christ as Lord and Savior. Packer was right when he stated, "The revelation to the believer that God is his Father is in a sense the climax of the Bible."[6] Since this is true, all people everywhere need to respond to God's eternal, redemptive, covenant scheme. Declaring that truth is what evangelism is all about.

Out of God's redemptive, creating fatherhood emerge several attributes, or characteristics. The Scriptures make them clear, and each has a definite evangelistic implication.

God as Father Is Holy

Were it possible to behold face-to-face the very essence of God, one overwhelming impression would be: God is holy. This is especially seen in the Old Testament, but it is certainly not attenuated in the New Covenant. Isaiah's experience of God (chap. 6) forms the classic example of the truth. What did Isaiah hear the Seraphim constantly cry as they hovered over the throne? "Holy, holy, holy is the Lord of hosts" (6:3). Not only that, when God reveals Himself as Spirit, it is as *Holy* Spirit that He comes to His people. Holiness is the Father's primary attribute.

Holy (*hagios*, Greek; *qodesh*, Hebrew), the key term describing God, essentially means "separateness." God is qualitatively and radically different, set apart from His creation. This "separateness" from all other reality is akin to God's *glory*. It speaks of His greatness (Heb. 1:3; 8:1),

His moral purity and excellence (Hab. 1:3), His utter transcendence (Isa. 55:8-9), and His "holy otherness," as Karl Barth expressed it. The Father's holiness makes Him the absolute standard of Himself.

Out of God's holiness, four facts surface:

1. God is righteous (Ps. 145:17, KJV). It is not a mere static righteousness; it is a righteousness that reaches out and delivers the unrighteous.

2. God is just (1 John 1:9). He judges evil, but God's perfect justice also vindicates the penitent faithful in Christ through the Lord's sacrifice.

3. God is wrathful (Rom. 1:18-32). Wrath is God's holy revulsion against all sin and evil. Although it is unpopular in many circles to speak of the wrath of God today, such sentimentalism does not mitigate the many biblical passages on God's anger.[7] The prophet Nahum said:

> The Lord is a jealous God and avenging,
> the Lord is avenging and wrathful;
> the Lord takes vengeance on his adversaries
> and keeps wrath for his enemies.
>
> . . . .
>
> Who can stand before His indignation?
> Who can endure the heat of his anger?
> His wrath is poured out like fire,
> and the rocks are broken asunder by him.
>
> . . . .
>
> But with an overflowing flood
> he will make a full end of his adversaries,
> and will pursue his enemies into darkness (1:2-8).

A. W. Pink was correct when he said, "A study of the concordance will show that there are **more** references in Scripture to the anger, fury, and wrath of God, than there are to His love and tenderness."[8] For example, see Romans 1:18; 2:5; 5:9; 12:19; 13:4-5; 1 Thessalonians 1:10; 2:16; 5:9; Revelation 6:10-17.

It is important to understand God's wrath and anger are not arbitrary or emotional reactions. Wrath grows out of the self-consistent nature of God. It is the consistent outcome of human beings sowing the seeds of sin. We reap what we sow (Gal. 6:7). Yet, wrath is more than the mere working out of impersonal moral law, as some argue. God's *active* judgment is involved; He overtly judges sinners who refuse His grace of forgiveness. God's wrath is His active righteousness in its judicial manifestations. His holiness moves against evil in a moral way. God is "jealous" for the vindication of righteousness (Num. 25:11; Josh. 24:19; Ps. 78:58; 1 Cor. 10:22).[9] Those who seemingly tend to avoid the obvious, biblical teaching on God's wrath are perhaps clinging to a partial or overly sentimental view of God's love, often implying there is an antithesis between active love and active wrath. However, that is not the case at all. Actually, God's love shines forth in all its compassionate grace in the light of His judgment toward sin. What sort of universe would it be if sin were not rampant?

4. God is good. Out of His holiness comes benevolence. "God is love" (1 John 4:7). Both holiness and benevolence stem from the very essence of God's nature. They are not contradictory, for God has no contradictions in His personhood.

There are those question, or at least play down, this absolute "otherness" of holy God. For example, Jürgen Moltmann declared, "God is not somewhere in the Beyond, but he is coming and as the coming One he is present."[10] When one speaks of God's holiness, it in no sense is meant to negate God's immanence, as Moltmann implied. Immanence is what the incarnation and redemption are all about; but in essence, God is holy: He is beyond.

In the light of the essential holiness of God, forgiveness of sin becomes the basic need of all people (Acts 2:38). Cleansing (Isa. 6:7) and a new acceptance with holy God emerges as vital. The universe the Father created is a moral universe. It reflects His own moral nature. So when people sin—and they do sin (Rom. 3:23)—forgiveness and restoration to the Father's presence is essential. Therefore, all are to respond to God's gracious call for cleansing and forgiveness (Isa. 1:16). Moreover, God's forgiven people are to declare that forgiving love to others. As Isaiah expressed his experience: " 'Your sin [is] forgiven.' And I heard the voice of the Lord saying, 'Whom shall I send, and who will go for us?' Then I said, 'Here am I! Send me' " (6:7-8). That is true evangelism.

God as Father Is Love

In light of the above principles on God's utter holiness, one should realize immediately God is also infinite love. A superficial understanding of divine holiness or love in isolation tends to put the two attributes in opposition, but that dichotomy will not hold. Love and holiness are completely compatible. Holiness (*hagios*) and love (*agape*) mix well, and both are central to God's basic nature.

Anders Nygren in his classic work *Agape and Eros* tells us *agape*, God's quality of love, is the central motif of the New Testament. John 3:16 alone is enough to verify such a contention. What unique love this love of God is! The common Greek term *eros* speaks merely of love for an object deemed worthy of love. Any well-meaning person can produce that sort of love. Even *philos*, brotherly benevolence, is possible on a human plane. But *agape*, God's self-giving love, is love for an *unworthy* object. Only God can consistently love on that level.[11] Thus, the Bible says, "God shows his love for us in that while we were yet sinners

Christ died for us" (Rom. 5:8). The perfect picture in the Old Testament is Hosea's love for his straying wife.

God's quality of love implies several things: (a) *agape* is selfless (1 Cor. 13:5); (b) *agape* is accepting (1 Cor. 13:7); (c) *agape* is giving (1 Cor. 13:5); (d) *agape* is benevolent, seeking the best for others (1 Cor. 13:7); (e) *agape* never ends, it loves to the end (1 Cor. 13:8); and (f) *agape* is suffering (1 Cor. 13:7). In a word, *agape* is Godlike: self-giving, regardless of how lovable or unlovely the object of that love may be.

There are three other aspects of *agape* that are important to realize. One, love centers in God's kindness and goodness; God benevolently cares for His creation. Two, God's mercy and grace emerge out of His love. The cross makes it all clear. Three, the covenant idea that is so central to biblical theology grows out of God's initiating love. As Milne pointed out:

> This aspect of the love of God is the Christian's ultimate security: If we are faithless, he will remain faithful (2 Timothy 2:13). Our standing with God does not depend on our grasp upon Christ, and is not finally qualified by our disobedience and half-hearted responses. God's almighty heart beats forever and in that fact we find our final security and peace.[12]

This give us the clue as to how holiness and love so perfectly conjoin in the inseparable unity of each Person of the Trinity. In the covenant relationship with God through our Lord Jesus Christ, divine holiness and self-giving love are beautifully displayed and revealed. Love and holiness come together in the Father's covenant of grace as the Son empties Himself (*kenosis*; Phil. 2:7) and in love, by the Spirit, dies for our sins. If God loves like that, the world desperately needs to share in it, thus finding security and acceptance. Such is the heart of evangelism's message.

God as Father Is Righteousness

God's righteousness is akin to His holiness. His righteousness is dynamic, the *outflow* of His holy nature touching lives to make them righteous. God's righteousness delivers and vindicates people (Jer. 23:6). It transforms them. This is why the righteous God is always the saving Father. As shall be seen in detail later, God's provision of righteousness stems from His grace. Our gracious Father imparts His righteousness to sinners who repent and believe.

It is important to realize, however, the outgoing righteous purpose of God also condemns sin, and not in an abstract, nonpersonal manner. The Bible clearly teaches that the righteous God judges people who sin. Sin cannot be divorced from people who willfully commit it. God condemns sin as a principle, but sin must be personified before it can do its destructive work. Those who engage in sin thus stand condemned. Still, the redemption of sinners stands right at the core of God's outgoing righteousness.

In light of the foregoing principles, how vital it is to be touched by the Father's saving righteousness? This is one's only hope. Evangelism shares that dynamic truth.

God as Father Is Power

The fact of the righteousness of God reaching out and redeeming rebellious people implies that God is power. His power is limitless (Gen. 17:1). As traditional theological terminology has it, God is omnipotent. The New Testament declares, "With God all things are possible" (Mark 10:27, KJV). This all-pervasive power is rooted in God's own person and manifest in His creative, sustaining, controlling hand on the universe. As theologian Fisher Humphreys put it: "The logic is quite straightforward. The One who created and controls this large, complex universe must have a knowledge and wisdom of awesome proportions. . . . power beyond the imagining of most of us."[13]

This means God is the sovereign Lord. As the transcendent God, He inhabits eternity and stands before His universe as absolutely unlimited and unconditioned. The Father truly has "the whole world in His hand." After all, He created all things; therefore, He controls all reality as its Sovereign Ruler. The dictionary defines sovereignty as: "Supremacy of authority or rule, as exercised by a sovereign." That is our God. As Job said, "I know that thou canst do all things, / and that no purpose of thine can be thwarted" (Job 42:2). Nothing in all creation happens beyond the ultimate purpose and will of God.

A clarification is called for here. God's limitless power is not to be seen in a mere abstract manner. Omnipotence means God has power to act. His power moves toward real objectives. This limitless power of God impacts everything that constitutes "the real." No segment of reality exists outside of His rule.

The power of the Lord is a personal power. As implied, it is not power like electricity or the atom. God exercises personal power. Actually, all the attributes of God have this basic personal quality. The perfections of our Lord are never abstract nor divorced from His person, hence, from His actions. Therefore, God does exactly what His sovereign will decrees. He wills to do "his good pleasure" (Phil. 2:13). That includes redemption.

Moreover, God's limitless power is not to be understood in the sense that He can do the ridiculous. For example, to ask whether or not God could make a stone so large He could not move it is a nonsensical question. Omnipotence does not mean that. Nor does God's sovereign power eliminate human freedom and subsequent responsibility. That dynamic tension shall be discussed later, but human freedom places no ultimate limitation on God's power. It should be recognized that the seeming "limitations" on God, such as human will or the problem of evil and suffering, are *self-imposed* limitations. To put it in old Greek philosophical terms, God is the "self-moved Mover," not the "unmovable Mover" or the "moved Mover." That which appears as a human situation over which God seemingly cannot exercise sovereignty never reflects on His omnipotence. He can do all things, but some thinkers disagree with that precept today.

A Deviation. Right here a quite serious aberration of biblical theology on God's omnipotence has emerged. "Process theology," as it has come to be called, has gained considerable popularity in recent years as the mystery of God's sovereignty is faced. This particular theological deviation takes its lead from various considerations. The evolutionary hypothesis made its impact on the movement. Not the least of influences on process thinkers is God's seeming inability to cope fully with the perplexing problem of evil and suffering. This particular issue moved Edgar S. Brightman of Boston University many years ago to lay some early foundation stones in process theology structures. He projected the idea of the "limited God." Be that as it may, process theology takes much of its current clue from philosopher Alfred North Whitehead (see Whitehead's *Process and Reality*). As leading process theologian John B. Cobb, Jr., confessed, "I become more of a Whiteheadian than [ever] before."[14]

Whitehead projects the basic tenet that God is in the process of becoming as we are. In other words, there are aspects of reality (like evil and suffering) God is not quite able to handle at this stage. Whitehead tells us God is "growing"; therefore, the day may come when He can cope, but such problems God simply cannot fully and completely handle at this stage in His "development." In a word, God is *not* at the moment omnipotent, and His sovereignty is *not* ultimately all pervasive. He certainly is *not* immutable. Consequently, "absolutes" are virtually eliminated. Although these statements on process theology are something of an oversimplification of the idea, they do express the basic thrust of the view.

One of the key leaders of this movement is Norman Pittenger of Cambridge University. He devised his thought system as something of a reaction to the extreme "secularized gospel" of the 1960s as epitomized in the so-called death of God theology of Thomas Altizer and William Hamilton.[15] We commend a reaction to that radical theology, but did Pittenger go far enough in propounding his "process" view of God? It seems he did not. He still wants to make peace with the secular, rational thinkers of the day, and he does so in a fashion which compromises the biblical revelation of the nature of God. For example, Pittenger has said:

He [God] is always *related*, hence always *relational*; he is eminently *temporal*, sharing in the ongoing which *is* time. His transcendence is in his sheer faithfulness to himself as love, in his inexhaustibility as lover, and in his capacity for endless adaptation to circumstances in which his love may be active. . . .

We live in a "becoming world," not in a static machine-like world. And God himself is "on the move." Although he is never surpassed by anything in the creation, he can increase in the richness of his own experience and in the relationships which he has with that creation. He is the *living* God; in that sense, we may say (as the title of a book of mine dared to do) that God is "in process."[16]

Although Pittenger's emphasis on the love of God and God's benevolent involvement in the affairs and struggles of His creation is most admirable, in the very emphasis He has drained God of His immutability by his failure to grasp all the revealed characteristics of the sovereign God. Pittenger seems so eager to "resurrect" the "dead God" of the secular theologians and get God projected into the affairs of His creation (while making peace with the positivists of the day), he does not see God for *all* He is declared to be by the Scriptures.

Pittenger seemingly rejected the idea of a theology built on the biblicism we have contended for in the first three chapters of this book. He declared, "We cannot work with . . . sheer biblicism in its fundamentalist dress."[17] In that rather cavalier statement, he apparently meant the biblicism of traditional evangelicalism, but he fell short in making his case for rejecting biblicism. His arguments seemed to be that modern secular people simply cannot accept historic scriptural models, but his reasoning fails to convince. To evangelize our generation Christians must, of course, take into serious account so-called modern man. Communication must be to a secularized mind-set. However, those who say, as did Paul Tillich, "The Protestant message cannot be a direct proclamation of religious truths as they are given in the Bible"[18] are wrong. The Bible does speak, even to a secular world. Actually, it is the only thing which really does profoundly and powerfully speak to secular people where they really are in life.

Moreover, process thought leaves one with disquieting theological and philosophical issues. Despite the popularity of the movement, these theologians project themselves into a precarious position. They place themselves on shaky theological and philosophical grounds, first of all, because most of them will grant that God is the Creator of all reality. But if their process presuppositions are true, then God has created an order of reality (time and space) He is subject to, and cannot quite cope with, at least at this stage in time. They make God the Creator of time and yet subject to it. The question then immediately rears its stubborn head: How could God possibly create something, like time,[19] greater or "stronger" than Himself? Anything God is subject to and cannot "handle" surely stands as "stronger" or greater than He. How could God who created time be subject to it? That, of course, is nonsense. If God truly did create the entire time-space order, how could it ascend and hold sway over God? How could *any* creator create *any* order greater than self? Actually, process thought makes time the ultimate principle, not God, if God is subject to it. The goal of process thus becomes all but God itself. That is philosophically very questionable, let alone unbiblical. The Bible says, "With the Lord a day is like a thousand years, and a thousand years are like a day" (2 Pet. 3:8, NIV). God certainly transcends time, not vice versa.

However, these thinkers may retort, there are certain situations God has created that by their very nature ascend above God; thus He cannot cope with them—like the "inevitability" of evil and suffering in the light of human freedom. That line becomes a very dubious admission, for if they say God is ultimate, that precipitates a sort of ultimate dualism: God and the "inevitable situation." No serious Christian theologian or philosopher can abide such a dualism. It all but produces a quasi-philosophical polytheism.

The process thinkers state, however, God will one day conquer all foes; therefore, it is not an *ultimate* dualism. God has not constructed something He will not be able to handle, at least sometime in the future, they argue. It is almost as if they are quoting an old proverb, "Time will heal all wounds." Their argument still leaves God on a finite time-space plane (Again, even the secular scientists know that time and space are finite, relative, and interrelated realities.), with God creating something "greater" than Himself in that He is subject to it. Either that is true or the "time process" is an ultimate entity, and one is left once more with a dualism or time as God. Process positions are simply untenable. There are better ways to solve the problem of evil and suffering.

Let it be stressed, if any entity like time and space is greater or as great as God, then that entity is actually God. If the process thinkers argue correctly that time and/or space are not really greater than God but only appear to be "at the moment," then God is playing games with us, and He just appears to be in process. It is very difficult to believe God engages in these deceptive games, and if to save themselves from contradictions or a dualism they further agree that this time "process" innately resides in the actual nature of God, such becomes tantamount to saying God is transcendent in the first place and thus can hardly be in "process." That leads back to God playing games or some strange sort of pantheism.

Thus, process theology falls to the ground in a shambles of inner contradictions if not outright absurdities. God relates to people in their changing attitudes and actions, but God in His essence is true to Himself, a constant personhood that does not change. The God of the Bible is ultimate, infinite, transcendent, sovereign, and immutable. He is infinitely beyond the bounds of creation and infinitely above the reasonings of all intelligent creatures. He is Lord!

The infinite, ultimate, unchanging God can do as He pleases; He can cope. That should inspire faith. One of the negative practical spin-offs of process theology is that it not only degrades God by putting Him on a process plane, but it also defuses the life of faith generally and the prayer of faith particularly. How could a God who is still attempting to deal adequately with life's pressing issues be a God who inspires one to seek His aid? I might find myself in a situation that God cannot handle, so why pray at all? To retort that prayer should be made anyway hardly kindles one's trust; but the Bible says God is infinite in power, and prayer actually does change things. Faithful intercession is not a mere psychological exercise to get our spiritual psyches right—although it does that too. Prayer changes *things*. Things take place through faith and prayer that will not take place if believers fail to launch out on God's promises. This is true because God has all power, and God has put His strength at the Christian's disposal in the intercessory prayer of faith.

Here emerges a great mystery: an infinite and ultimate God, who can do as He wishes, hears His peoples' prayers. Without that foundational reality, the prayer of faith rarely gets uttered. Praying in faith is essential to receiving answers. James said, "But let him ask in faith, with no doubting, for he who doubts is like a wave of the sea that is driven and tossed by the wind. For that person must not suppose that a double-minded man, unstable in all his ways, will receive anything from the Lord" (1:6-8).

God rules the universe, and God's sovereign reign is one of moral goodness and benevolent wisdom. Therefore, if God is the all-powerful, loving Lord of all creation, life will never have meaning or reality until people are properly related to the Lord of all. Without God's power, life simply overwhelms humanity, but everyone can become dynamically related to this sovereign God and thus become *overcomers* (1 John 4:4). To help people move into a life-giving relationship with the loving, sovereign God is what evangelism attempts to do. In that task, God will grant what is needed to His servants to accomplish the work because He is all wise and powerful in Himself. This leads to the next attribute of the Father.

God as Father Is Good and Wise

God the Father is the all-wise, all-knowing One. Not only that, God's infinite wisdom is always a *benevolent wisdom*. He is not just omniscient—

all-knowing—He acts in goodness as He apprehends and knows all that is an object of knowing.[20]

Furthermore, the omniscience of God does not mean He merely remembers the past perfectly and is a flawless prophet in foretelling the future. Nor does it mean He can just put the present moment together more coherently than human beings. Such a view does no more in principle than place God on our cognitive level, moving through time. God does not proceed through time in His knowledge, He encompasses and transcends time. Otherwise, the process theologians are correct, but we the weakness of their approach has been shown. God simply knows, encompassing all that is an object of knowledge.

Further, the fact that God's omniscience is *good* implies God communicates wisdom to us in a benevolent fashion. Wisdom is one of God's good, gracious gifts to people of faith (Jas. 1:5). Many theologians see this gift of wisdom as essentially moral in nature. Packer observed:

> Thus the effect of His gift of wisdom is to make us more humble, more joyful, more godly, more quick-sighted as to His will, more resolute in the doing of it and less troubled (not less sensitive, but less bewildered) than we were at the dark and painful things of which our life in this fallen world is full. The New Testament tells that the fruit of wisdom is Christ-likeness—peace, and humility, and love (Jas. 3:17)—and the root of it is faith in Christ (I Cor. 3:18; cf. I Tim. 3:15) as the manifested wisdom of God (I Cor. 1:24, 30). Thus, the kind of wisdom that God waits to give to these who ask Him, is a wisdom that will bind us to Himself, a wisdom that will find expression in a spirit of faith and a life of faithfulness.[21]

Therefore, to lead a person into the moral realm of wisdom is to lead them into a grasp of life that is unsurpassed. And this is what evangelism strives to do.

God as Father Is a Spiritual Person

The perfections of God are manifest in His personal omnipresence. The Fourth Gospel tells us "God is Spirit" (John 4:24). This concept is not limited to the third person of the Trinity, the Holy Spirit. The substantive nature of the entire Godhead is personal spirit as over against a limited, relative, materialistic entity. Thus, He can be in all places at all times.

Quite naturally, this attribute of the Father precludes every vestige of idolatry. As Paul stated, "We ought not to think that the Deity is like gold, or silver, or stone, a representation by the art and imagination of man" (Acts 17:29). God is not contingent upon any time-space reality. He is Spirit. Idols not only diminish and dishonor the infinity of the Father, hence His glory, but also they cloud people's understanding of who this great God actually is.

Yet, we all recognize the need of some manifestation of the Father we can "get a hold of," as it were. The perfect answer to that need is met in the incarnation of God in the person of His Son, the Lord Jesus Christ, but more of that glorious fact later.

It must be clearly understood that the essential spiritual nature of God does not diminish in any sense His perfect personhood. God's spiritual essence, which places Him everywhere at all times, does not mean He is not person. To the contrary, if God as Spirit is anything, He is Person. Of course, there are those who argue otherwise. In the Western world,[22] the modern objections to the personhood of the spiritual God probably has much of its roots in the Absolute idealism of Frederick von Hegel. Actually, Hegel's Absolute was something of a rational, Western version of Eastern pantheism. Pantheism has been with us for eons, but Hegel put a philosophical base under it for Western thought.[23] Are Hegel and the Absolute idealist thinkers that flowed from this basic stance right?

Arguments for the personhood of God can fill many volumes. Space again forbids the exercise here; nevertheless, a few statements are in order:

1. The highest concept we conceive is personhood. Surely God, the Ultimate Reality, must be at least person.
2. If God created us as persons, He of necessity must be a person or He is less than we are, thus hardly a Creator.
3. Our experience of God comes to us in the context of person-to-person encounter, the I-Thou relationship of Martin Buber (see *I and Thou* by Buber).
4. Above all, the Scriptures, our final authority in formulating theology, consistently presents God as person, even to the point of using anthropomorphisms. This is no doubt why the anthropomorphisms are so intensively used in the Bible.

And the arguments can go on. To view God as a mere impersonal spiritual power, or principle of love, is woefully inadequate to describe the personal Father God. The very term *Father* means Person.

Because God is person in an ultimate sense, He has limitless intelligence and wisdom. That follows because persons are intelligent beings, even on our level of personhood. Obviously, it must be so with God. "With him is wisdom and strength" (Job 12:13, KJV). Moreover, that wisdom is infinite: "There is no searching of his understanding" (Isa. 40:26-28, KJV). God's wisdom is active, active in such a way it cannot be frustrated.

Furthermore, God as infinite Person acts in complete freedom. Because God is ultimately free, He is ultimately responsible only to His ultimate Self; but because He is the loving Father, He imparts to us limited freedom. Consequently, because we are limited and yet free, we are responsible to the unlimited Bestower of these graces—God Himself. The fruit of that gift of free wisdom is to make us like God, that is, Christlike.

Finally, we must recognize that God's personal being is *purposeful*. The Father has a will, a purpose, and a goal for all His acts. We shall be exploring the ramifications of that basic and important reality throughout this book. One last general idea of God must be listed.

God as Father Is Sovereign

All which has been said up to this point may, in one sense of the word, be summed up in the statement that God is sovereign. He, as personal Creator and righteous Sustainer, rules all.[24] He created it; He controls it. Nothing happens outside of His will—absolutely nothing. He does whatever pleases Him (Ps. 135:6). He "works out everything in conformity with the purpose of his will" (Eph. 1:11, NIV). God has perfect freedom to exercise His sovereign purpose. There are no external constraints on His will. As pointed out earlier, God is only responsible to God.

God's sovereignty raises problems, of course. If God is sovereign, the argument runs, why does He not eradicate all evil? Theodicy issues are important in evangelism. One finds some help in the distinction between the *casual* will of God and the *permissive* will of God, as some have expressed it. The final answer rests in the fact that God is holy love. He always does the right and good and loving thing, even if people do not understand it all in this present life. The rational process theologians, who reject the idea of sovereignty, surely do not have the solution, as attractive as their humanistic system may seem. To deny the Father's ultimate sovereignty because of rational problems is no solution at all. If God is not sovereign, and is in some sort of "process," He may regress rather than progress. That would leave an untenable situation, but God *is* sovereign. He rules well, whether we understand it all or not. Faith declares He is Lord of all and does all things well. The self-existence of God, His lordship in one's personal life, and His eternity will be dealt with in other contexts. Now some clarifications must be noted.

Some Clarifications Concerning God's Attributes or Perfections

First of all—and most important—although the above concepts have been placed in the rubric of God as Father, the perfections or attributes discussed are equally and fully true of God as Son and Holy Spirit. For example, in speaking of the Son, Paul stated, "In him all the fullness of God was pleased to dwell" (Col. 1:19). The same principle is true of the

Holy Spirit, for the Spirit is also called the "Spirit of Jesus" (Acts 16:6-7). Of course, this opens up the "problem" of the divine Trinity again. The biblical doctrine of Trinity is a "problem" because of the nonrational thread that is woven throughout the concept. Perhaps a few more words would be helpful at this juncture.

Many analogies have been propounded to explain the mystery of the Trinity. For example, it has been suggested that the Trinity is as a tree with leaves, a trunk, and roots, each distinct from the other; yet one tree. Or, that human beings possess a body, a will, and a mind; yet are one person. It must be so with God. But these types of approaches finally break down. Perhaps the best thing to say is simply that the infinite Triune God has perfect, self-contained communication and love, and thus He can have "fellowship" with Himself. Therefore, the Trinitarian revelation is called for.

It is also good to recognize that the concept of the Trinity is one of the ways the Scriptures use to emphasize the personal qualities of God's nature. As the Bible makes evident, each person of the Trinity—Father, Son, and Spirit—are referred to as a personal God in the Scriptures: *the Father*: Matthew 6:8-13; 7:21; Galatians 1:1; *the Son*: John 1:1-18; Romans 9:5; Colossians 2:9; Titus 2:13; Hebrews 1:8-10; *the Holy Spirit*: Mark 3:29; John 15:26; 1 Corinthians 6:19-20; 2 Corinthians 3:17.[25] The Athanasian Creed declared: "We worship one God in Trinity and Trinity in Unity, neither confounding the persons, nor dividing the substance."

In the final analysis, explaining the Trinity thrusts persons back on the suprarational nature of God as He reveals Himself to human finitude. Rational statements concerning the Most High never exhaust Him. In saying this, let it be stressed again, such a move is not a cowardly retreat into a safe epistemological harbor so as to avoid tough issues. Mystery surrounds the ultimate God; He reveals Himself in a personal Trinitarian manner, and that is the sum and substance of the issue. To go beyond this is all but an exercise in futility, and most have little energy for futile theological endeavors.

Another needed clarification grows out of issues like the Trinity. The analogical nature of language generally—and theological language in particular—must be borne in mind. That is to say, talk of God always fails to exhaust Him. To some extent people always speak of God's ultimate nature in analogies, and human language is true as far as it can depict reality. In speaking of God's perfections, one does not speak ultimately or perfectly but does "the best one can."

This leads to another issue: the use of anthropomorphisms—attributing human qualities to God, like the "arm of the Lord" (Isa. 51:9). The Bible abounds with these literary devices, and such is what they are, literary devices to communicate some attribute or action of the personal God. The Trinitarian God wants human beings to understand His self-revelation, so He speaks our language. That is what enables revelation to make sense and be logical. It is understood that anthropomorphisms are to be taken for what they are, not final representations of God, but true within the limits of human language and rational grasp. As previously pointed out, they speak of and emphasize His personal qualities.

One final clarification is needed. Humphreys expressed it well: "No one can provide a complete list of God's attributes. . . . we must make no claims for completeness."[26] To attempt to exhaust God with descriptive words is presumptuous, if not arrogant. The above ideas are mere outlines and thus only a beginning. The Father is infinite: How can finite people describe Him? However, the faithful say what they can because *He has spoken*.

Moreover, there is even a serious danger in attempting to delineate God's attributes in too much detail. A long list can generate an air of unreality; it can even come over as contrived. More than one theologian has sailed his or her ship on these treacherous rocks. It is unintentional, of course, but if the list gets too long, it begins to look as if God is not a real Person, and the whole procedure collapses.

Conclusion

It thus seems wise to break off the exercise at this stage and make the primary point of it all: if God is a creating Father, the sort of Father the Bible tells us He is, then to become His child is the fulfillment of life's reason for existence. To know Him in filial relationship is what human life is all about (John 1:12). This surely follows from His creative perfections. How vital it is to grasp that God the Father in grace and love has, out of His very nature, provided redemption and a personal relationship with Himself for all who will call upon Him through Christ. The Father is the Source of salvation, and there evangelistic mission is set. To have a part in helping alienated people into a Father-child relationship with God is the highest service and honor one could possibly imagine. That is exactly what the Father has commissioned believers to do. He sends His people forth with the message of His love and redemption. Paul said, "We are ambassadors for Christ" (2 Cor. 5:20). The very nature of God the Father thrusts believers into whitened fields to reap the harvest (John 4:35). This is what evangelism is.

Notes

1. R. B. Kuiper, *God-Centered Evangelism*, (London: The Banner of Truth Trust, 1966), 13.

2. Ibid., 14.

3. That is, as much as people can in their finitude grasp the revelation of the ultimate God.

4. J. I. Packer, *Knowing God* (London: Hodder and Stoughton, 1973), 16.

5. To speak of God as "Father" as over against a concept like God as "Mother" is not meant to imply sexist bias or language. It is the way the Bible reveals God, and thus I accept that.

6. Packer, *Knowing God*, 182.

7. "Anger" in God is not to be understood in a human, emotional sense. It is His high displeasure with sin.

8. A. W. Pink, *The Attributes of God*, (Swengel, Pa.: Reiner Publications, 1968), 75.

9. Jürgen Moltmann, *Theology of Hope* (New York: Harper and Row, 1967), 164. In Moltmann's stress on the hope of a new world, he seems to have overplayed the role of God's immanence in the above quotation. One need not sacrifice God's otherness for His immanence. They are fully compatible, as the whole Christ event testifies.

10. The problem of all these anthropomorphisms will be dealt with later.

11. As *agape* is at the core of God's nature, His redeemed people are also to love on that level, even if imperfectly (Rom. 5:5).

12. Bruce Milne, *Know the Truth* (Downers Grove, Ill.: InterVarsity Press, 1982), 70-71.

13. Fisher Humphreys, *The Nature of God*, Layman's Library of Christian Doctrine, 16 vols. (Nashville: Broadman Press, 1985), 4:99.

14. James, M. Wall, ed., *Theologians in Transition* (New York: The Crossroad Publishing Co., 1981), 77.

15. It seems so much theology is, in the final analysis, a "reaction" theology, that is, reacting against theological fads. The "death of God" theology was certainly a fad and now quite dead itself. How important to realize a true biblical theology never passes off in a faddist fashion.

16. Norman Pittenger, *Catholic Faith in a Process Perspective* (Maryknoll, N.Y.: Orbis Books, 1981), 21-22. This brief quotation from Pittenger is not to imply that Pittenger's entire approach is found in such a few words.

17. Ibid., 15. It seems clear that Pittenger uses the term *fundamentalist* far too broadly and glibly.

18. Paul Tillich, *The Protestant Era* (Chicago: The University of Chicago Press, 1983, 202).

19. Remember, Einstein has shown us time and space are interrelated, relative aspects of reality. Human beings are in a "time-space capsule," in Einstein's words. Thus if God created space, He created time.

20. Some process thinkers would deny God knows all things,

21. Packer, *Knowing God*, 97.

22. Eastern thought has always seen "God" in an impersonal way. The so-called "transcendentalists"; Emerson, Whitman, etc., projected the idea in American literature (See Ralph Waldo Emerson's "The Oversoul.").

23. Some fallout of Hegel's thought has not been positive. It precipitated dialectical materialism and crass rationalism.

24. God the Father as Creator should probably be listed as one of the divine attributes, but that opens up vistas of theology beyond the scope of this book. It is sufficient to see here that God is the Creator of all. Moreover, some aspects of this truth will be approached in the Christological section to follow.

25. Bruce Milne, *Know the Truth*, p. 80. Milne lists these passages. Many others can be cited.

26. Fisher Humphreys, *The Nature of God*, 4:93.

5

God as Son:
Provider and Means of Redemption

"You are the Christ" (Matt. 16:16).

Introduction

"In the beginning was the Word, and the Word was with God, and the Word was God. . . . And the Word became flesh and dwelt among us, full of grace and truth; we have beheld his glory" (John 1:1,14).

The eternal Word became flesh! Jesus Christ, the Logos of God, came and dwelt among us; and the wonderful truth is that he came to live, die, and live again in order to redeem sinners. An entirely new concept of God and His power and love has now been revealed. As T. F. Torrance has correctly declared, "So far as the New Testament Scriptures are concerned, the incarnation and resurrection of Jesus Christ constituted the ground on which they were understood and validated, brought about a radically new conception of God and a complete transformation of man's outlook in terms of a new divine order."[1]

Three tremendous redemptive terms emerge out of the all but inconceivable condescension of Jesus Christ: incarnation, substitution, and resurrection. *Incarnation*: God's Son became human. *Substitution*: Christ died in mankind's place for their sins. *Resurrection*: Jesus conquered death and is alive. Now life can never be the same again. Each term demands a careful and humble study.

I
Incarnation

Herein rests the ultimate paradox: the omnipotent, creating Son became a man of flesh and blood. Can God become man? It seems incredible! If it is true, how are we to come to grips with that divine act with our limited, cognitive abilities? Of course, as so often pointed out in these sorts of matters, the paradoxical nature of incarnational truth dictates that human beings can never arrive at a full understanding. Yet, there is much to be said because Jesus did come to *reveal* God. Revelation implies knowledge, even if limited in scope. The biblical revelation of God in

Christ gives persons the best grasp of the mystery and wonder of the incarnation.

There are actually two basic incarnational issues in approaching the person of Jesus Christ: the Christological problem and the historical issue. Both clearly relate dynamically to evangelism. We shall approach the Christological issue first.

The Christology of the New Testament

The crucial question in Christological theology is, what does the Bible mean by "the Word was made flesh," or what is the meaning of the incarnation? New Testament scholar, George Beasley-Murray, contended, "In my judgment, the key Christological issue is the reality of the true manhood and real divinity of Christ (more exactly, his deity). The tendency of many is to insist that if Jesus is man, he cannot be God."[2] In this dynamic and controversial area of study, three significant ideas have emerged: *anhypostasia*, *kenosis*, and *lordship*. Of course, in the entire arena of Christological thought, theologians have set forth many concepts, but this study is restricted to the three afore-mentioned approaches.

The Anhypostasia Concept of the Incarnation

This view, quite current in some theological circles today, is hardly new. It centers around the idea that in the person of Jesus Christ there was no true *full* humanity, no distinct human *personality*. Adherents to this concept contend that Jesus of Nazareth was a divine Personality merely assuming a human nature. That is to say, Christ was not really a *human* person, but a *divine* Person who took upon Himself a human nature but not a human personality. This ancient approach to Christology first found followers during the church's controversy with the Nestorians in the fifth century. Some say it had an even earlier expression, at least in incipient form, among the Apollinarians. At any rate, Cyril of Alexandria in his polemic against the Nestorians gave the concept its first full airing during the fifth-century theological controversies.

What the Nestorians were saying is that Mary gave birth to the human Jesus but not to the eternal Son of God. This was untenable to Cyril. According to D. M. Baillie, Cyril worked out the following solution to the Nestorian heresy:

> There was no man Jesus existing independently of the Divine Logos: the human element in the Incarnation was simply human *nature* assumed by the Second Person of the Trinity. There was no human *hypostasis* or *persona*: the *persona* was the Divine Son, while the human nature was . . . "impersonal humanity."[3]

On the surface, this approach seemingly routed the error of the Nestorians. It was widely embraced and became official Catholic dogma. However, it is difficult to know just what is meant by the formulation. It is plagued with the problem that, as R. C. Moberly put it, "Human nature which is not personal is not human nature."[4] What can "impersonal humanity" possibly mean? Some adherents to anhypostasia thought declare that Jesus is not *a* man but *Man*. Yet what does that mean? It, too, lacks real substance in describing the real Jesus.

Emil Brunner, something of a follower of the view, brought his unique interpretation to the issue by declaring there is a distinction to be drawn between the "personality" of Jesus, which is a historical reality, and His "Person," which is the ultimate, nonhistorical mystery of the Godhead. That is, the "personality" of Jesus is no more than "human nature" assumed by the Second Person of the Godhead, thus taking the place of a human "person" in Jesus.[5] This seems to be close to C. A. Campbell's distinction between what he called the "ontological self" (which is to some degree unknowable) and the "self *qua* man," or the empirical self.

The obvious weakness of Brunner's approach centers in the fact that any attempt to divide the ego is a sheer abstraction, for the ego is clearly a unity. As Baillie expressed it:

> It must be sheer nonsense to maintain that in the case of Jesus the one [nature] was divine while the other was human. For the transcendental and the empirical ego are not distinct entities at all, but the two sides of the same entity. . . . That is meaningless, for "human nature" thus separated is an abstraction.[6]

The problem with anhypostasia concepts centers in the apparent reluctance of the advocates to make Jesus genuinely and fully human. They find it difficult, seemingly, to bring the human and divine together in such a way that the human remains genuinely human. To overemphasize the divinity of Christ at the expense of His true humanity is not the answer; that causes the old Docetic heresy to assert itself again.

Still, this much can be said for the anhypostasian view: it did form a bulwark against any sort of "adoption theory" of the incarnation. Nonetheless, the biblical view contends that Jesus was truly human. He was in essence one with humanity. He was surely divine, but He did become *a man*. This leads us to the next important approach.

The Kenotic Theory of the Incarnation

The *kenotic* concept is a relatively modern theory, born in the current quest for a viable Christology.[7] It takes its primary lead from the use of the Greek term *emptied* (*kenosis*) in Philippians 2. Paul wrote, "Who, though he was in the form of God, did not count equality with God a thing to be grasped, but *emptied himself*, taking the form of a servant, being born in the likeness of men" (Phil. 2:6-7, author's italics). The biblical language of the *kenosis* theory is obvious. However, can the passage in Philippians, which is clearly poetical (or even a hymn), support all the theological weight it is called to bear in modern versions of the *kenotic* theory? What are supporters of the view asking of the words of Paul?

The basic thrust of this idea revolves around the contention which holds that the Son of God, the Divine Logos, laid aside His full divine attributes (omniscience, omnipresence, omnipotent, etc.), emptied himself of His ultimacy for a period of time, and lived on earth with all the limitations of humanity. In other words, He "emptied" Himself (*kenosis*) of His transcendence and became a man. Thus we can see Jesus as a true God-Man, at least ostensibly.

Will this theory, however, hold up to all the word *incarnation* demands? It is quite questionable. Granted, Paul was absolutely correct when he stated Christ "emptied" Himself. Moreover, Vincent Taylor argued correctly that at least some form of *kenotic* Christology is essential to any "worthy doctrine of the Incarnation."[8] But can the *whole* answer to the incarnation be found in *kenosis* alone? I think not, for several reasons.

First, as Donald Baillie[9] asked, "What happened to the rest of the universe during our Lord's self-emptying period?" The Bible tells us clearly the omnipotent Son of God continually sustains the universe (Col. 1:17). What then went on while He laid aside His omnipotence during the days of His flesh? The question is not a naive one. It must be answered.

Second, *kenotic* theory sounds perilously close to an incarnation which is no more than some sort of a theophany. That is, the Son of God, formally the Transcendent One, changed Himself temporarily into a man as He laid aside His full divinity and took up humanity to reveal God; but, as Baillie properly contended, this is even akin to the pagan idea of metamorphosis. It is hardly the Christian doctrine of incarnation. Baillie said, "The relation between the divine and the human in the Incarnation is a deeper mystery than this."[10]

The baseline issue rests on the clear implication that in the *kenotic* view we do not have God and Man simultaneously in hypostatic union, but rather, in *succession*, that is, first divine, then human, and then divine again. This precludes the permanence of the manhood of Christ, and that denies what the Bible says about the incarnation. He is forever the resurrected Jesus Christ who walked on earth before His ascension to the Father's right hand, and He will so come again in like manner as He went up.

Moreover, one cannot sidestep the above criticisms by saying God transcends time. He is above time, but Jesus is and will remain the Son of *man*.

This does not deny the truth in the *kenotic* concept. Jesus did lay aside His splendor, but not His deity. He surrendered His position. The word *kenosis* can be translated "made empty." This implies Paul was stressing the humility of Jesus in the incarnation. Although the *kenosis* idea is important, one dare not put all the weight of incarnational truth on *kenosis* alone and present a *complete* rationale to the incarnation. Perhaps the best approach to Philippians 2:6-7 is to take as the core of the issue the phrase "taking the form of a servant." Such is the general circumstantial experience of the whole idea. The phrase is the explanation of how the divine Son emptied Himself; He became a servant in the fashion of man. This is what constitutes the *kenosis*. He did not lay aside the nature of what the Godhead is; He *subordinated* Himself to the Father as a servant during the days on earth.

Lordship and the Incarnation

Karl Heim of Tübingen formulated this Christological concept some years ago. In Heim's book *Jesus der Herr* (Jesus the Lord), an interesting and rather existentially oriented theory is worked out.

Heim began his argument by contending that humanity is so corrupted by original sin that no one can ever rise above that stultifying situation and direct one's life along God-directed pathways. Therefore, all need a Leader and Lord whom they can unquestionably and unreservedly follow. That Leader is the Lord Jesus Christ. He alone is Leader and Lord.

Heim went on to say that the leadership of the Lord must be personally direct and existential. The experience is an "I-Thou" relationship between the Lord and His followers. Furthermore, there must be absolute obedience on the part of His disciples. That raises a serious question. Is it possible to follow Christ in absolute obedience all the time? Yes, argued Karl Heim, for it is actualized in the Person and presence of the Holy Spirit. Through the inner work and witness of the Spirit, we gain a dynamic knowledge and a personal experience of God. In that sense, Jesus became our constant contemporary. Consequently, our relationship to God is forever changed, because Jesus came and by the Spirit has become our contemporary thus continually leading us to God. That is what *leadership* and *lordship* means, and such became the basic idea underlining Heim's Christology.

Heim's approach has many internal problems. The basic problem, however, is simply this: Heim had no Christology. Actually, his approach cannot yield a true Christology for it failed to attempt an answer to the pressing question of how divinity and humanity combine in Jesus. He made Christ our existential Leader and no more. Agreed,

Christ should become one's Leader, but Heim went nowhere in solving the Christological issue.

Of course, such an approach appeals to our existential age which subtly tends to downplay metaphysics and theological absolutes. Heim treaded even beyond the existentialism of the Ritschlian school; he did not seem to be interested in any metaphysical issues at all. He would not even tell us why Jesus is a better Leader than others. However, can one avoid the metaphysical question as to *why* Jesus is Lord? Hardly! Moreover, the Scriptures declare Jesus is Leader and Lord because of who He is: all God, all man, one hypostatic union. Jesus of Nazareth is the eternal Logos made flesh. That is what makes Him Lord.

At the same time, however, Heim was absolutely right to stress obedience to the Lord, even if He never solved the problem of "absolute obedience" which few would claim to have attained. Moreover, Heim's insistence on the inner work and witness of the Spirit to give knowledge of God and make Jesus our "contemporary" is most worthy, but the incarnation surely means more than the believers' existential experience of Jesus, although that is not to be neglected. After all, bringing people existentially to the Lord Jesus Christ is what evangelism is all about. Still, it is because we come to realize, at least in a measure, what the incarnation truly means that we are led to give obedience and devotion to Jesus as Leader and Lord.

There are, of course, many other approaches to incarnational theology today. Space forbids taking them up here, but they have all been discussed in detail in a myriad of writings. The above concepts are mere samples of what has been and is being said at the moment on this central Christian doctrine. Now look at what I consider the best biblical approach to the whole scheme of God being in Christ reconciling the world into Himself (2 Cor. 5:19).

A Biblical-Evangelical View of the Incarnation

The incarnation (and the resurrection), faces humanity with the "supreme paradox."[11] The incarnation addresses people with the unbelievable fact that the transcendent "Holy Other" became supremely immanent and in flesh dwelt among us. Here the world confronts "mystery."[12] Failure to humbly admit the mystery invariably spawns trouble. For example, an inordinate desire to explain and simplify all things rationally, or an undue impatience with the paradoxical or an extreme stress on the existential elements of Christian faith, can lead to error. The constant recurrence in one form or another of the ancient Arian and Docetic heresies is witness to the fact. Nonetheless, what can be said about the incarnation from the source of God's revealed truth should be said. After saying all that can be said on the basis of the Bible, the mystery of the Godhead remains. Such an approach is not a dogmatic rigidity coupled with a retreat into mystery and paradox when this position is challenged. It is all believers can do, given the supremacy of revelation.

Mystery and paradox imply, in one sense, the incarnation cannot be explained at all. This being the case, the theological task becomes somewhat negative. That is, one is forced to begin by declaring what is *not* meant by the incarnation. Something of this sort of exercise has been attempted along with a declaration of what can be said positively about God becoming a man. As startling as the phrase *God becoming a man* may be, such is what the incarnation means. That is positive and constitutes the primary truth of the incarnation. God truly did incarnate Himself. Actually, this is what the very word *God* means. For the Christian believer, *God* means incarnation. Believers understand and come to know Him in such a manifestation. How vital it is for the Christian thinker to realize this basic reality. The following are some historic, positive statements.

Positive, Historic Creedal Statements on the Incarnation

With the incarnational God of the paradox now set forth, it will probably prove helpful to outline some of the outstanding historical statements on the incarnation. They are admittedly quite old and no doubt need a fresh restatement from time to time; still, they can aid in getting to the heart of the biblical Christological issue.

One of first important declarations concerning the incarnation came from Athanasius. In the context of the theological controversies of his day, Athanasius wrote:

> For he [Jesus Christ] did not simply will to become embodied, or will merely to appear. For if he willed merely to appear, he was able to effect his divine appearance by some other and higher means as well. But he takes a body of our kind, and not merely so, but from a spotless and stainless Virgin, knowing not a man, a body clean and in very truth pure from intercourse of men. For being himself mighty, and Artificer of everything, he prepares the body in the Virgin as a temple unto himself, and makes it his very own as an instrument, in it manifested, and in it dwelling. And thus taking from our bodies one of like nature, because all were under penalty of the corruption of death he gave it over to death in the stead of all, and offered it to the Father—doing this, moreover, of his loving-kindness, to the end that, firstly, all being held to have died in him, the law involving the ruin of men might be undone inasmuch as its power was fully spent in the Lord's body, and had no longer holding-ground against men, his peers, and that, secondly, whereas men had turned toward corruption, he might turn them again toward incorruption, and quicken them

from death by the appropriation of his body and the grace of the Resurrection, banishing death from them like straw from the fire.[13]

The Chalcedonian Creed was something of a continuing affirmation of the basic ideas set forth by Athanasius. The Council of Chalcedon met in A.D. 451 and formulated a time-honored statement of the incarnation. It reads as follows:

Wherefore, after the example of the holy Fathers, we all with one voice confess our Lord Jesus Christ one and the same Son, the same perfect in Godhead, the same perfect in manhood, very God and very man, the same consisting of a reasonable soul and a body, of one substance with the Father as touching the Godhead, the same of one substance with us as touching the manhood, like us in all things, sin except; begotten of the Father before the worlds as touching the Godhead, the same in these last days, for us and for our salvation, born of the Virgin Mary, the Mother of God, as touching the manhood, one and the same Christ, Son, Lord, Only-begotten, to be acknowledged in two natures, without confusion, without conversion, without division, never to be separated; the distinction of natures being in no wise done away because of the union, but rather the characteristic property of each nature being preserved, and concurring into one Person and one subsistence, not as if Christ were parted or divided into two Persons, but one and the same Son and Only-begotten God, Word, Lord, Jesus Christ; even as the Prophets from the beginning spake concerning Him, and our Lord Jesus Christ hath instructed us, and the Symbol of the Fathers hath handed down to us.[14]

Emerging out of the British reformation, the Westminster Confession formulated a similar Christological statement:

The son of God, the second person in the Trinity, being very and eternal God, of one substance, and equal with the Father, did, when the fullness of time was come, take upon man's nature, with all the essential properties and common infirmities thereof, yet without sin; being conceived by the power of the Holy Ghost, in the womb of the Virgin Mary, of her substance. So that two whole, perfect, and distinct natures, the Godhead and the manhood, were inseparably joined together in one person, without conversion, composition, or confusion. Which person is very God and very man, yet one Christ, the only Mediator between God and man.[15]

A more modern statement, from A. H. Strong, is as follows:

The Scriptures represent Jesus Christ to have been possessed of a divine nature and of a human nature, each unaltered in essences and undivested of its normal attributes and powers, they with equal distinctness represent Jesus Christ as a single undivided personality in whom these two natures are vitally and inseparably united, so that he is properly, not God and man, but the God-man. The two natures are bound together, not by the moral tie of friendship, nor by the spiritual tie which links the believer to his Lord, but by a bond unique and inscrutable, which constitutes them one person with a single consciousness and will, this consciousness and will including within their possible range both the human nature and the divine.[16]

Many other Christological statements could be presented, but this brief sampling represents the efforts of the church through the centuries to declare who Jesus was. What can be said about such formulations? They have been criticized to be sure.

The Chalcedonian formulation, for example, has suffered many severe blows. In recent years Pannenburg and Moltmann, though wanting to retain something of the tradition, certainly went beyond Chalcedon. Some current thinkers, Roman Catholic and Protestant alike, have in Klaas Runia's words completely "abandoned" the time-honored formula, declaring, as Runia put it, "Jesus as man, [is] no more than a man."[17] This all sounds quite Arian which will be discussed shortly, and must be rejected, but Chalcedon sought to preserve the mystery of the incarnation holding both to the divinity and the humanity of Jesus.

Charles Hartshorne argues that *all* the traditional Christological statements like Chalcedon are in bondage to a set of metaphysical presuppositions. He feels these presuppositions pervert the distinctive Christian idea that formed the essence of incarnational doctrine, that God is love. Even if that pitfall has ensnared some, Hartshorne's criticism is surely far too much of a blanket indictment and seems to grow out of a retreat into an existentialism that would avoid any real objective, theological statements about the incarnation. Of course, the formulators did have a set of presuppositions. They had no choice. Part I of this book shows that no one can even begin to formulate theology without epistemological presuppositions. Hartshorne had his, even if he failed to make them explicit. His existential approach is presuppositionary. Be that as it may, the above confessions do have something positive and helpful to say to us for they get at the essence of what the Bible declares concerning Christological truth. However, incarnational concepts have their pitfalls.

There are two errors in Christological thought that seem to lurk about to snare the unwary thinker. The historical formulations given above were sensitive to those issues. This is probably why they were written. First, the docetic heresy has claimed many victims. This view centered in a basic denial of Jesus' full humanity. *Docetism*, as a term, takes its lead from the Greek word *dokeo*, "to seem or appear." Based essentially on Greek thought, docetism propounded the idea that Jesus only *appeared* to be human. It infected Gnosticism and Marcionism within the Christian

community. The heresy grew specifically out of the influence of Platonic and Aristotelian thought. Both of these Greek philosophers, though
coming from different starting points, held that the visible, physical,
material world is innately evil. They viewed God, therefore, as transcendent and totally disparate from the material world. Thus they concluded
there could never be an intrinsic connection between God and anything
material. It is easy to see why such a philosophical presupposition pre-
cluded a true "God-man." Man, yes; God, yes; but never God-man! So,
if Jesus were God, He could never be a real man.

The Docetics, however, were left with a serious quandary on their
hands: How did Jesus, the Son of God, arrive into this world? The Bible
clearly states He was born of Mary. Docetism resolved its problem by
contending that Jesus merely passed through Mary "like water through
a tube."[18] He was not born of her in a human way. The virgin was
merely a vehicle who did not contribute anything of substance to the
existence of Jesus. This approach, of course, resolves the paradox of traditional Christology, but the price is too high. Fortunately, pure Docetism is held by few today; yet, the tendency to exalt the divinity of Jesus
at the cost of His Humanity still persists in rationalistic ultra-conserva-
tism. One need not attenuate the full humanity of Jesus to exalt His
divinity.

On the other hand, philosophical Arianism, the second Christological
error, stressed Jesus' humanity to the point of virtually denying His divinity. Let it be stressed that the importance of Jesus' humanity cannot
be set aside. The humanity of our Lord as it relates to soteriological issues is central, but Jesus was not a mere man who just understood God
better and experienced Him more profoundly than the rest of us. He was
fully divine.

British theologian Michael Taylor verbalized this Arian approach recently. It must be granted that Taylor was insightful and absolutely correct when he called the incarnation the "central nervous system of
Christianity."[19] He had grasped the importance of the issue. However,
in an address to the British Baptist Union on the subject, "How Much of
a Man was Jesus?" Taylor declared our Lord was in kind merely human,
just as others are. He contended Jesus differed only in that He had more
of God in Him than others. Thus Taylor denied the unique divinity of
Jesus. Taylor's approach is followed by many thinkers today as expressed, for example, in the radical British work, *The Myth of God Incarnate*,
edited by John Hick. Some of the most radical views have been expressed in this series of essays. In one chapter Hick tells us:

> It was natural and intelligible both that Jesus, through whom men had
> found a decisive encounter with God and a new and better life, should
> come to be hailed as son of God, and that later this poetry should have

hardened into prose and escalated from a metaphorical son of God to a metaphysical God the Son, of the same substance as the Father within the Triune Godhead. . . . And because of the inherent conservatism of religion, the way in which the significance of Jesus was expressed in the mythology and philosophy of Europe in the first three centuries has remained the normative Christian language which we inherit today. But we should never forget that if the Christian gospel had moved east, into India, instead of west, into the Roman empire, Jesus' religious significance would probably have been expressed by hailing him within Hindu culture as a divine Avator and within the Mahayana Buddhism . . . one who has attained to oneness with Ultimate Reality but remains in the human world out of compassion for mankind and to show others the way of life.[20]

In other words, according to Hick, the first-century dynamics of Jesus really does not conform to our Christological statements at all. Christologies like that expressed in Chalcedon were developed from the effort of the early church to extol Jesus, and they made Him Son of God in the unique sense the historic creeds present Him. Many of these theologians take their lead from Schleiermacher. Russell Adwinckle said, Schleiermacher "preferred to speak of a perfect God-consciousness in Jesus, a perfect without the deviations and imperfections which mark our development."[21] One of the strange aspects of Schleiermacher's theology is: he signed a doctrinal statement that affirmed the five points of Calvinism formulated by the Council of Dort but never reflected it, at least in writing.

Of course, many modern New Testament critics maintain there is no evidence that Jesus thought of Himself as God, or even as one equal with God. Yet, the prologue to the Fourth Gospel states, "The Word was God" (John 1:1), and Jesus said, "He who has seen me has seen the Father" (John 14:9). What about this? The critics argument runs that John's Gospel is a wholly later tradition which just put such words into the mouth of Jesus. They contend that even the Synoptic Gospels' tradition of Jesus as the "Son of man" is unauthentic. In other words, Jesus was simply not God in human flesh and the Gospels say nothing to the contrary.

Such an approach to Christology has, of course, surfaced often. The Ebionites of the second century denied the essential reality of Christ's divine nature. This ancient view emerged out of Jewish philosophy. It invaded early Christian thought because of the Hebraic insistence on monotheism. To declare Jesus as divine was to destroy their basic theistic view, so they thought.

Doctrinaire Arians of all ages deny in some fashion the essential integrity of the divine nature in Jesus Christ. Early thinkers regarded the Logos, who united himself to humanity in Jesus Christ, as not absolute

God. They thus viewed Jesus as merely the first and highest of created beings. Arias, the author of the doctrine, was condemned at Nicea in A.D. 325 ; and his views have been considered heresy in orthodox circles ever since.

The Nestorians, another version of Arianism, denied the intrinsic union between the divine and human in Jesus. They contended the union was a moral one rather than essentially organic. Nestorius was condemned in A.D. 431; and, of course, there has been a variety of "adoptionists" views of the incarnation.

Appollinarianism, somewhat paradoxically infected with Arianism and Docetism both, became something of a "halfway house" in its Christological stance. That is to say, they too truncated Jesus' divine-human nature. They held Jesus took on genuine humanity, but not the *whole* of human nature. Therefore, Jesus, though human, was in some respects different from other human beings.[22]

Another attempt to resolve the issue, commonly termed "the doctrine of dynamic incarnation," also falls short. This view holds that:

> The presence of God in the God-man was not in the form of a personal hypostatic union between the Second Person of the Trinity and an individual human being, Jesus of Nazareth. Rather, the incarnation should be thought of as the active presence of the power of God within the person Jesus.[23]

It should now be clear that the effort to resolve on a purely rational basis the "supreme paradox" of the incarnation leads to perversion. The contemporary age is no exception. For example, Karl Barth, who certainly was not as cavalier as some, though granting the full humanity of Jesus, saw nothing particularly remarkable about it. He felt getting any real historical data on Jesus was difficult and that even if the true historical Jesus could be seen, people would not see much. Barth stated:

> Jesus Christ in fact is also the Rabbi of Nazareth, historically so difficult to get information about, and when it is got, one whose activity is so easily a little commonplace alongside more than one other founder of a religion and even alongside many later representative of His own "religion."[24]

Growing out of his view of historical revelation, Barth precipitated a rather strange form of a quasi-Docetism.

Rudolf Bultmann[25] was far more radical than Barth concerning the historical Jesus. Following the historical philosophy of Martin Kähler, Bultmann held that virtually nothing can be known of the historical Jesus. He can only be known in existential encounter. As Erickson put it, "Bultmann's Christology, therefore, does not focus on an objective set of facts about Jesus, but on his existential significance."[26] In other words, Christological statements about the historical Jesus are not really important. What we need to do is *experience* the Christ. Thus Bultmann's Christology is almost an emotional view.[27]

Rationalism leads into a perfect cul-de-sac, but we cannot rest in refuting inadequate views in developing a Christology. The pressing issue is: How do believers explain the hypostatic union of the truly divine and absolute human natures in Jesus? Many attempts have obviously been made, and many failures occurred. So our question is still, "What can be positively said in the light of the paradoxical nature of the incarnation?"

Some Positive Points

First, as Erickson pointed out,[28] the incarnation is to be seen essentially as the eternal Son of God assuming or gaining human qualities rather than giving up divine attributes. This is where an undue stress on *kenosis* (Phil. 2:6-7) can lead to error. Paul was not arguing that Jesus ceased to possess a divine nature during the days of His flesh. Colossians 2:9 makes this quite clear: "For in him the whole fullness of deity dwells bodily." The Son accepted some limitations while on earth because of His taking the form of a servant, but not at the loss of essential divine attributes. Incarnation was far more than some sort of Old Testament theophany. Actually, in the incarnation the second Person of the Trinity took on genuine human attributes.

Second, the incarnation does not mean the two natures of Jesus, human and divine, functioned independently of each other. Rather, in all the acts of our Lord, the acts were always divine *and* human, never human on one occasion and divine on the next. He was omniscient as God; but, because He was incarnated, He limited Himself and was subjected to the human organism and process of acquiring knowledge through time. This is true of all the divine and human attributes in Jesus. Granted, the idea is very difficult to conceive because human rationality is limited. Nonetheless, full meaning must be given to the divine-human hypostatic union in the incarnation.

Third, preconceived ideas as to what constitutes true humanity and divinity must be laid aside. The normal view is to say God is infinite and humans are finite, and the two are incompatible. From our present existential, empirical perspective, that is true, but in an ontological sense, it may not be. There was certainly a profound affinity between God and Adam and Eve in the garden. The results of the fall of our first parents has corrupted our humanity. None of us are truly human in the original, created sense. When Jesus came as a "servant, being born in the likeness of men" (Phil. 2:6-7), He did not take on a sinful nature; to the contrary, He acquired the sort of humanity Adam and Eve enjoyed before they sinned. Paul said that Jesus, the "second Adam," was truly human, human as God originally intended.

Moreover, God is found and understood in Jesus Christ; He is what God is like. Human concepts of God are wrong if they are adverse to what Jesus is like. In Him "the whole fullness of deity dwells bodily" (Col. 2:9). God is the incarnate God. God came in Jesus. This is how God revealed Himself. The incarnation *is a fact*, and believers must accept it and cope with it as best they can, even if human efforts fail to explain it completely.

Fourth, the above argument stresses the point that the incarnation originated and stemmed from God, not from earth. Therefore, it is not a human being becoming God: it is God becoming a human being. True, no human could ever become God, but it does not follow that the reverse is impossible. Remember, with God nothing is impossible, even the Son of God being born of a woman. Right here a word is in order about the "virgin birth" of Jesus.

The Virgin Birth of Jesus

At the turn of the twentieth century, this particular doctrine became a symbolic issue. In what was called the fundamentalist-modernist controversies, the acceptance or rejection of the concept of the virgin birth stood as the barometer of orthodoxy in the minds of many. It virtually became tantamount to the acceptance or rejection of Jesus' divinity. That is not quite the situation today. Nonetheless, it is an issue to consider seriously.

From a biblical perspective, the idea of Mary being a virgin is mentioned only twice in the New Testament—in Matthew and Luke. Moreover, Paul never referred to it. Some have made much of this in their denial of the entire doctrine. They seemingly cannot bring themselves to say Mary was a pure virgin when she conceived Jesus. Thus they raise the scarcity of biblical references, especially in Paul. However, it must be remembered Paul was writing primarily to solve problems in local churches. That doctrinal issue probably never arose. This implies the tradition of the virgin birth must have persisted previously and been commonly and firmly accepted. After all, it was incorporated in two of the three Synoptics. How often must something be said in the Scriptures to be true? If the Bible is God's revelational truth, once is surely enough. Thus I accept the truth of the doctrine.

On the other hand, caution is called for lest we make more of the concept than the Bible itself. Some Roman Catholic theologians say Jesus as a babe was not only conceived miraculously by the Holy Spirit in the womb of Mary, the birth itself was a miraculous birth. That is, they argue Jesus' actual birth was not a natural birth in the sense of the Babe coming into the world through the birth channel of Mary. Rather, they say Jesus came into the world directly and miraculously through the wall of Mary's womb much as He could pass through the walls of buildings after His resurrection. Thus the hymen of Mary was never broken, and she therefore remained a virgin throughout life. Roman Catholic dogma tells us Mary never consummated her marriage to Joseph and was a virgin forever. They take the doctrine of the "virgin birth" very literally, not only stressing a virginal conception but a virginal birth as well.[29] What can be said about these two extreme polarized views.

First, I reject outright any denial of the doctrine. The Bible clearly teaches it, so that should settle the basic issue. Secondly, however, Christians do not have to ascribe validity to the extreme view. Jesus surely had a natural birth after His divine conception. Thus it is probably far better to call the doctrine the "virgin conception," not the "virgin birth." This seems more in line with the biblical presentation, but what does it mean, especially as it relates to the incarnation?

Again, theologians present a variety of ideas as to the incarnational significance of the divine conception of Jesus—even among Evangelicals who accept the doctrine. As a case in point, Millard Erickson does not see the importance of the doctrinal content of the issue as some do. Erickson rejects the common Evangelical argument which holds if Jesus had been born through a natural conception between Joseph and Mary, our Lord would have inherited a sinful human nature, and thus the incarnation would have been flawed or even impossible. Apart from the divine conception, the old argument runs, Jesus would not have been the sinless, incarnation of God.[30] Erickson speaks against such an approach by pointing out that *both* Adam and Eve sinned and inherited a resulting evil nature; thus Jesus could have inherited an evil nature from Mary as well as from Joseph, if God had not otherwise overcome the problem in the incarnation. He contends the incarnation could have occurred even if Joseph had been responsible for the conception. In other words, the incarnation was not dependent on the virgin conception but on the power of God. Other Evangelicals hold the contrary and see the divine conception in a virgin as essential to the incarnation.

Perhaps Carl F. H. Henry has the best approach, resting somewhat between the two Evangelical poles. Henry states:

> It may be admitted, of course, that the Virgin Birth is not flatly identical with the Incarnation, just as the empty tomb is not flatly identical with the Resurrection. The one might be affirmed without the other. Yet the connection is so close; and indeed indispensable, that were the Virgin Birth or the empty tomb denied, it is likely that either the Incarnation or the Resurrection would be called in question, or they would be affirmed in a form very different from that which they have in Scripture and historic teaching. The Virgin Birth might well be described as an essential, historical indication of the Incarnation, bearing not only an analogy to the

divine and human natures of the Incarnate, but also bringing out the nature, purpose, and bearing of this work of God to salvation.[31]

Nevertheless, Erickson is correct when he says the virgin conception clearly demonstrates that salvation is all of God's grace and is a supernatural gift of His love and mercy. Moreover, it clearly points up the uniqueness of Jesus and becomes a clear token of God's absolute sovereignty over nature and His entire creation. The fact Mary conceived Jesus by the Holy Spirit is the main point, not simply her virginity. Still, the Bible surely says that Mary's virginal conception had a definite role to play in the incarnation of God's Son; therefore, we accept the truth and thank God for it, even if a mystery yet remains.

Conclusion to Christology

Much more could and perhaps should be said concerning the incarnation of God in Christ. But again, space forbids the exercise. Perhaps it is best to summarize by stating it is most wise to realize Jesus was a very complex personality. All He was and is humanity shall never know from our empirical perspective. Our task is to accept what the Holy Scriptures state and avoid the heresies. As Erickson expressed it:

> There are basically six [heresies], and all of them appeared within the first four Christian centuries. They either deny the genuineness [Ebionism] or the completeness [Arianism] of Jesus' deity, deny the genuineness [Docetism] or the completeness [Apollinarianism] of his humanity, divide his person [Nestorianism], or confuse his natures [Eutychianism]. All departures from the orthodox doctrine of the person of Christ are simply variations of one of these heresies. While we may have difficulty specifying exactly the content of this doctrine, full fidelity to the teaching of Scripture will carefully avoid each of these distortions.[32]

So rest on the Word, thank God for the glorious reality of the incarnation that God became man, and realize some day believers will grasp it fully when they see Him face-to-face.

Why all this stress on Christology? The answer is simple, yet most profound and essential: redemption rests upon it. However, before moving to investigate this significant area of incarnational theology (and its obvious implications concerning evangelism), the second vital issue concerning the incarnation, the historical question, must be raised. Here the basic issue is: What can be grasped historically about this God-man called Jesus of Nazareth?

The Jesus of History

The early so-called quest for the historical Jesus by New Testament scholars such as Albert Schweitzer ended in something of a quagmire. It was finally given up by Bultmann and similar schools of thought.[33] For example, Ernst Käsemann said, "We only make contact with the life history of Jesus through the *kerygma* of the community."[34] Käsemann claimed that the New Testament does not yield direct, authentic history concerning the life of Jesus. In like manner Martin Kähler stated, "I regard the entire Life of Jesus movement as a blind alley."[35] This is not to mention men like Paul Tillich, John Knox, and a host of others. Yet Evangelical orthodoxy declares people do know much about the historical Jesus from the pages of the Bible.

Granted, people learn of the historical Jesus from the church's *kerygma*, but that means the Bible to Evangelicals. Does this preclude actual historical facts, as some say? A serious polarization between conservative Evangelicals and many modern scholars has arisen over this issue. These contrary approaches stand a great distance apart. How did New Testament studies get into this polarized stance?

The presuppositional sources of the modern critical views on the historicity of the New Testament's presentation of Jesus must be recognized. Although these thinkers' philosophical presuppositions have their roots in the ancients, they sprang from modern soil in David Hume. Speaking from a typical British empirical stance, Hume argued strongly against miracles. Taking Hume's approach, and reinforced by the growing influence of the scientific method of the day and linguistic analysis philosophy, these New Testament critical historians believe that a miracle would allow an irrational element to intrude into history, and this cannot be permitted under the ordinary laws of history. This presupposition resulted in a philosophy of history which contends that for every historically verifiable event there must be a rational-empirical cause. History is a natural, causal continuity that allows no intrusion of anything supernatural. Stated in its most hard-nosed expression: for every earthly *effect* there is an earthly *cause*.

This philosophy of history precludes a historical explanation or acceptance of miracles because it demands a purely natural explanation for all occurrences. Thus the historian lives in and records a world where supernatural events simply do not take place. Clearly, such a concept will inevitably demand a quite radical approach to recorded biblical history, especially the life of Jesus. It has led critical theologians to seek for a "historical" Jesus in the sense of the "uninterpreted Jesus," that is, a Jesus somehow free of the religious supernatural elements that are ordinarily attributed to Him by the Gospels. The Gospel writers, the more

extreme critical school tells us, interpreted Jesus. These writers attributed miracles to Him, but such acts did not actually occur historically.
These critics seek a Jesus who did things just like any other person,
limited to the natural cause-effect course of history. That is the *real* historical Jesus, in their thinking.

The implications of this approach are formidable. The only satisfying
accounts of Jesus are the Gospels, and they are filled with supernatural
accounts and instances concerning this Man of Galilee. The recorders of
the Nazarene's life attributed all sorts of miracles and nonrational
events to the Lord, but if history is as Hume and his followers argue:
What is left "historically" in the Gospel narratives? Very little.

Bultmann and his school, for example, were quite consistent in their
views of Jesus based on this philosophy of history. They have said little
can be known about the real historical Jesus, what He actually said and
did historically. After all the accretions of the interpretative narrators
are sluffed off, very little historical substance remains. As New Testament scholar I. Howard Marshall has told us:

> When R. Bultmann and other scholars claim that we can know next to
> nothing about the historical Jesus, they are in effect saying that although
> Jesus really lived he is hardly a historical figure in the sense of a person
> who can be known by the historian or by the historian's readers. For Bult-
> mann, we can know next to nothing about the personality and career of
> Jesus, indeed little more than a handful of his sayings have come down to
> us; in that sense there is for him no "historical Jesus." The point is a valid
> one. *If* the evidence is as meager as Bultmann claims, then there is no "his-
> torical Jesus" in the sense of a person who can be known by later genera-
> tions of men.[36]

This skeptical view has been quite influential in New Testament
studies of late, but Bultmann must at the same time be credited with a
real consistency in his view of history. He carried out the implications of
his presuppositions to the end. This is commendable whether one agrees
with him or not.

It was this philosophical consistency of the Bultmannian school that
ended the earlier search for the historical Jesus. Schweitzer and his followers were on a futile quest, Bultmann contended. He argued there is
so much supernaturalism in the Gospel accounts of Jesus, and because
there is virtually nothing else of any real importance about the life of
Jesus in other sources, to find a true historical Jesus is simply impossible.
Bultmann's form-criticism with its demythologizing methodology put
the death blow to the old quest. Schweitzer's approach was to attempt
to trace step by step the story of Jesus from His birth to the resurrection.
The *formgeschichte* school held that the stories and sayings of Jesus were

circulated as separate narratives by the early church. They were put together by the Evangelists with no knowledge or concern for their proper
chronological order. The Gospels are "faith documents," not histories.
They are *kerygma*, proclamation, not historical presentations of Jesus'
life. Bultmann's theories make it impossible to accept the Four Gospels
as historically valid.

This extreme existential approach, existental more than purely rational, has been somewhat revised in recent years, however. In 1953 Ernst
Käsemann, himself a former pupil of Bultmann, produced a paper on
"The Problem of the Historical Jesus." In the paper he quite strongly
criticized his former teacher. This opened up a new, less hard-nosed approach to the historicity of Jesus. Käsemann was joined by other continental thinkers like Fuchs and Bornkamm. It was introduced to the
English-speaking world by James Robinson in his *New Quest of the Historical Jesus*. This percipitated a less rigid approach to the historicity of Jesus
as recorded in the Gospels.

The new quest was born through the recognition that the early *kerygma* itself was rooted and grounded in history; therefore, the essentials of
the teaching, ministry, and travels of the Lord can be reconstructed.
Granted, such a study of the Gospels cannot produce a pure, connected
biography of Jesus. Nonetheless, real history can be found in the Gospels. As a consequence, a number of books with the simple title *Jesus*
began to be written once more. No doubt the most outstanding of the
works is *Jesus Christ* (Mercer University Press) by Eduard Schweizer. Being a one-time student of Bultmann, Schweizer's lectures show how
much the situation has changed in recent years. Along with Schweizer,
Heinz Schurmann, E. Schillebeeckx, J. Jeremias, and E. Jungel have all
made their contributions in this new quest for the historical Jesus. Bultmannian radicalism is in many circles being laid to rest, at least to some
degree.

A further aspect of the new quest is recognition of the fact that the
parables of Jesus give historical validity to the ministry of our Lord.
Here Jeremias stands out, as did C. H. Dodd before him. Crossan, an
American, has likewise done notable work in this area. This new appreciation of the historicity of the Gospels is to be welcomed. Bultmannian
form-criticism has been, at least to some extent, replaced in significance
by redaction-criticism. Yet, form-criticism in a less radical expression is
still used by some more orthodox thinkers, as Jeremias does.

Nonetheless, the basic philosophy of history propounded from Hume
through Bultmann, and up to the contemporary moment by many
thinkers, significantly influences much New Testament study. For example, in just recent days a group of biblical scholars met at Saint Mein-
rad Catholic Seminary in Indiana, U.S.A., to discuss which sayings attributed to Jesus in the Four Gospels are actual, authentic sayings of the

Lord. This philosophy of history, at least some form of it, has pretty well captured the hermeneutical approach of the day for more than a few.

This presuppositional approach is, of course, quite legitimate for scientific research and for scientific everyday history, but is it adequate for the study of Christianity? That is the crunch. Obviously, it presents real problems, because the Gospels clearly relate many supernatural, or "nonhistorical," events associated with Jesus. Moreover, the writers recorded the events in Jesus' life as if they actually happened that way in the real history of a real Jesus. It must be acknowledged, of course, that miracles are not the result of natural causes. They break out of the cause-effect course of natural history. Yet, they are recorded in the Gospels as if they really happened. What do Christians do then with that quandary? Various approaches have been taken.

Some of the empirical-rational theological historians first of all make a distinction between the "historical Jesus" and the "Christ of faith," but that stance is very dubious indeed. This approach does violence to a biblical Christology. Jürgen Moltmann argued we dare not divide "the crucified Jesus . . . from the risen Christ, or the risen Christ from the crucified Jesus."[37] Still, many in the critical school strongly disagree, some even going so far as to say we can completely dispense with the "Christ of faith," that is, Christological dogma: the "Jesus of history" is enough. The teaching, ethics, and example of Jesus is all we need, the argument runs. T. R. Glover, for example, painted this sort of portrait of Jesus.[38] Marshall described these advocates well when he said, "The concept of Jesus as a present Saviour and spiritual presence is either denied or retreats into a position of comparative insignificance."[39] Thus they actually reject any real Christology. Others put all the stress on the existential "Christ of faith."

To resolve the aforementioned dilemma, Bultmann and his school projected the idea of *heilsgeschichte*: sacred history. *Heilsgeschichte* is not *Historie* (German word for natural cause-effect historical events); rather, it is an *interpretation* of the significance of *historie*. The supernatural elements of the Jesus narratives are to be understood on the *heilsgeschichte* level. Natural, "real events" in our Lord's life rest on *historie*. For example, concerning the stories of the miraculous resurrection of Jesus, Bultmann stated, "Jesus has risen in the *kerygma*." That is to say, Jesus was not actually and literally historically raised from the dead; in *historie* His body still decays away in some unknown Palestinian grave. Jesus was depicted as raised from the dead in the preaching of the church to extol and describe the tremendous existential experience the disciples had of Jesus, even though He was actually, physically dead. He was "raised" in the *heilsgeschichte* sense. He was simply declared historically "raised" so as to interpret the impact of His life on believers. The Jesus of *history* (*historie*) was not raised, but the Christ of *faith* (*heilsgeschichte*) was.

Thus Bultmann saw two streams, or levels, of utterances concerning reported events. We have *historie*, that which actually occurred in casual time and space, and *heilsgeschichte*, interpretation of events which did not really happen historically. And *historie* and *heilsgeschichte* do not intersect except existentially in proclamation.[40] This is why Bultmann declared that Jesus was raised "in the *kerygma*":

> It is often said, almost always in criticism, that according to my interpretation of the kerygma, Jesus has risen in the kerygma. I accept this proposition. It is entirely correct, assuming that it is properly understood. It presupposes that the kerygma itself is an eschatological event, and it expresses the fact that *Jesus* is really present in the kerygma, that it is *his* word which involves the hearer in the kerygma. If that is the case, then all speculation concerning the modes of the existence of the risen Jesus, all the narratives of the empty tomb, all the Easter legends, whatever elements of historical fact they may contain, and as true as they may be in their symbolic form, are of no consequence. To believe in the *Christ* present in the kerygma is the meaning of the Easter faith.[41]

This approach gave rise to the well-known critical method of "demythologizing." It was a historical quest to get to the original forms of the traditions.

Of course, the outcome of the view is not only the rejection of a high Christology, but also the abandoning of any hope of discovering the historical Jesus. As Hugh Anderson observed:

> Bultmann's de-historicized version of the kerygma, in which Jesus has become a hollow name, a ghostly figure abstracted from our world and our history, is to some extent an inevitable outcome of the idea of human nature with which existentialists theology operates. For Bultmann, appropriating Heidigger's categories, *Dasein*, human being, is choice, free personal decision. . . . True human existence is thus comprised of broken and unrelated moments of encounter and decision, so that there is denied to it any temporal continuity and participation in the relativities of history. . . . The acosmic overtone in existentialist theology's understanding of man makes it virtually impossible to give specific content to the figure of Jesus Christ as one involved in his world, the historical events of his time and place, or in a particular nexus of ordinary human relationships. The Christ of the kerygma must accordingly remain *unworldly* and non-historical . . . [even if] the actual historical person of Christ is the origin, the point of departure, for Christianity.[42]

Everything now rests essentially on an existential base. To *experience* the Christ of faith is all which really matters.

The question thus becomes: Is this Bultmannian critical approach really consistent? D. M. Baillie thought not, as he pungently pointed out:

> It is common in certain theological circles to-day, partly through the influence of Form Criticism, to maintain that it is illegitimate to use the Gospels as historical "sources" for the reconstruction of the Jesus of history, since they were never meant to serve the purpose of historical evidence, but that of Christian witness. Yet in those very circles (one cannot help noticing) the Gospels are used precisely as historical "sources," not indeed for the reconstruction of the figure of Jesus, but for the reconstruction of the *kerygma* and the attitude of the early Church—though the early Church itself, in producing the Gospels, was supremely interested in the figure of Jesus![43]

The problem of the whole approach is, to quote Baillie again:

> This is a fertile source of confusion in the whole matter: the habit of setting "history" and "faith" too sharply against each other, with the assumption . . . that a really historical study of Jesus could not give us the kind of figure that would be of any use to faith![44]

In other words, one simply cannot dismiss out of hand the historical narrative of the Gospels, not even the existentialists, for they must use the Bible to formulate their *kerygma*. Actually, how can we build any sort of a concept of Jesus, historical or Christological, or any sort of valid existential experience, apart from viewing the Gospel records seriously as historical? To fail to do so seems to thrust one into a land of mere speculation or an existentially oriented, non-objective world.

It is most important to realize that how we understand the historicity of Jesus ultimately raises the "whole problem of the basis and rationale of our Christian belief in the Incarnation."[45] Relative to the entire question of the historicity of the recorded biblical events, Roland DeVaux argued, "If the historical faith . . . is not in a certain way founded in history, this faith is erroneous and cannot command my assent."[46] If the vital thing in Christian religion is no more than a mere "Jesus of history" about whom very little can be known, why did the first-century church not see it that way? They developed a very definite incarnational Christology, and they did it on the basis of the historicity of what they declared about Jesus' miracles, resurrection, etc. On such a foundation they understood the existential experience of God in Christ to be true and valid.

Moreover, what do Christians do with the pervasive principle of God revealing Himself by acting dynamically in real historical events? If the Bible says anything, it says that. It surely seems the concept of a God who saves and redeems historical people in a historical event demands a true historical account of the incarnation.[47]

Actually, the Bible knows nothing of a rationalistic, existential, double stream or level of "history" such as *historie* and *heilsgeschichte*. What Bultmann projected is, in some sense, a very sophisticated deism. If the God of the so-called *heilsgeschichte* plane never, except existentially, intersects with natural cause-effect *historie*, it really amounts to an esoteric sort of deism.[48] Even the view of some neoorthodox theologians like Karl Barth is inadequate when they present the Christ of faith (*heilsgeschechte*) as breaking in *only* at certain special times into *historie*. God does not just break into the natural, causal continuity of history at given times, as some contend; our Lord even sustains and permeates that naturalistic process. When He sees fit to do the supernatural, He just does it. He is omnipresent and ominipotent in all historical reality. Pannenburg has put it far better when he declared, "Increasingly it seemed to me inconsistent with the assumptions that Barth presented God's revelation as if God had entered a foreign country instead of 'his home,' as the Gospel of John tells us."[49] In those words, Pannenburg has expressed the real biblical view. After all, history is God's creation and in Christ "all things hold together" (Col. 1:17).

Thus to divide the Christ of faith (often called the "cosmic Christ") from the Jesus of history is a truncation of biblical history and biblical Christology. It radically weakens the incarnation. It cannot be correct from a scriptural standpoint to argue against the continuity between the historical Jesus and the eternal Christ. This falls woefully short of the scriptural view. In the New Testament, Jesus and Christ are one and the same. To separate them is not only biblically unfounded, but also philosophically inconsistent because the very meaning of God means One who incarnates Himself. It seems correct to say that Bultmann's approach strikes right at the heart of the whole redemptive plan of God.

Furthermore, the critical school's limited, narrow view of history is very difficult to square with actual facts. Miracles really do happen, and they happen in historical reality. There is simply too much genuine historical evidence to deny that. The philosophy of history propounded by Bultmann, and even to some extent by some of the neoorthodox school, is actually a tunnel vision approach to history. History simply is more than mere cause-effect. Why cannot God the omnipotent Creator do as He pleases with and in His creation?

The real sting in a purely casual view of history centers in the fact that it tends to make the incarnation quite weak at best. It falls into the two-thousand-year-old trap of trying to resolve rationally the paradox of the ultimate miracle of the glorious incarnation. Such an approach can easily weaken that wondrous act of God when Christ robed Himself in flesh. Paul Tillich saw these issues clearly, even if he was not an Evangelical himself, when he stated the problem of the historical reality of the incarnation is "the most immediate problem of our present existence."[50] Our understanding of history is vitally important to our view of Jesus.

Another important principle emerges from one's approach to the historicity of the Christ event. Understanding incarnation as the Bible presents it, makes all other scriptural declarations concerning the miraculous acts of Christ become viable. Kierkegaard recognized this when he said, "He who in faith has accepted the most absurd, humanly speaking, of all absurdities—that a simple human being is God—finds it impossible to be baffled by some detail [like the miracles]."[51]

The Jesus of history as recorded in the Scriptures is the eternal cosmic Christ and visa versa. Never is He to be "cut in two." It was against this separation that John argued in his writings (1 John 2:22; 4:1-3; 2 John 7). One must not sever Christ and Jesus: "Jesus is the Christ" (John 20:31). What the Gospels say of the incarnate Christ are *historically true*.

The implications for evangelism of the above principle are obvious and exceedingly significant. For example, there are those who would tell us people can be saved and redeemed through the "cosmic Christ" apart from hearing the "good news" of the historical Jesus. This subtle syncretistic approach is rejected, and not because of a narrow conservatism. It is because the New Testament reveals nothing of such an approach. The Bible takes its stance because of the meaning of the historical incarnation in Christ's redemptive activity. A weak Christology based on a weak historical view of Jesus will make for a shallow experience of God. Therefore, the world needs to know all it means to call the incarnate God by His incarnational, historical name: *the Lord Jesus Christ*. The whole *kerygma* (proclamation) must be shared.

The Place of Faith

All of this reasoning is not to imply that faith plays no role in the apprehension of the historical Christ event. History by itself does not "prove" that the Jesus of history is fully God Incarnate. It does take God-inspired, God-imparted faith (Eph. 2:8-9) to grasp Jesus Christ for all He is, but real history is not incompatible to the affirmation of faith. Faith is not a blind existential leap in the dark. It is a leap, but it is a leap based on historical realities. History is important. George E. Ladd affirms:

> There must be interaction between historical evidence and faith. Faith is not a blind leap in the dark without any historical evidence. Neither will historical evidence demand faith, for the man of unbelief will always

come up with different historical explanations. However, faith is support-
ed and reinforced by historical evidences.[52]

Keeping this balance and dynamic tension is vital. For example, an
uncritical view can easily accept everything as simple, forth-right history and conclude that is all one needs to affirm Christ. God is always, in
one sense, "nonhistorical." He is never limited to the "cause-effect" empirical world nor "proved" by it. Christians *believe* in God; they do not *see*
Him (Heb. 11:1). So they must exercise faith to grasp what God has
done, and who He is. Yet, God deals in real history; He is the God of
Abraham, Isaac, and Jacob. History and faith mix. So the incarnation of
Jesus the Son is an act of God which surely happened in history, but it
did not happen in terms of mere historical causality. It was a *miraculous*
occurrence. However, because the incarnation took place in history, we
are duty bound to investigate the historical accounts. How are these accounts to be explained, if they are to be explained?

Perhaps there is a simple existental explanation, as Bultmann argued.
This school tells us it was essentially existential subjectivism on the part
of the disciples when they said Jesus is God fully incarnate and was
literally resurrected from the grave. However, Bultmann's "historical"
approach failed to give a convincing explanation, even if it did present a
rationale for the situation. In the incarnation the disciples were convinced they actually met God the Son face-to-face. Thus, the Gospel
accounts force the belief that they are literally true when they say God
actually came into the course of human history, in human form, and was
bodily resurrected from the dead. Still, faith has the final answer, make
no mistake about that. Why? Because the incarnation is not fully explained on pure historical grounds. That is the point: accounts must be
investigated as far as possible, realizing a full, rational explanation is
not to be found.[53]

In reality, if adequate empirical evidence to answer questions concerning the incarnation and the resurrection on a purely rational basis
existed, it would create a biblical bind and a theological muddle. It
would eliminate the necessity of faith. Explanations do away with faith.
"Without faith it is impossible to please" God (Heb. 11:6), but Christians *believe* God acted in history and truly incarnated Himself in Jesus
Christ, even if they cannot explain it fully.

Even though history does not prove or rationally explain the miraculous Christ, the Holy Spirit uses history to help undergird faith, as Ladd
argued. Not only that, when believers say, "Christ came in the flesh,"
such a confession is actually the best answer to the historical accounts

themselves. It certainly does more justice to the narratives that the existential school, or any other school for that matter. In that sense, therefore, our declarations are logically consistent with the evidence. Still, faith has the last word.

Yet, why did the Word leave the "glory place," the Father's presence, to come to the "gory place," Calvary, as one preacher pungently put it? Jesus expressed it in His own words, "For this cause came I into the world" (John 18:37, KJV). What cause? The Cross! He came to die; and, of all wonders, He died in the sinner's place. He became humankind's redeeming Substitute. This leads to the next significant word in the salvific work of Christ in the theology of evangelism.

II
Substitution

Substitution, the often-used word in describing the saving work of Christ, centers in the idea of atonement. Yet substitution is but one of the so-called theories of the atonement, systematized by the theologians throughout the Christian era. Some thinkers see it as just one view among many. Some even reject the general idea. Others argue it is the heart of the atonement. A careful study is clearly called for.

Theories of the Atonement

Perhaps the best place to start would be to review briefly the various historical views of the atonement. It may well be true, as some contend, that the early declarations of the death of Jesus were not meant to present a theory of the atonement. They were simply presented to declare a saving reality. Nonetheless, the formulation of theological concepts such as the theories of the atonement fulfill a purpose. Moreover, a historical overview of the theories should help set the doctrine of substitution in proper theological and historical context. It will be seen that the various theories can be categorized under three basic themes: law (Athanasius), love (Abelard), and victory (Augustine).

The Example (Socinian) Theory.—This view of the atonement states that by Christ's example, people are motivated to reconcile themselves to God. It has precipitated the debate as to whether the Greek word *hilasmos* in 1 John 2:2 should be translated "propitiation" (KJV) or "expiation" (RSV). That debate will be taken up in more detail later. The Socinian theory is a quite popular view today. However, the weakness of this approach rests in its apparent failure to grasp the fact that God must be seen as reconciled to sinful, rebellious people as well as visa versa.[54] Vincent had apparently grasped this essential truth when he spoke of God's "transformed face" towards sinners as a result of Christ's atoning work. The example theory does point out the desperate need of sinful humanity to be reconciled to God, and the personal responsibility people have to see it accomplished. Further, this theory emphasizes that the death of Christ is a sterling example of faithfulness to truth and duty and thus has a powerful influence on one's own moral improvement. Christ's example of love and sacrifice should obviously kindle a similar love in us. The cross is far more than example, but it surely is that also. Peter Abeland (1079-1142) was a proponent of this approach.

The Commercial (Anselmic) Theory.—Emphasized by Anselm of Canterbury (1033-1109), the impact of this conception of the atoning work of Christ rests in its grasp of the fact that the divine honor was grossly sinned against in the fall of Adam and Eve. Infinite punishment must therefore attend the offender, the argument runs. That degree of punishment Christ bore. This approach, however, suffers from a lack of understanding that more than divine honor was involved in the fall. The atonement of Calvary accomplished more than merely meeting the divine claims in an exact equivalent. The work of Christ on the cross was not that formal and external, and divine honor cannot become anymore prominent than divine holiness. Yet, one must grant that God's honor was involved in it all, and in that sense the concept has something to say.

The Dramatic (Patristic) Theory.—Here the emphasis is on the struggle between the forces of God and the encroachments of evil. The theory holds that when Christ died, Satan and his hosts were unseated and routed. There is rich truth here. In one sense, however, this approach tends to leave men and women somewhat out of the picture. It so fixes one's vision on the divine struggle against evil, one wonders where needy people are involved, if at all. Surely, all of humanity was deeply involved in the entire affair. At the same time, however, it is clear a great battle was being waged, and the forces of evil were soundly defeated and destroyed in the Christ event. Our Lord has overcome the world (John 16:33). This view of the atonement dominated the patristic period.

The Ransom Theory.—This concept is also called the patristic view, something of a variation of the above approach. The theory propounds that if we are redeemed through a ransom of blood paid by God in Christ (1 Pet. 1:18-19), the one who was paid off must have been Satan. Few, if any, hold such a morally repugnant view today although Aulen in his *Christus Victor* proposes something of a demythologized view of the concept. It is true that our salvation was very costly to God, but He hardly paid a ransom for captive people to the devil or anyone. The question as to who received the ransom price is never raised in the New Testament. The truth to be stressed in the concept of ransom is that the atonement price was the very costly blood of Christ, and God paid that price, thus becoming the great Deliverer.

The Ethical Theory.—In more recent times, A. H. Strong attempted to bring together some of the strengths of these various views in the approach he conceived and called the ethical theory. He made the following points: (a) the atonement must be seen as rooted in the holiness of God; (b) it must answer the ethical demands of the divine nature; (c) in the humanity of Christ and His sufferings all claims of justice are met; (d) Christ suffered vicariously; (e) the atonement was accomplished through the solidarity of the race; (f) it satisfies people's ethical needs; and (g) the atonement is for all, but people must avail themselves of it.

Whether or not one agrees with all Strong asked for, he has at least grasped something of the principle of gleaning from the various theories the aspect of truth presented and then incorporating it into a fuller system. John Driver was correct when he stated, "The plurality of images used to understand the work of Christ is essential. The apostolic community allowed all to stand in a complementary relationship rather than attempting to reduce them to a single theory or dogmatic statement."[55] As Robert Jackson reminded us, "Often the images overlap . . . sometimes several will come near to being conflated (cf. I Peter 1:18,19). But the crux of the gospel cannot be reduced to one image."[56] This approach has obvious value, for the atonement of Christ is as a many-faceted jewel. To fix one's gaze upon just one facet is to neglect the beauty of the whole. Actually, so profound is the scriptural presentation of the atonement that a completely satisfying theology is most difficult, if not impossible. The more we look into its wonders, the more glorious it becomes, but we must continue our gaze and continue to pass on to others what beauties we discover.

There are other interpretations of the atonement.[57] These are of interest, but they will have to be left to more critical studies. We now come to "substitution." It is the contention of this author that the underlying core of the atonement, as it is presented in the Bible, revolves around the idea of substitution: *Christ died for us.* If all the other theories are facets of the jewel of atonement, *substitution* is the core of the stone from which all the facets are cut.

This view, sometimes called the governmental (Grotion) theory, tells us that Christ was essentially a *substitute* for us. On Calvary He hung in our place, took our iniquities on Himself, and bore the penalty for our sins. It sees the atonement as a satisfaction to God's justice and holiness.[58] The Law and its demands had to be met. Sin must be judged. Christ accomplished this when He died in our place and bore our judgment in Himself. We are pardoned because Christ bore the just penalty of our sins and satisfied the Law's requirements.

The penal substitutionary theory of the atonement has received stress through the years, especially since the Reformation. Luther and Calvin understood it as the heart of the atoning work of Christ. Both these reformers saw the atonement as something of a combination of Christ as the victor and as the victim. In His substitutionary death, Jesus defeated death. This theory has recently been defended by John R. W. Stott in his work *The Cross of Christ.* What does it all mean? It means far more than human beings can ever comprehend; still, there are several things that can be positively stated.

Christianity is a religion of the cross. The crucifixion is at the center of our faith. The supreme question is not, as Anselm asked, "Why did God become man?" but, "Why did Christ die?" The New Testament reveals Christ died for our sins. He died in our place.

However, words like *substitution* and *satisfaction,* although right at the heart of biblical and Reformation theology, are not exceedingly popular today, at least in some scholarly circles. Vincent Taylor, for example, raised questions about the idea of substitution.[59] He is indicative of many, although not nearly as cavalier as some; for he grants some form of substitution is found in the atonement, and he realizes the cross is central.

Jesus knew He came primarily to die (John 12:27). Although He seemingly wanted to keep His messiahship something of a secret (Matt. 16:20), He labored to instruct His disciples that He was to die on a cross. He strove to get them to see the Messiah was also the Suffering Servant of Isaiah 53. This He dramatized in the institution of the Lord's Supper. Actually, the cross event was the focal point in all our Lord said and did. This is biblically beyond serious dispute. Matthew tells us:

> From that time on Jesus began to explain to his disciples that he must go to Jerusalem and suffer many things at the hands of the elders, chief priests and teachers of the law, and that he must be killed and on the third day be raised to life.
> Peter took him aside and began to rebuke him, "Never, Lord!" he said. "This shall never happen to you!"
> Jesus turned and said to Peter, "Get behind me, Satan! You are a stumbling block to me; you do not have in mind the things of God, but the things of men" (Matt. 16:21-23, NIV).

Our Lord knew He was to die for three obvious reasons (at least obvious to Himself): (1) because of the hostility of the Jewish religious leaders, (2) to effect the fulfillment of Scriptures, for example, Isaiah 53, Psalm 22, and (3) by His own choice, the Son of man personally determined to be also the "Suffering Servant." The dominant motivation in Jesus' ministry was Calvary: "He steadfastly set his face to go to Jerusalem" (Luke 9:51, KJV). For our Lord, hence for us, Christianity centers in a cross.

Moreover, it is correct to state: the cross is the focal point of all history. Heaven raised the question: "Who is worthy to open the scroll [of history]" and look into it? (Rev. 5:3). The answer rang through the courts of glory, "Worthy art thou to take the scroll and to open its seals" (Rev. 5:9). Who is this "worthy" one? The Lamb of God! Notice, it is the sacrificially *slain* Lamb of God—humanity's great Substitute. He alone is worthy to open up history. The crucified Lord is the central figure of all time.

Further, Jesus as the Lamb not only occupies the central position in history, but God will also sit center stage in all eternity. The cross truly is central. P. T. Forsyth was absolutely correct when he wrote in *The Cruciality of the Cross:* "Christ is to us just what his cross is. All that Christ was in heaven or on earth was put into what he did there . . . . Christ, I repeat, is to us just what his cross is. You do not understand Christ till you understand his cross."[60] Brunner had it right when he stated:

> The cross is the sign of the Christian faith, of the Christian Church, of the revelation of God in Jesus Christ . . . The whole struggle of the Reformation for the *sola fide* the *sili deo gloria*, was simply the struggle for the right interpretation of the Cross. He who understands the Cross aright—this is the opinion of the Reformers—understands the Bible, he understands Jesus Christ.[61]

The cross is the glory of Christ. Our Lord said on the night of the Supper: "Now is the Son of man glorified, and in him God is glorified; if God is glorified in him, God will also glorify him in himself, and glorify him at once" (John 13:31-32). The old rugged cross displays the glorification of Christ and the love of God as nothing else. His scars are eternal (Rev. 13:8) and will cry throughout eternity, "God so loved the world that he gave his only Son" (John 3:16).

As central as the cross may be to Christian faith, the atonement question must still be faced: *Why* did Christ die? Of course, from the human perspective, Judas betrayed the Lord, and some Jewish religious leaders, out of jealousy, by the hands of Rome put Him to death.[62] Moreover, Jesus did not resist the cross. The Bible even makes it clear the crucifixion was in the predetermined will of God (Rom. 8:32). Thus Jesus submitted to that will as seen in the Gethsemane struggle. But why?

The Heart of the Atonement

The word is *substitution:* Christ "who knew no sin," became sin for us (2 Cor. 5:21). In that self-imposed act, he bore *in our place* our deserved punishment and divine judgment on sin.[63] He is the slain-risen *Lamb,* an idea used twenty-eight times in the Book of Revelation. He is the scapegoat who bears our sins and takes them on Himself, goes outside the camp, and purchases our redemption.

Theologians have for ages attempted to mitigate the harsh reality of substitutionary truth. For example, New Testament scholar Frank Stagg has told us:

"Jesus became a curse for us, yet surely not in the sense that he himself became a sinner. The picture of the Father's turning from the Son because the Son had become sin does not come from the New Testament."[64] William J. Wolf has observed: "God did not punish Christ. It is monstrous to picture the Father deliberately inflicting punishment on his beloved and obedient Son as a scapegoat."[65]

What then is the meaning of the cross, why did Christ die? Stagg stated, "The death of Jesus is ultimate in confronting us with God's *way of life* for us. . . . The cross alone would *show* us how to die in order to love."[66] This is really no more than the old moral influence theory of the atonement in a bit of modern garb. We granted the death of Christ does have moral influence in one's life, but there is far more involved in Calvary than merely a demonstration and inspiration on how to live and die. Jürgen Moltmann, hardly a conservative reformed theologian, recognized the necessity of at least some form of substitution in the atonement when he said, "The meaning of his [Jesus] giving of himself to death on the cross is the liberation of the sinner from the burden of sin by virtue of reconciliation; and his liberation from the power of sin by virtue of substitution."[67] Millard Erickson emphatically declared, "Because he [Jesus] has come to be sin, we have ceased to be sin or sinners. *The idea of substitution is unmistakable.*"[68] If substitution therefore lies at the heart of it all, what does it actually mean?

John R. W. Stott has told us there are several things we can say.[69] First, although Jesus died at the hands of human beings, it was really the fulfillment of divine decree and purpose. He was "delivered up according to the definite plan and foreknowledge of God" (Acts 2:23). It was all accomplished "according to the scriptures" (1 Cor. 15:3-4, KJV). It was God's redemptive scheme from the beginning.

Second, the substitutionary death of Christ abounds in rich doctrinal content. For example, the cross is set forth in the context of Old Testament teaching on the curse of God upon anyone who hung on a "tree." Being familiar with Old Testament legislation, the New Testament writers saw Jesus as dying under God's curse. Yet, they well knew Jesus was undeserving of a curse; therefore, they theologized the event by stating: "Christ redeemed us from the curse of the law by becoming a curse for us, for it is written: 'Cursed is everyone who is hung on a tree' " (Gal. 3:13, NIV). Peter wrote, "He himself bore our sins in his body on the tree" (1 Pet. 2:24).

Third, in the light of the resurrection, the empty tomb declares the defeat of the entire death syndrome. Because Jesus submitted Himself to a sacrificial, substitutionary death, God raised Him to the place of honor at His right hand and made Him both Lord and Christ. In that, the glorious fact emerges: "Death is swallowed up in victory" (1 Cor. 15:54).

Thus it is little wonder that Paul boasted in nothing save the sacrificial cross of Jesus Christ (Gal. 6:14). It is the heart of Christ's work. Brunner was absolutely correct when he told us in *The Mediator*:

> [The cross] *is* the Christian religion itself; it is the "main point"; it is not something alongside of the center; it is the substance and kernel, not the husk. . . . And there is no other possibility of being a Christian than through faith in that which took place once for all, revelation and atonement through the Mediator.[70]

The substitutionary view of the atonement also has significant and profound implications, Erickson pointed out, because Christ died in our place:

1. We see in bold relief the depravity of human sin.
2. We see God as both loving and just, and these attributes are in perfect oneness.
3. Salvation comes from the pure, sovereign grace of God. Pelegianism is forever laid to rest.
4. There is security for the believer in the grace of God.
5. We are motivated to not "neglect so great salvation" (Heb. 2:3, KJV).[71]

All of this theologizing about the cross means God can justly forgive sins, and that means *satisfaction*. His Law is satisfied. It must be realized, however, that "satisfaction" does not mean there is some moral external principle, that is, external to God, that must be met so God can be "satisfied." We have learned God is the *only* ultimate, and all moral standards exist *internal* to God. Moreover, because words like *substitution* and *satisfaction* appear strange, if not offensive to some, does it really mean God could not forgive unless some appeasement of His anger or wrath against sin was forthcoming, thus seemingly reflecting on His infinite love for sinners? How do we answer this criticism?

In the first place, God's love is a *holy* love. It is certainly a love that reaches out to sinners, yet never a love that condones sin or compromises His holiness. God must be true to His righteous nature. So the penalty for sin had to be meted out and paid for. Someone had to bear the punishment, either the sinner or a substitute. Holiness demands such. Satisfaction had to be met. Such is what God is like in being true to His own righteous, holy Being. What love is demonstrated in the cross! Actually, when the atonement is really understood, the love of God stands out in bold relief as never before realized. As Stott put it:

> At the cross in holy love God through Christ paid the full penalty of our disobedience *himself*. He bore the judgment we deserve in order to bring us forgiveness we do not deserve. On the cross divine mercy and justice were

equally expressed and eternally reconciled. God's holy love was "satisfied."[72]

There is always, it seems, a tendency to attenuate the seriousness of sin. The old Puritans were accustomed to speaking of the "exceeding sinfulness of sin." Apparently we have lost something of that in our contemporary understanding, but sin is serious—deadly serious. The Bible calls it rebellion, defiance, arrogance, missing God's mark, perversion, transgression, unbelief, wickedness, and vileness. If such is God's evaluation of our self-willed actions—and if God is consuming holiness—sin is serious beyond imagining. It cannot be lightly dismissed by God or humanity. Sentimentalism is not to be confused with *agape*.

But is the judgment of God against sin real? Does God actually punish sinners? Yes, He does. Judgment is far more than sin just running its natural course. It goes infinitely beyond the impersonal outcome of our perverseness. God actively condemns our rebellion. Paul spoke of sin in impersonal terms at times, but the apostle adopted such language to emphasize that God's wrath is never tainted with personal malice. Nor is God's anger ever arbitrary; it is principled and controlled.

How then can we understand God's anger or wrath? Leon Morris put his finger on it: "The words describe a positive revulsion. . . . they speak of God's . . . personal, vigorous opposition"[73] to sin. Granted, to speak of God's wrath and anger is to use anthropomorphisms, but the principle is still true. God is holy, hates sin, and judges evil sinners. Wrath is real. Contemporary people need to grasp this biblical truth. It cannot be dismissed on psychological or shallow theological grounds. Stott said,

> We must, therefore, hold fast to the biblical revelation of the living God who hates evil, is disgusted and angered by it, and refuses ever to come to terms with it. In consequence, we may be sure that, when he searched in his mercy for some way to forgive, cleanse and accept evil-doers, it was not along the road of moral compromise. It had to be a way which was expressive equally of his love and of his wrath. As Brunner put it, "where the idea of the wrath of God is ignored, there also will there be no understanding of the central conception of the Gospel: the uniqueness of the revelation in the Mediator." Similarly, "only he who knows the greatness of wrath will be mastered by the greatness of mercy."[74]

Therefore, the absolute necessity of "satisfaction" by "substitution" is seen. Actually, if God were not provoked by sin, He would probably lose our respect; we might in some sense even consider Him immoral. God's righteousness must be "satisfied" on God's own moral grounds. Those demands must be met, and it was fully accomplished when Christ died and endured God's wrath on the cross as our great "substitute." Further, if God did nothing about our sad situation, we would seriously question His love. But notice, Jesus *willingly* suffered. The only compulsion was His great love and desire to redeem all humanity. In that divine act of fathomless love, the Law was satisfied, God's holiness, justice, honor, and love met, and believers are set free. God, whose actions are the definition of what is right, moral, and loving, has utterly satisfied Himself. God answers only to God. His Law has been met by Himself in the cross. God is "just, and the justifier" of those who believe (Rom. 3:26, KJV).

Thus in the cross of Christ, fathomless love and divine justice meet. Actually, they more than meet. They are one and the same. Consequently, Christians never need be morally embarrassed by God's full forgiveness and loving redemption. The moral price has been paid. God morally and lovingly forgives. He acts on the basis of all His attributes at all times simultaneously. Therefore, God was completely consistent with God. What a message to proclaim! When Jesus cried out on the cross, "It is finished," He said more than can ever be realized.

> Beneath the cross of Jesus
> I fain would take my stand,
> The shadow of a mighty rock
> Within a weary land;
> . . . .
> And from my smitten heart with tears
> Two wonders I confess,
> The wonders of his glorious love
> And my unworthiness.
> —Elizabeth C. Clephane

Substitution and satisfaction thus stand out in bold relief when one speaks of the atonement. Yet, certain theologians still get involved in the gymnastic exercise of retaining substitutionary terminology when in reality they avoid the idea of *penal* substitution in the atonement. This exercise goes as far back as Abelard's polemic against Anselm in the twelfth century. More recent writers like John McLead Campbell in *The Nature of the Atonement*, Howard Bushnell in *The Vicarious Sacrifice*, and R. C. Moberly in *Atonement and Personality*, attempt similar efforts.[75] Their arguments are hardly convincing for several reasons.

First of all, these authors clearly fly in the historical face of the reformed thinkers who expressed and argued so convincingly for the doctrine of penal substitution. How do they deal with Calvin, for example, who reminded us: "This is our acquittal: the guilt that held us liable for punishment has been transferred to the head of the Son of God (Isaiah 53:12). We must, above all, remember this substitution, lest we tremble and remain anxious throughout life, that is, in fear of God's judgment" (Institutes, II. xvi. 5).

Far more important, however, what do the modern deniers of penal substitution do with the Scriptures themselves? The biblical writers constantly use sin-bearing language. The Old Testament abounds in the idea. As Stott pointed out,

> It is clear from Old Testament usage that to "bear sin" means neither to sympathize with sinners, nor to identify with their pain, nor to express their penitence, nor to be persecuted on account of human sinfulness (as others have argued), nor even to suffer the consequences of sin in personal or social terms, but specifically to endure its penal consequences, to undergo its penalty.[76]

The Old Testament declares reconciliation between God and sinners comes about by penal substitution, substitutionary sin-bearing.

Moreover, Isaiah 53 personifies the sin-bearing principle. In Isaiah a man dies to take away sin. This particular passage became central to New Testament Christians (Acts 8:32-35), and strikes at the heart of it all. Joachim Jeremias said, "No other passage from the Old Testament was as important to the church as Isaiah 53."[77] One thing is quite clear: the apostolic age certainly saw Jesus as the fulfillment of Isaiah's prophetic word. Regardless of the fact some scholars deny that Isaiah speaks of Christ's suffering, there can be only one conclusion: Jesus the Suffering Servant died as our substitute to satisfy God's righteous Law, and that is penal substitution.[78]

Therefore, to view the atonement of Christ on the cross as essentially a penal substitution for the sins of the world seems unavoidable biblically. That view honors both God's holiness and love. Stott correctly concluded, "We strongly reject, therefore, every explanation of the death of Christ which does not have at its centre the principle of 'satisfaction through substitution,' *indeed* divine self-satisfaction through divine self-substitution" (author's italics).[79] The Reformers saw this clearly. The Bible makes it plain. Substitution ought to be accepted in holy humility, seeing the cross for all it is. In the observance of the Lord's Supper, the church has regularly realized the centrality and wonder of Christ's substitutionary sacrifice of Himself. As Moltmann expressed it,

> The messianic anticipation of eating and drinking in the kingdom of God are linked with Christ's giving of himself to death for the world's salvation. The breaking of the bread and the pouring out of the wine acquire significance through the self-giving of the Messiah.[80]

Of course, it must be granted, many secondary questions cluster around the substitutionary concept: Since the idea of the Trinity is taken seriously, how could God pour out wrath upon Himself? How could God be separated from God in the cry of dereliction: "My God, my God, why have you forsaken me?" (Ps. 22:1, NRSV). How could the death of one man redeem all people? These and kindred quandaries shall be taken up in part III of this work in the consideration of words like *propitiation, justification*, and *reconciliation*. It must be sufficient to say here the Bible makes it clear that Christ died for our sins. The preposition *for* should be taken as seriously as the New Testament writers took it. No wonder Paul said, "God forbid that I should glory, save in the cross of our Lord Jesus Christ, by whom the world is crucified unto me, and I unto the world" (Gal. 6:14, KJV). Jesus died, endured the wrath of God for sins, experienced separation from the Father, and agonized for us all. What love!

From a practical proclamation perspective, it may be wise to *begin* the story of salvation by emphasizing some other aspect of the atonement, such as the defeat of demonic forces. For a very primitive, animistic people who live out their lives in fear of demons, to realize Christ defeated the enemy on the cross is extremely relevant and captivating. So the proclaimer should begin where people are, emphasizing that aspect of atonement which appeals to them, and then, when they are open, declare all the truth of Christ's work. That is good evangelistic methodology. Perhaps the penal-substitution concept may not be the immediate idea that captivates the mind of some in today's secular world. Nevertheless, it is the essence of the atonement; and, even if one pragmatically begins some place else in the relevant proclamation of salvation, one must eventually help people to see what lies at the heart of it all.

The cross, though central, is not the whole story, however. There is another great word to consider in Christ's redemptive work.

III

Resurrection

"He is not here, but is risen" (Luke 24:6, KJV). The angels' words filled the women with fear, wonder, awe, confusion, amazement, hope, and a host of other human emotions. What sort of a declaration was this? The Teacher was dead. He was buried. Hope was gone. What could this startling message be saying? What did it mean to the women who first heard it? What did the disciples think when first told? What does it communicate to us today? These questions must be answered.

The immediate biblical answer to the vital queries raised is that Jesus Christ was resurrected from the grave. Moreover, that startling declaration has, from a scriptural perspective, become a foundational stone in the entire Christian faith. For example, there is little question how much weight Paul placed on the resurrection of our Lord. He said:

Now if Christ is preached as raised from the dead, how can some of you say that there is no resurrection of the dead? . . . if Christ has not been raised, then our preaching is in vain and your faith is in vain. We are even found to be misrepresenting God, because we testified of God that he raised Christ, whom he did not raise if it is true that the dead are not raised. For if the dead are not raised, then Christ has not been raised. If Christ has not been raised, your faith is futile and you are still in your sins. Then those also who have fallen asleep in Christ have perished. If for this life only we have hoped in Christ, we are of all men most to be pitied (1 Cor. 15:12,14-19).

Rare indeed is the New Testament theologian who would not, at least in principle, agree with Paul. Michael Green stated, "The resurrection of Jesus Christ from the dead is the cornerstone of Christianity."[81] But what did the apostle mean by "resurrection"? What had really happened when the tomb was found empty? A myriad of ideas have been set forth by various scholars in answer to these pertinent questions, and serious disagreements have arisen.

Some Rational Approaches

Several speculative, rationalistic explanations for the empty tomb have been propounded, some rather ludicrous ones.[82] For example, the "swoon theory," concocted by Paulus in 1828, is a very elaborate scheme. The theory states that a man with His last breath could hardly cry so energetically. A virile young man could last several days on the cross, and Jesus was a fine physical specimen. Paulus concluded that the Roman soldier's spear inflicted only a mere surface wound on Jesus, and the Lord passed out in a swoon. When the Lord was then placed in the cool grave with the aroma of spices, He came out of His faint that had been mistaken for His death. Next an earthquake opened the grave, and He walked out. Our Lord consequently put on some old gardener's clothes, and Mary mistook Him for the gardener (John 20:15), and that was how the resurrection story got started. This scheme was "resurrected" recently in a religious novel *The Passover Plot* by Schonfield. If such were the actual events, then Jesus must have spent the rest of His life in hiding, for He was never seen again around Galilee after forty days (Acts 1:3).

Another view by Kirsopp Lake argued that Jesus was laid in a tomb which was only one among several others. The women who came on the first day of the week merely saw the wrong tomb, an empty one, and a young man said, "He is not here; see the place where they laid him" (Mark 16:7, pointing to another tomb where the body of Jesus actually laid). The women misunderstood the entire episode. In fear they ran to the disciples to tell their partial understanding of what actually happened. Hence, the idea of a resurrection emerged in the early church's traditions.

Such explanations to account for the empty tomb border on nonsense. This type of reasoning comes perilously close to falling under Paul's judgment of being "found to be misrepresenting God" (1 Cor. 15:15). It is really quite ridiculous to think that first-century believers would put their lives on the line, endure persecution and ridicule, or be so naive as to think they could keep such a hoax alive. The disciples, who endured so much for their belief in the resurrection, were not that unrealistic. People could flog them, imprison them, or kill them, and still they declared Jesus actually arose. They must have believed it, but what sort of a "resurrection" did they believe in? That is the question.

The Historical Issue

When one attempts to answer the key questions raised above, the historical issue once again surfaces. Of course, what contemporary, rational, historical thinkers say is common knowledge. As might be surmised, they take essentially the same line concerning the resurrection as they do regarding the incarnation. They drain it of its true, corporeal, historical bite. For example, Bultmann declared, "Jesus has risen in the *kerygma*." His view of history *(historie)* forced him to declare, "A historical fact which involves a resurrection from the dead is utterly inconceivable."[83] What can we say about this? Can modern men and women really accept the idea of a historical, bodily resurrection from the dead?

The bedrock issue to face is: Does the testimony concerning Jesus' resurrection speak of an event in any real historical sense, or is it merely a faith expression to eulogize the greatness of Jesus or preserve His memory? A second vital issue then arises. Does it matter? Several things need to be said.[84]

First, pure historical evidence in itself does not automatically produce faith. It may well undergird faith, but the Holy Spirit gives birth to faith. Even if there is strong historical evidence that Jesus arose, that in itself will not demand faith. The Pharisees did not believe the report of the soldiers who guarded the tomb; they even gave the soldiers money to lie (Matt. 28:11-15). It takes the Holy Spirit to generate genuine faith.

Second, the early disciples were absolutely convinced Jesus had been raised. They testified He was alive even at the cost of their own lives. Why? Because they had gone to the tomb and found it empty, and even more, they had literally seen Jesus alive. Above all, the Holy Spirit was active in it all. Consequently, in complete Spirit-inspired faith they could say, "The Lord has risen indeed" (Luke 24:34).

Third, it seems reasonable to believe a resurrection actually did occur in history, but, as in the case with the incarnation, the event transcended history. It was a supernatural event. As Walter Kunneth put it, "The resurrection of Jesus is clearly rooted in history, although it is not in itself a historical fact."[85] In other words, Jesus was actually raised, but it transcended mere historical causality. This is why the Holy Spirit must aid us to grasp all that is meant by the historical resurrection of Jesus.

Fourth, it thus seems sensible to conclude that belief in the resurrection is "interaction between historical evidence and faith."[86]

If Ladd is correct, it becomes important to ask, what "evidences" from history do people have respecting the resurrection? Some, of course, say little if any. For example, Brunner declared, "The Resurrection communications of Christ . . . allows no objectivity."[87] But can that be true? The answer is no for several reasons.

Initially, the resurrection of Jesus is recorded in the New Testament exactly as are other historical events. There is no different literary style employed when presenting the resurrection narratives as over against obvious historical events such as Jesus' teaching by the seaside. Bishop Westcott pointed this out in his *Gospel of the Resurrection:*

> Nothing can be more simple history. What we call the miraculous facts are placed beside the others without any difference. The Resurrection of the Lord and His appearances after the Resurrection are taught as events of the same kind essentially, and to be received in the same way as His Death and Burial.[88]

Simply put, the New Testament writers apparently thought they were recording a true event in history, even if it was a transcending miracle. That stubborn fact must be faced by the positivistic historians.

Second, we have to deal with the empty tomb. Frank Morrison raised that issue years ago in his popular work *Who Moved the Stone?* Someone did move the stone, and the grave was found to be empty. Several issues need to be realized in the light of that fact:

1. Jesus actually died and was given a proper burial. "Christ died . . . [and] he was buried" (1 Cor. 15:3-4).
2. The grave had been sealed and guarded by the authority of Rome itself.
3. On the third day the women came to the garden tomb expecting to find the body of Jesus. They discovered the stone rolled away, and the body gone. It completely baffled them. Strange as it seems in the light of Jesus' prophecy, they did not anticipate anything like a resurrection.
4. Even the Sanhedrin acknowledged the tomb was empty and bribed the soldiers to say the body of Jesus was stolen (Matt. 28:11-15).
5. There is no trace of any early Christian group paying homage to a tomb of Jesus. After the disciples found the tomb vacated, the grave

of Jesus simply faded out of history. This constitutes a complete repudiation of most religious customs and systems.

6. Then there is the shroud. John 20:7 tells us the grave clothes were left
   in the tomb and the turban "not lying with the linen cloths but rolled
   up in a place by itself." Beasley-Murray raises the question, "Does
   that signify it had retained its shape? What an extraordinary sight!
   The stone was moved, the body had disappeared, the clothes were
   left untouched!"[89] George Ladd thinks this is the case as do other
   New Testament scholars.

7. The Apostles often spoke of the empty tomb in their preaching of the
   gospel.

A number of issues are obviously raised in the context of the empty
tomb. Who moved the stone? What happened to the body of Jesus?
What did the angels really say? How does one account for all of these
realities? Could it be Jesus was truly resurrected? All the evidence seems
to say so, and there are the postresurrection appearances. This issue is
most important.

The Appearances of the Resurrected Christ

Several things need to be said relative to the reported "appearances"
of Jesus after the tomb was discovered to be empty. C. H. Dodd argued
the appearances were of a different order and nature than any other sort
of experience. He states "The 'appearances' of the risen Christ . . . are
represented as a series limited in time, and distinct from any subsequent
type of 'Christian experience.' "[90] The vital question in this arena is: Did
the disciples actually have true objective experiences they understood as
verifiable appearances of their crucified Teacher? The biblical narratives
present the appearances as objective, historical events which the disciples experienced, and all that while in their sane, rational minds. But can
we take it for literal fact?

A full reading of 1 Corinthians 15:3-8 is helpful here:

> For I delivered to you as of first importance what I also received, that
> Christ died for our sins in accordance with the scriptures, that he was
> buried, that he was raised on the third day in accordance with the scrip-
> tures, and that he appeared to Cephas, then to the twelve. Then he ap-
> peared to more than five hundred brethren at one time, most of whom are
> still alive, though some have fallen asleep. Then he appeared to James,
> then to all the apostles. Last of all, as to one untimely born, he appeared
> also to me.

The New Testament beyond doubt declares the historical, verifiable appearances of the resurrected Lord. However, does the New Testament
tell us the unabashed historical truth? Can the documents be relied
upon? Not really, say some critics. This type of narrative, the positivists

argue, is a device the church added later to the Jesus narratives to eulogize and perpetuate the impact of Jesus on their lives. However, we
know the Corinthian letter is one of the earliest New Testament documents. It was composed around A.D. 53 or 54, less than a quarter century after the reputed appearances. Moreover, Paul was converted probably in A.D. 34, just four years after the death of Jesus. He had declared
the resurrection since his Damascus Road experience. Three years later
he went up to Jerusalem. There he got much of his detailed information
on the narratives of the appearances from the Jerusalem disciples themselves. At the outside, Paul's testimony was only seven years after the
fact. Therefore, it seems safe to conclude that seven years after the event
is close enough for some real, objective accuracy. Not many legendary
accretions could have grown up around the resurrection narrative in that
short a time. That fact alone should lay to rest the contention of certain
New Testament scholars that the resurrection narratives were added
later by the church to strengthen their claim to the deity of Jesus.

We might also add what is basically true of Paul is likewise verifiable
in the narratives of the Four Gospels.[91] A redating of the New Testament is occurring in biblical studies. For example, Bo Reicke wrote, "An
amazing example of uncritical dogmatism in New Testament studies is
the belief that the Synoptic Gospels should be dated after the Jewish
War of A.D. 66-70 because they contain prophecies *ex eventi* of the destruction of Jerusalem by the Romans in the year 70."[92] C. F. D. Moule
argued along the same line, stating:

> It is hard to believe that a Judaistic type of Christianity which had itself
> been closely involved in the cataclysm of the years leading up to A.D. 70
> would not have shown scars—or, alternately, would not have made capi-
> tal out of this signal evidence that they, not non-Christian Judaism, were
> the true Israel. But in fact our traditions are silent.[93]

Even the highly critical scholar, John A. T. Robinson, has done a major
redating work. He dated the *Revelation* at A.D. 68 and James as early as
A.D. 47-48. He declared:

> One of the oddest facts about the New Testament is that what on any
> showing would appear to be the single most datable and climactic event of
> the period—the fall of Jerusalem in A.D. 70, and with it the collapse of
> institutional Judaism based on the Temple—is never once mentioned as a
> past fact.[94]

All this is obviously significant in giving validity to the historicity of the
biblical statements concerning the resurrection.

Much more could be said in this same vein of argumentation. Beasley-Murray summed it up:

Could any ancient historical document of so brief a compass be produced, more fully authenticated? We have every right to believe that this document [1 Corinthians 15] *is an unimpeachable witness* to the fact that the men concerned believed they saw Jesus alive after His burial; to refuse to accept its testimony would be tantamount to denying that we can know anything of the history of the past centuries?[95]

So the evidence is conclusive the disciples recorded early what they thought were historical experiences of the kind narrated in Scriptures. Did they really see Jesus *objectively*? Or, were the "appearances" some sort of purely *subjective* event, perhaps an "objective vision" as Pannenberg thought? In other words, were the disciples a credible, capable group upon whom people can rely as giving a true objective account? Clearly, it has to be either an objective or subjective experience to which the disciples gave testimony. What Pannenberg meant by an "objective vision" is a bit of a puzzle.

I reject any *purely* subjective experience for several reasons. In the first place, when the initial proclamation of Jesus' resurrection was made, the disciples did not believe it; actually, they refused to believe the story. Luke told us that when the report of the resurrection was heard, "These words seemed to them an idle tale, and they did not believe them" (24:11). Thomas's reaction, for example, is well known (John 20:24-29). Actually, he reacted much like a first-century empirical rationalist, but he got his opportunity to see the print of the nails and thrust his hand into the Lord's side. Then he believed. Paul's case is even more startling, for he was an avowed enemy of the Lord. He was not about to accept the testimony of shallow subjectivists. All that hardly sounds like the reaction of a deeply grieving group who were ready to be worked up into some sort of unrealistic, subjective emotional state and thus project a hallucination on themselves.

Furthermore, when Jesus first appeared to the women and to the disciples on the road to Emmaus, they did not even realize it was Jesus. Not only that, all sorts of people from various backgrounds reported they actually saw Jesus alive. A large number of the disciples—in one case five hundred at the same time—declared Jesus was out of that grave (1 Cor. 15:6). How could so many be suffering from the same subjective deception at the same time? It really does not make sense to say they were. Moreover, these appearances spanned a forty-day protracted period. The disciples could hardly have kept having subjective visions going on for that length of time. To say they did, all but implies they were neurotic or even psychotic. What then can be said? Again Beasley-Murray put his finger on it: "There is only one explanation of these facts. The appearances of the Risen Jesus were historical objective, and catastrophic in their effects. *Jesus is Alive*" (author's italics).[96]

The arguments can go on. In the final analysis, however, it reduces itself to this: the New Testament documents—the earliest ones—clearly and distinctly state that the tomb was empty, and the disciples saw Jesus alive. There can be only one reason why the Bible states it so emphatically. The disciples believed He was actually and literally and historically raised from the dead, despite the purely rational problems the fact of the resurrection raises. Theologian and philosopher D. M. MacKinnon of Cambridge University was correct when he stated, "Now let us be fair. The Gospel writers do make clear that on Easter Day events happened which were qualitatively similar to previous events. . . . What, then, is wrong with the simple down to earth realism of those who say that either Christ rose or he did not?"[97]

When the Bible speaks clearly and emphatically, the most coherent epistemological approach is to accept it. Faith grasps what may puzzle the mind, and the idea of a resurrection is a rational mind boggler.[98] Still, *Christians believe.* But even as the above argumentation demonstrates, faith in the resurrection is not a blind, irrational leap of faith. It does make sense that the Lord is actually alive. Historical evidences abound. So believers accept God's Word as true when borne home to their minds and hearts by the Holy Spirit. God is then praised for His redemptive grace wrought in the resurrection of Jesus Christ.

> Up from the grave he arose,
> With a mighty triumph o'er his foes;
> He arose a victor from the dark domain,
> And he lives forever with the saints to reign.
> He arose! He arose!
> Hallelujah! Christ arose!
>
> —Robert Lowry

The Nature of the Resurrection

Granted Christ arose, yet the question as to the actual nature of the resurrection remains. Was it a *bodily* resurrection, a *spiritual* one, or what? Evangelical believers have contended through the years that the resurrection of Jesus was essentially a bodily resurrection. In other words, that which was laid to rest on the cold stone slab as dead and buried, came out as alive in resurrection form. The tomb was empty. Of course, this flies in the face of much modern theological thought and all purely rational, existential presuppositions. For example, G. W. H. Lampe, though not as radical as the Bultmannian school, declared, "A Resurrection of his physical body, such as is implied by the empty tomb and by some of the stories of the Gospels of his appearances, would point towards a docetic Christ who does not fully share the lot of men."[99] Lampe argued for his position by stating, "Such a Resurrection . . . would offer in itself no promise of risen life beyond death for those who

have to face both death and corruption."[100] Many contemporary thinkers see the resurrection more as a resurrection of the *spirit* of Jesus, rather
than a bodily raising from the dead. They are akin to the Greeks in their
view of the immortality of the soul. They tell us Jesus is certainly alive
in some sense, but the body of the Lord is unknown. These scholars
argue from both philosophical and theological vantage points. Philosophically, they share kinship to the Kantian view of the distinction
between "fact" and "meaning," the phenomenal and noumenal worlds.
With that philosophical base laid, these positivists tell us that the
"meaning" or "significance" of the resurrection (noumenal) idea is what
really matters. Whether or not Jesus was actually, bodily resurrected as a
phenomenal fact is not important. The theological impact and meaning
of the living Christ is what matters, not the nature of the resurrection.
However, the weakness of rationalistic philosophical positivism has already been seen. To place all the meaning of the resurrection in some
sort of "spiritual" event is almost tantamount to once again separating
the "historic Jesus" from the so-called eternal Christ. This the Scriptures
never allow.

Evangelicals hold Jesus was *bodily* resurrected, and therein is its *real*
meaning. Can that contention be sustained, and is it truly important?

Let it be made clear initially that Evangelicals speak of a bodily *resurrection*, not a resuscitation. Jesus was *not* brought back to life as He had
known it, limited by time and space as He had experienced it in the
incarnation. Our Lord had infinitely qualitatively more happen to Him
when He came out of the tomb than did Lazarus when He was resusci-
tated. The Lord did not come back to mere earthly life where He could
die again. He was bodily *resurrected.* As Ladd expressed it, "The resurrection itself did not mean the revivification of a dead corpse; it meant the
radical transformation of the body of Jesus from the world of nature to
the world of God."[101] This is surely what is implied by Paul's language
about a "spiritual body" (1 Cor. 15:44). "Spiritual" in some real sense;
still, a *body.* But is this what the narrative really says? Nowhere does the
New Testament distinctly call Jesus' resurrection a *bodily* resurrection.

In answer to the above questions, look first at the entire mind-set of
Jewish religious life. If ever there were a gutty, corporal group of religionists, it was the Jews. They thought and theologized in those earthly
terms. The Prophets were far from the Greek mentality with their "spiritual" approach to God. The Greeks saw the material world as evil;
hence all things related to God must be conceived in spiritual ways. Not
Israel! God had created this material universe; it was His handiwork,
and it was "very good" (Gen. 1:31). This view of God and creation
emerged out of the conviction that God created all there is ex nihilo.
What God does is always good, the act and the product. Thus they rev-
erenced the human body. It was from God. One can thus historically

trace the development of the Jewish idea of a *bodily* resurrection. Many able scholars have done so.[102]

Granted, the Sadducees denied the resurrection principle. The grave ended it all for them, but what they denied was a bodily resurrection; they well knew what Judaism taught. Of course, the Sadducees denied many things—they were the "positivists" of their day; but the Pharisees held firmly to a bodily resurrection, as did the vast majority in Judaism.

Consider who Paul was as you look at his resurrection theology in 1 Corinthians 15: a Pharisee of the Pharisees, a Jew from the tribe of Benjamin, schooled under Gamaliel (Phil. 3:5). There is no indication whatsoever that in the matter of a resurrection from the dead he changed his underlying philosophy after he was converted to Christianity. Becoming a Christian did not make him a Greek, regardless of the fact he was the apostle to the Gentiles. Actually, he built his whole theology on his Jewish grounding. Were we able to ask Paul today if what he referred to in the Corinthian letter was a *bodily* resurrection, I believe he would look rather perplexed and reply, "I did not think there was any other sort of resurrection."

Furthermore, what can be said of Paul holds for the rest of the New Testament narrators, Luke notwithstanding, even though he was a Greek. The beloved physician had been with Paul and other Jewish believers long enough to know what they were talking about.

The entire anthropology of Israel is important to grasp. The Jews never "chopped up" human personhood into component parts such as spiritual and material, as did the Greeks. They saw people as unified "living beings" or "souls." If persons were raised from the dead, all they were shared in the new life. The Bible does not enter into the argument between a trichotomist (body, soul, and spirit) or a dichotomist (body and soul) view of the human person. The theologians argue over that. The Jewish view is, what Erickson called, a "radical unity," a monism.

Moreover, what do we mean by the empty tomb? Jesus was literally out of Joseph of Arimathea's grave, and if He were out of the tomb, all He was came out of that grave. That means *bodily* resurrection. What does it mean when Jesus ate fish before the disciples (Luke 24:36-43). A pure spirit would hardly do that. So either we have a bodily resurrection or no resurrection at all. That is the crux of the matter. Bultmann's often-quoted statement, "Jesus has risen in the *kerygma,*" is purely rational, Greek thought and a far cry from Jewish understandings, and hence from the New Testament. It is a serious deviation of the basic gospel of Christ.

But why this insistence on a bodily resurrection? Why is it so important? First, that is what *resurrection* means. Then, in the second place, it once and for all demonstrates that Jesus conquered all that death and hell could hurl at Him. As Eric Sauer put it:

> By a return to heaven without a resurrection of the body, Christ would not have been displayed as the complete conqueror of death (Psalm 16:10) ... Without bodily resurrection Christ would not have been revealed as *in any degree* the conqueror. ... Therefore, without bodily resurrection *no sort of* triumph of life (1 Corinthians 15:54-57), without bodily resurrection *no* plain fruit of the victory.[103]

Well said; because He lives, death has died. God has put everything that is wrong in creation fully right because of the resurrection.

This obviously strikes at the heart of the meaning of the resurrection of Jesus. Just because some theologians deposit all their account in the meaning column, thus attenuating the historicity of the event, does not mean there is no profound meaning in Christ's rising. To the contrary, there is great significance in the glorious Easter message. True, there is in-depth mystery here. McKinnon was surely correct when he told us, " 'His Father raises him.' . . . What do these words mean? . . . They indicate the ultimate mystery."[104] Still, there are some very meaningful things that can be said.

First of all, death has been vanquished in the resurrection of Jesus. "O death, where is thy sting? O grave, where is thy victory?" (1 Cor. 15:55, KJV). Thank God, death does not have the final word.

Further, by the resurrection of our Lord, the Father put His seal on His Son's person and work. It demonstrated incontestably that Jesus is the Son of God (Rom. 1:4; Acts 13:33). Moreover, He is King (Acts 13:34); He is Messiah (Acts 2:36); He is Prophet and Son of man (Rom. 1:4); He is Judge (Acts 17:31); and He is Lord (Acts 2:25).

The resurrection also means that all who have faith now share in Jesus' resurrected life. Paul stated, "We were buried therefore with him by baptism into death, so that as Christ was raised from the dead by the glory of the Father, we too might walk in newness of life. For if we have been united with him in a death like his, we shall certainly be united with him in a resurrection like his" (Rom. 6:4-5). Paul declared believers have become so intrinsically united with Jesus Christ that they are *in Him* as truly as He is in us by His Spirit. Union with the crucified, resurrected Christ makes Christians one with Him. When Jesus was raised, He was raised into full humanity, becoming the second "Adam" (Rom. 5:12-21). He is thus the head of the "new humanity." In Him believers share in that "new creation" (2 Cor. 5:17) and therefore in the victory of Christ. A. H. Strong put it well many years ago when he said:

> As Christ's union with the race involves atonement, so the believer's union with Christ involves *Justification.* The believer is entitled to take for his own all that Christ is, and all that Christ has done; and this because he has within him that new life of humanity which suffered in Christ's death and rose from the grave in Christ's resurrection—in other words, because

he is virtually one person with the Redeemer. In Christ the believer is prophet, priest and king.[105]

Every person should view with wonder the truth that eternal redemption is now possible. Again, as Strong expressed it, "His resurrection from the grave gave proof that the penalty of sin was exhausted and that humanity in him was justified."[106] From death came life; from judgment came vindication; from alienation came reconciliation; from sin came forgiveness; and from hell came heaven. All these truths are bound up in the resurrection. He was "raised for our justification" (Rom. 4:25).

Our Lord's victory means Christians will also rise. The believer's resurrection is predicated upon Jesus' resurrection. Christ is the "firstfruits of them that slept" (1 Cor. 15:20, KJV). A. H. Strong has again expressed it well:

> The nature of Christ's resurrection, as literal and physical, determines the nature of the resurrection in the case of believers (Luke 24:36; John 20:27). As in the case of Christ, the same body that was laid in the tomb was raised again, although possessed of new and surprising powers, so the Scriptures intimate, not simply that the saints shall have bodies, but that these bodies shall be in some proper sense an outgrowth or transformation of the very bodies that slept in the dust.[107]

The Christian's resurrected body will actually be fashioned like unto His glorious body. John said, "We shall be like him, for we shall see him as he is" (1 John 3:2). Of course, to behold fully the glorified Christ face-to-face demands that believers be like Him. Since the Lord passed by resurrection from the self-imposed "boundaries of finitude" into His eternal infinite personhood in the resurrection,[108] if believers are to apprehend Him for all He is as the resurrected Christ, they must of necessity be like Him in resurrection. They must in some way share His infinite nature to grasp, in any meaningful sense, His infinite personhood. That is exactly what John was talking about. Therefore, as Jesus bodily arose, so shall Christians bodily arise. That Day is set in heaven. The *parousia*—the Lord's return—shall one day come; and His people will rise, just as He did. This is why Paul talked about the "revealing of the sons of God" (Rom. 8:19). The Scriptures declare that His people will sit on His throne with Him to judge the nations (1 Cor. 6:2). What a position! Believers will be like Him when their bodies come out of the grave.

A brief clarifying word seems appropriate here. The resurrection of the body is never meant to imply that the body alone is resurrected. Resurrection means the whole person. The entire unified personhood is resurrected. But as personal identity is in some way dependent on the body, that fact underscores the necessity of a bodily resurrection.

Furthermore, the resurrection means believers are no longer spiritually dead. That reality is experienced at the present moment. True, physical death still prevails, but such is surely not the end. Moreover, it is a strength to know that Christians have already been freed from spiritual death (Eph. 2:1). Christ bore the death penalty for sin and, through the resurrection, made believers alive in the contemporary moment.

It is wise to remember, "The Bible does not know the distinction, so common among us, between a physical, a spiritual, and an eternal death; it has a synthetic view of death and regards it as separation from God."[109] Perhaps it is best simply to say apart from Christ people are dead and dying, but in Christ all are made alive and are living, and one day will see the whole redemptive plan culminated in resurrected bodies.

Furthermore, the resurrection of Jesus not only authenticated God's claims concerning the person and work of His Son, it also put credence in the actual claims Jesus made concerning Himself. He did make fantastic statements about Himself:

1. He claimed to be the Messiah (Luke 4:17-21).
2. He claimed to be the Son of God (Matt. 27:43).
3. He claimed to be equal with God (John 14:7).
4. He claimed oneness with the Father (John 14:9-11).
5. He claimed to be the "I am" (John 8:58).

How could this be? What sort of man would make such declarations? If people are to believe them at all, God must confirm them. If God did not confirm them, Jesus must be written off as either a deceiver or a fanatic. Pannenburg was right when he said, "Everything depends upon the connection between Jesus' claim and its confirmation by God."[110] Did God confirm the Man of Galilee's statements? Yes, He did it in the glorious resurrection. Everything turns on that. Millard Erickson has correctly stated:

> The resurrection of Jesus means, then, that God gave his approval to the claims of Jesus and that these claims, which would be blasphemous unless Jesus really is the Son of Man, are true. Thus, not only the historical fact of Jesus' resurrection, but also the theological truth of his deity, have been established.[111]

Furthermore, the resurrection puts revelation on the highest of planes. If God ever spoke, it was at the empty tomb. There God can be seen as never before. The full divinity of the revealed Christ shone all around that sacred spot. There God manifested Himself in a way all new and exalted. No one can ever again deny that Jesus, the Teacher from Nazareth, is the revealed Lord of Glory. As Lewis and Demarest recently expressed it, "The supreme event that demonstrated Jesus to be the all-powerful Son of God [cf. Romans 1:4] was his resurrection from death and the grave."[112]

So a new era has arisen on the wings of Easter's morning sun. The Last Days have arrived. By resurrection Jesus entered into the life of the "age to come." As Ladd put it, "It was the emergence of eternal life in the world of mortality."[113] The consummation has commenced, and Christians can become citizens of that heavenly realm (Eph. 2:19). Believers do existentially share in His resurrected life. This is existentialism in a profound biblical sense. We "must be born again" (John 3:7) to enter the Kingdom age.

Finally, the resurrection was the prelude to the ascension of Jesus Christ. Without the resurrection there could hardly have been an ascension as the New Testament depicts it. It certainly was a vital moment when the Son returned to the Father, as He had said He would (John 16:5)[114] He is there now, seated at the Father's right hand to intercede for His people. Thus the Prophet-King became the Priest as well. Bruce Milne saw the resurrection and ascension of our Lord as directly related to His priestly, intercession work. Milne stated, "In the resurrection God the Father in effect pronounced His divine 'Amen' on the priestly work of his son" (2 Cor. 1:20).[115] Moreover, the New Testament itself declares: "This Jesus God raised up, and of that we all are witnesses. Being therefore exalted at the right hand of God, and having received from the Father the promise of the Holy Spirit, he has poured out this which you see and hear" (Acts 2:32-33). "The God of our fathers raised Jesus whom you killed by hanging him on a tree. God exalted him at his right hand as Leader and Savior, to give repentance to Israel and forgiveness of sins" (5:30-31).

Conclusion

Thus, because of the resurrection, Christians can confidently conclude that nothing will ever be the same again. Neville Clark wrote: "The empty tomb stands as the massive sign that the eschatological deed of God is not outside this world of time and space or in despair of it, but has laid hold on it, penetrated deep into it, shattered it, and has begun its transformation."[116]

In that transformation believers have shared. Therefore, they are deeply and profoundly obligated to share the wonderful message with others. Jesus' resurrection absolutely demands Christian commitment to world evangelization. In reality, the entire Christ event places the evangelistic challenge before all believers. If what the Bible declares concerning the incarnate life, substitutionary death, and bodily resurrection of Jesus be true, failure to herald that message is akin to gross insensibility, if not outright callousness. The theology that surrounds the Christ event demands evangelization.[117] The Gospel is good news; our world desperately needs to hear and experience it.

Notes

1. T. F. Torrance, *Reality and Evangelical Theology* (Philadelphia: The Westminster Press, 1982), 105.

2. From personal correspondence.

3. D. M. Baillie, *God Was in Christ* (New York: Charles Scribner's Sons, 1948), 86.

4. R. C. Moberly, *Atonement and Personality* (New York: Longman's Green and Co., 1901), 93.

5. This is how Baillie in *God Was in Christ* interpreted Brunner. There are other versions of the anhypostasia concept as well, for example, views expressed by H. M. Retton, Leonard Hodgson, etc. They cannot be approached in this limited space, however, but it is correct to say they are all variations of the same basic idea.

6. Baillie, *God Was in Christ*, 89.

7. The theory had some early beginnings in Zinzendorf and the Moravians, but it took its full form in the last century and has been employed quite extensively since.

8. Vincent Taylor, *The Person of Christ in the New Testament Teaching* (London: Macmillan Publishing Co., 1958), 270.

9. Baillie made three very good points in his setting out the weakness of *kenosis* ideas as the full answer to the incarnation problem.

10. Baillie, *God Was in Christ*, 97.

11. Ibid., 65. Baillie agreed that our faith is full of the paradox. The incarnation is the peak of the issue. But believers have learned this is inevitable because they are faced with the suprarational God.

12. William Temple said, "If any man says that he understands the relation of Deity to humanity in Christ, he only makes it clear he does not understand at all what is meant by Incarnation." William Temple, *Christus Veritas* (London: Macmillan Publishing Co., 1924), 139.

13. Saint Athanasius, *The Incarnation*, ed. A. Robertson (London: D. Nutt, 1891), 14-15.

14. *Documents Illustrative of the History of the Church*, vol. II, A.D. 313-461, ed. B. J. Kidd (New York: Macmillan Publishing Co., 1938), 298-299.

15. *The Westminster Confession of Faith for Study Classes*, G. I. Williamson (Philadelphia: Presbyterian and Reformed Publishing Co., 1964), 72-73.

16. A. H. Strong, *Systematic Theology* (Philadelphia: The Judson Press, 1912), 683-684.

17. Klaas Runia, *The Present-Day Christological Debate* (London: IVP, 1984), 47. This small volume gives an excellent summary of the current debate and its leading thinkers.

18. This is how Millard J. Erickson interpreted this idea in *Christian Theology* (Grand Rapids: Baker Book House, 1984), 712-714.

19. Michael Taylor, *A Plain Man's Guide to the Incarnation* (a pamphlet), 1.

20. John Hick, "Jesus and the World Religions," *The Myth of God Incarnate*, ed. John Hick (Philadelphia: The Westminster Press, 1977), 176.

21. Russell F. Aldwinckle, *More Than Man: A Study in Christology* (Grand Rapids: William B. Eerdmans Publishing Co., 1976), 134.

22. A. H. Strong, *Systematic Theology*, 670-671.

23. Millard J. Erickson, *Christian Theology*, 753. Erickson has a very good discussion of all these views in his work *Christian Theology*, 726-734. The reader is referred to this excellent critique of the views.

24. Karl Barth, *Church Dogmatics* (Edinburgh and T. Clark, 1936), vol. 1, part 1, 188. Quoted by Millard J. Erickson in *Christian Theology*, 716.

25. An excellent critique of Bultmann's basic approach is found in *The Scottish Journal of Theology*, vol. 18 (1965). In an article entitled "The Role of Jesus in Bultmann's Theology" George E. Ladd examined the entire issue.

26. The historical question will be approached shortly.

27. This is using the word *emotional* in a more pervasive and profound manner than is done in casual conversation. More of Bultmann's views will be discussed later.

28. The author follows Erickson on the following positive points regarding the incarnation. Erickson's treatment seems most helpful and satisfying.

29. As is well known, the Roman Catholic Church contends Mary had an "immaculate conception." This restored her prefall nature, many believe, enabling her to conceive a sinless Son of God.

30. Some say Jesus did have a fallen nature but never yielded to it and overcame all temptation and was thus sinless, for example, Karl Barth.

31. "Our Lord's Virgin Birth," *Christianity Today*, 7 December 1959, 20.

32. Erickson, *Christian Theology*, 738.

33. Although several references to Bultmann have been made, and will be made, it should be realized the succeeding generation of Bultmannian thinkers have departed in some significant ways from their mentor. Yet, Bultmann and his basic approach is influential still. So he must be taken into account, hence the references.

34. Ernst Käsemann, *Essays in the New Testament Theme* "Studies in Biblical Theology," No. 41, trans. by W. J. Montague (London: SCM, 1964), 24. This brief quotation does not, of course, exhaust Käsemann.

35. Martin Kähler, *The So-Called Historical Jesus and the Historic Biblical Christ*, ed. and trans. Karl E. Braaten (Philadelphia: Fortress Press, 1964), 19.

36. I. Howard Marshall, *I Believe in the Historical Jesus* (Grand Rapids: William B. Eerdmans Publishing Co., 1977), 34.

37. Jürgen Moltmann, *The Church in the Power of the Spirit* (New York: Harper and Row Publishers, 1977), 31. Of course, Moltmann had much more to say than these few words.

38. Marshall, *I Believe in the Historical Jesus*, 66.

39. Ibid. Glover did not reject the Christ of faith, however.

40. This presentation of the general view is somewhat oversimplified, and there are varying degrees of the skepticism among such scholars. It is presented in this fashion to set out the basic philosophy clearly.

41. Rudolf Bultmann, "Das Verhältnis der urchristlichen Christusbotschaft

zum historischen Jesus," *Sitzungsberichte der Heidelberger Akademie der Wissenschaften*, Heideberg, 1960.

42. Hugh Anderson, *Jesus and Christian Origins* (New York: Oxford University Press, 1964), 37-38.

43. Baillie, *God Was in Christ*, 46-47.

44. Ibid., 47. Baillie's criticism is directed pointedly at Emil Brunner, but the principle is surely applicable to Bultmann and others.

45. Ibid., 50.

46. Roland DeVaux, "Method in the Study of Early Hebrew History," *The Bible in Modern Scholarship*, ed. J. Hyatt (Nashville: Abingdon, 1965), 16.

47. That is, an event in real history but not necessarily having an empirical-rational cause.

48. That is, God acting "up there" in *heilsgeschichte*, while the world "down here" moves along on its naturalistic cause-effect *historie* plane.

49. Wolfhart Pannenburg, "God's Presence in History," *Theologians in Transition* (New York: The Crossroad Publishing Co., 1981), 95.

50. Quoted by Baillie in *God Was in Christ*, 72. This is also seen, according to Baillie, by Barth, Gogarten, Otto Piper, C. H. Dodd, and Reinhold Niebuhr.

51. *Sören Kierkegaard's Journals and Papers*, II, 234, no. 1642, eds. and trans. Howard V. and Edna H. Hong (Bloomington, Ind.: Indiana University Press, 1970). If God can become flesh, "walking on the water" is hardly a problem.

52. Ladd, *I Believe in the Resurrection*, 12.

53. Let it be said again, all this argumentation is not to make a case for antirationalism. It is set forth to emphasize rationalism simply cannot exhaust the truth of God, but it can be used as far as it can go. Actually, rationalism should be used where it is true.

54. This failure is often not realized because of a rather sentimental view of God's love.

55. John Driver, *Understanding the Atonement for the Omission of the Church* (Scottdale, Penn.: Herald Press, 1986), 18-19.

56. Robert Jackson, "Biblical Interpretation and Theology: Bringing the Bible to Life," in *The Proceedings of the Conference on Biblical Interpretation*, 177.

57. It should be stressed that in the actual, practical proclamation of the cross (the gospel), one need not necessarily *start* in an apologetic framework on the atonement or even on biblical authority (see chs. 2 and 3 of this book). Even the issue of inordinate stress on theology may be pragmatically out of place. The wise proclaimer begins where people are and communicates those truths of Christ that are relevant and helpful to the hearers in their real life situations. Then one moves to the entire gospel presentation.

58. Both terms *substitute* and *satisfaction* are central to the theory.

59. John R. W. Stott may be correct when he said, "What Vincent Taylor shrank from was not the doctrine itself, but the crudities of thought and expression of which the advocates of substitution have not infrequently been guilty." John Stott, *The Cross of Christ* (Downers Grove, Ill.: InterVarsity Press, 1986), 10-11.

60. Quoted by John R. W. Stott in *The Cross of Christ*, 43.

61. Ibid., 44.

62. This is not to be understood as an anti-Semitic statement. It is simply a

fact of history. The Roman Catholic pronouncement absolving the Jews of the death of Christ does not eradicate the fact that Jesus died at Jewish instigation. That does not mean contemporary, individual Jewish people are guilty of Jesus' death.

63. Stating that "substitution" is the heart of the atonement does not mean Christ bore our sins in a *purely* legalistic manner *alone*, although the forensic motif predominates. As has been said, there has always been a cross in the heart of God. Christ was the Lamb slain "before the foundation of the world" (Rev. 13:8). Yet, to effect our redemption it was absolutely essential and necessary that Jesus Christ die and shed His blood in our place in our time frame. After all, He prayed in the garden, "My Father, if it be possible, let this cup pass from me; nevertheless, not as I will, but as thou wilt" (Matt. 26:39). Surely, if there had been any way other than the cross, Jesus' prayer would have been granted, but on Calvary, believers see the eternal purpose and heart of God worked out in history—and the interaction of the one upon the other.

64. Frank Stagg, *New Testament Theology* (Nashville: Broadman Press, 1962), 144-145.

65. William J. Wolf, *No Cross, No Crown* (New York: Doubleday and Co., Inc., 1957), 87.

66. Ibid., 122-123 (author's italics). This approach, quite clearly, is a modern version of the old "moral influence" theory of the atonement. Good as far as it goes, failure to see Christ as enduring judgment on the cross is to that extent a serious error. Paul Tillich saw a supposed weakness in the substitutionary idea in that it could attenuate moral and ethical motivations. This hardly holds, however, because the indwelling Holy Spirit constantly motivates believers to live ethical lives. Moreover, when one receives the atonement, that one is *transformed* and identified with Christ in life and death (Rom. 6:1-12).

67. Moltmann, *The Church in the Power of the Spirit*, 30.

68. Erickson, *Christian Theology*, 813, author's italics.

69. Stott, *The Cross of Christ.* This work on the atonement is an excellent presentation of the concept of substitution.

70. Emil Brunner, *The Mediator*, trans. Olive Wyon (Philadelphia: Westminster Press, 1947), 40.

71. Erickson, *Christian Theology*, 822-823. These are the concepts Erickson brought forth, not his exact words. See this work for a development of these essential ideas.

72. Stott, *The Cross of Christ*, 89, (author's italics).

73. Leon Morris, *The Cross in the New Testament* (1965; reprint, Grand Rapids: William B. Eerdmans Publishing Co., 1977), 191.

74. Stott, *The Cross of Christ*, 109.

75. Listed by Stott in *The Cross of Christ*, 141-142. See this work for a discussion of these theologians.

76. Ibid., 143.

77. Joachim Jeremias, *Eucharistic Words*, trans. N. Perrin (New York: Charles Scribner's Sons, 1966), 228.

78. Perhaps it goes too far to say, as some have, Christ "went to hell" for us; hence, the "cry of dereliction." Still, something of that must be true if we take substitution seriously.

79. Stott, *The Cross of Christ*, 159. We must be careful in making too crude statements concerning this truth, for example, "God in anger punished Jesus." We do well to express it exactly as the Bible expresses it. Such crudities may be what Taylor rebelled against.

80. Moltmann, *The Church in the Power of the Spirit*, 249-250.

81. Michael Green, "Foreword" in George Eldon Ladd, *I Believe in the Resurrection of Jesus* (Grand Rapids: William B. Eerdmans Publishing Co., 1975), 7.

82. Ladd discussed several of the concepts in *I Believe in the Resurrection of Jesus*.

83. Ladd, *I Believe in the Resurrection of Jesus,* 11.

84. This line of argumentation follows the lead of George E. Ladd in *I Believe in the Resurrection of Jesus.*

85. Walter Kunneth, *The Theology of the Resurrection* (London: S.C.M., 1965), 107.

86. Ladd, *I Believe in the Resurrection of Jesus*, 12.

87. Quoted by G. R. Beasley-Murray, *Christ Is Alive* (London: Lutterworth Press, 1947), 18.

88. Ibid., 20. Although Westcott argued this point some years ago, it still remains a fact to be reasoned with. Everything that is old is not thereby necessarily invalid today.

89. Ibid., 39.

90 C. H. Dodd, *The Founder of Christianity* (London: Collins, 1971), 171.

91. It must be recognized that there are problems with the various resurrection narratives, for example, their harmonization. Space precludes taking up the issues here. Suffice it to say, many evangelical New Testament scholars have faced the problems and worked out a way to formulate a harmonization. See Beasley-Murray's arguments for the historical veracity of the Gospel narrative in *Christ is Alive*, 53 *ff.*

92. B. Reicke, "Synoptic Prophecies on the Destruction of Jerusalem" *Studies in New Testament and Early Christian Literature* (New Testament Supplement 33) (London, 1972), 121-341.

93 C. F. D. Moule, *The Birth of the New Testament* (London, 1962), 123.

94. John A. T. Robinson, *Redating the New Testament* (Philadelphia: The Westminster Press, 1976), 13.

95. G. R. Beasley-Murray, *Christ Is Alive*, 50 (author's italics).

96. Ibid., 65.

97. D. M. McKinnon, (G. W. H. Lampe), *The Resurrection, A Dialogue*, (Philadelphia: The Westminster Press, 1966), 63.

98. Some scholars feel the resurrection of Jesus is not a difficult mental problem at all. For example, Machen stated: "What we are trying to establish . . . is not the resurrection of any ordinary man, not the resurrection of a man who to us is a mere *x* or *y*, not the resurrection of a man about whom we know nothing, but the resurrection of *Jesus*. There is a tremendous presumption against the resurrection of any ordinary man; but when you come really to know Jesus as He is pictured to us in the Gospels you will say that whereas it is unlikely that any ordinary man should rise from the dead, in His case the presumption is exactly reversed. It is unlikely that any ordinary man should rise; but it is unlikely that *this* Man should not rise: it may be said of this Man that it was impossible that He 'should be holden' to death. This was the heart of the appeal made by Peter

on the first occasion of the preaching of the resurrection. Addressing men who themselves probably had known Jesus, certainly who knew a good deal about Him, he said: 'Ye men of Israel, hear these words: Jesus of Nazareth, *a Man approved of God unto you by mighty works and wonders and signs* which God did by Him in the midst of you, even as ye yourselves know; Him, being delivered up by the determinate counsel and foreknowledge of God, ye by the hand of lawless men did crucify and slay: whom God raised up, having loosed the pangs of death: because *it was not possible that He should be holden of it* (Acts 2:22-24).' " George Beasley-Murray, *Christ Is Alive*, 108-109 (Beasley-Murray's italics).

99. G. W. H. Lampe, (D. M. McKinnon), *The Resurrection, A Dialogue* (Philadelphia: The Westminster Press, 1966), 97. It is only fair to say about Lampe that he did believe in an "objective" resurrection. He did not argue the resurrection narratives were just the disciples' way of eulogizing Jesus. Yet, somewhat like Bultmann, he seemingly could not fully accept the bodily resurrection. See 30-32.

100. Ibid., 97-98.

101. Ladd, *I Believe in the Resurrection of Jesus*, 125.

102. Ibid., see chapter 4.

103. Erich Sauer, *The Triumph of the Crucified* (Grand Rapids: William B. Eerdmans Publishing Co., 1951), 40.

104. D. M. McKinnon, *The Resurrection*, 65.

105. A. H. Strong, *Systematic Theology*, 805. Union with Christ will be discussed in detail shortly.

106. Ibid., 657.

107. Ibid., 1018.

108. This terminology needs some clarification. See the previous section on the incarnation so as to grasp the meaning of this kind of language.

109. Louis Berkhof, *Systematic Theology* (Grand Rapids: William B. Eerdmans Publishing Co., 1946), 258-259.

110. Pannenburg, *Jesus—God and Man* (Philadelphia: The Westminster Press, 1968), 66.

111. Erickson, *Christian Theology*, 671.

112. Bruce Demarest and Gordon Lewis, *Integrative Theology*, vol. 1 (Grand Rapids: Zondervan Publishing House, 1987), 105.

113. George E. Ladd, *I Believe in the Resurrection of Jesus*, 128.

114. This is probably the "lifting up" idea which Jesus expressed (John 12:32). Therefore, much more should be made of the reality.

115. Bruce Milne, *Know the Truth*, 160.

116. Neville Clark, as quoted by C. F. D. Moule and recorded in George E. Ladd's work: *I Believe in the Resurrection of Jesus*, 101.

117. A good work on the theology of evangelism is found in William J. Abraham's work: *The Logic of Evangelism* (Grand Rapids: William B. Eerdmans Publishing Co., 1989).

6

God as Holy Spirit:
The Implementer of Evangelism

"Not by might, nor by power, but by my Spirit" (Zech. 4:6).

Introduction

When the day of Pentecost had come, they were all together in one place. And suddenly a sound came from heaven like the rush of a mighty wind, and it filled all the house where they were sitting. And there appeared to them tongues as of fire, distributed and resting on each one of them. And they were all filled with the Holy Spirit and began to speak in other tongues, as the Spirit gave them utterance.

. . . So those who received his word were baptized, and there were added that day about three thousand souls. . . . And the Lord added to their number day by day those who were being saved (Acts 2:1-4,41,47).

Pentecost is evangelism in action. God revealed Himself as Holy Spirit and multitudes came to faith in Jesus Christ. That Day inaugurated the Age of the Spirit, and the implications are obvious: powerful evangelization is now possible. Therefore, to understand who the Holy Spirit is and how He implements and energizes the evangelistic enterprise is of vital importance. It marks the difference between success and failure in the grand endeavor, both theologically and pragmatically.

The doctrine of the divine Holy Spirit takes on an immediate relevance perhaps not felt by the church for some time. As a single case in point, the phenomenal growth of Pentecostalism in both its denominational expression (Assemblies of God, Church of God of Prophecy, Pentecostal Church of God, etc.), and its "charismatic" mode—which has touched every old mainline denomination including Roman Catholicism—certainly gives credence to the claim we are living in the "age of the Spirit." After the "quest for the historic Jesus" was laid to rest in the early decades of the twentieth century,[1] it seems the focus—at least experientially—has shifted to the Person and work of the Holy Spirit. The so-called Azuza Street Revival[2] of 1906 gave birth to modern Pentecostalism and ushered in a new era of interest in pneumatology. No segment of the Christian church can really ignore these realities any longer.

This phenomenon is something of a fluke of history, for the evangelical church has had considerable to say about the person and work of the third Person of the Trinity. Even John Owen, the seventeenth-century Puritan theologian preoccupied with the sovereignty of the Father, had a large section in his theological works on the "gifts of the Spirit"; and rightly so, for all our experience of God as Father and Son is revealed, inspired, mediated, and carried on through the Spirit of God. Therefore, when we talk about the Godhead in evangelism, we must give proper space—particularly pragmatic space—to the work of the blessed Spirit. Without the Spirit's activity, there is no evangelism. The enigma of the hour, however, centers in the fact that while multitudes of professing Christians have all but overemphasized the Holy Spirit and His work, many others have maintained very vague ideas, even at times calling the Holy Spirit an "it."[3]

We must keep in mind, therefore, that the Spirit of God embodies all the attributes of the Father and the Son. He is variously called the Spirit of God (Matt. 3:16), the Spirit of His Son (Gal. 4:6), and the Holy Spirit (Rom. 5:5). The unity of the Trinity is preserved in the Bible. Still, the Spirit is seen as a distinct Person in the Godhead with a distinct and dynamic office-work to do.

It is further interesting to see the Spirit's involvement in the life and ministry of our Lord Himself. The Scriptures tell us:

1. The Holy Spirit was responsible for Mary's conception of Jesus (Matt. 1:18-21).
2. At Jesus' baptism the Holy Spirit came upon the Lord (Mark 1:9-11).
3. The temptation scene in the wilderness was orchestrated by the Spirit (Luke 4:1-2).
4. Jesus returned from the temptation battle in the power of the Spirit (Luke 4:14).
5. Jesus' mission was undertaken in the power of the Spirit (Luke 4:18-19).
6. Jesus' whole life was filled with the Spirit (John 3:34).
7. Jesus gave up His life on the cross by the Spirit's power (Heb. 9:14).
8. He was resurrected in the power of the Holy Spirit (Rom. 8:11).

In a word, *all* Jesus did in the days of His flesh was Spirit permeated.

The person and office function of the Spirit must be left to other works. The divine Spirit's work, primarily through an evangelistic prism, is the subject of this chapter. Three primary topics are considered in this evangelistic pneumatology: (a) the Spirit's work in respect to unbelievers, (b) the Spirit's work regarding converts, and (c) the Spirit's work enabling the church to evangelize effectively. This outline will be followed.

The Holy Spirit's Work Towards Unbelievers

The key passage to consider on this topic is found in John 16:7-11. Jesus said:

> Nevertheless I tell you the truth: it is to your advantage that I go away, for if I do not go away, the Counselor will not come to you; but if I go, I will send him to you. And when he comes, he will convince the world concerning sin and righteousness and judgment: concerning sin, because they do not believe in me; concerning righteousness, because I go to the Father, and you will see me no more; concerning judgment, because the ruler of this world is judged.

The passage is quite difficult to interpret, as Raymond E. Brown pointed out: "Several interpretations are possible. Augustine even avoided it because of its difficulties."[4] Yet, this important passage not only presents one of the great "Paraclete" dissertations of John but also has the obvious profound touch of the Spirit Himself on it. One can hardly disagree with Rudolf Schnackenburg's statement:

> The evangelist [John] . . . saw himself chiefly as one who interpreted Jesus' words and actions as well as his appearances and his person, and he did not make this interpretation on the basis of his own ability and power, but because he was guided and enlightened by the Spirit.[5]

Not everyone would agree with all Schnackenburg holds or with all his presuppositions; yet, the above quotation is essentially on target and worthy of note. One further word from Schnackenburg should also be kept in mind in approaching this significant Johannine passage: "The Spirit, whose presence causes the Johannine community to rejoice is, however, inseparably bound to Jesus Christ. . . . He thus becomes Jesus' representative and in this way continues his revelation of salvation . . . and makes it effective and fruitful."[6] The Spirit of God is seen as the Presence of the resurrected Christ.

This Johannine paraclete passage reveals the threefold work of the Holy Spirit towards the unbelieving world. In fact, according to Leon Morris, it is "the one place in Scripture where the Spirit is spoken of as performing a work in 'the world' "[7]

In the light of this basic principle, it becomes clear from the passage that the Holy Spirit speaks to people about their actual condition before God with a threefold thrust.

The Holy Spirit Convinces of Sin

C. H. Spurgeon correctly said, "The Spirit alone has power over man's heart."[8] Only the power of God can convince the human mind and heart of its sin and thereby reveal to persons their true self. Melancthon, the great Lutheran theologian and companion of Martin Luther, once thought that by persuasion he could convince persons of their sin and need of Christ. He learned differently when he entered the arena of the battle for souls. He said, "Old Adam is too strong for young Melancthon." The Holy Spirit, the *parakletos*, the advocate who comes along by our side to aide us, alone is the great "Convincer."

The word *convince* (*elegcho*) used by the Fourth Gospel writer is a quite interesting term. Etymologically, it had broad connotations in the secular world. In the historical development of the word, it first meant "to scorn" or "to bring into contempt." Later it merged into the idea of "to shame," "to blame," or "to expose." Finally, it came to mean "to investigate," thus developing a forensic motif. In the Bible, however, it has more pointed meanings. In the Old Testament, the LXX, it connoted the idea of God disciplining and educating a person as a result of Yahweh's judicial activity, including chastisement and punishment. The forensic idea predominated.

In the New Testament, though based on these Old Testament concepts, *convince* is more restricted and is attributed almost exclusively to the Holy Spirit. Buchsel has told us:

> The use of *elegcho* in the NT is restricted. . . . it is almost always used with the acc[usative] of person, . . . It means "to show someone his sin and to summon him to repentance." . . . The word does not mean only "to blame" or "to reprove," nor "to convince" in the sense of proof, nor "to reveal" or "expose," but "to set right," namely, "to point away from sin to repentance." It implies educative discipline.[9]

Because of the pungency of the word *elegcho*, the writer chose the term *Comforter* (*parakletos*) to describe the convincing Holy Spirit of God, but with a twist. As Leon Morris argued, the word *parakletos* "normally . . . denotes a person whose activities are in favor of the defendant. Here, however, the meaning is that the Spirit will act as prosecutor and bring about the world's conviction."[10] C. H. Dodd put it this way: "The tables are turned. The Advocate becomes a prosecuting council and 'convicts' the world."[11] Obviously, much is packed into the provocative words John used to introduce this key passage.

Now of what does the Holy Spirit convict people? Of what do they stand guilty? Obviously, their sins! The Holy Spirit, who alone can do so, indicts the whole world, exposes people's sins, and leads them in the direction of "repentance to God and of faith in our Lord Jesus Christ" (Acts 20:21). Spurgeon had it right in a personal testimony when he said:

I knew what sin meant by my reading, and yet I never knew sin in its heinousness and horror, till I found myself bitten by it as by a fiery serpent, and felt its poison boiling in my veins. When the Holy Ghost made sin to appear sin, then was I overwhelmed with the sight, and I would fain have fled from myself to escape the intolerable vision. A naked sin stripped of all excuse, and set in the light of truth, is a worse sight than to see the devil himself. When I saw sin as an offense against a just and holy God, committed by such a proud and yet insignificant creature as myself, then was I alarmed.[12]

This is exactly what the Bible declares about the nature of sin. In the Old Testament several descriptive, disturbing words are used by the writers to depict the horror of human sin against God. There are four main Hebrew roots used to depict this rebellion. *Chata* is the most common term and its essential meaning is "to miss the mark" or "deviate from a goal" (Gen. 20:9). The implication is that all people miss God's moral and spiritual plan and goal for their lives. In its substantive form, *chatta'eh*, the emphasis is not so much on motivation but on the formal aspect of deviation from the moral norm.

Pasha' refers to breaking of a relationship; hence, a "rebellion" or revolution (Isa. 1:28). This term is perhaps the most profound picture of sin as it demonstrates that human sin is rebellion against God Himself, defiance of His holy lordship and rule in one's life.

'Awah connotes a deliberate perversion or "twisting." It implies deliberate wrongdoing or committing iniquity (2 Sam. 24:17). In noun form it stresses the idea of guilt which arises from that deliberate twisting of one's life away from the will of God.

The final key root in the Old Testament is the word *shagah*. This denotes a person straying away from the proper path. It can be translated "erring" or "creaturely going astray" (see 1 Sam. 26:21; Job 6:24). It appears at times, in the cultic context, as sin against the rituals of God.

Two other Old Testament terms are worthy of mention. *Rasha'* means to act "wickedly" (2 Sam. 22:22). *'Amal* connotes "disaster or trouble caused for others" (Prov. 24:2; Hab. 1:13).

The New Testament is hardly bereft of picturesque words to describe the human plight. The principle term in the New Testament is *hamartia*. It is equivalent to the Hebrew *chata'* and means "missing the mark" or to "fall short" (Rom. 3:23). It implies concrete wrongdoing, a violation of God's law (John 8:46; Jas. 1:15; 1 John 1:8).

Paraptoma stresses the moral error of a misdeed or trespass. In Ephesians 2:1 we are told we are "dead" through *paraptoma*, our misdeeds.

A similar term to that above is *parabasis*. This means "to go beyond the norm" or "to transgress" (Rom. 4:15).

Asebeia is perhaps the most profound New Testament word as *pasha'* was in the Old Testament. In the LXX, *asebeia* is usually the Greek word used for the Hebrew *pasha'*. It implies ungodliness or impiety as, for example, in Romans 1:18 and 2 Timothy 2:16.

Another term, *anomia*, means lovelessness or contempt for the law (Matt. 7:23).

Spiritual and moral depravity are depicted in two terms *kakia* and *poneria* (see Acts 8:22; Rom. 1:29; Luke 11:39). At times *ho poneros* is translated "the evil one" and refers to Satan (Matt. 13:19).

Adikia is a classical Greek term defined as "doing wrong to one's neighbor." In the koine Greek of the New Testament it is usually translated "injustice" (Rom. 9:14), "unrighteousness" (Luke 16:9), "falsehood" (John 7:18) "wickedness" (Rom. 2:8), or "iniquity" (2 Tim. 2:19).

A few other terms are used such as *enochos* meaning "guilty" (Mark 3:29) and *opheilema* (Matt. 6:12) meaning "debt."

Still, the issue is: "The definition of sin . . . is not to be derived simply from the terms used in Scripture to denote it. The most characteristic feature of sin in all its aspects is that it is directed against God. . . . It is a violation of that which God's glory demands and is, therefore, in its essence the contradiction of God."[13]

This rather dismal picture the Bible paints of the human heart has a vivid point to make. It demands that people face the reality of their true position before God and look to Him for mercy. In other words, to grasp fully the good news of the gospel, one must come to understand deeply the bad news of personal sin.

What lies behind all this iniquity, rebellion, wickedness, and debt? The answer is, according to our Lord, unbelief. The root of all specific sins is the sin of unbelief. As Raymond Brown expressed it, "All other sins find expression in or are related to this basic sin of disbelief."[14] Disbelief is a willful, evil act on our part. John said, "And this is the judgment, that the light has come into the world, and men loved darkness rather than light, because their deeds were evil" (John 3:19). The condemnation of the basic sin of unbelief is the thrust of Jesus' words when He said the divine Spirit would convince the lost world of its heinous crime of refusing to believe on Jesus.[15] Unbelief is not mere ignorance of Christ, it is the willful rejection of the Lord and His salvation. Sin is rebellion against God for all He is. Barth put his finger on it when he said, "As an event, sin is that interchanging of God and man, that exalting of men to divinity or depressing of God to humanity, by which we seek to justify and fortify and establish ourselves."[16]

How can a person become convinced that lack of faith is such a serious evil? It goes against the grain in our pluralistic society where many feel one "faith" is as good as another so long as one is sincere. Ethelbert Stauffer commented, "It was *necessary* that the Holy Spirit himself should open our eyes."[17] This forensic work of the Spirit is absolutely essential to see unbelief for all it really is in God's sight. God sees the refusal to submit to Christ in faith as a permanent choice of evil which merits His eternal wrath. On their own, human beings simply refuse to face up to that reality. It is right there, however, that the Holy Spirit steps in and convinces people of their sin of unbelief. Brown has told us:

> The Paraclete will focus on the expression of disbelief that culminated in putting Jesus to death, but those who are guilty are a much wider group than the participants in the historical trial of Jesus. Those participants are only the forebears of men in every generation who will be hostile to Jesus.[18]

The whole idea in John's passage is of a world on trial before God. Through the witness of the disciples to the Christ event (*kerygma*), the world will have unveiled before its own eyes the true nature of sin and righteousness and judgment. Only the probing finger of God can tap the deep recesses of the human heart and bring a person to that realization.

The Holy Spirit Convinces of Righteousness

The Spirit of God does more than convict of sin; He convicts of righteousness. This term (Hebrew: *tsedeq*, Greek: *dikaiosune*) is most interesting. The Hebrew *tsedeq* is probably derived from the old Arab root meaning "straightness." It implies action that conforms to a norm. The New Testament uses *righteousness* in the sense of conforming to the demands and will of God. At times, righteousness is attributed to people, at times to God, "the righteousness of God" (Rom. 1:17).

This understanding of the righteousness of God was in the mind of Jesus when He stated the Spirit would "convict the world of . . . righteousness" (John 16:8, NIV). What convinces the world of God's righteousness? The Son's work on the cross and His ascension! Of course, the Jewish religious leaders thought Jesus unrighteous because of His claim of equality with the Father. The entire purpose of the authorities was to prove Him guilty of blasphemy and not truly God's Son. Yet, Jesus proved Himself as righteous in a most profound way: the cross and ascension. As Raymond Brown put it:

> The Paraclete will demonstrate to the disciples that this same death sentence really showed that Jesus was what he claimed, for after his death he is with the Father; and by glorifying Jesus . . . , the Father has certified him. "The return to the Father is God's imprimatur upon the righteousness [justice] manifested in the life and death of his son."[19]

Beasley-Murray saw the relation of the cross and the ascension when he told us it is all "bound up with the mode of Jesus' departure: the lifting up of Jesus on the cross . . . it was at once God's reversal of the

verdict of men."[20] Morris has summarized it well: "The righteousness
which is shown by Christ's going to the Father is surely that righteousness which is established by the cross."[21] Christ's life, death, resurrection, and ascension established and demonstrated the righteousness of
our Lord.

God's righteousness is not only a static norm as seen in Christ, however; it reaches out, and because of the cross, others can now stand before God as righteous. God declares people righteous as they trust Jesus
Christ. The righteousness of God is dynamic, making and declaring
righteous those who have faith. The Spirit strives to make people see
this essential, redemptive principle.

The point is: the Holy Spirit must convince the world their righteousness before God does not depend on their own human efforts. Even the
Old Testament told us "all our righteousnesses [deeds] are as filthy
rags" (Isa. 64:6, KJV). Righteousness, or a "right standing" before God,
depends on the atoning work of Christ on Calvary. Our Lord's words,
"Ye see me no more" (John 16:10, KJV), "might refer to the cross, . . . or
through the cross to the ascension."[22] It all has to do with God reaching
out through the life, death, resurrection, and ascension of Jesus Christ to
atone for sins and thereby enable God to establish people as righteous
before His justice and holiness. It is basically a forensic idea: believers
are *declared righteous* because of Christ's atoning work. Thus His righteousness is set to the Christian's account. This right standing with God
is imputed through faith; blessed is the person to whom the Lord im-
putes righteousness (Rom. 4:6). Such is the dynamic, "reaching-out
righteousness" of God redeeming repentant, believing sinners (Rom.
4:1-8). Of course, in Christ, believers are not only declared righteous,
but in regeneration they are also *made* righteous. As Hoskyns emphasized, "The witness of the Spirit . . . is focused upon Jesus, and the nature of Sin, of Righteousness, and of Judgement (sic) is exposed in relation to Him, and thereby shown to be present, concrete realities."[23]
"Therefore, if any one is in Christ, he is a new creation; the old has
passed away, behold, the new has come" (2 Cor. 5:17).

These salvation truths, however, do go against the grain of humanistic pride. Many feel they can do enough good things to be acceptable in
God's sight! That line is the grand satanic deception. It is the blindness
of the mere moralist. It is the core of all other world religions, and the
mind-set of the masses. Will people ever learn He "saved us, not because of deeds done by us in righteousness, but in virtue of his own
mercy, by the washing of regeneration and renewal in the Holy Spirit"
(Titus 3:5)?

William Temple put his finger on the issue when he said, "The
world's notion of righteousness is wrong in the same way as its notion
of sin."[24] Only the Holy Spirit can cause those scales to fall off one's

eyes, as He did for self-righteous Saul of Tarsus. The power of God alone can make people see the efficacy of the work of Christ, their positions before God, and the utter need of Christ's righteousness, but that is exactly what the Spirit came into the world to do. He came to reveal the Jesus of the cross.

> This righteousness is proclaimed by Jesus as a gift to those who are granted the Kingdom of God (Matt. 5:6). By faith in Jesus Christ and his work of atonement man, unrighteous sinner though he is, receives God's righteousness, i.e. he is given a true relationship with God which involves forgiveness of all sin and a new moral standing with God in union with Christ "the Righteous One" (Rom. 3:21-31; 4:1-25; 10:3; 1 Cor. 1:30; 2 Cor. 5:21; Phil. 3:9).[25]

The Holy Spirit Convinces of Judgment

This final work of the Holy Spirit in relationship to the world also has direct reference to the cross. Jesus said, "The prince of this world is judged" (John 16:11, KJV). The "prince" is, of course, Satan; the judgment is clearly the cross. Leon Morris stated, "The work of judgment is referred to the defeat of Satan on the cross."[26]

Now the defeat of the devil was not one of sheer power but of a *just* judgment. Justice was done on the cross (substitution or satisfaction) in the overthrow of the "evil one." In that moment, Satan was "thrown out." As Beasley-Murray expressed it: "The ejection of the latter [Satan] from his vaunted place of rule took place as the Son of Man was installed by God as Lord of creation and Mediator of the saving sovereignty of God to the world."[27] Here is the sting: this judgment on Satan "involves the judgment *of the world.*"[28] Why? Because the world has subjected itself to its "prince" and joined in the rejection of the Son of God and became the tool for His murder.[29] So like the devil himself, the world's cause is lost; it has been judged. When the world condemned Jesus to death, it condemned itself. Brown summed it up well:

> If the hour of passion and death represented the confrontation of Jesus and the Prince of this world, . . . then in being victorious over death, Jesus was victorious over the Prince of the world. The very fact that Jesus stands justified before the Father means that Satan has been condemned and has lost his power over the world.[30]

Victory has now come, but in the strange way of a cross. No one will ever believe it, let alone accept the idea that, in the cross, human beings are judged with Satan (1 Cor. 1:18). However, the power of the mighty

Holy Spirit can break through that fog and reveal the truth. A. M. Hunter said, "The Holy Spirit initiates men unto the whole meaning of the word made flesh."[31]

The Spirit's work all centers in the Christ of the cross, our "hope" (1 Tim. 1:1). Christ becomes our "passover" (1 Cor. 5:7, KJV). Christ is seen as the wisdom of God and our "life" (Col. 3:4). Christ is recognized as the "power of God" (1 Cor. 1:24). Christ is the gospel. Jesus said the "Spirit of truth" would testify of Him to a world who needs His grace desperately (John 16:12-15).

Therefore, if there is no deep profound enlightening, convincing, convicting work of the Holy Spirit to address lost humanity with all these realities, there will be no conversions at all. W. T. Conner was correct when he said:

> Pentecost [the giving of the Holy Spirit] was just as essential for the realization in the lives of men of the values of gospel as was Calvary and the resurrection. Without the death and resurrection of Jesus there would be no gospel. Without Pentecost there would be no gospel so far as our apprehension and experience are concerned.[32]

The witness of the church has power only as the gospel is communicated in the strength and wisdom of the Holy Spirit. Jesus said, "No one can come to me unless the Father who sent me draws him" (John 6:44); "Power belongs to God" (Ps. 62:11). How vital, therefore, that those who would evangelize be "filled with the Holy Spirit," as was the first-century church (Acts 2:4). Then they can speak "the word of God with boldness" (Acts 4:31). More of that later. Now we must see what the blessed Spirit of God does for the person who, after being convinced by the Spirit of sin, righteousness, and judgment, repents and believes.

The Holy Spirit's Work in Converts

Several beautiful realities of the Spirit become the believer's experience the moment they receive Christ as Savior by faith. Jesus said He would not leave His children alone; He would come to them (John 14:18). The Spirit, the Accuser, now becomes the Spirit, the Advocate. Several things can be said.

The Holy Spirit Regenerates New Believers

"He saved us. . . by the washing of regeneration and renewal in the Holy Spirit" (Titus 3:5). Jesus said, "Do not marvel that I said to you, 'You must be born anew' " (John 3:7). The Holy Spirit truly does make one a new person (2 Cor. 5:17), giving a whole new life. So dramatic is the change it can only be described as being "born again" (KJV). We who were once "dead through the trespasses and sins" in which we walked, "he [Christ] made alive" (Eph. 2:1). Through the "Crucified God," to use Moltman's terminology, believers have come to new life. Christians have been regenerated.

The compound word *regeneration* finds its root in the Greek terms *palin* and *genesis*, meaning " 'coming back from death to life' "[33] Philo used the word to describe the reconstitution of the world after the flood. Josephus called the reestablishment of God's people in the Holy Land after the exile *paliggensias*. Although the term has roots in Greek Stoicism, the Jews filled it through and through with their own religious content. Judaism saw it as entry into an existence in which righteousness dwells. It was a personal and present experience for the devoted Jew. Therefore, Nicodemus should have known, at least in principle, what Jesus was talking about in John 3:7 (although that is not the exact word Jesus used: *dei humas gennethenai anothen*). The entire concept is the entering into a whole new experience of God. Buchsel told us: "It does not mean only attainment to a new life with the end of the old life, nor does it mean only moral renewal; it embraces both."[34] But what are the implications for new Christians who are regenerated by the power of the Holy Spirit in the moment of their conversion?

Being "in Christ."—In answer to the above query a multitude of wonderful realities emerge. Perhaps it can be best summarized by using Paul's favorite expression to denote what happens to persons when they are regenerated. Paul used "in Christ" over 100 times in the body of his letters. James Stewart declared "in Christ" to be the essence of the apostle's understanding of Christian experience. When people are "born again," they are born "into Christ." When a person is regenerated, he or she is immediately, by the agency of the Holy Spirit, taken *out of Adam* and put *into Christ*. Paul expressed it like this: "For since by man came death, by man came also the resurrection of the dead. For as in Adam all die, even so in Christ shall all be made alive" (1 Cor. 15:21-22, KJV). What does that imply?

The "in Christ" motif of Paul's writing equates with his view of regeneration. This is true because the apostle often relates the "in Christ" experience to Christian baptism, which is obviously the symbol of regeneration. For example, Paul wrote:

> Know ye not, that so many of us as were baptized into Jesus Christ were baptized into his death? Therefore we are buried with him by baptism into death: that like as Christ was raised up from the dead by the glory of the Father, even so we also should walk in newness of life (Rom. 6:3-4, KJV).
> For as many of you as have been baptized into Christ have put on Christ (Gal. 3:27, KJV).
> Buried with him in baptism, wherein also ye are risen with him through

the faith of the operation of God, who hath raised him from the dead (Col. 2:12, KJV).

Some have even seen Titus 3:5 in this light.

Hans Conzelman defined the personal spiritual aspects of being in Christ in this way: "The phrase expresses the objective foundation and the inner-worldly intangibility of Christian experience."[35] In other words, *in Christ* describes the essence of our spiritual experience of God through Jesus Christ. It is the heart of "being saved." The primary thrust of the idea centers in the fact that saved believers are brought into a dynamic, spiritual, personal *union* with Christ. As surely as Christ is *in* the believer by the Holy Spirit, so the believer is *in* Christ. There is a real, genuine union between Christ and people of faith. Paul said, "For ye are dead, and your life is hid with Christ in God" (Col. 3:3, KJV).[36] By the Holy Spirit, converts are "fused" in union with Jesus Christ through the salvation of God. This mystical union—"mystical" in the profound biblical sense of the word—is so radical and real that believers are actually made "one" with Christ.[37] Therefore, everything Christ has experienced, God's redeemed share. Someone has said:

> "In Christ" denotes our situation; where he is, we are—"in the heavenly places" (Eph. 1:3).
> "In Christ" defines our status; what he is, we are—"children of God" (John 1:12).
> "In Christ" describes our substance; what he has, we share—"heirs of God" (Rom. 8:17).
> "In Christ" determines service; what he does, we do—"seek and save the lost" (Luke 19:10).

The principle covers all aspects of one's Christian experience.

> God's people are chosen in Christ: Ephesians 1:4.
> God's people are baptized into Christ: 1 Corinthians 12:13.
> God's people are crucified with Christ: Galatians 2:20.
> God's people are resurrected with Christ: Colossians 3:1.
> God's people have life in Christ: Colossians 3:3.
> God's people have standing in Christ: Colossians 2:10.
> God's people are righteous in Christ: 1 Corinthians 1:30.
> God's people are glorified in Christ: Romans 8:30.

All this is true because God was in Christ (2 Cor. 5:19), and now the redeemed are in Christ. The Scriptures make it very evident that all humanity shares in the Adamic race, and that means death in every sense of the word. "In Adam all die" (1 Cor. 15:22); but being uprooted out of the condemned Adamic family and grafted into Christ in regeneration, believers are "crucified with Christ," made alive, and thus set free. Ernest Best saw this clearly when he stated:

> Into Christ implies . . . the death of the believer with Christ and his resurrection with Christ in the new life of the corporate personality of Christ; it is a participation in his death . . . [it] brings us into our share in Christ's death; it therefore makes us a part of the inclusive personality which is Christ.[38]

Note, however, not only do those in Christ share in their Lord's death by identification, they share in His resurrection as well. Romans 6:11 implies it; Ephesians 2:1 makes it explicit. As John Murray stated, "Union with Christ must mean also union with Christ in his resurrection and therefore in his resurrection life. . . . As surely as Christ rose from the dead so surely shall we walk in newness of life."[39] In Christ believers have died and are now resurrected. As a devotional writer expressed it, we are "Born Crucified."[40]

Paul went even further and said believers share in Christ's ascension. In Christ they are seated in the heavenly places with their Lord on God's right hand—on the throne no less. Paul wrote the Ephesians: "[God] hath raised us up together, and made us sit together in heavenly places in Christ Jesus" (Eph. 2:6, KJV). What a sublime thought; Christians are destined for the throne.

Now when did all of this happen? In the ontological sense, it occurred "before the foundation of the world" (Eph. 1:4, KJV). It also took place when Christ died on the cross and was resurrected in the first century (Gal. 2:20). However, in the believers' personal time frame, being on God's throne pragmatically and dynamically happened at conversion, when they were regenerated by the Holy Spirit and fused into Christ. At that very moment believers died—literally spiritually died—and were raised to newness of life in Christ and thus became a member of God's own personal people.

In Romans 6:1-14 Paul so identified believers with Christ (*Identification* is a key word in the concept.), that all who are regenerated have been crucified with Christ to the old nature and race and raised in Christ to the new race. The practical implications of this are most profound.

The ethical aspects of being in Christ are significant and far reaching. As God constantly reminded the Israelites that He brought them up out of the land of Egypt, and they should therefore live like God's own redeemed people, Paul constantly used the "in Christ" motif to spur regenerate believers to ethical and moral living. Christians are a new people in a new race with a new Head, the Lord Jesus Christ. Thus they ought to live like it. George E. Ladd declared:

> The ethical significance of union with Christ is . . . illustrated in Ephesians 2, where this union is expressed in terms of new life through identification with Christ in his resurrection and ascension. The believer is raised into newness of life, and even exalted to heaven to be seated with Christ at the right hand of God. The contrast between the old life and the new life is expressed primarily in ethical terms. Outside of faith in Christ, men are dead—but dead through trespasses and sins, living under the domination of "the passions of [the] flesh, following the desires of body and mind" (Eph. 2:3). The new life in Christ, which is a new creation, expresses itself in good works (Eph. 2:10). Here are the indicative and the imperative: the believer who was dead in sins is now alive with Christ (indicative); he is therefore to live a life of good works (imperative).[41]

This is why Paul asked the Romans: "Are we to continue in sin . . . ? By no means! How can we who died to sin still live in it?" (Rom. 6:1-2). Paul argued that believers are thus so identified with their Lord in His death that they, too, died *to* sin. We are dead to sin in Christ. It has no more dominion over us: "You also must consider yourselves dead to sin and alive to God in Christ" (Rom. 6:11). Therefore, concluded the apostle, "Let not sin . . . reign in your mortal bodies, to make you obey their passions. . . . For sin will have no dominion over you, since you are not under law but under grace" (vv. 12,14).

So the "in Christ" union effected in regeneration in the grace of God not only forms the motive for ethics and morals but also becomes the basis of pragmatically living out those principles in everyday life. By the grace of God in Christ, believers have victory over the power of sin. Barth commented on Romans 6:3 with these words:

> The man who emerges . . . is not the same man. . . . One man dies and another is born. . . . Overwhelmed and hidden by the claim of God, he disappears and is lost in this death. . . . The man over whom sin has power and dominion has died. . . . In the Resurrection, the full seriousness and energy of the veritable negation, of our being buried, are displayed and ratified. By the creation of the new man, the truth of the redemption which Christ effected is made known . . . ; by our existence in Him our existence in Adam is manifestly dissolved.[42]

Faith's Struggle.—Life is a real struggle against the world, the flesh, and the devil. "Old Adam" still persists. Paul himself knew it well and confessed, "For that which I do I allow not: for what I would, that do I not; but what I hate, that do I. . . . For I know that in me (that is, in my flesh,) dwelleth no good thing: for to will is present with me; but how to perform that which is good I find not. For the good that I would I do not: but the evil which I would not, that I do. . . . O wretched man that I am! who shall deliver me from the body of this death?" (Rom. 7:15,18-19,24, KJV).[43] How often we find ourselves there! Is there any hope to live out the ethical demands of our Lord as expressed, for example, in the Sermon on the Mount?[44]

Paul told us there is hope. He did not leave us in the despair of crying out "Who will deliver me from this body of death?" (Rom. 7:24). He declared, "Thanks be to God through Jesus Christ our Lord!" (Rom. 7:25). In Christ, the principle of victory through our identification with Him in death is manifest. But how is it worked out? How can one live pragmatically the ethical, moral life one's position in Christ demands?

The answer rests in *faith's appropriation*. John said, "This is the victory that overcomes the world, our faith" (1 John 5:4). Failure to appropriate by faith the fact of union with Christ, and thus to engage in fighting the world, the flesh, and the devil by human strength alone, will thrust one into the despair of Paul's own plight; but if one stands on faith, appropriating union in Christ and declaring oneself dead to sin and alive to God, victory by the power of the indwelling Holy Spirit effects victory. Believers can actually become conquerors in Christ.

Another Approach

Perhaps the principle can be further illustrated this way: there are two laws that seek for ascendancy in the Christian's life. One is the "law of sin and death" (Rom. 8:2). That law operates through the unrenewed mind. The law of sin functions constantly if given ascendancy through lack of surrender to Jesus Christ and His daily lordship in our lives. It also fails if there is no recognition that our "old man" is dead in Christ. The other principle is the "law of the Spirit of life in Christ Jesus" (Rom. 8:2). This law works through the new, redeemed nature as the new mind is constantly renewed and enlarged. In this latter law lies the victory.

The interaction of these two principles is similar to ascending in a balloon. The law of sin functions like the law of gravity. Its pull cannot be escaped. Still, the balloon ascends because of a higher law that counteracts the law of gravity. The gas in the balloon is more powerful than the downward pull. In like fashion, the law of the Spirit of life in Christ Jesus is the higher law that overcomes the pull of sin and death through the unrenewed mind. If the Holy Spirit is allowed to function in believers' lives by faith, they can ascend to spiritual heights. "There is therefore now no condemnation for those who are in Christ Jesus. For the law of the Spirit of life in Christ Jesus has set me free from the law of sin and death" (Rom. 8:1-2). Moreover, the wind of the Spirit carries us along over obstacles in the way God would have us to travel.

Two or three insights emerge out of the above analogy. First, the old mind that is open to the law of sin and death remains present. It is never eliminated. Absolute, complete sanctification and perfection wait for heaven. Second, the law of the Spirit of life in Christ Jesus overcomes the downward pull of the law of sin and death because of its great power. This process cultivates the new mind of Christ in believers. If the higher law ever ceases to be operative in experience, believers fall to earth again. So Christians must stay "in the balloon," that is, *exercising faith* in their identification in Christ. Thus the mind is constantly renewed, and the process of sanctification moves along.

The Holy Spirit actualizes these truths in one's daily experience. For example, suppose that a Christian is confronted by one of his old weaknesses. The unrenewed mind, accustomed to foster the things of the flesh, exerts itself; but now one recognizes the reason the temptation has an appeal is because of the old, yet unrenewed part of one's "mind" (Rom. 8:7). This is what moves a Christian to think, feel, and decide contrary to God's purpose. Then the new truth of one's identification with Christ is pressed home to one's consciousness by the Holy Spirit. Realizing the believer's union with Christ in death and resurrection, and by faith in that biblical reality, each one can confront the temptation and say, "This sin has no more power over me. I am dead to it. I am a new person. The old nature is crucified. I am alive to God, and the resurrected life of Jesus Christ is mine." Each can take the ground of faith and stand against the temptation. Thus trusting Christ's promise, a Christian looks to God and His power for the victory. A willful submission to the will of God, a trust in the fact of one's death to sin, and a vital look in faith to God, assures the victory. That act of faith involves the twin aspects of the grounds for belief: biblical truth and our powerful Lord.

There is a battle, of course, but the battle is not to fight sin directly. That spells defeat. Christians dare not fight temptation on its own ground. The war to be fought is to yield absolutely to the will of God and strive to stay in the field of faith. The battle is the Lord's (2 Chron. 20:15). The believer rests in faith. The devil will do anything and everything to get Christians to surrender their position of faith. As it has been put: "His aim is to get the believer to forsake faith's position . . . for the moment the believer quits faith's position, he falls under Satan's power. Hence the fight is not merely 'the good fight' . . . but 'the good fight of faith' " (1 Tim. 6:12).[45]

Christians do not work *toward* victory. By faith they work *from* victory as already theirs in Christ. They are new people—righteous before God in Christ, and they live and battle in a new arena, an arena of the freedom of faith. Not only in eternity are believers delivered from the penalty and presence of sin, but now by faith they are saved from its power. Deliverance from sin's dominance is as much a part of salvation as deliverance from its penalty. All of these beautiful realities are bound up in the conversion experience. God's people need to know they are accepted by God in Christ, and a whole new nature is theirs. Therefore, they permit the Holy Spirit to renew their minds constantly, and sanctification naturally follows. Redemption is as much in the present tense as in the past or the future. This is one of the Spirit's gifts and work in salvation.

The Normal Christian Life

This quality of living is not to be thought of as unusual for the Christian. As one writer put it: it is just the "normal Christian life." Being crucified with Christ and raised to walk in newness of life is not a position one attains by ardent spiritual striving. It is not the end result of much maturing and gigantic growth in Christ. Every believer holds this marvelous position by virtue of the fact of being born again by the grace of God and of being possessed by the Holy Spirit. Every believer is "born crucified." The Christian's part is merely to appropriate by faith what is already his and start living like it. As Paul said, "I have been crucified with Christ; it is no longer I who live, but Christ who lives in me; and the life I now live in the flesh I live by faith in the Son of God, who loved me and gave himself for me" (Gal. 2:20).

This entire new sphere of victories, moral living, effected by the Holy Spirit, is possible because of one's regeneration in Christ. One truly is, in Christ, "born again."[46] But the Spirit does more in the marvelous moment of conversion.

The Holy Spirit "Seals" New Believers

> In him you also, who have heard the word of truth, the gospel of your salvation, and have believed in him, were sealed with the promised Holy Spirit, which is the guarantee of our inheritance until we acquire possession of it, to the praise of his glory (Eph. 1:13-14).

A brief look at the term that describes the "sealing" work of the Spirit of God is in order. It was a very common word in first-century usage. *Sphragis, seal,* was the simple instrument that people or authorities used to put their marks (or the mark of whom they represented) on documents or articles. The actual instrument of sealing was at times a signet ring, or a stamp, or a cylinder. The act of sealing normally carried legal significance, giving the article sealed the stamp of authority, guarantee, or ownership. The use of seals was very common, as was their misuse in attempts of fraud.

The act of sealing took on metaphorical, figurative usages, and religious connotations. It was an apt figure for many situations. The religious usage is the concern here.

In the Old Testament the term *sealing (chatham)* is used *both* in a literal sense and in a figurative manner. It carries ideas like "to stop up," "to hold secret," "to finish," and even to end a letter as a signature. Most often it refers to sealing a letter prior to sending or to a signet ring used to seal and validate a document. One of the important Jewish rabbinic metaphorical usages was to describe the rite of circumcision as a "sealing," basing the interpretation on Genesis 17. For the Jew the seal of circumcision became the stamp of identity, membership in the covenant, and ownership by God, thus ensuring the power and protection of God. It was God's "brand" on His people.

The New Testament picks up on these basic ideas. Of course, there are times where the word is used in a literal sense, such as the sealing of Jesus' tomb by Pilate (Matt. 27:66); but as in the Old Testament, the term is also used in its religious metaphorical connotations. In this word we see a marvelous work of the Holy Spirit upon the new convert.

Sealing has a connection with Christian baptism, as did circumcision in the old covenant. Baptism speaks of the initiating of redemption for the Christian as circumcision did for the Jew. Gottfried Fitzer pointed out, "On the same plane of usage are expressions in Paul's epistles in which circumcision on the one side . . . and endowment with the Spirit on the other are linked to the image of the seal."[47] When believers are initiated into Christ, as pictured in baptism, God stamps His seal on them. Alan Richardson saw this when he wrote: "The idea of baptism as the seal of the Spirit appears in II Cor. 1.22; Eph. 1.13 and 4.30. . . . St Paul teaches that God has firmly established us in Christ and has anointed us . . . and sealed us and given us in our hearts the earnest . . . of the Spirit."[48] That immediately implies that one aspect of sealing is the receiving of the Spirit Himself. R. E. O. White in *The Bible Doctrine of Initiation* argues for this understanding. The Spirit not only seals believers, the gift of His presence is the seal in itself (Eph. 1:13-14). Thus the Spirit becomes the believer's surety, guarantee, the pledge, and the down payment ("earnest" in KJV) of their redemption. Fitzer developed this one step further and told us: "This seal does denote membership, yet not simply of the people as God's people, but of the *justified* people."[49] When God justifies a person, He seals the believer as a mark of justification. Paul said that God has sealed us for Himself and given us the pledge of the Spirit in our hearts (2 Cor. 1:22; 5:5). This means several things.

First the seal means Christians are *God's own personal possession*; He has put his "stamp" on each one. Paul told Timothy: "God's firm foundation stands, bearing this seal: 'The Lord knows those who are his' " (2 Tim. 2:19). The Book of Revelation abounds with the idea of the sealing of God's people. For example, we read, "Do not harm the earth or the sea or the trees, till we have sealed the servants of our God upon their foreheads" (Rev. 7:3). The same idea is expressed, albeit negatively, in Revelation 9:4 where those who do not have the seal on their foreheads are to be tortured for five months.

All these passages, along with others, make it very clear that when

individuals are saved, those persons receive God's stamp of possession
on their foreheads. They belong to God. They have become one of God's
own personal "people" (Titus 2:14). As Paul told the Corinthians: "Do
you not know that your body is a temple of the Holy Spirit within you,
which you have from God? You are not your own" (1 Cor. 6:19). Simply
put, when God seals His redeemed with His Holy Spirit, in that moment
of redemption they thereafter belong to Him.

Second, the seal of God is the mark of *authenticity*. As Fitzer pointed
out, believers are a justified people. The parable of the wheat and the
tares (Matt. 13:24-30) makes it clear that different sorts of people, lost
and redeemed, grow up together and may in many respects look much
alike. The same idea is back of the Lord's parable of the ten virgins
(Matt. 25:1-13); nonetheless, there is a vast difference between people.
Wheat bears a different sort of kernel than tares. The five wise virgins
have oil in their lamps, the foolish ones do not. What is the mark, the
"oil" or "kernel," that identifies true justified believers? The "oil" is the
seal of the indwelling presence of the Holy Spirit Himself. Paul declared, "Any one who does not have the Spirit of Christ does not belong
to him" (Rom. 8:9). Barth had it right when he said, "Spirit [that is, the
Holy Spirit] means the eternal decision by which God decides for men
and men for God."[50] The Holy Spirit is God's stamp of authenticity on
His people. God has decided for them, justified them, and sealed them.
As Anders Nygren expressed it, "One cannot belong to Christ without
sharing in His death and resurrection and having His Spirit *resident in
him*" (author's italics).[51] When the Spirit is present within, the seal of
authentic faith is upon the believer.

This basic idea has something of a forensic motif, as dynamic and
existential as the inner presence of the Spirit is. The authentication of
the sealing of God points to the new standing one has before God in
justification. The justified enter into covenant with God. The Reformed
theology of the covenant concept is taken up elsewhere in this book, but
it is also important to see here that the authenticating seal of the Spirit
has to do with the assurance which a believer enjoys as part of the new
covenant in Christ.

In the third place, sealing has to do with security. In the literal, natural
sense when something was legally sealed in the first century, it was considered secured. For example, when Jesus' tomb was sealed by Pilate, it
meant no one had any right to enter the tomb; it was secured by the
authority of Rome. Therefore, when the Bible says Christians are
"sealed" by the Holy Spirit (2 Cor. 1:22; Eph. 1:13; 4:30), it implies they
are secure in the new covenant relationship with God. Thus the eschatological element of the giving of the Spirit emerges. As often seen, the
Spirit is the "earnest" or the "down payment" of redemption. Consequently, believers have the assurance that God Himself, who gave the

down payment, will surely give the "full payment" of salvation in the "fullness of time" (Eph. 1:10).

All are aware, however, of the persistent theological debate that goes on concerning the doctrine of the security of the believer. Nonetheless, it is true to say that fervent evangelism is not dependent on one's theological perspectives concerning the doctrine. A multitude of writings have been produced on both sides of the question. A recent book from the Arminian perspective has been produced by Professor Dale Moody under the title *The Word of Truth*. Dr. R. T. Kendall has done a fine work from the Calvinist viewpoint entitled *Once Saved, Always Saved*. These and similar works should be investigated by the interested reader.

Yet, it does seem the sealing of the Spirit is an eternal act of God. "The gifts and the call of God are irrevocable" (Rom. 11:29). That is a very strong word from Paul, and it surely means God gives His gifts, including the gift of salvation (Eph. 2:8-9), for eternity. As paradoxical as some life situations may seem, even certain passages of Scripture themselves, the weight of the Bible rests on the side of eternal security, not to mention the whole theology of conversion. We are "sealed," hence, safe and secure in Christ forever. God's true people persevere in their faith to the end.[52]

Finally, the sealing of the Spirit has to do with *service to Christ*.[53] In addressing the Corinthian church, Paul said, "You are the seal of my apostleship in the Lord" (1 Cor. 9:2). The apostle may even have something of the metaphor of sealing in mind when he told the Galatians, "I bear on my body the marks of Jesus" (Gal. 6:17). One thing is clear: the indwelling Holy Spirit, which constitutes the essence of the sealing, leads and directs God's people in service. Christians are set apart and stamped so as to magnify Jesus Christ in ministry. This leads to another major element of the activity of the Spirit in a new convert's life.

The Holy Spirit "Gifts" the New Believer

Three major passages from the pen of Paul clearly outline the theology of the Holy Spirit's bestowal of ministering gifts: Romans 12:3-8; 1 Corinthians 12—14; and Ephesians 4:4-16. Along with other passages like 1 Peter 4:10, the New Testament teaches that gifts of the Spirit or "grace gifts" (*charismata*) are given to every believer. These gifts are supernatural endowments of the Spirit of God that enable God's people to serve Him effectively and efficiently. No believer is exempt in receiving a gift or gifts; therefore, no one in Christ is excused from ministering in the Lord's name.

Furthermore, the New Testament implies these spiritual gifts are received at the moment of conversion, because Paul related them to being baptized by the Spirit into the "body of Christ," the church (1 Cor. 12:13). That is not to say the Spirit cannot bestow His ministering gifts later as well, but it does mean every new believer has a gift and can serve Christ.

The Holy Spirit Baptizes the New Believer into the Body of Christ

Paul told the Corinthian church: "For by one Spirit we were all baptized into one body—Jews or Greeks, slaves or free—and all were made to drink of one Spirit" (1 Cor. 12:13). Every new convert is baptized by the Holy Spirit into the church of Jesus Christ. This is a great and powerful work of the Spirit. Of course, "Spirit baptism" is a quite controversial doctrine today. Study of this doctrine will be discussed in detail in a later chapter when looking at phrases like "filled with the Spirit" and "anointed by the Spirit." It should be pointed out in this immediate context that one of the blessed works of the Holy Spirit is this "baptizing" of the new convert into Christ's body. From a practical perspective, it means the new believer should identify with a local "body"—a local church—where he or she can worship, serve, and mature in Christ.

The Holy Spirit Indwells New Believers

"The fellowship of the Holy Spirit be with you all" (2 Cor. 13:14). The key word is *fellowship* (*koinonia*). The Spirit is in believers and they are in Him. "The communion of the Holy Ghost," as the *King James Version* has it, is a significant experience for a number of reasons.

To begin with, the indwelling Spirit constantly leads God's people into His perfect will for their lives. "All who are led by the Spirit of God are sons of God" (Rom. 8:14). God's plan and purpose for life is directed by the Holy Spirit. To be led into a daily experience of performing the will of God is quite complex. It initially means the Holy Spirit aids one in discovering God's will. To find God's will in the practical affairs of life is not easy. The Spirit uses several means to reveal the purposes of God. Here are ten sources, or principles, in assisting one to discover God's will:

1. The Holy Scriptures: Psalm 119:105.
2. Circumstances of life: Acts 20:22-24.
3. Advice of others: Acts 21:10-12.
4. Common sense: Ephesians 5:15-17.
5. Prayer: Psalm 143:10.
6. Conscience: 2 Timothy 1:3.
7. Lessons learned in the past: Philippians 4:9.
8. "Closed doors": Acts 16:7.
9. "Open doors": 1 Corinthians 16:9.
10. Inner witness of the Spirit: Acts 8:29.

It is good to pray with the psalmist:

> Teach me to do thy will,
> for thou art my God!
> Let thy good Spirit lead me
> on a level path! (Ps. 143:10).

All this, of course, presupposes that one is yielded to the will of God and seeking His glory (Ps. 13:3). When one is determined to perform the purpose of God in daily living, one will be able to find God's will. Jesus said, "If any man's will is to do his will, he shall know whether the teaching is from God or whether I am speaking on my own authority" (John 7:17). Coming to know God's will requires a surrender to that will. The Holy Spirit steps in and reveals the Lord's will, and then empowers one to yield to the will of God (1 Cor. 15:10). As W. T. Conner expressed it: "We need to bring ourselves under the control of a *living* Person, Jesus Christ, made available to us in an immediate experience of transforming power. This can only be done by the Holy Spirit. To bring us under the control of the living Christ is the function of the Spirit."[54] It proves to be a delight to do His will (Ps. 40:8), for then it is His power at work within.

Second, the Holy Spirit leads believers into all truth. In the Old Testament, *wisdom* is often personified. Many see this as an allusion to the Spirit. In the New Testament, however, it all becomes very explicit. Jesus called the Holy Spirit the "Spirit of truth" (John 16:13) who would guide God's people into all truth. As Stouffer put it, "The Holy Spirit brings the truth to light, and the Church can recognize him by that. And it is for this reason that John calls him the Spirit of truth."[55] In the final analysis, only the Holy Spirit can reveal the truth of God. He does this essentially through the Word of God. The Bible is the "sword of the Spirit" (Eph. 6:17). If the Spirit is the ultimate source of all Scripture (2 Tim. 3:16), He alone is the final Interpreter. The Bible is not just like any other book to be held up to mere historical criticism alone, making that critical method the final arbitrator of truth. The interpreter should use the critical tools, of course, but these tools must be used with a sensitivity to the leading and inspiration of the Holy Spirit. He reveals God in a manner our human ingenuity never could. Paul said, "The natural man receiveth not the things of the Spirit of God: for they are foolishness unto him: neither can he know them, because they are spiritually discerned" (1 Cor. 2:14, KJV). We need to remember that. Alan Richardson said, "Without the inward testimony of the Holy Spirit at the reading or the preaching of the Scriptures their message would remain locked up in the written or spoken words. . . . The Risen Christ . . . is the true interpreter of Holy Scripture; apart from his presence and inspiration the Scriptures are a mysterious enigma."[56] Of course, this does not mean Christians put their minds in neutral; it does mean they humbly accept the Spirit's instruction.

There is an important issue relative to the Spirit's guiding into basic truth. Failure to submit the mind to the Spirit of truth can easily lead to theological error. Doctrinal deviations are spiritual problems as well as intellectual ones. It will not do to say believers simply see things differently on an intellectual level, hence departing from the essential gospel (Gal. 1:6-7). Heresy grows out of not submitting to and following the Spirit's lead.

The Holy Spirit places barriers in the pathway of error concerning the essentials of the faith as they center in Jesus Christ. Therefore, doctrinal deviation has a moral connotation as well as a theological one in that it implies resisting the Spirit of truth's leadership. To depart from the bedrock essentials of the Christian faith is a sin as much as to depart from the moral and ethical basis of the faith.[57] The Spirit guides into all truth, ethical and doctrinal. The psalmist said, "Lead me in thy truth, and teach me,/for thou art the God of my salvation;/ for thee I wait all the day long" (Ps. 25:5). When one learns God's truth, it forms a firm foundation of growth and development in Christ.

The above statement leads to a third reality: the indwelling Spirit sanctifies the believer. (See the "in Christ" motif discussion in an earlier chapter.) The root word *sanctify* (Hebrew, *qadosh*; Greek, *hagios*) means simply "to set apart." Its root is variously translated "holy," "saint," "separate," and "sanctified." The Bible uses it in relationship both to God and His people.[58] In relationship to God in the Old Testament, as Procksch put it in his discussion of the history of *hagios* in the Old Testament, "Yahweh's holy name contrasts with everything creaturely."[59] He is "set apart" in the ultimate sense. By the same token, those whom God redeems and grants the gift of the Holy Spirit, they too are "set apart," made holy by the indwelling Spirit. It is important to see the centrality of holiness in the practical Christian experience.

In this context the Holy Spirit bears His "fruit" in the lives of redeemed saints (Gal. 5:22-23). Madame Guyon, a deeply spiritual French Christian, said:

> I had a deep peace which seemed to pervade the whole soul, and resulted from the fact that all my desires were fulfilled in God. . . . I desired nothing but what I now had, because I had full belief that, in my present state of mind, the results of each moment constituted the fulfillment of the Divine purposes. . . . I had no will but the Divine will. One characteristic of this higher degree of experience was a sense of inward purity. . . . My mind had such a oneness with God, such a unity with the Divine nature, that nothing seemed to have power to soil it and to diminish its purity.[60]

Mature saints of God develop a holy life-style. God by His Spirit attempts to effect Christian growth into the beauty of Jesus Christ. Paul put it this way: "This is the will of God, your sanctification" (1 Thess.

4:3). J. B. Phillips translated: "God's plan is to make you holy." God's design for life is maturation in winsome holiness and attractive consecration. God places the standard before His people; their part is to meet it.

Such an in-depth work of the Holy Spirit cannot be effected overnight, however. Although Christ through the Spirit enters one's life in a moment, that is just the beginning. After regeneration, the mind-renewing, sanctifying process of becoming formed into Christ's beautiful image is inaugurated by the power of the Holy Spirit. This process continues until the day one is made perfectly Christlike at the resurrection. In the meantime, believers are to permit God to nurture them in Christ through the renewing of their minds (Rom. 12:1-2).

The Fruit of the Spirit

Now if Christians are to be like their Lord, they must obviously bear the same fruit of holiness He did. In the end, fruit bearing is the crux of the whole matter. The fruit of the Spirit—the quality of fruit that Christ epitomized in His character—centers in holy living. This principle is fully outlined in Galatians 5:22-23: "The fruit of the Spirit is love, joy, peace, patience, kindness, goodness, faithfulness, gentleness, self-control; against such there is no law." Paul urged God's people to permit the Holy Spirit to develop a quality of Christlike holiness in their lives through His indwelling fruit-bearing work. This is sanctification.

Important implications immediately emerge from Paul's foundational passage. The Christian, as a branch grafted into the Vine, Jesus Christ, is to abide and draw life-giving sustenance from the Vine. When this abiding state is maintained, fruit is produced on these grafted branches. A brief look at each aspect of the Spirit-empowered, fruitful life will give insight.

The Fruit of Love.—The first fruit which blooms on Christian "branches" is love. Most significant is the fact that love is placed as the primary fruit of the Spirit. This implies there is really only one fruit of the Spirit: God's kind of love (*agape*). The rest of the Galatian passage then becomes a definition or ramification of the one essential quality of love. There is a certain validity to this approach in the light of how Paul defined love in 1 Corinthians 13:

> Love is patient and kind; love is not jealous or boastful; it is not arrogant or rude. Love does not insist on its own way; it is not irritable or resentful; it does not rejoice at wrong, but rejoices in the right. Love bears all things, believes all things, hopes all things, endures all things (vv. 4-7).

Paul's hymn to love implies that the fruit of love is basic to all other Christlike graces, but there are other "fruits" that demand a brief word, for each reflects the indwelling Spirit's work of creating *agape* in the believers' experience.

The Fruit of Joy.—Joy is a beautiful blossom that sends forth its fragrance in the Christian life. The prophet Nehemiah said, "The joy of the Lord is your strength" (Neh. 8:10). There is nothing quite so contagious or winsomely attractive as Christian joy. It is not an earthly, temporary, human joy. Abiding in Christ and drawing on His life-giving strength gives a much deeper meaning and reality to life than that. Christian joy is a deep-seated satisfaction, welling up in the heart because of the Holy Spirit and His abiding inner work.

The Fruit of Peace.—Faithfully abiding on the Vine and drawing on His strength will produce peace. Paul described it as "the peace of God, which passeth all understanding" (Phil. 4:7, KJV). Notice again, it is *God's* peace. One does not strive for it, nor will work produce it. This sort of peace is Christ's gift to those who faithfully rest in Him.

The Fruit of Patience.—Another fruit growing on the branches of those who abide in Christ is patience. One writer has defined this term as "the strength to defer anger, and the contentedness to bear injuries." The word depicts a patience in regard to people. Chrysostom said that patience is the quality of grace God gives to the Christian who could in justice seek revenge, but refuses to do so. The concept is constantly used concerning the Lord Jesus Christ and His attitude toward the people He encountered.

The Fruit of Kindness.—Kindness is another beautiful fruit which Christian branches bear. This word is akin to "goodness" and is sometimes translated that way. It implies a particular sort of goodness that is very kind. One definition expresses it as a sweetness of temper that moves believers to be gracious and courteous and easy to reconcile when wronged. The word appears solely in the New Testament. It is not found in secular Greek. Only the fruit-bearing Christian can display it in any real depth.

The Fruit of Goodness.—The fruit of goodness takes its rightful place on the believer's branch. This word appears often in the Christian gospel. Of course, there is One alone who is good: God (Matt. 19:16-17).He is the fountainhead of all true goodness. So doing good and being good is to be Godlike. Paul said, "So then, as we have opportunity, let us do good to all men, and especially to those who are of the household of faith" (Gal. 6:10).

The Fruit of Faithfulness.—Faithfulness is a fruit of the Spirit which displays the manifestation of God's love. This term is the common word for "trustworthiness." It denotes a person who is totally reliable, just as God is. Honesty and justice and fidelity in what one professes and promises is implied.

The Fruit of Gentleness.—With faithfulness as a basic stance before God, a proper attitude and relationship to people becomes the next lovely fruit of the Spirit: "gentleness." Jesus said, "I am gentle and lowly in heart" (Matt. 11:29). He further stated, "Blessed are the meek, for they shall inherit the earth" (Matt. 5:5). This grace is threefold. In the first place, it signifies submission to the will of God (Matt. 11:29). It further means that a gentle Christian is teachable, one who is not too proud to learn (Jas. 1:21). Finally, it exalts the attitude of consideration (1 Cor. 4:21). The adjectival form of the word refers to an animal trained and brought under control. For the fruit-bearing Christian it means when one is wronged, there is no display of resentment or vengeance.

The Fruit of Self-Control.—The final fruit blooming on the Christian branch because of constant abiding in the Vine is termed "self-control." The philosopher Plato used this word to convey the concept of self-mastery. It applies to persons who have mastered all their desires and their love of pleasure. Paul employed the term in relationship to an athlete's discipline of his body (1 Cor. 9:25) and to the Christian's mastery of sex desire (1 Cor. 7:9). Strength of character is at the heart of the idea. Thus, it is possible for Christians to control themselves so they are able to be the right kind of self-giving servants to others. That is what it is like to be a fruit-bearing branch. In simplest terms, we live the exchanged life: the Christ-life for the self-life.

One of the primary works of the indwelling Holy Spirit is to make believers holy through bearing the fruit of the Spirit. We shall never be sinlessly perfect in this life (1 John 1:8,10); nonetheless, we can be "sure that he who began a good work in [us] will bring it to completion at the day of Jesus Christ" (Phil. 1:6). That is most encouraging.

The Graces of the Spirit

Along with fruit-producing grace, the indwelling Holy Spirit graciously empowers the believer in service for Christ. Discussion of this wonderful truth is left to to a later chapter. It must merely be mentioned here that there is real power (*dunamis*) for the believer who would serve Jesus.

Another beautiful grace of the indwelling Spirit is that He makes prayer vital and dynamic. Paul said:

> Likewise the Spirit helps us in our weakness; for we do not know how to pray as we ought, but the Spirit himself intercedes for us with sighs too deep for words. And he who searches the hearts of men knows what is the mind of the Spirit, because the Spirit intercedes for the saints according to the will of God (Rom. 8:26-27).

In commenting on these verses, Conner pointed out, "As the Christian thus prays under the tuition of the Spirit, Paul indicates that God searches his heart and sees that he prays according to the will of God. . . . Since the Christian thus prays according to the will of God, God can and does answer his prayer. It is only the Spirit-inspired and Spirit-guided prayer that God hears and answers."[61] Prayer, therefore, demands discipline, knowledge, faith, commitment, compassion, and grace. Only the indwelling Spirit can supply those grace needs. This is why Paul constantly talked about praying "in the Spirit" (Eph. 6:18). Space again forbids delving into the doctrine of prayer, but many excellent works have been produced on the subject. We must be content to say here the Holy Spirit is the "Teacher" in the school of prayer and makes praise, thanksgiving, adoration, confession, intercession, asking, and all the elements of a deep prayer life vital and alive. Every new convert has the "Spirit of prayer" within and must learn to pray effectively.

Another marvelous reality of the indwelling of the Holy Spirit is His witness to our salvation. Paul put it this way: "For you did not receive the spirit of slavery to fall back into fear, but you have received the spirit of sonship. When we cry, 'Abba! Father!' it is the Spirit himself bearing witness with our spirit that we are children of God" (Rom. 8:15-16). W. T. Conner has an insightful comment on this important passage:

> This passage does not mean that the Spirit bears witness to our spirits, as if the Spirit were over against our spirit speaking to our spirit in an external or objective fashion. It is not the Spirit of God speaking with my spirit as one man speaks with another. The word for *with* in this connection means conjointly with, together with. It is the Spirit of God conjointly with my spirit that bears testimony that I am a child of God. It is not the divine Spirit saying to me that I am a child of God; it is rather the divine Spirit saying along with my spirit that I am a child of God. It is the indwelling and creative Spirit enabling me to realize for myself that I have this relationship with God.[62]

Paul told the Galatians: "Because you are sons, God has sent the Spirit of his Son into our hearts, crying, 'Abba! Father!' " (Gal. 4:6). Assurance of one's salvation comes not only by being knowledgeable of the Word of God (Rom. 10:17), the Spirit also bears witness with us. Assurance does not stem from ourselves alone, the Spirit confirms it. Stouffer was correct when he said, "It is certainly not myself, but the Spirit in my heart" that spawns assurance; and because the Spirit does this, the new convert can know he or she is saved. That will keep one from the judgment of Hebrews 6:1-8 and enable one to mature in Christian grace.

The indwelling Spirit also forms believers into the body and temple of Christ. Paul stressed this to the Corinthians (see 1 Cor. 10—12). This is to be understood in a twofold sense. First, the Holy Spirit makes all believers a part of the body of the Lord (1 Cor. 12:13). In a word, the

Spirit creates the church, the body of Christ. The Christian experience is never an isolated, individual experience alone. We are born into a family, a fellowship, the household of faith. John emphasized *"our* fellowship" with God (1 John 1:3, author's italics), not simply *my* fellowship, "for we are members one of another" (Eph. 4:25, KJV). H. Wheeler Robinson pointed out, "If we ask what is the most characteristic and comprehensive work of the Holy Spirit, according to the New Testament, there can be little doubt that we should answer in the one word, 'fellowship.' . . . But fellowship with God essentially means fellowship with men . . . that he makes this fellowship of Christians with one another in the Spirit the basis of his service."[63]

Because the Holy Spirit indwells the individual bodies of each believer, (as He did the temple in the old dispensation), the body of the Christian thus becomes the very temple of God on earth (1 Cor. 6:19-20). Therefore, in Paul's word, Christians are to "glorify God in [their] body" (1 Cor. 6:20). The moral and ethical implications of the truth are most profound, bringing on the necessity of holiness.

Many other things should be said concerning the inner working of the gracious Holy Spirit in a new convert's life: forming Christ within (Gal. 4:19), the Spirit as the "first-fruit" of the coming "harvest" (Rom. 8:23), the prophetic call of the Spirit (1 Sam. 3:1-9), the Spirit giving wisdom in persecution (Mark 13:11), and the freedom the Spirit imparts to believers (2 Cor. 3:17). Space simply forbids going into these areas of study, but enough has been said on the work of the Holy Spirit that it is clear: without the Holy Spirit there is simply no evangelism or new life.

Conclusion

Therefore, God is vitally and centrally involved in the entire evangelism enterprise. He is, in the final analysis, the Great Evangelist. Father, Son, and Holy Spirit all work toward the redemption of all humanity. Why? Because "God so loved the world that he gave" (John 3:16). That is what God is like. Since this *is* true, believers ought to be engaged in evangelism.

Notes

1. As discussed in chapter 5, even though the old "quest" has been by and large given up, it must be granted that the "new quest for the historical Jesus" has made an impact through scholars like Ernst Kaseman, G. Ebelong, E. Fuchs, etc. See *The Present-day Christological Debate* by Klass Runea (London: IVP, 1984).

2. The Azuza Street Revival of 1906 in Los Angeles, California, is something of the beginning of the widespread growth of Pentecostalism, even though it had some incipient manifestations earlier. See Frank Bartleman, *Azuza Street* (Plainfield: Logos International, 1980).

3. One cannot help but feel at times this vagueness, if not ignorance, grows out of either fear or reaction, or both, to the extreme emphasis of some.

4. Raymond E. Brown, *The Gospel According to John* (XIII-XXI), The Anchor Bible, 44 vols. (Garden City: Doubleday and Company, Inc., 1970), 29A:711.

5. Rudolf Schnackenburg, *The Gospel According to St. John*, (New York: Crossroads Publishing Company, 1982), 3:149.

6. Ibid., 149.

7. Leon Morris, *Commentary on the Gospel of John*, The New International Commentary, ed. F. F. Bruce (Grand Rapids: William B. Eerdmans Publishing Co., 1971), 697.

8. C. H. Spurgeon, *Twelve Sermons on the Holy Spirit* (Grand Rapids: Baker Book House, 1973), 23.

9. Friedrich Büchsel, *"elegcho"* in *Theological Dictionary of the New Testament, 10 vols.*, ed. Gerhard Kittel and Gerhard Friedrich, trans. Geoffrey W. Bromily, (Grand Rapids: William B. Eerdmans Publishing Co., 1964), 2:474.

10. Morris, *Commentary on the Gospel of John*, 697.

11. C. H. Dodd, *The Interpretation of the Fourth Gospel* (Cambridge: University Press, 1953), 414.

12. Spurgeon, *Twelve Sermons on the Holy Spirit*, 137.

13. *The Illustrated Bible Dictionary*, Part 3. (Leicester: IVP, 1980), 1456. The author followed the general presentation of this fine work in the word study on sin in the Scriptures.

14. Brown, *The Gospel According to John*, 29A:712.

15. The depth of the word (*pisteuo*) will be discussed in a later section on the *call* of the Gospel.

16. Barth, *The Epistle to the Romans*, 6th ed., trans. Edwyn C. Hoskyns (London: Oxford University Press, 1932), 190.

17. Ethelbert Stauffer, *New Testament Theology* (London: SCM Press Ltd., 1955), 167, author's italics.

18. Brown, *The Gospel According to John*, 29A:712.

19. Ibid., 713.

20. George R. Beasley-Murray, *John* (Waco: Word Books Publisher, 1987), 282.

21. Morris, *Commentary on the Gospel of John*, 698.

22. Ibid., 699.

23. Edwyn Clement Hoskyns, *The Fourth Gospel*, ed. Francis Noel Davey, rev. ed. (London: Faber and Faber, Ltd., 1947), 484.

24. William Temple, *Readings in St. John's Gospel* (London: McMillian and Co., Ltd., 1950), 285-286.

25. *The Illustrated Bible Dictionary*, 1341. More will be said concerning all these great truths as we progress.

26. Morris, *Commentary on the Gospel of John*, 699.

27. Beasley-Murray, *John*, 282.

28. Ibid., 282.

29. Ibid.

30. Brown, *The Gospel According to John*, 29A:714.

31. A. M. Hunter, *Introducing New Testament Theology* (London: SCM Press, Ltd., 1957), 140.

32. W. T. Conner, *The Work of the Holy Spirit* (Nashville: Broadman Press, 1949), 57-58.

33. Friedrich Büchsel, "paliggenesia" in *Theological Dictionary of the New Testament*, 1:686.

34. Ibid., 688.

35. Hans Conzelman, *An Outline of the Theology of the New Testament* (London: SCM Press, Ltd., 1969), 211.

36. The Greek prepositions normally used in Paul's phrase are *en* and *eis*. Williams saw the clear implication of these prepositions and translated them "in union with." See his translation of the New Testament.

37. This "oneness" does not eradicate individuals in some Eastern, mystical sense. People retain their essential personhood, yet, paradoxically, they are one with Christ.

38. Ernest Best, *One Body in Christ* (London: SPCK, 1955), 66.

39. John Murray, *The Epistle to the Romans*, The New International Commentary of the New Testament, ed. F. F. Bruce (Grand Rapids: William B. Eerdmans Publishing Co., 1968), 216.

40. See L. E. Maxwell, *Born Crucified* (Chicago: Moody Press). Other writings on this line include *Bone of His Bone* by Hugel and *Life on the Highest Plane* by Ruth Paxon, etc. It has been called the foundational truth of the "Keswich Convention" approach to holiness of life.

41. George E. Ladd, *A Theology of the New Testament* (Grand Rapids: William B. Eerdmans Publishing Co., 1974), 517.

42. Barth, *The Epistle to the Romans,* 193,195.

43. There is a long-standing debate over whether this was Paul's "pre" or "post" Christian experience. Commentators differ. The point seems to be that any person, believer or unbeliever, who is not appropriating by faith the power of Christ ends in a "Romans 7" experience.

44. The author is following his own work: *The Revived Life* (Nashville: Broadman Press), 121-126, in this practical section.

45. Evan Hopkins, *The Law of Liberty in the Scriptural Life* (Philadelphia: Sunday School Times, 1955), 108.

46. As is well known, Jesus' statement to Nicodemus is perhaps translated as well "born from above" (NRSV). This emphasizes even more clearly the divine act in regeneration. People do not regenerate themselves. There is no place for Pelegianism in biblical Christianity.

47. Gottfried Fitzer, "*sphragis, sphragizo, katasphragizo,*" in *Theological Dictionary of the New Testament,* 7:949.

48. Alan Richardson, *An Introduction to the Theology of the New Testament,* (London: SCM Press Ltd., 1958), 351.

49. Fitzer, in *Theological Dictionary of the New Testament,* 7:949.

50. Barth, *The Epistle to the Romans,* 283.

51. Anders Nygren, *Commentary on Romans*, trans. Carl C. Rasmussen (Philadelphia: Fortress Press, 1949), 321-322.

52. More of this will be taken up in a later chapter on predestination and election.

53. By the same token it relates to morals and ethics because of the sealing gift of the Spirit, but that has been discussed earlier under another heading.

54. W. T. Conner, *The Work of the Holy Spirit,* 104.

55. Ethelbert Stouffer, *New Testament Theology,* 168.

56. Richardson, *Theology of the New Testament,* 113.

57. This applies essentially to the *kerygma.* There may be differences on minor points of doctrine, but not in the area of the *kerygma.* Paul made this most clear and explicit in Galatians 1.

58. The use of the term is largely personal, although it is used in relationship to the Scriptures, artifacts of the temple, etc.

59. Otto Procksch and Karl Georg Kuhn, *"hagios—hagiazo—hagiasmos—hagiotes—hagiosune"* in *Theological Dictionary of the New Testament,* 1:91.

60. James Lawson, *Deeper Experiences of Famous Christians* (Chicago: Glad Tidings Publishing Co., 1911), 87-104.

61. W. T. Conner, *The Work of the Holy Spirit,* 108.

62. Ibid., 95.

63. H. Wheeler Robinson, *The Christian Experience of the Holy Spirit* (London: Nisbet Co., Ltd., 1928), 141.

Part III

Key Biblical Words in Evangelism:
A Scriptural Survey

Introduction

The biblical presentation of the evangelistic message and ministry of the church is varied and in many senses all-encompassing. When one searches the Scriptures, there is scarcely any aspect of Christian reality that is not in some way permeated with an evangelistic flavor. The entire Bible is a Book of redemption.

Having seen how the Trinitarian Godhead is involved in effecting salvation, the purpose of this section in developing a theology of evangelism is to investigate three foundational scriptural terms: *kerygma* (proclamation), *soteria* (salvation), and *basileus* (kingdom). From a systematic perspective, the attempt shall be made to discover what these key words communicate concerning God's grace in evangelization. The venture is hardly inclusive of all that could be said; yet, the words and subjects to be discussed strike at the heart of an emerging evangelistic theology.

This study is undertaken primarily from an etymological and doctrinal viewpoint with a pragmatic application. The rationale for practical application centers in the fact that biblical evangelism must work itself out in actual ministry, never being merely theological and abstract. Although the last section of this work deals with pragmatic affairs exclusively, it will be impossible not to draw some practical conclusions in the study of crucial biblical terms. In this way alone can one be faithful to what each key word means and implies. So with these principles in mind we proceed.

7

The Message of God's Grace: *Kerygma* The Proclamation

"God decided, through the foolishness of our proclamation [kerygma], to save those who believe" (1 Cor. 1:21, NRSV).

Introduction

Paul's word to the Corinthians bristles with stimulating ideas and principles. One of the most vital truths the apostle would have the entire church to grasp is that, in all evangelistic endeavors, God uses as His primary instrument in redemption what Paul called "our proclamation" (*kerygma*). In other words, the *kerygma* is the "sword of the Spirit" God wields to bring people to saving faith in Jesus Christ. If this is true, those who aspire to evangelize effectively need to know all that is compacted in this key word.

Since by the means of *kerygma* people are brought to a saving knowledge of our Lord, it must be a powerful word, a word which reveals truth about lostness and truth about the Savior. Further, it must be a word in which one can have full confidence. This is surely what Paul meant when he wrote to the Romans: "I am not ashamed of the gospel [*euaggelion*]: it is the power of God for salvation to every one who has faith" (Rom. 1:16). The gospel was fully tested in the laboratory of life when on the Day of Pentecost, "Those who received his word were baptized, and there were added that day about three thousand souls" (Acts 2:41). If the *kerygma*, in the hands of the Spirit through the agency of men and women, can accomplish those sort of results, Christians do well to have it at their finger tips and be ready to share it gladly.

Kerygma

The root of *kerygma* boasts various ideas. In its verbal and substantive forms it becomes the basis of terms like "herald," "proclaimer," "to preach," "to declare," "news," "enquiry," "order," and "decree." In general Greek usage, such as in Philo, both the act and the content of proclaiming are implied. The *ma* suffix to *keryk* (the root) gives the two-fold sense to the word. As Gerhard Friedrich stated, it signifies "both the result of proclamation (what is proclaimed) and the actual proclaiming. . . . In many cases it is hard to say where the emphasis falls."[1]

Something quite profound emerges in the dual meaning of the term when used in the New Testament. It implies the proclamation of the gospel is not a mere reciting of theological dogmas; it also speaks of a positive faith response with definite results. Gospel declarations contain an existential element. Results are forthcoming because of the Spirit's activity in addressing real needs in the dynamic of proclamation. The total person is touched by the ministry of Christ. For example, when Jesus sent out the disciples (Luke 9:2), He charged them to preach and heal in the power of the Spirit. Friedrich expressed the principle in these words:

> If preaching is true proclamation in which God is at work, so that His rule is a reality, then signs and wonders occur. It is not that miracles usher in the new age. Miracles take place because the efficacious Word of God has declared the divine rule, and in it everything is sound and well. . . . [And] the important thing is the message which effects it. . . . Hence the NT crowd is not simply astonished at the miracles. . . . It is also astonished at the doctrine or word proclaimed.[2]

Therefore, when the *kerygma* was preached, miraculous results occurred. The most glorious miracle of all was the conversion of lost sinners. Preaching in the biblical sense does not attempt to persuade hearers by clever oration. True preaching does far more: the Word comes in "demonstration of the Spirit and of power" (1 Cor. 2:4).[3] The reason for such a "demonstration" is clear: "That your faith might not rest in the wisdom of men but in the power of God" (1 Cor. 2:5). Once more Friedrich is helpful: "The foolish message of Jesus crucified saves those who believe. . . . [It is a] message with a very definite content. The gospel of Paul is identical with that which Jesus Himself preached during His earthly life."[4]

When we thus read in 1 Corinthians about the "foolishness" of the *kerygma*, even through the emphasis in Paul's mind at that moment was probably on the content of the message (hence the RSV and other translations render it "what we preach"),[5] this by no means implies there is no active power or expected results as the proclamation is heralded. To the contrary, conversions are to be fully anticipated. Paul could thus say to the Romans, the gospel is "the power of God for salvation" (1:16). That leads to a brief look at *euaggelion*.

Euaggelion

This key word also holds a host of ideas. In its earliest usage in the Greek world, it simply meant a "reward for good news."[6] Later it developed into a more specific, technical term meaning "news of victory."[7]

The term paints a graphic picture: a messenger appears and raises his right hand holding a beautiful palm branch. With face shinning and the other hand lifting up a spear bedecked with a laurel wreath, he calls out in a loud triumphant voice, "Victory!" The city goes wild! Sacrificial feasts are held. The temples are draped in garlands. The herald is highly honored. Good news has arrived at his hands.[8]

In the oldest Greek Old Testament, the Septuagint, two words appear: the feminine *he euaggelia* meaning good news and the plural of *euaggelion* meaning reward for good news. The good news causes great joy, for the word carries power and brings about rewarding results.

Of course, the New Testament gives the term the full meaning intended. The four Gospel writers employed it to connote the essence of the entire teaching-preaching ministry of Jesus, whether or not Jesus Himself actually used the word. The gospel is fully equated with Jesus Christ and the kingdom He came to usher in.

Gospel stands as a favorite term of Paul. Actually, the majority of the New Testament passages where the word occurs are found in the Pauline corpus. The apostle used the term in a threefold sense. As Gerhard Friedrich pointed out: "It describes the act of proclamation: 2 C. 8:18; praise at the preaching of the Gospel Phil. 4:15; the beginning of activity as an evangelist, 2 C. 2:12."[9] Paul, following the line of traditional usage, implied both the content of the news and the effect of the proclamation when he employed *euaggelion*. This principle was obviously most important for all the biblical writers. Friedrich made that clear:

> The Gospel does not merely bear witness to a historical event. . . . Nor does it consist only of narratives and sayings concerning Jesus which every Christian must know, and it certainly does not consist in a dogmatic formula alien to the world. On the contrary, it is related to human reality and proves itself to be living power. . . . The Gospel does not merely bear witness to salvation history; it is itself salvation history. It breaks into the life of man, refashions it and creates communities. . . . Through the Gospel God calls men to salvation.[10]

This principle is not meant to imply there is no definite theological, historical content in the gospel. Paul's word in 1 Corinthians 15:1-4, makes it plain that theology is important:

> Now I would remind you, brethren, in what terms I preached to you the gospel, which you received, in which you stand, by which you are saved, if you hold it fast—unless you believed in vain.
>
> For I delivered to you as of first importance what I also received, that Christ died for our sins in accordance with the Scriptures, that he was buried, that he was raised on the third day in accordance with the Scriptures.

That speaks of content, but it is powerful content. The Holy Spirit takes the historical events of Jesus Christ and brings them home to the heart and thereby effects conversions. The evangelist, therefore, must keep both aspects of the gospel in dynamic balance. If one fails to do so, a swing to either a rigid scholasticism or an existentialism with no objective mooring becomes inevitable. Such a swing either way perverts the gospel and leads to evangelistic disaster. Paul knew the gospel contained both theological facts and Spirit-filled power. Therefore, when one sums up the gospel, several significant truths immediately surface:

1. The gospel brings salvation (Eph. 1:3).
2. The gospel brings the kingdom of God (Luke 4:21).
3. The gospel brings immortality to light (2 Tim. 1:10).
4. The gospel brings affliction (2 Tim. 1:8).
5. The gospel brings truth (Col. 1:5).
6. The gospel brings grace (Acts 20:24).
7. The gospel brings peace (Eph. 6:15).
8. The gospel brings labor (Col. 3:17).
9. The gospel brings responsibility (1 Thess. 2:4).
10. The gospel brings God (Rom. 15:16).

Simply put, the gospel brings everything that pertains to life in the God-given sense because it brings men and women face-to-face with Jesus Christ. This is why it is called the "eternal gospel" (Rev. 14:6). *Kerygma* and *euaggelion* are obviously most significant terms.

Now we need to answer the question raised at the outset: What is the actual content of the proclamation, the good news?

The Content of Evangelistic Proclamation

Although few appreciate the type of proclamation that grows out of a bigoted and narrow dogmatism, there must be no "uncertain sound" when the gospel is declared. As Webster reminded us:

A mood of uncertainty about the heart of the Gospel, the Lord of the Church, and the Savior of the world, is unworthy of Christians and bodes ill for the future of missions if it is allowed or encouraged to persist. Describing the first mission to Thessalonica St. Paul wrote: "When we brought you the Gospel, we brought it not in mere words but in the power of the Holy Spirit, *and with strong conviction,* as you know well" (I Thess. 1:5, NEB). Christian, even theological, humility is not synonymous with vagueness (Webster's italics).[11]

What then is the message? What is the "foolishness of our proclamation" (1 Cor. 1:21, NRSV) God uses to save the lost?

C. H. Dodd's Approach to the Kerygma

Ever since C. H. Dodd gave us *The Apostolic Preaching and Its Development*,[12] much interest in New Testament studies has centered on the *kerygma*.[13] Dodd approaches this central concept by first making a rather rigid distinction between *kerygma* and *didaskein*. *Didaskein* he defined as "teaching"—ethical and moral instructions on the Christian life. *Didaskein* certainly contains theological doctrine and apologetics, but *didaskein* is quite distinct from "proclamation." *Kerygma* is essentially the public declaration of Christianity to the non-Christian world with the view of converting that world. Dodd told us that much of the so-called preaching in the contemporary church would not have been recognized by the early Christians as *kerygma*. What is heard in large measure on Sunday morning in many congregations is either teaching, exhortation (*paraklesis*), or a *homilia*, that is, a discussion on the Christian life directed to those who already believe.

Dodd contended that proclamation, in the New Testament sense of the word, has for its content the gospel of Jesus Christ. He deduced:

> For the early church, then, to preach the Gospel was by no means the same thing as to deliver moral instruction or exhortation. While the church was concerned to hand on the teaching of the Lord, it was not by this that it made converts. It was by *kerygma*, said Paul, not by *didache*, that it pleased God to save men.[14]

Dodd discerned six basic elements in the *kerygma* in early Acts. First, the age of fulfillment has dawned. The messianic age has come (Acts 2:16). Second, this new age has come through the ministry, death, and resurrection of Jesus Christ. Moreover, a brief account of these central acts of Christ's passion is always given. The concepts of the Davidic descent, the Lord's ministry of healing and helping, His vicarious death, and His glorious resurrection are presented without fail. Further, these truths are presented in the context of scriptural prophecy fulfilled as determined by the foreknowledge of God. Third, by virtue of the resurrection, Jesus has been elevated to the right hand of God as messianic head of the new "Israel" (Acts 2:33-36). In the fourth place, the Holy Spirit is given as the sign of Christ's present power and glory (Acts 2:33). Fifth, the messianic age will reach its consummation in the return of Christ (Acts 3:21). Sixth, the *kerygma* in early Acts closes with an appeal for repentance, the offer of forgiveness, the gift of the Holy Spirit, and the assurance of salvation in the life of the age to come (Acts 2:38-39). This emphasis had relevance to the Jewish mind-set. Dodd then summarized, "We may take it that this is what the author of Acts meant by 'preaching the kingdom of God.' "[15]

Dodd saw some development upon the early Jerusalem proclamation in the *kerygma* of Paul. The apostle often spoke of "my gospel." He had a very definite view of the content of the proclamation. Not only that, he uttered a curse on anyone who declared any other message contrary to his gospel. He told the Galatians:

> But even if we, or an angel from heaven, should preach to you a gospel contrary to that which we preached to you, let him be accursed. As we have said before, so now I say again, if any one is preaching to you a gospel contrary to that which you received, let him be accursed (Gal. 1:8-9).

Those were very strong words. The apostle must have had great confidence in the *kerygma* as he understood it, and he was prepared to defend it at all cost. How did he view the message to be proclaimed? Paul's gospel, according to C. H. Dodd, can be summarized as follows:
1. The prophecies are fulfilled, and the new age is inaugurated by the coming of Christ.
2. He was born of the seed of David.
3. He died according to the Scriptures to deliver us out of the present evil age.
4. He was buried.
5. He rose on the third day according to the Scriptures.
6. He is exalted at the right hand of God, as Son of God and Lord of [the] quick and dead.
7. He will come again as Judge and Savior.[16]
Dodd granted that the evangelistic message of Paul probably contained more than the above, but it had at least these seven points if it could be called evangelistic proclamation at all.

   To contrast the Pauline proclamation to the Gentiles with the "Jerusalem *kerygma*" makes it clear that Paul emphasized three things which are not explicit in the preaching found in the early chapters of Acts. First of all, in early Acts Jesus is not normally called the "Son of God." His titles are more in line with the prophecies of Isaiah. But Dodd admitted that the idea of Jesus as Son of God is deeply embodied in the Synoptic Gospels, and the first three books of the New Testament were probably little influenced by Paul. Thus the preachers of Acts were certainly not adverse to the idea of Jesus as Son of God, but they were preaching to Jews, hence Old Testament terminology was more relevant and communicable. Second, the Jerusalem *kerygma* as over against Paul's preaching does little in declaring that Christ died *for* our sins. As Dodd put it, "The result of the life, death, and resurrection of Christ is the forgiveness of sins, but this forgiveness is not specifically connected with his death."[17] Third, the Jerusalem *kerygma* does not emphatically assert the ascended

Lord intercedes for us, as does Paul. As for the rest of the points in Paul's gospel, they are all found in the early sermons of Acts.

The reasons for the contrast between the Jerusalem and Pauline *kerygma* are obvious. Paul was preaching primarily to Gentiles. Presenting Jesus as Son of God rather than Messiah was far more relevant. Furthermore, Paul had time to work out a theory of the atonement relative to the cross. Consequently, he could say, "Christ died for us," that is, *for* our sins (see Rom. 5:6-11). In the days of the early Jerusalem proclamation, time simply did not allow for that sort of theological reflection. The practical implications for today are clear: good evangelism is relevant and thoughtful.

Since the time Dodd wrote his classic, bookshelves have been filled with volumes that build upon his essential thesis. Wide and varied have been the approaches in these works. Criticism and development of Dodd's ideas have naturally arisen. Michael Green is a case in point.

Michael Green and the Kerygma

Green began his presentation by an analysis of Dodd. He argued, "There has been undue concentration on what has become technically known as the '*kerygma.*' "[18] He held that Dodd made the *kerygma* far too wooden and fixed. At one point, Green raised the question as to whether there was a fixed *kerygma* at all. He argued that "the probabilities of the situation would militate against undue fixity in the presentation of the message."[19] What is to be grasped, Green contended, is that the background and understanding of the listeners significantly determined which aspect of the truth of Christ was to be shared. Green was not alone in this contention. Professor C. F. D. Moule in his book *The Birth of the New Testament* and Eduard Schweizer in an essay found in *Current Issues in New Testament Interpretation* take this line of argumentation. Perhaps the best treatment of this idea is found in R. C. Worley's work *Preaching and Teaching in the Early Church*. According to Green:

> It would be a mistake to assume from studies such as those of Dodd that there was a crippling uniformity about the proclamation of Christian truth in antiquity. That there was a basic homogeneity in what was preached we may agree, but there was wide variety in the way it was presented. Nor was this variety always the result of the supposedly rigid and conflicting theologies which were prevalent in different sections of the ancient Church. . . . But much of the variety will have been necessitated by the needs and understanding of the hearers. Evangelism is never proclamation in a vacuum; but always to people, and the message must be given in terms that make sense to them.[20]

Still, Green granted, there was a "basic homogeneity" in what was preached. What then was this "basic homogeneity" as Green saw it? He suggested three basic points as essential to the Word the first-century church proclaimed.

First, the early church preached a Person. Their message was frankly and unapologetically Christocentric. This gospel message was not so much on Jesus' life and public ministry; rather, it centered on His death and glorious resurrection.

In the second place, Green held that the infant church proclaimed the gift of forgiveness, the gift of the Holy Spirit, and the gracious gift of adoption and reconciliation. That kind of grace made "no people" the "people of God." Concerning the idea of gift in the gospel, the emphasis was placed upon the gift of forgiveness and the gift of the Holy Spirit.

Third, the first-century church looked for a positive response on the part of its hearers. The apostles were anything but shy in asking people to decide then and there, for or against, Christ. They expected results. These early preachers declared all people must do three things in the light of the gospel:

1. They must repent. This was first and foremost.
2. They must exercise faith. A continuing life of faith was called for, but it must begin by a "leap of faith." Moreover, true faith was viewed as inseparable from repentance.
3. The apostles preached baptism. This act of obedience was seen as the seal on God's offer of forgiveness and the essence of one's response to that offer in repentance and faith.

Green thus presented his understanding of the *kerygma*, and though there is probably validity in his criticism of Dodd's rather inflexible approach, it is clear he also saw the essential proclamation as a definable, propositional body of theological truth.

James Stewart and the Kerygma

Another interesting approach to the theme of proclamation is found in James Stewart's work. In his helpful book *A Faith to Proclaim*, Stewart declared the first axiom of evangelism is that the evangelist must be sure of his message. However, he did not, on his own admission, attempt to traverse again the ground that Dodd and others have done in attempting to discover the primitive *kerygma*. His purpose was to find the bearing the *kerygma* has on present-day questions. From this pragmatic perspective, Stewart presented what he felt was the essential gospel proclamation. He raised the key issue:

What, then, was the essence of this proclamation by the original heralds of the faith? Quite briefly it was this. They proclaimed that prophecy was fulfilled; that in Jesus of Nazareth, in His words and deeds, His life and death and resurrection, the new age had arrived; that God had exalted

Him, that He would come again as Judge, and that now was the day of salvation.[21]

From the above statement Stewart derived five principles that should be found in all evangelistic proclamation. It begins with the evangelist proclaiming the *incarnation*. The facts of the *kerygma* are historical facts, that is, the doctrine of the incarnation means that "God has come right into the midst of the tumult and the shouting of this world."[22] Furthermore, the facts of the incarnation are not only historic, they are unique. The kingdom of God, itself, has actually broken into the here and now. That is unique and unrepeatable.

The evangelist also proclaims *forgiveness*. This truth is always relevant to people's lives, for "wherever the Church truly proclaims the forgiveness of sins there the healing ministry is veritably at work."[23] The feeling of meaninglessness and "cosmic loneliness" which is characteristic of our existentially oriented society must be recognized as essentially a problem of sin. Iniquity stands as the ultimate culprit in the contemporary loss of identity and feelings of utter futility, for sin separates one from God who is the source of all meaning. Therefore, as the church preaches forgiveness it strikes at the heart of many present-day problems. This brings the modern-day application of the gospel to the fore.

In the third place, Stewart stated that the proclaimer preaches the *cross*. The veil has been rent, the veil which kept people out of God's presence and that which shut God in. The darkness and mystery of God's "wholly otherness" has now been opened. Reality can be touched. As Stewart expressed it: "The death of Christ gives me the very heart of the eternal, because it is not words at all, not even sublime prophetic utterance: it is an act, God's act, against which I can batter all my doubts to pieces. We preach Christ crucified, God's truth revealed."[24] Moreover, the cross speaks of atonement, guilt-bearing, and expiation. Not only that, the demonic forces of the universe were once and for all defeated. Christ has overcome the world. "We preach Christ crucified" is always to be the cry of the evangelist (1 Cor. 1:23).

Fourth, "the hour cometh, and now is" (John 4:23). The new age, the long expected hope has taken place: *Christ has been raised*. We declare a resurrected, living Lord. "This was indeed the very core of the apostolic *kerygma*," Stewart argued.[25] It was the theme of every early Christian sermon. The fact of the resurrection was no mere appendix tacked on the end of their proclamation. The resurrection is a cosmic event. It is far more than just a personal victory for our Lord: all history was shattered by this creative act of God Almighty. The resurrection means the whole world has died, and a glorious rebirth has taken place. Nothing can ever be the same again. It must be clear, the apostolic message did not see

Good Friday and Easter as two isolated events; they were always presented as one mighty stroke of God, but now time has been baptized into eternity. Things on this side have been immersed into things on the other. God has effected His great act of justification. Stewart contended, "This is our gospel. For this is what Christianity essentially is—a religion of Resurrection."[26]

Finally, and in summary, Stewart declared the evangelist simply proclaims *Christ*. The message is not a cold, conceptualized theology or philosophy. A Person is preached, and He is the Helper, Shepherd, Companion, Friend, Light, and Bread of life, our *Paraclete*. If Christianity is anything, it is an experience of a vital relationship to a living Christ. This is the great discovery the world needs to make. How different contemporary society would become if it truly understood what the Christ event means.

Stewart thus cast the *kerygma* in a pragmatic context. He applied all the essentials of the gospel to the living human situation. Surely this is what must be done in actual proclamation. Believers must thoroughly understand the message theologically, but it must be related in terms that addresses the *kerygma* to real life.

Douglas Webster and the Kerygma

Douglas Webster in *Yes to Mission* presented his grasp of the *kerygma* in four basic principles. He began by reminding us that "mission implies that the church does have something to say."[27] He stated that evangelistic preaching must center upon:

1. "The person and character of Jesus Christ. He really did live."[28] He was unique above all men.
2. "The teaching of Jesus Christ. He said certain things about God, about life, about the Kingdom of God, and about human destiny . . . [as] no one had [ever] spoken before."[29]
3. "The death of Jesus Christ. The death of our Lord was a turning point in history. . . and God was active in it."[30]
4. The resurrection of Jesus Christ. Death did not end it all for the Lord, rather it was the end of death, for He is a living Savior.

Webster correctly pointed out that though some may wish to add more to the gospel than the above four essential points, it is certain that "we cannot have less, if we are to retain the Gospel at all."[31]

Conzelmann and the Kerygma

From a more critical perspective, Hans Conzelmann has told us: "No primitive Christian preaching has been transmitted to us. But the gist of the preaching is to be found in the epistles, from which types and patterns can still be reconstructed."[32] What then, according to Conzelmann, are these "types and patterns" of the primitive *kerygma*? He stated:

(*a*) Promise of salvation . . . This pattern, recognizable in Romans, Galatians, Colossians and Ephesians, depicts the primacy of the saving event (of the gospel); this is actualized in ethics.

(*b*) The connection with scripture appears in surveys of the history of the people of God which end with a didactic conclusion: Acts 7; 13.1ff.; Heb. 11; cf. I Clement.

(*c*) The newness of Christian existence in contrast to the past is depicted in the pattern 'once-now'; once Gentiles in blasphemy and darkness, now enlightened (Rom. 7.5; Gal. 4.3ff.). Paganism is not described neutrally, but is evaluated exclusively from the perspective of what is new.[33]

We need to be reminded right here that several critical New Testament scholars today would view much of the foregoing study of theologians like Dodd, Green, Stewart, and Webster as in some sense missing the target. They feel the implied historicity of all the elements of the primitive *kerygma* are so dubious that to undertake an exercise like the above diverts the whole point and purpose of the *kerygma*. The proclamation, in their thinking, is primarily and simply a dynamic existential experience of the living Christ. Therefore, they argue, the historical rootage in actual fact of the various elements of the *kerygma* are unimportant. Coming from the Heidiggerian existential philosophy of Heidegger, they agree that Christians should preach Jesus because the early church did, but the actual historicity of such declarations as death and resurrection are not important to the *kerygma*. The historical Jesus is not a vital consideration; it is the Christ of the *kerygma* people encounter in the proclamation that is the essence of the preaching. For example, concerning the actual historicity of the resurrection of Jesus, Hugh Anderson stated, "Our source material with the witness to specific historical events and concrete details, events and details which the historian, when put to this acid test, has seemed quite incapable of verifying."[34]

The weakness of such extreme existential positions continues to be seen. Even the "new quest of the historical Jesus" motif of the school that in some respects grew out of the older Bultmannian approach falls short. Those arguments will not be traced again. I accept the genuine historicity of the *kerygmatic* events and declare them as essential redemptive acts because that is exactly what the early church believed and did; and they did it in the wisdom, inspiration, and power of the Spirit.

Lessons from the Study

Now what is to be learned from these varied approaches to the *keryg-ma*? Two lessons seem vital. To begin with, whether we take a more rigid view of men like Dodd or a more flexible approach similar to Green or Webster, there is still an essential and basic content to evangelistic proc-lamation if it is to be biblical in nature. There are certain theological and historical redemptive realities to be clearly understood and declared in the presentation of the message. The *kerygma* does have historical con-tent; it is more than an existential encounter as Conzelmann, Bultmann, and others would tell us. The German school has tended to emphasize strongly the existential, experiential elements in proclaiming Christ. Consequently, the objective truth of Jesus Christ all but gets lost at times. For Bultmann, all that matters is: we die with Christ. The English school, Dodd, Stewart, and others, stresses the historical, objective side as well. Although no one wishes to eliminate the demand for an existen-tial response to the gospel, there is history and objective truth in the proclamation.

The balance between the cognitive content of truth and the experien-tial element of coming to know God is beautifully displayed in Paul's prayer for the Ephesian church (3:17-18). In his intercession Paul prayed that "being rooted and grounded in love" they might be able "to com-prehend" (*katalabesthai*, that is, with the mind) the breadth, length, height, and depth of God's love, and "to know" (*gnonai*, that is, know by experience) his love which "passes all knowledge." This is how one is thus "filled with all the fullness of God." A balance between objective truth and subjective experience predicated on that truth must be kept at the heart of the *kerygma*, for that is what the term means. This sort of proclamation has impact and effect. Moreover, the objective aspects of the *kerygma* center in the historic person and salvific work of Jesus Christ.

Second, it must be stressed that evangelistic proclamation must con-tain the essential *kerygma* to expect God's full blessings upon Christian communication. Today, much that goes on in the name of evangelism seems rather bereft of the biblical content of the *kerygma*. Mere appeals to the imagination and emotions are not what the New Testament un-derstands by preaching. "We preach Christ" (1 Cor. 1:23). This is to be the theme in all our attempts to win people to faith. Great gospel procla-mation, if it is true to the biblical idea, must be filled with dynamic *kerygmatic* content.

Furthermore, the message and ministry of evangelism must not be-come equated with other aspects of Christian ministry, as legitimate and vital as those aspects of ministry may be. In other words, evangelism must not be understood as *any* sort of ministry. There is a definite, specific work the Bible defines as evangelism *per se*. The broadening out of the *kerygma* to include social ministries, for example, can often dilute evangelism so that it tends to lose its punch. As a case in point, the contemporary "liberation theology" has at times leaned in that direction. John R. W. Stott addressed that issue at the International Congress on World Evangelization in Lausanne:

> The salvation which Christ brought, and in which we participate, offers the comprehensive wholeness in this divided life . . . God's liberating power changes both persons and structures . . . therefore we see the struggle for economic justice, political freedom and cultural renewal as elements in the total liberation of the world through the mission of God. Humanization, development, wholeness, liberation, justice: let me say at once that all these are not only desirable goals, but that Christians should be actively involved in pursuing them, and that we Evangelicals have often been guilty of opting out of such social and political responsibilities. We are to blame for this neglect. We should repent of it and not be afraid to challenge ourselves and each other that God may be calling many more of us than hear His call to immerse ourselves in the secular world of politics, economics, sociology, race relations, preventive medicine, development and a host of other such spheres for Christ.
>
> But these things do not constitute the salvation which God is offering the world in and through Christ. They could be included in "the mission of God," in so far as Christians are giving themselves to serve in these fields. But to call socio-political liberation salvation and to call social activism "evangelism"—this is to be guilty of a gross theological confusion. It is to mix what Scripture keeps distinct—God the Creator and God the Redeemer, justice and justification, common grace and saving grace, the reformation of society and the regeneration of man. It is significant that the main, Biblical argument with which . . . [some try] to buttress . . . [their] position was the liberation of Israel from the oppression of Egypt, which is not only an embarrassing topic for residents in the Middle East, but a misuse of Scripture. The Exodus was the redemption of God's covenant people. It is used in Scripture as a foreshadowing of redemption from sin through Christ. It offers no conceivable justification or pattern of national liberation movements today.[35]

Social liberation and action—or any other aspect of Christian ministry—has a legitimate place in the service of Christ; however, such cannot be equated with doing evangelism. It can certainly become the context of evangelistic proclamation, but it is not evangelizing *per se*. Social ministries are most important, but it is not evangelism in the pure biblical sense of the word.

Thus believers have a definite gospel to proclaim. It need not be defended, just proclaimed. There is an anecdote from the life of Charles H.

Spurgeon that well illustrates the point. On one occasion a young man studying for the ministry asked the great London preacher how to defend the gospel. Spurgeon insightfully responded with a question: "How do you defend a lion?" Obviously, one does not; the lion can defend itself. So can the gospel!

This, of course, does not mean to ignore Peter's admonition, "Always be prepared to make a defense to any one who calls you to account for the hope that is in you" (1 Pet. 3:15). Believers should be ready to present a rationale, an apologetic, to those who think the gospel is foolish (1 Cor. 1:21). The discipline of apologetics is most important, especially in a secular age; but in the final analysis, all argumentation at best only knocks down other human arguments. It does not convince of God's truth without the Spirit's work. The gospel itself is as a strong lion of truth, and when borne home to the human heart by the Spirit of God, barriers are broken down; people see their need and the ultimate solution to their problems in the glorious gospel of Jesus Christ.

One of the tragedies of the current hour, however, is that the same detractors of the orthodox gospel number themselves in the ranks of the church. Therefore, in Marvin Anderson's words, there will always be a need to engage in the "Battle for the Gospel."[36] Renaissance humanism initiated the ongoing battle and gave us two results, one most positive, one quite negative.

The positive factor led to a new hermeneutical approach to the Scriptures. The old allegorical method was sloughed off, the original texts were critically examined, outmoded traditions were questioned in the light of the light of the Bible and its times, and the gospel was thereby well served. The Reformation itself used the principles of historical criticism, but new exciting things have a way of getting out of control. The historical critical approach in humanistic hands became far too rational and empirical. Eventually, for the more radical humanist, the gospel itself was lost. This is the battle faced today, and Christians ought to defend the essential gospel of Christ at any cost. There have been those who gave their lives for it. Can believers today do less?

At the same time, however, Christians must never subtly become negative and polemical. The gospel is good news: it is "good," and it is "news" to many. God has designed it for positive proclamation. Therefore, with a firm grip on the essential *kerygma*, may every Christian evangelize in the power of the Holy Spirit. But, how is that done effectively so as actually to win people to faith in Christ?

The Methodology of Effective Proclamation

As important and fundamental as the content of *kerygma* is in evangelistic communication, that in itself alone falls short of the whole story of effective proclamation. The proper spiritual dynamic is vital to the success of evangelistic declaration. Proclamation is more than merely a means of conveying the content of the Christian faith. Declaring the gospel becomes a unique activity in the Christian context, whether it be formal preaching, personal witnessing, writing, use of the media, or any other means of communication. True evangelization is an event: an event wherein God meets sinners. Proclamation is a form of God addressing Himself to people in their need. As H. H. Farmer put it:

> Preaching is telling me something. But it is not merely *telling* me something. It is God actively probing me, challenging my will, calling on me for decision, offering me His succour, through the only medium which the nature of His purpose permits Him to use, the medium of a personal relationship. It is as though, to adapt the Apostle's words, "God did beseech me by you." It is God's "I—thou" relationship with me carried on your "I—thou" relationship with me, both together coming out of the heart of His saving purpose which is moving on through history to its consummation in His Kingdom.[37]

Right here the distinctive nature of effective evangelistic proclamation appears. This is why it can be seen in some sense as a sacrament. Proclamation is only distinctively Christian communication insofar as it is both uttered and listened to in faith. In other words, evangelization is, in the final analysis, God's activity. God encounters men and women in the extreme and supreme crisis of their lives. Real preaching depends upon the communication conveying the sense of the living, saving activity of God in Christ.

It should be said here, incidentally, the distinction between *kerygma* and *didache* is not to imply the two never blend as Dodd seems to hold. Nor should this distinction be understood as dictating methods of communication. The preacher in the pulpit can be in the context of *didache*, and a layperson in dialogue with one individual can surely be in the spirit of proclamation. *Kerygma* is not to be understood as always a monologue, nor is *didache* always dialogue. What is to be sought is communicating the truth in the method the immediate situation calls for. And as emphasized above, declaring God's Word is to be done in faith and heard in faith. This implies that all genuine Christian communication is something of a dialogue whether it be *kerygma* or *didache*. And, of course, there are personal and social ministries that play a vital role in evangelism.

These principles of Christian communication indicate a number of things. Initially, it should be understood that proclamation of the gospel is to be viewed as a personal encounter. God confronts people in the communicative situation on a Person-to-person level. As Farmer expressed it, "God's 'I—Thou' relationship with me is never apart from, but is always in a measure carried by, my 'I—thou' relationship with my fellows."[38]

In this light one can see the position of the proclaimer. In the first place, the herald must be intimately related to God in an "I—thou" sense. If one loses the reality of God's presence in proclamation, all is lost. Not only that, the Christian communicator is also to be dynamically related to the hearers in this "I—thou" manner of understanding relationships. The proclaimer stands, as it were, at the corner of a right-angle triangle, being related vertically to God and horizontally to the hearers. In the context of this setting, God completes the triangle and confronts and addresses people. Moreover, there is give and take in all directions on the triangle. It is an existential encounter *par excellence*: existential as the Bible presents the dynamic of existential encounter. As Miller observed, "Men . . . are confronted by the living Christ himself, who chooses to make his eternal redemptive deed effectual by making the word of the preacher become his own word in the fellowship of the members of his body."[39]

The immediate implication of this kind of declaration is that proclamation is costly. Effective sharing does not come easy. The very giving of oneself is involved. That has its price! Effective proclaimers pour out themselves to God on the vertical dimension and give themselves also on the horizontal to the people. Real proclamation of the gospel can be painful when people give of themselves as they ought. It is no place to be cool and casual in spirit and attitude. It was Paul who said, "Therefore be alert, remembering that for three years I did not cease night or day to admonish every one with tears" (Acts 20:31).

Therefore, the proclaimer must keep God and people—not just truth—in view. People must be seen as central as should be pointed to God. Christ is not declared in a vacuum. The proclamation of Christ is to people. To them the saving message is addressed in love, compassion, and understanding, with an attempt to relate to them meaningfully. Believers speak to people in their real-life situation. Thus, all other aspects of methodology are secondary to the basic existential situation described. The Christian witness should understand and attempt to cultivate people where they are in life, for this is the context in which God works in bringing people to faith.

Therefore, a word about the person who declares God's message is in order here. Dr. Raymond Brown reminded us that the effective proclaimer today must have three essential qualities. He or she must first be an acute observer. It takes more than just understanding the Scriptures to be an effective witness in today's world. The proclaimer must be a student of contemporary society. The late D. T. Niles said, "If we want to talk with God we had better find out something about the world because that is the only subject in which God is interested."[40] The same surely is true if Christians want to speak *for* God. Roger Schutz has correctly confessed that often "we allow ourselves to be caught up in a Christian environment that we find congenial and in the process create a ghetto of like-minded people who are quite unmindful of the real world."[41] Believers are to witness to real people in real life.

The proclaimer should also be a compassionate listener. As Brown put it: "Before he talks he must learn again to listen."[42] Witnesses for Christ listen on a twofold level: one must listen to God, and also listen to people. How can one effectively communicate unless one is genuinely open to both? We need to emulate the spirit of Ezekiel when he said, "I sat where they sat, and remained there astonished among them" (Ezek. 3:15, KJV). That was where the prophet learned to be God's spokesman.

Finally, the witness for Christ ought to be a discerning teacher. The need is obvious. If ever there were a day of alarming ignorance concerning the Word of God, this is that day. May God make of His spokesmen those who are faithfully "holding forth the word of life" (Phil. 2:16).

Conclusion

By way of summary, the effective witness is simply a man or woman of God declaring His Word. Proclaimers are those who walk with God and share His message. Good witnesses know by daily experience the One for whom they speak, and they speak with relevance to real people. As Farmer has said, "I suppose in the end the secret lies in the quality of our own spiritual life and the extent to which we are ourselves walking humbly with God in Christ."[43] Effective proclaimers know the Lord and His powerful "word of the cross."

Notes

1. Gerhard Friedrich, *"kerux (hierokerux), kerusso, keruagma, prokerusso"* in *Theological Dictionary of the New Testament*, 10 vols. (Grand Rapids: William B. Eerdmans Publishing Co., 1964), 3:714.

2. Ibid.

3. That is not meant necessarily to rule out the "signs and wonders" that took place throughout Acts and take place today, even if some have overemphasized the fact.

4. Friedrich, *Theological Dictionary* 3:716.

5. It may be true the KJV rendering of 1 Corinthians 1:21 is somewhat misleading in translating *kerygma* "preaching." That seems to put all the emphasis on the act, not the content of the preaching.

6. Friedrich, *Theological Dictionary* 2:722.

7. Ibid.

8. Ibid.

9. Ibid., 729.

10. Ibid., 731. One must be cautious here and not denigrate the historical realities to which the gospel gives witness, as some have done.

11. Douglas Webster, *Yes to Mission* (London: SCM Press, Ltd., 1966), 20.

12. The concern here is not with the strengths and weaknesses of Dodd's "realized eschatology." The help Dodd gives is in the study of the *kerygma*. His systematizing of the various elements of the proclamation and the subsequent impact of his findings is most significant.

13. The author follows his own work: *Leading Your Church in Evangelism* (Nashville, Broadman Press, 1975), 95-106.

14. C. H. Dodd, *The Apostolic Preaching and Its Development* (London: Hodder and Stoughton, 1936), 8.

15. Ibid., 24.

16. Ibid., 17.

17. Ibid., 25.

18. Green, *Evangelism in the Early Church*, 48.

19. Ibid., 61.

20. Ibid., 115.

21. James S. Stewart, *A Faith to Proclaim* (New York: Charles Scribners' Sons, 1953), 14-15.

22. Ibid., 18.

23. Ibid., 50.

24. Ibid., 82.

25. Ibid., 104.

26. Ibid., 110.

27. Webster, *Yes to Mission*, 18.

28. Ibid.

29. Ibid., 19.

30. Ibid.

31. Ibid.

32. Hans Conzelmann, *An Outline of the Theology of the New Testament* (London: SCM Press, Ltd., 1969), 88. It is interesting that Conzelmann does not see the sermons in Acts as primitive preaching, even if he rejects the authorship Luke assigns them.

33. Ibid., 88-89.

34. Hugh Anderson, *Jesus and Christian Origins* (New York: Oxford University Press, 1964), 187. Despite this statement, Anderson is not as radical as some, for example, Rudolf Bultmann. Anderson saw the danger in Bultmann of "undervaluing the theological significance of the historical Jesus."

35. *Evangelicals* (Australia: Continuation Committee, International Congress on World Evangelization, 1975), 41-42. It seems a gross presumption to dismiss liberation theology in such a few words, especially in the light of its impact today—especially in Latin America. However, space dictates it. Further, much has been written on the subject.

36. See Marvin W. Anderson, *The Battle for the Gospel* (Grand Rapids: Baker Book House, 1978).

37. Ibid., 22.

38. Hubert H. Farmer, *The Servant of the Word* (New York: Charles Scribner's Sons, 1942), 27-28.

39. Ibid., 56.

40. Donald H. Miller, *Fire in Thy Mouth* (New York: Abingdon Press, 1954), 34.

41. From an unpublished lecture, "Preaching Today," presented by Raymond Brown at Spurgeon's College, London.

42. Ibid.

43. Ibid.

44. Farmer, *Servant of the Word*, 90.

8

The Goal of God's Grace: *Soteria* Salvation

"By grace you have been saved" (Eph. 2:8).

Introduction

"Saved, Saved" is a hymn that continues to be sung because the dramatic word *saved* speaks volumes. Many books have been written on the meaning of salvation. The grace of God in redemption is fathomless. Thus it seems rather presumptuous to attempt to cover such a profound subject in one short chapter. Yet, this entire book is actually a work on salvation. This particular chapter, therefore, will attempt to cover only those aspects of salvation not discussed elsewhere, realizing that it still has only "touched the fringe of [the] garment." Still, that touch helped the woman of old (Luke 8:43-48).

The Meaning of Salvation

Salvation (Hebrew: *Yesha'*, Greek: *soteria*, from which we derive our English theological word *soteriology*) is revealed in the Bible in a threefold manner, particularly in the New Testament. It is presented as historical: people are saved by God's action in one's personal history through the person of Jesus Christ. This aspect of redemption takes place in a moment of time (Eph. 2:8; Titus 3:5). Salvation is also "present tense" in that it becomes a continuing experience of deliverance from sin, guilt, and judgment. That is, salvation is moral, ethical, and spiritual (Phil. 2:12; Heb. 2:3). Finally, salvation is eschatological. Redemption will be consummated in the perfecting of the moral life and in the resurrection of the body at the return of the Lord (Rom. 13:11; Rev. 12:10). As it has been expressed, being saved is past, present, and future; or, the spirit has been saved, the life (soul) is being saved, and the body shall be saved in the resurrection. In a word, God's salvation is all-inclusive and all-encompassing. The total person is saved by God's fathomless grace. When one says, "I am saved," he or she is making life's most profound statement. What does it all mean? Again, a word study is a good place to seek some initial answers.

Etymologically, the term *salvation* in its various forms connotes concepts like "safe," " 'to make safe or sound,' . . . 'to deliver from a direct threat,' . . . 'to bring safe and sound out of a difficult situation,' "[1] "keeping," and "benefiting." The word is very broadly used and obviously covers a multitude of situations. It was employed in common everyday speech as well as by philosophers and religionists.

Religious connotations abound in the various uses of *soteria*. For example, in the Greek pagan world it meant "an acutely dynamic act in which gods or men snatch others by force from serious peril."[2] At times, the ideas of *keeping, benefiting,* and even *pardoning* are attached to the term.

In the Old Testament, the concept of "deliverance from a bad situation," "to free," or "the experience of help," and similar ideas predominated.[3] The actual Hebrew stem meant originally "to be roomy, broad."[4] To be hemmed in is most uncomfortable, to be given space or room is to be *delivered;* hence, the idea of salvation as help to escape from a difficult situation arose. It can refer to freedom from disease (Isa. 38:20), from trouble (Jer. 30:7), or from enemies (2 Sam. 3:18).

The Old Testament Scriptures are consistent in the belief which views deliverance into space and room as coming essentially from God. A person without strength needs deliverance (Job 26:2). They may well be oppressed and ready to fall because of being hemmed in (Job 5:4). Therefore, help is desperately needed from without, so God is called upon, and the Lord saves, delivers, opens up space, and gives one room and freedom. Only Yahweh can do that in the full sense of the word. God saves His flock (Ezek. 34:22); He rescues His people (Hos. 1:7); and He alone can save them (Hos. 13:10-14). Idols of wood and stone are of no help (Isa. 45:20). Only God gives victory (Ps. 44:3-8). God is the one who saved His people from Egypt (Ps. 106:7-10), and the exiles from Babylon (Jer. 30:10). The exodus became the archtype of God's great deliverance, and when Yahweh uses human instruments in His deliverance, even this is "connected with the idea of God's heroic strength (Ps. 80:2) and also with the concept that Yahweh is the King (Is. 33:22). . . . so the intercessor comes to God with the cry: 'save,' 'help.' "[5] Therefore, to know God is to know salvation. "God" and "Savior" are virtually synonymous terms. That is the kind of God He is.

The idea of salvation developed as the Hebrew grasp of God grew and matured. Earlier concepts of deliverance from earthly enemies and different situations gave way to the understanding of salvation in an eschatological sense of being saved to eternal life. What Israel had seen God do in the past, by faith they believed He could do in the future. He had shown Himself to be Lord of all creation; He must, therefore, be Lord of the future—even of eternity. Space forbids tracing this interesting long development, but it has been well done by others.[6] Suffice it to say, by the first century in certain strains of Judaism, the idea of eternal salvation was becoming full-blown. It found its ultimate expression in the belief that God's deliverance would come through His Savior, the Messiah. It bloomed out completely and bore final fruit in the New Testament.

In the Gospels and Epistles, *soteria* is used various ways, as in the Old Testament. In a nonreligious sense, it often connotes being saved from some sort of physical danger—much as the word is used today. The Synoptics employ the root word several times to denote the physical healings by Jesus. People were saved from the ravages of disease. Actually, our Lord's name means "deliverer" or "savior." Interesting to note is the fact that in the healings of Jesus, where the word is widely used, it denotes the healing of the whole person, not just a single member of the body; hence the phrase, "Thy faith hath saved thee" (Luke 7:50, KJV). Nonetheless, the idea of eschatological salvation is the most profound use of the term in the first three Gospels. As Foerster put it: "In the Synoptists, then, *soteria* is a future event denoting entry into the (future) kingdom of God, and yet it is also a present event in the sayings about that which was lost and is found."[7]

In the fourth Gospel, along with the Synoptics, salvation is presented as present in the person of Jesus. He is the Source and expression of God's salvation. He is "the way, and the truth, and the life" (John 14:6).

Paul's Understanding

Salvation for Paul was essentially a dynamic relationship between God and humanity. The matter is primarily spiritual, and God's saving truth is found in the Scriptures which "are able to instruct you for salvation through faith in Christ Jesus" (2 Tim. 3:15). When Paul sought God's deliverance from earthly temporal danger, he used another word entirely (*hruomai*). The content of *soteria* as Paul saw it is twofold: (1) salvation from the approaching wrath (1 Cor. 3:15; 5:5), and (2) the endowment of the saved person with the divine *doxa*, the "glory of God." The apostle did not directly merge salvation with terms like *justification, reconciliation,* and *forgiveness.* He employed *soteria* in a more restrictive sense. Still, he certainly did not exclude such ideas from the grace of God's saving mercy in Christ.

In the Pauline corpus, *soteria* also possesses a definite eschatological note. This was important to the apostle. The eschatological element in Pauline theology, however, did not rule out the present aspects of salvation. This is plain in 2 Corinthians 1:2: "Grace to you and peace from God our Father and the Lord Jesus Christ." In the Pastorals, Paul stressed the present benefits of salvation (see 1 Tim. 2:4; 2 Tim. 1:9).

In Revelation, the idea of salvation as victory predominates. In the last book of the Bible, salvation belongs to God, much like the Old Testament. The overcomers, the victorious ones, attribute their deliverance to God. After the fall of the accuser, the power and glory and victory and the kingdom all belong to God.[8]

Salvation, as used by the biblical writers, contains a multitude of marvelous realities. The idea of deliverance is so prominent in salvation, however, it must be asked what one is delivered from in the salvation of Christ. In this context, three words immediately surface: *sin, self,* and *standing judgment.*

Salvation as Deliverance from Sin

When those who heard the gospel proclaimed on the Day of Pentecost were "cut to the heart" (Acts 2:37), they cried out, "What shall we do?" Peter said they were to repent, and they would receive the "forgiveness" of their sins (v. 38). Sin, the archenemy of the human race, can be fully and finally dealt with in God's forgiving grace.

In the concept of salvation from sin, look back on the earlier study of the nature of sin (see chap. 6). To appreciate God's deliverance, one must be vividly conscious that sin alienates from God (Col. 1:21). Sin kills (Rom. 6:23), but with the many words for *sin* in the Bible, the Scriptures couple the beautiful word *forgiveness.* God's forgiveness is a pungent idea in the biblical witness.

In the Old Testament, the writers employ three words to expound God's mercy in forgiveness. *Kipper* normally connotes the idea of atonement. It is often used with the cultic practice of sacrifice. In the sacrifice of the animal the atonement is made, and sin is forgiven. The second word is *nasa'* meaning "to lift" or "carry away." The colorful picture is painted of sins being lifted up and carried off. Third, *salach* gets at the actual heart of the word *forgiveness.* God absolves sins and remembers them no more. This word is always used in conjunction with God's forgiveness.

In the old dispensation, God's forgiveness was not a light matter. Mercy was to be received with gratitude and thanksgiving. Sin deserved punishment, and the forgiven should show appreciation to the One who forgave.

How then does God forgive the offender? Yahweh is a God of grace. He is "ready to forgive" (Neh. 9:17). He is "merciful and gracious, slow to anger, and abounding in steadfast love and faithfulness" (Ex. 34:6-9). He blots out transgressions (Isa. 43:25). When God deals with sins, He deals with them completely.

In the New Testament the reality of forgiveness shines forth even more brightly. Two main verbs are used: *charizomai,* meaning "to deal graciously with," and *aphieme,* connoting "to send away" or "to loose." The noun *aphesis,* "remission," is found at times, as are *apoluo,* "to release," (Luke 6:37) and *paresis,* which means "a passing by" as used by Paul in Romans 3:25.

Forgiveness in the New Testament is clearly linked to the Christ event, especially the cross. For example, Ephesians 1:7 states: "In him we have redemption through his blood, the forgiveness of our trespasses." In a word, forgiveness rests essentially on the atonement of Christ in death and resurrection. "Through this man forgiveness of sins is pro-claimed to you" (Acts 13:38). Forgiveness on the basis of the atoning work of our Lord is a dynamic part of the essential *kerygma*.

Two important considerations grow out of the New Testament concept of forgiveness of sins. First, if believers have been forgiven, they are to forgive others. The Model Prayer clearly teaches this (Matt. 6:12), as does our Lord's parable on the ungrateful servant (Matt. 18:23-35). Peter asked the Lord how often he should forgive his brother. Jesus told him seven times seventy, that is, continually (Matt. 18:21). Our Lord went so far as to say, "If you do not forgive men their trespasses, neither will your Father forgive your trespasses" (Matt. 6:15). This is true for two reasons. One, forgiven people are grateful for their forgiveness, and it reflects in forgiving others. It is living like God. Godless people know little or nothing about forgiveness. Two, if one does not forgive, that is a sin in itself; hence, God cannot forgive the offended until the person repents and forgives the offender.

The Unpardonable Sin

There is one New Testament consideration relative to forgiveness that proves somewhat disturbing. The Bible informs us that some sins *cannot* be forgiven. John talks about a "sin unto death" (1 John 5:16, KJV), and Jesus warned that blaspheming the Holy Spirit has no forgiveness (Mark 3:28-30). A myriad of interpretations have been given to these enigmatic passages. A full exegesis is impossible here; a few comments must suffice.

In the so-called sin against the Holy Spirit, the context makes it clear that the Pharisees were attributing to Satan the *obvious* work of the Holy Spirit that was taking place through the ministry of Jesus. Our Lord was the personification of the very kingdom of God in their midst, and He was presenting Himself as the "door" to that kingdom. He was offering people life in the kingdom. All His miracles and teaching clearly attested to the fact. Then, right in the face of it all, the Pharisees attributed the entire affair to the devil himself. What blasphemy! They must have had a heart so calloused and corrupt that they would have called black, white. Therefore, forgiveness was impossible for them.

Two primary possible interpretations from this situation can be drawn. First, the Pharisees were so immune to God's truth there was no hope for them as long as they harbored that rebellious attitude. Unless they softened their hearts, they would never find forgiveness. Second, it has been argued the sin of attributing the clear, obvious work of the

Holy Spirit to Satan so grieves the Spirit that He departs, never to draw that guilty person to Christ and forgiveness. Hence, the sin is an eternal sin. In support of the first interpretation, Sherman Johnson said:

> To curse the Holy Spirit is similar to the blasphemy of the name of God, which the Pharisees considered a capital offense. In the context (cf. verse 30) it means ascribing to Satan what is perhaps the greatest gift of the Holy Spirit, that of rescuing those who are in Satan's power. One who takes such an attitude overturns all moral values and says, "Evil, be thou my good." So long as a man is in this position he has not forgiveness, for he has shut God out from his life.[9]

It is probably correct to say, as Henry E. Turlington stated:

> The sin can hardly be just any railing or angry word against the work of God's Spirit—in Jesus or through any Spirit-led man. . . . The sin against the Spirit which brings permanent alienation must be not one act or series of acts, but a perversion of one's self which utterly denies and defies moral values and characteristically thinks of good as evil and light as darkness.[10]

Moreover, it does appear possible that after a protracted period of striving by the Holy Spirit to bring certain people who continue to resist to repentance, God's Spirit finally gives them up as they degenerate spiritually and morally. Paul certainly seemed to view this as a possibility when he told the Romans:

> For the wrath of God is revealed from heaven against all ungodliness and wickedness of men who by their wickedness suppress the truth. . . . for although they knew God they did not honor him as God or give thanks to him, but they became futile in their thinking and their senseless minds were darkened. Claiming to be wise, they became fools, and exchanged the glory of the immortal God for images resembling mortal man or birds or animals or reptiles.
> Therefore God gave them up (Rom. 1:18,21-24).

Some commentators tend to sidestep this knotty issue. Other interpretive approaches have been set forth concerning the issue. However, it appears wisest to realize the blasphemy of the Spirit is a most solemn situation that should be taken seriously.

The "sin unto death" (KJV) of 1 John has also been dealt with in various ways. Some equate it with the sin against the Spirit,[11] but this is doubtful. Edward A. McDowell believed the "mortal sin" was "either the sin in which all unregenerate men live, or the sin of apostasy in which the gnostic false teachers (antichrists) lived. The latter are the people John likely had in mind."[12] Raymond E. Brown agreed, arguing that John is speaking of "brothers," that is, those who remained within the fellowship for a period and then apostized.[13]

Some have seen the mortal sin in 1 John as possible for true believers, restricting it to physical death. They site the passage in 1 Corinthians 11 where Paul told the church because of their abuse of the Lord's Supper: "That is why many of you are weak and ill, and some have died" (1 Cor. 11:30). Along with that there is also the sin of Ananias and Sapphira (Acts 5:1-11). Therefore, Christians can so grieve the Spirit that they are taken out of this life, but their spirits do not eternally die.

McDowell's point seems to be well taken on a careful reading of 1 John 5:16. McDowell has reminded us that "in John's view, a Christian brother *can* be guilty of ***committing what is not a mortal sin*** . . . [but he] *excludes* the Christian brothers from those who would be guilty of committing 'sin unto death.' "[14] It is another stern warning and should be taken seriously by all. All sin is exceedingly serious, even if there are "degrees" of sin, as John apparently wished to show.

The glorious truth to be realized in all this, however, is that our sins can be forgiven if we repent. This is the scriptural stress. The Bible says, "As far as the east is from the west, / so far does he remove our transgressions from us" (Ps. 103:12). Hymn writer Elisha A. Hoffman put it well: we are "washed in the blood of the Lamb." Forgiveness brings peace; we experience peace with God (Rom. 5:1) and the peace of God (Col. 3:15). Knowing I am accepted by God, I can accept myself and others. There truly is a peace that "passes all understanding" (Phil. 4:7). Life becomes rich and meaningful.

Salvation as Deliverance from Self

The fact of forgiveness through Christ also means one experiences deliverance from one's own lower self. The "old man" is crucified with Christ (Rom. 6:1-14). The salvation of Jesus Christ is a moral salvation. Redemption makes one different. The sanctifying work of the Holy Spirit does go on continually (1 Thess. 5:23). Sinners are delivered from the bondage of sin and the old self. "Therefore, if any one is in Christ, he is a new creation" (2 Cor. 5:17).

Salvation as Deliverance from Standing Judgment

The final consideration in answer to the question from what one is delivered in God's salvation centers around the problem of eternal judgment—hell. The very term itself bristles with issues: What is hell? Is it a real place? Is hell eternal? Does God send people there? How could a loving God eternally condemn people? Is hell just annihilation? The queries go on. Obviously, a knotty problem has arisen. The interpreter must be faithful to the Scriptures. Philosophy and speculation are of little help here. Rationalism also fails. The ultimate question becomes: What does the Bible say?

It should be made clear at the outset that the Scriptures clearly indicate that all, even Christians, will be judged (2 Cor. 5:10). This presents little difficulty. Judgment in principle stumbles few. What causes concern is the biblical statements about the *eternal* punishment of the unbeliever (Heb. 6:2). So the subject is approached, attempting to say only what the Word of God declares. Then, the deliverance of God must be kept in mind.

To speak of hell and eternal judgment creates in the minds of many the caricature of the fanatical "hell-fire and damnation" preacher. It is thus quite easy to reject the entire idea. Yet, the Bible has much to say on the subject. Our Lord spoke of it often:

> If your right eye causes you to sin, pluck it out and throw it away; it is better that you lose one of your members than that your whole body be thrown into hell. And if your right hand causes you to sin, cut if off and throw it away; it is better than you lose one of your members than that your whole body go into hell (Matt. 5:29-30).
> But I will warn you whom to fear: fear him who, after he has killed, has power to cast into hell, yes, I tell you, fear him! (Luke 12:5).
> And if your eye causes you to sin, pluck it out; it is better for you to enter the kingdom of God with one eye than with two eyes to be thrown into hell (Mark 9:47-48).
> You serpents, you brood of vipers, how are you to escape being sentenced to hell? (Matt. 23:33).

The word Jesus used in these passages is *gehenna*. The term is taken from the Hebrew word meaning "the Valley of Hinnom." This valley lies geographically south of Jerusalem. By Jesus' day, it had become the place of refuse for the city. In former years children had been sacrificed in fire to the pagan god Molech (2 Kings 23:10; 2 Chron. 28:3). It became a symbol for the place of punishment for sinners by the first century B.C. The unquenched fire of the place depicted to the Jewish mind the judgment of God (Deut. 32:22, Dan. 7:10).

Although there are early Old Testament references to a punitive conflagration (Deut. 32:22), it was during the Greco-Roman period of Jewish religious life that the distinct concept of an eternal hell emerged. With these traditions quite well set in Jewish understandings by the first century, Jesus and the other New Testament writers seem to have picked up on the theme.

Another term for judgment is used in 2 Peter 2:4: *tartaroo*, often translated "hell." It was visualized as a place of "nether gloom" where fallen "angels" are kept until the final judgment.

The Old Testament word, at times translated "hell," especially in the

King James Version, is *sheol*, but it simply meant the "realm of the dead," or the "grave." It was a rather nebulous place. Here people waited for the final judgment. Still, there seems to be a division in sheol, a place of rest and a place of suffering, but it was not as well defined as the New Testament presentation of separation between the righteous and wicked. The New Testament equivalent to *sheol* is *hades*.

The rabbinic literature produced various ideas concerning who would suffer God's eternal judgment and of what judgment actually consisted. For example, some writings espoused annihilation; others saw the fire of *gehenna* as purgatorial, but there were those who saw God's judgment of sinners as eternal punishment, as do some writings in the Apocrypha (Wisd. of Sol. 3:1-10; Judith. 16:20-21).

But what does the New Testament itself teach? One writer has summed up his understanding by stating, "The fire of hell is unquenchable (Mark 9:43), eternal (Matt. 18:8), its punishment is the converse of eternal life (Matt. 25:46). There is no suggestion that those who enter hell ever emerge from it."[15]

Can this sort of position be sustained?

There are many who say the doctrine of an eternal hell cannot be legitimately held by the church. For example, Oxford professor R. H. Charles stated:

> The doctrine of eternal damnation . . . is a Judaistic survival of . . . grossly immoral character. . . . this doctrine originated in Judaism when monotheism had become a lifeless dogma, and Jewish particularism reigned supreme, and when a handful of the pious could not only comfortably believe that God was the God of the Jews alone, . . . but also could imagine that part of their highest bliss in the next world would consist in witnessing the torment of the damned.[16]

Professor Charles went on to say the doctrines of eternal hell "in the New Testament Canon can give them no claim on the acceptance of the Church."[17] He was bold to state, "As for hell, the final eternal abode of the damned, such a conception is impossible in the cosmos ruled by the God of justice and love."[18]

This dogmatic approach is held by various thinkers, but it seems far too cavalier to be taken seriously. One cannot dogmatically dismiss what the New Testament states on the subject and refuse to deal with it.

Annihilation Theories

Another less radical objection to eternal punishment comes from the ranks of those holding the doctrine of annihilation: the unrighteous are simply eradicated and cease to exist after the final judgment. For example, in an article entitled "Fire, then Nothing," Professor Clark Pinnock argued for the annihilation of the unrepentant masses on the Day of Judgment.[19] He began his case with a rather emotional argument, stating:

> How can one imagine for a moment that the God who gave his Son to die for sinners because of his great love for them would install a torture chamber somewhere in the new creation in order to subject those who reject him to everlasting pain? It is hard enough to defend the Christian message apologetically in relation to the problem of evil and suffering without having to explain this doctrine, too. My point is this: The popular tradition concerning the nature of punishment that some of the wicked will have to suffer is morally and scripturally flawed, and is accelerating the move toward universalism.[20]

One can appreciate Pinnock's concern for apologetics, but does he make his case?

Pinnock raised the question: Cannot the "fire" of God's judgment simply consume the lost? In this view, God raises the lost dead at the end of the age not to torment them forever, but simply to declare his judgment and condemn them to extinction. Pinnock believes this is what the Bible means by the second death (Rev. 20:11-15).

Several passages of Scripture are cited to support this annihilation view. In Matthew 3:10,12, John the Baptist talked of the lost as chaff thrown into the fire. Pinnock argued that Jesus used the term *gehenna* to depict the place where the garbage was finally consumed. Surely, he contended, this speaks of the utter consuming of sinners (Matt. 5:22). Not only that, Pinnock pointed out that Jesus spoke of a God "who can destroy both soul and body in hell" (Matt. 10:28). Notice, the person is *destroyed*. Many other passages in the New Testament use similar expressions. Pinnock thus concluded, "The dread possibility here is surely the annihilation and extinction of the whole human person subject to this judgment."[21]

Still, Pinnock had to face the key phrase "eternal punishment" (Matt. 25:46). His argument was simple; he told us:

> That is precisely what it is—not everlasting punishing, but eternal punishment. God sentences the lost to a final, irrevocable, definitive death. It is indeed an everlasting punishment. The fire of hell does not torment, but rather consumes the wicked. As Paul put it, the wages of sin is death (Rom. 6:23).[22]

This hardly seems good exegesis. Surely the idea of eternal punishment means an *eternal state* of punishment. Regardless of the argument that a

God of purposeful love would not perpetuate the endless torment of anyone, Pinnock's use of the Bible fails to convince. The constant emphasis on everlasting punishment stands right beside everlasting life. That fact cannot be dismissed so easily.

Other arguments have been made. Tillich contended, "Participation in the eternal makes man eternal; separation from the eternal leaves man in his natural finitude." Tillich continued, "In estrangement man is left to his finite nature of having to die."[23] Bultmann also took a similar stance, telling us: "If God is the sole reality . . . the world . . . turns away from life . . . which . . . is simultaneously death."[24] Of course, both Tillich and Bultmann felt this fact leads to a universal salvation. As J. H. Leckie argued, the idea "the Creator will slay His own creatures"[25] is untenable, but more of that in a moment. Suffice it to say, the arguments against eternal punishment have been continually made throughout the history of theology. Outstanding thinkers like Irenaeus, Socinius, Spinoza, and Ritschl have all held such positions. What then can be said?

Most of the arguments for annihilation rest on two ideas. The first contention is that words like *death, perish,* and *destruction* are to be taken literally, but such is a pure supposition. The word *eternal* (*aionion*) is set side by side as an adjective of both life and death. If eternal life means everlasting bliss, surely eternal death means everlasting sorrow. The *everlasting* quality the writers mean by use of the terms simply cannot be sidestepped.

Second, the argument is made that everlasting punishment is immoral, and to say God punishes people forever is simply unethical. However, what is the ultimate meaning of ethics? *Whatever* God does is ethically right, whether we understand it and agree or not. Furthermore, what did Jesus mean when He described *gehenna* as a place where "their worm does not die, and the fire is not quenched" (Mark 9:44,46,48)? In Jesus' parable, the rich man in hell was very conscious and in real torment (Luke 16:19-31). It is well to remember Jesus Himself made those statements, and what He said is right, true, and moral.

Moreover, it is vital to realize that in the atonement Christ accomplished on the cross, He accomplished by suffering God's full judgment on sin. Did He experience annihilation? Obviously not! In arguing against Pinnock's view of the destruction of the lost, David Wells stated:

> A gospel, then, that trades on a diminished view of sin, a modified notion of divine righteousness, and a restructured Atonement is not one that is more appealing, as Pinnock thinks, but one that is less. It is a gospel that has lost its nerve because it has lost its majesty.
>
> Pinnock has tried to revive the old argument that the judgment of God

raises moral problems. I assert the opposite: God's judgment settles all moral problems.[26]

The annihilation doctrine has little to support it, both theologically and biblically. Thus, it must be rejected.

Universalism Theories

The final issue to consider in the doctrine of eternal punishment is *universalism,* that is, all will be saved and enjoy the benefits of Christ's redemptive work. Some see this concept in a very broad manner, and define it as such. They hold not only will all humanity be reconciled to God, but even the "fallen heavenly spirits" will enjoy the fruits of redemption. For example, R. H. Charles declared, "Since in the world of spiritual beings some have sinned or apostatised they too must share in the Atonement of the Cross of Christ, and so obtain reconciliation."[27]

Some see no final judgment at all, at least not in any historical sense. C. H. Dodd, from his so-called realized eschatology presuppositional position, stated, "The notion of a last day and a second advent are not to be taken literally at all. . . . It is impossible to think of Dooms day as a coming event in history."[28] This does not necessarily imply universalism, but it certainly undercuts the idea of a final judgment and leaves the idea of universalism quite intact. It is interesting to see what lies back of all these thoughts.

Universalism has an immediate appeal to some probably because they have heard "hell-fire" judgmental preaching to the point they have rebelled. Others seemingly give in to the general contemporary trend to reject objective truth, and thus they overlook the seriousness of sin. Still others have a quite sentimental view of God's love, but there are different opinions as to how the concept of universalism is to be understood. A brief historical sweep of the doctrine will help in grasping those differences.

Universalism as a doctrine has an interesting background. The doctrine had something of its beginnings in Origen (A.D. 185-254). He is a highly respected church father but a highly controversial theologian. As one put it, "Where Origen was good, no one was better; where he was bad, no one was worse."[29] As a young man, Origen desired to be a martyr for Christ. His father actually did give his life for Jesus' name.

After becoming a school master at the age of 18, Origen devoted himself to reading and writing. He prepared the first critical edition of the Old Testament, along with ten commentaries and several homilies on the Bible. His apologetic writings were outstanding as well as his work on systematic theology.

Origen's concept of universalism was predicated on three ideas: (1)

God is good; (2) God is just; and (3) God is powerful. Origen saw God's goodness as extending even to the divine desire that the devil be saved. Moreover, because God is just, *all* thinking beings have free will. Finally, God possesses such power that He can accomplish His purpose. Therefore, God in His goodness and justice purposes to save all thinking beings, and it will certainly be accomplished. Thus, his rational conclusion became the bedrock of his view.

Origen taught that God's punishment for sin (sin had to be punished) lasts only until such punishment has accomplished it's purpose. The purpose is to persuade sinners to repent. God never infringes upon human freedom, but eventually He will bring all thinking, willing creatures to Himself. When God's ultimate purpose is thus accomplished, the world will end. There was a strange twist in all this, however. Because free will is an eternal principle, Satan could rebel once again and start the same process all over again, *ad infinitum*.

The universalistic theology of Origen was condemned at the Council of Constantinople in A.D. 543. As a result, the doctrine essentially died out for several hundred years with the exception of a few thinkers like Gregory of Nyssa, Theodore of Mopsuestia, and John Cassin, but in the ninth century a revision of the theory arose from the thought and pen of Johannes Scotus Erigena (810-877). His universalistic view centered in his eschatology.

Erigena was born in Ireland and became an able Greek scholar. He was a prolific writer, translating the Greek Fathers into Latin and producing a notable commentary on the Gospel of John. Because of Erigena's scholarship, the bishop of Rheims asked him to write a refutation of Gottschalk's work on "double predestination." Gottschalk, a monk, had gone so far as to say God not only predestines some to heaven and the rest to hell, God predestines *every* human action.

Erigena went to work, but as Charles E. White put it, Erigena's "antidote to Gottschalk's doctrine . . . the bishop found worse than the poison."[30] Erigena argued that God is one; therefore, His will must be one. Thus there is only one predestination, and God's one predestination elects all people to salvation.

Erigena moved on from that point, and, influenced by Pseudo-Dionysius, he became a virtual pantheist. Basing his views on 1 Corinthians 15:28, God will "be all in all," (KJV) he held that the entire creation will be reconciled to God and united into His nature. When faced with the Scriptural passages concerning eternal punishment, Erigena replied the wicked will be punished for eternity by having their wicked desires frustrated. Of course, not many in his day followed this line of argumentation.

Since the time of Erigena's work, universalism has surfaced many times and in various forms in the works of Johannes Tauler, Jan van Ruysbroeck, and Albert the Great.

An early and influential advocate of the doctrine in American Christianity was Hosea Ballou. Born in New Hampshire in a Baptist preacher's home, he was brought up on high Calvinism. As a young man he was influenced by Ethan Allen in the skeptical work *Reason the Only Oracle of Man.* At the same time, young Ballou heard a farmer named Caleb Rich say God wanted all people to be saved. After reading Allen and hearing Rich, Ballou discarded his Calvinism and began preaching universalism. Through a rigorous study of the Bible, strangely enough, he became a classic nineteenth-century "liberal." He concluded Christ's divinity was a creation of the early church. This view, coupled with his universalism, moved him into unitarian-universalism. He was a fervent "evangelist" of his doctrine, riding over the hills of New England preaching his views.

In the meantime, in Boston, many intellectuals were moving in the same theological orbit. All this gave rise to the Unitarian and universalist denominations founded by John Murray of Gloucester. Other advocates of the doctrine followed like J. H. Peterson, S. Huber, C. Chauncy, and E. Winchester.

Universalism has further contemporary roots in the liberal theology of Immanuel Kant, Schleiermacher, and Ritschl. Barth, Emil Brunner, K. Rohme, and others are in some sense products of this basic orientation, although some debate that contention. This ferment is also found in the writings of Vatican II and in the thought of Hans Kung and E. Schillebeeckx.

With this very brief, historical overview, several things can be deduced. First of all, it is true that the gospel possesses a universal appeal: "God so loved *the world*" (John 3:16, author's italics); "make disciples of *all* nations" (Matt. 28:19, author's italics); "[God] commands *all* people everywhere to repent" (Acts 17:30, NRSV, author's italics).

Furthermore, God clearly desires the salvation of all: "not wishing that any should perish" (2 Pet. 3:9). God loves all humanity and therefore wishes to see them come to Christ's redemption.

Not only that, the Bible seems to make it clear that Jesus died for all (1 John 2:2). This passage in 1 John is extremely difficult to square with the Reformed doctrine of the "limited atonement" which holds that Christ died *only* for the elect. His death on the cross reaches out to all, not just the elected few.

However, over the years many thinkers have held to a reformed view of the doctrine of predestination. They look to Paul's statement in Ephesians: "He hath chosen us in him before the foundation of the world, that we should be holy and without blame before him in love: Having predestinated us unto the adoption of children by Jesus Christ to himself, according to the good pleasure of his will" (1:4-5, KJV). This is one of the mysteries of the church that theologians have grappled with for centuries.

This work is not the venue for this debate between divine sovereignty and human responsibility. There are discerning minds adhering to both sides of the issue. The point is: Christians are to take the gospel to the ends of the earth. Even the five-point Calvinist will admit this. After all, we do not have the insight as to who the elect are.

There is thus a biblical case that can be made for the doctrine of universalism. One can appeal to the Bible for the view that all will be saved. Roger Nicole makes four points on this fact:

> The concept of universal salvation has a ring of orthodoxy to it. Consider the manner in which universalists appeal to Scripture:
>
> 1. They build their case on Scriptures that are construed to teach a universal saving will of God (Ezek. 18:23,32; John 3:16-17; 1 Tim. 2:4; 2 Pet. 3:9).
>
> 2. They use Scriptures that suggest the death of Christ had a universal intent articulated by the words *world, all, everyone,* and *whoever.*
>
> 3. They quote passages that represent the final state as one of total subservience to God: "the renewal of all things" [sic] (Matt. 19:28; Acts 3:21); "all flesh shall see the salvation of the Lord" [sic] (Isa. 40:3; 52:10; 62:2; Luke 3:6); "to bring all things in heaven and earth together under one head, even Christ" (Eph. 1:10; cf. Col. 1:20); "that every knee should bow, . . . and every tongue confess . . ." (Phil. 2:10-11); "He has put everything under his feet" (1 Cor. 15:27-28); ". . . that God may be all in all" (1 Cor. 15:28).
>
> 4. They quote passages where death is represented as subdued in the eschaton (1 Cor. 15:26; Rev. 20:14).[31]

What can be said to the universalists' claims? First, it is extremely dubious to say, as Clark Pinnock stated, "I wish universalism were true."[32] Or, as Kenneth Kantzer put it even more strongly: "I wish I could say that God is too loving, too kind, and too generous to condemn any soul to eternal punishment."[33] These men, even though they are conservative thinkers, imply there is a "goodness" and a "level of love" which God does not quite reach. Such an approach thrusts one back on the philosophical dualism that there is an ultimate ethical standard alongside God to which He must adhere. We have seen how untenable that position is, but even worse, in the issue of eternal punishment, Kantzer and Pinnock implied God apparently is not as loving as the standard demands in ethical "conduct." To claim He is not loving enough to save all would make God unethical. Such a thought must be soundly rejected.

What God does is the description of what is loving and good. There is no higher love or goodness than God's actual acts. God cannot be "too loving" to conceive of something other than what He actually does. God is love, and all His actions are expressions of the highest form of love which is Himself. If God condemns unrepentant sinners to eternal punishment, that is the highest form of love and goodness that can be expressed, just as the bringing into glory of repentant sinners is an expression of His love and goodness. Therefore, the rather sentimental view of *agape* that says "I wish God were . . ." is philosophically untenable, not to mention its lack of a biblical base. Actually, it makes God less than God.

The Scriptural View

The biblical base itself shows the final folly of universalism, for the Bible constantly speaks of God measuring out judgment. A look at some scriptural terms and expressions that speak of the fate of those who in this life reject God's offer of salvation will be rewarding.

The essence of the idea of eternal punishment is *separation from God*. Jesus said, "Depart from me" (Matt. 25:41). Paul described the future state of the unrepentant as shut out of "the presence of the Lord and from the glory of his might" (2 Thess. 1:9). As physical death is essentially the separation of the spirit from the body, eternal death is the thrusting of the human personality from God.

It must be made clear, spiritual death does not mean cessation of existence. See the section on annihilation. In some sense, the spirit lives on by the sustaining power of God. This is not meant to say people are immortal in themselves. People are not immortal in that they have an immortal soul, in the Greek understanding of the word. "The King of kings and Lord of lords, . . . alone has immortality and dwells in unapproachable light" (1 Tim. 6:16). God alone is eternally immortal in Himself. People, therefore, live on forever because they have a *conditioned* immortality. They exist forever because of the sustaining immortality of God which He imparts, but they do live on, even though such an existence is exclusion from the face-to-face presence of God. That can only be described as separation, exclusion, destruction, and death. If the presence of Jesus Christ is what makes heaven what it is, separation from the Lord is what makes hell, hell.

Darkness is another word describing the fate of the lost. Paul told Timothy that God dwells in unapproachable light. Thus, to be excluded from God's presence means darkness—darkness forever (Matt. 8:12; Jude 13).

Another term of judgment is *fire*. There has been a measure of debate as to whether or not the fire of judgment is literal fire as known it on earth today, or figurative. The debate will probably continue. The issue is, however, separation from God; being a recipient of His wrath is the essence of the torment. Nonetheless, the rich man in Jesus' parable cried out to Abraham, "I am tormented in this flame" (Luke 16:24, KJV). Notice, the man was in a real, literal conscious state, and in anguish. Hell is a real place as surely as heaven is a literal place.[34] The eternal state of those rejecting Jesus Christ must be taken as literally as those who receive the Lord and live with Him forever. The Scriptures require this.

"Everlasting chains and dungeons" is another expression to describe the fate of unbelievers. Only believers are truly free people.

Futility is a further significant term to describe the eternal state of those who reject Christ. "What does it profit a man, to gain the whole world and forfeit his life?" (Mark 8:36). To make a wrong choice about Christ in this life means a futile existence forever. This is why the Bible speaks of judgment as everlasting shame and contempt. The lost will see what they lost in rejecting Christ (Isa. 66:24). It is a most serious matter.

Implied above are words like *trouble, distress, torment,* and *agony.* In the same vein, expressions arise like "weeping," and "wailing and gnashing of teeth" (Matt. 8:12; 13:42,50, KJV). All these terms can be summed up in Jesus' word *punishment* (*kolasis,* Matt. 25:46). Moreover, Revelation 20:10 tells us clearly this state is eternal: "tormented day and night for ever and ever." The everlasting aspects of judgment is surely what Jesus was talking about in His description concerning *gehenna* as the place where the "worm does not die, and the fire is not quenched" (Mark 9:48).

The Wrath of God

All that has been said can be epitomized in the fearful phrase "the wrath of God." This particular expression appears more than 600 times in the Scriptures. Universalists must face that weighty fact. As Roger Nicole said:

> Though some Scripture appeals to a universalistic understanding of salvation, in the final analysis the universalist must face the more consistent scriptural treatment of a final judgment to which all humankind is summoned and which issues into a *bifurcation of destiny.*
>
> The universalist faces further difficulties with passages relating to the unpardonable sin, the great chasm between the rich man and Lazarus over which no one could cross. Jesus' statement "Where I go, you cannot come," and particularly with his remark about Judas: "It would be better for him if he had not been born." How could someone who is ultimately going to be saved be called "the son of perdition?" How can a universalist fairly deal with the many Scriptures that show that life's decisions have everlasting and irrevocable consequences in the life to come?[35]

The reality is hard to avoid. One must face the biblical facts.

But, other universalists argue, surely an endless punishment is not proportionate to the crime of sin. Two things can be said on this point. First, many decisions in life have lifelong consequences. Not only that, as previously emphasized, sin is exceedingly sinful in God's sight. This must not be forgotten in our relativistic age. Second, sinners in hell are just that: sinners. They remain as impenitent in judgment as in life. They continue in their wicked rebellion. To let such people into heaven would destroy the moral fabric of the universe.

Surely, the argument is raised, those who have never heard the gospel cannot be lost. Granted, this is a big hurdle to clear for those who accept the biblical idea of eternal judgment for those who do not receive Jesus Christ. What can be said?

It is the acts of God themselves that speak. It is not correct to say, "God will do right," implying there is a standard of right God lives up to. What God does *is* the right. So whatever the outcome of the lost may be, it will be right, loving, and of God. There is a biblical passage, however, that fully deals with the issue. It is a weighty passage, but it must be understood to be truly biblical. The passage comes from the pen of Paul to the Roman church:

> For the wrath of God is revealed from heaven against all ungodliness and wickedness of men who by their wickedness suppress the truth. For what can be known about God is plain to them, because God has shown it to them. Ever since the creation of the world his invisible nature, namely, his eternal power and deity, has been clearly perceived in the things that have been made. So they are without excuse; for although they knew God they did not honor him as God or give thanks to him, but they became futile in their thinking and their senseless minds were darkened. Claiming to be wise, they became fools, and exchanged the glory of the immortal God for images resembling mortal man or birds or animals or reptiles.
>
> Therefore God gave them up in the lusts of their hearts to impurity, to the dishonoring of their bodies among themselves, because they exchanged the truth about God for a lie and worshiped and served the creature rather than the Creator, who is blessed for ever! Amen.
>
> For this reason God gave them up to dishonorable passions. (Rom. 1:18-26).

First, in all human sin, the divine honor is at stake. God will not, cannot, condone sin regardless of the sinners' circumstances. Sin is rebellion. Sin is an affront to holy God. Sin willfully despises God and spurns His love and grace. Therefore, *sin will be judged*. The Holy One will not ignore it. We must make no mistake here. In the permissive spirit of the age, it is easy to forget the vileness of all human sin before God.

Furthermore, it is an indisputable fact that *all* sin—people who have heard the truth and those who have not heard the gospel. The hearing of the gospel has no direct bearing on whether or not people are sinners (Rom. 3:23). Therefore, and here is the point, "they are without excuse" (Rom. 1:20). Barth saw this clearly when he said:

> Inexcusable is their godlessness, for the *clearly seen* works of God speak of His *everlasting power* and they have already risen up in protest against the service of the "No-God," by which God is ranged in the midst of the natural and "spiritual" and other forces of this world. Inexcusable also is their unrighteousness, for the *clearly seen* facts bear witness to the *everlasting divinity* of God.[36]

Arnold and Ford, many years earlier, would have agreed to Barth's assessment. They pointed out:

> This seeing or perception of the divine attributes through his works, was so ordained, or purposely established that sinning men should have no excuse. . . . Dr. Gifford [says], "God's *purpose* was to leave nothing undone on his part, the omission of which might give men an excuse for sin."[37]

The Lutheran commentator Lenski went so far as to say:

> This idea is widely held . . . [that] Heaven is opened to noble pagans. But this is not Biblical teaching. Moreover, Paul is not speaking only of the final judgment and as being without excuse at the last day. Men have been, are now, ever will be without excuse.[38]

William Sanday stated, "God did not design that man should sin; but He did design that if they sinned they should be without excuse: on His part all was done to give them sufficient knowledge of Himself."[39]

In a word, *no one* can honestly say, either "I have not sinned," or, "I did not know anything about God, nor that I was sinning against him." That is simply not true. So, all are without excuse. What can be known of God, whether one has heard the whole gospel or not, is manifest, and *everyone* has sinned against the light they have received. Not only have they sinned against the light they have, but they actually suppressed "the truth" (Rom. 1:18) and "did not see fit to acknowledge God" (Rom. 1:28). The human situation simply cannot be ignored by holy God.

Therefore, "the wrath of God is revealed from heaven against all ungodliness and wickedness of men" (Rom. 1:18). Not only that, if people persist in turning from the light they have and continue to suppress the truth, God will give them up (Rom. 1:24,26,28). What a stern warning!

Does not all this fly in the face of God's love. No, for as Roger Nicole pointed out:

We must remember that the very person who revealed most stunningly God's love, our Lord Jesus Christ, is also the one who spoke most frequently and in most frightening words of the tragedy of the lost. It is dangerous to be more generous than God has revealed himself to be!

If the plight of the unbelievers is what the Bible reveals it to be, it is not an act of love to hide their fate from them. To do so further blinds them from the remedy God provided. If a person is struck with a deadly disease for which there is a known cure, it is neither wise nor loving to try and convince him that nothing is wrong.[40]

Again, let it be understood that *agape* is not sentimental; it is "tough love," tough in that it tells the truth. God is holy and will punish *all* sin.

Universalism means either there is salvation outside of the glorious appeal of Christ, or there is hope beyond the grave. Neither stance can stand the weight of Scripture. Moreover, such a stance undercuts the entire missionary-evangelistic thrust of the New Testament. Why go if they will be saved anyway? To say the hearing of the gospel gives one a better grasp on life hardly motivates many to go for that reason. Such is not the biblical motivation to seek the lost. The writer of Hebrews put it well when he reminded us, "It is a fearful thing to fall in the hands of the living God" (Heb. 10:31).

What then can be said? The answer is simple—yet so profound. Believers must carry the gospel to the lost. Proclaiming the good news breaks the power of sin and sets the captive free. The gospel is the power of God unto salvation (Rom. 1:15). Therefore, instead of retreating into an unbiblical universalism or annihilation stance, let Christians be brave and sacrificial and take the life-giving message to the lost millions. If they fail to do that and refuse to warn the wicked, God said, "his blood I will require at your hand" (Ezek. 3:18). Evangelism is central in ministry.

The Dynamic of Salvation

It has become evident that eternal salvation rests in the gospel of Christ. God's great love sent the Son to redeem the world. To the divine salvific act the Holy Spirit constantly testifies. There is one aspect of the manifestation of the grace of God in Christ needing elaboration, however. The issue—and the problem—is set forth by John in his first Epistle. There is a significant word used by the beloved apostle that strikes right at the heart of the situation. John wrote, "If any one does sin, we have an advocate with the Father, Jesus Christ the righteous; and he is the expiation [*hilasmos*] for our sins, and not for ours only but also for the sins of the whole world" (1 John 2:1-2; also 4:10).

Expiation or Propitiation?

The key word to be addressed in the dynamic of salvation is *hilasmos,*
"expiation" as the *Revised Standard Version* translates it; "propitiation" as
the *King James Version* has it. These two different translations of *hilasmos*
pose the problem. To avoid the issue the *New International Version* translates the key word: "the atoning sacrifice." Why the divergence in
translations? Jesus Christ is the source of our redemption, but what was
it He actually did as implied by the controversial term *hilasmos?* Why has
it precipitated controversy?

The root of *hilasmos* is only used four times in the entire New Testament (Rom. 3:25; Heb. 2:17; 1 John 2:2; 4:10). Therefore, the question
can be raised: Should so much be made over it? Definitely, because it
points up one of the key realities of the Christian faith. Buchsel was
right when he said, "For John the *ilasmos* is much more than a concept of
Christian doctrine; it is the reality by which he lives."[41] What does it
mean?

One definition of *hilasmas* is as follows: "An atoning action which
obliterates sin from God's sight and so restores to holiness and the divine favor."[42] Buchsel defined the term as "the action in which God is
propitiated and sin expiated. . . . Behind the use of *ilasmos* stands the
twofold sense of *ilaskomai* as both 'to propitiate' and 'to expiate.' "[43] In
the LXX, the word is regularly used to depict the "mercy seat" where the
blood was sprinkled on the Day of Atonement. Paul's use of the term in
Romans 3:25 places *hilasmos* at the cross of Christ where the full atonement was made. Obviously, the term has to do with the heart of the
atonement, hence salvation.

The theological issue, therefore, is this: Is God's wrath *propitiated?* Does
Christ's death move Godward and appease His wrath against human
sin? Or, is sin *expiated?* Is the power of the atonement essentially human-
ward as Christ's death moves us to reconcile ourselves to God? Is God's
attitude changed, or merely people transformed in mind through
Christ's atoning work?

The problem seems to center in the fact that people are prone to take
an either/or stance on the issue. This approach may miss the full impact
of Christ's atoning sacrifice. For example, Buchsel told us, "The work of
Christ is therefore, represented, not as the propitiation by the Son of the
Father's wrath, but as the divine act of 'covering' or 'blotting' sin."[44]

Buchsel stated in a similar vein: "John is obviously following the OT.
ilasmos does not imply the propitiation of God. It refers to the purpose
which God Himself has fulfilled by sending the Son. . . . The meaning,
then, is the setting aside of sin as guilt against God."[45]

Such approaches see *expiation* as the proper way to understand the
atonement. On the other side of the issue, George E. Ladd wrote:

The shedding of Christ's blood, i.e. his sacrificial death, provides the means of *propitiation* on the ground of which acquittal or justification can be bestowed upon man as a free gift. This *propitiatory* death of Christ was an act of divine righteousness (v. 25). Previous to the death of Christ God had appeared to pass over sins. . . . In the death of Christ, God is no longer passing over sins but is dealing with them as a righteous God ought to do. . . . The death of Christ was an act of righteousness on God's part; and we can only conclude that this act of righteousness consisted in visiting upon Christ, who was ethically sinless, the guilt and doom that sin deserves, namely, death. . . . It is because God manifested both his righteousness and his love by visiting upon Jesus the guilt and the doom of sin that he can now in perfect righteousness bestow the vindication of acquittal upon the sinner.[46]

This lengthy passage is obviously weighted on the propitiation side of the issue.

The reluctance of some to embrace the idea that *hilasmas* has a propitiatory element seems to stem from two primary sources. First, propitiation is a view that was held my many crude pagan religions. They felt their angry, vengeful god needed to be appeased because of their sins. Surely, Christians do not understand the true God in those kind of terms; He is a God of love. Second, the passages in 1 John do seem to refer essentially to Christ forgiving sins and drawing people into fellowship with Himself. Hence, the expiation motif surfaces.

However, we must realize God's wrath is as real as His love. Wrath, as seen, is a biblical concept as much as divine love. Of course God is not "angry" in a pagan sense. God does not get "mad" at someone and must be appeased as a human might, but He is a God of holy wrath and has been grossly offended by human sin. He is estranged from us just as we are alienated from Him. Reconciliation in the full scriptural sense has to do with God being reconciled to sinful humanity as well as human beings finding themselves ready to reconcile to God. This is a clear element in the atonement. Reconciliation is to be seen as a "two-way street," as it were. God moves to us as well as we move to God, and what makes both moves possible is the full sacrifice of Christ. Donald G. Bloesch comments:

The doctrine of atonement includes both the dimensions of propitiation—averting the wrath of God—and expiation—taking away or covering over human guilt. By the expiation of human guilt, the wrath of God is turned away, the holiness of God is satisfied. Yet it is God who in the person of His Son performs the sacrifice of expiation.[47]

Therefore, the solution to the theological dilemma is that both propitiation *and* expiation ideas are presented in the biblical view of atonement. In the actual exegesis of John, the expiation idea predominates, but in the larger full biblical concept of the atonement, propitiation is also present. In Christ's life, death, and resurrection, substitution and satisfaction as well as moral influence is present. In Christ, believers come into full fellowship with God as He comes into blessed fellowship with them. In other words, *hilasmos* is not an "either/or" concept, it is "both/and." Such an approach seems to do justice to the scriptural scheme.

This leads to the final consideration.

Aspects of Salvation

In this area of thought, three prominent words immediately come to the fore: *justification, redemption,* and *eternal life.*[48] This study approaches them in that order.

Justification

The well-known Greek root of this significant term is *dik* (Hebrew *tsedeq*). It is variously translated "justified," "righteousness," "acquitted," or "declared righteous." Essentially, a forensic, legal motif dominates the term. Thus it could also mean "to get the acquittal" as opposed to being condemned.

The LXX carries the forensic idea almost exclusively. It is "constantly used in the positive sense of 'to pronounce righteous,' 'to justify,' 'to vindicate.' "[49]

The New Testament basically follows suit. At times, however, the forensic idea is absent (see Gal. 5:4). Still, "It should also be noted . . . that to think of *dikaiousthai* one-sidedly in terms of experience is to imperil the forensic objectivity of the process."[50] Forensic justification takes place primarily as "an act of grace from which it is not to be severed."[51] Several things have already been said about God's gracious justification of sinners in previous chapters, but a systematic presentation of the concept is called for here. It was a favorite word of Paul. It ought to be a favorite of believers.

Paul used many words to describe the work of Christ in atonement, but in his most "theological" epistles like Romans and Galatians, he labored the ideas of justification or righteousness. In all his writings, Paul used the verbal form of the word fourteen times and the substantive form fifty-two times. The bulk of his use of the verbal form rests in Romans and Galatians.

The background of Paul's thought can be discovered in the Old Testament. Basically, *righteousness* in the Old Testament is a term of relationship. A person is righteous, or justified, because he or she fulfills the demands or standard of relationships. The theological implications are obvious. God establishes the standard of righteousness, and those who meet the standard thus stand in a right relationship with Him. The principle is that straightforward.

Here the forensic idea becomes central to the concept. The righteous person is the one whom the judge *declares* to be free from guilt of failing the standard. It is well known that Judaism by and large defined righteousness in terms of obeying the Law. They could not believe God's standard was unattainable by human effort. This was what Jesus encountered constantly with the scribes and Pharisees.

Paul struck a death blow at the view of traditional Judaism. He held that God certainly does have a standard. Moreover, he argued if one is to be in fellowship with God, that standard must be met. However, no one is capable of ever meeting the standard. It never has been met, and never can be met by mere human effort. Paul said humanity is helpless. People are sinners. How then is a right relationship with God to be experienced? Right at that point God has done something: He sent His Son to meet the standard for sinful, helpless humanity. "For our sake he made him to be sin who knew no sin, so that in him we might become the righteousness of God" (2 Cor. 5:21). By faith, sinners are justified by and in Christ Jesus' perfect life and atoning death. Because of their faith in Christ's work, sinners are declared righteous. Therefore, as Ladd put it: "Paul asserts that in the very act of justifying the ungodly, God has shown himself to be righteous (Rom. 3:26). Furthermore, this acquittal comes entirely apart from the works of the Law (Gal. 2:16; 3:11)—by faith alone (Gal. 2:16)."[52] It thus becomes clear why this idea is essentially forensic: one is *declared righteous* in God's sight by faith, because of what was accomplished in the Son. The Judge acquits the sinner and thus effects relationship.

Not all thinkers agree to that basic, forensic thrust. For example, Vincent Taylor in *Forgiveness and Reconciliation* argues that forensic justification, mere *imputed* righteousness, is fictitious. Justifying faith results in real, life-changing righteousness. That is, believers are not so much *declared* righteous in Christ as actually *made* righteous in the Lord. He believes that in justification God does for sinful humanity what they cannot do for themselves, live pleasing to God.

Norman Snaith in *The Distinctive Ideas of the Old Testament* argued Taylor had not gone far enough in his rejection of forensic righteousness. Snaith felt there is no standard at all one must meet to be justified before God. Only one thing is required for salvation: faith. Justification, or meeting some standard, is *not* required for salvation, whether imputed or imparted. Justification is by faith alone. Snaith argued that if some sort of standard of righteousness were required for salvation, it would present a principle to which God Himself must bow in bringing people into relationship with Himself. Such could never be, Snaith told us. There is no standard to which God is subservient. He is ultimacy in

Himself. Isaiah said of God, "I am the Lord, and there is no other" (45:18). Therefore, God just grants salvation by faith.

Both Taylor's and Snaith's arguments miss, to some degree, the biblical idea. First of all, Taylor was wrong, because forensic righteousness is certainly *not* fictitious; it is real. A declared righteousness is the sinner's only hope. In Christ one truly enters into a new relationship with God by faith. The very word *righteousness* demands such an understanding of salvation. It is a new righteous relationship, as all who have entered into Christ well know. However, Taylor was right when he said God's regenerating power in salvation does give one a new mind and heart, even if one is far from all one should be. The point is, in Christ one is declared righteous and is also in the process of actually becoming righteous.

Snaith also seemed to miss the basic biblical point that Paul made. Granted, there is no standard God must live up to. God does not bow to any external standard of righteousness. In that Snaith was correct. However, God is the standard of righteousness in Himself (Rom. 6:5), and that righteous standard must be met if persons are to be in fellowship with Him. The standard that God is in Himself does not necessarily imply something "outside" of God. Through faith, therefore, God *declares* people righteous by imputing His own standard, the righteousness of Christ, to their account. This is one aspect of the "in Christ" motif of Paul. Moreover, God does this work in the here and now, thus bringing the faithful into relationship with Himself. Being "in Christ" means sharing in that innate standard God has in Himself.

Further, there is also a basic eschatological element in justification. There will be a final judgment on the last day in which the Judge shall pronounce who is justified and who is not. Only those declared righteous will receive the acquittal. Why? Because they are justified by faith (Rom. 5:1). This justification is certainly enjoyed at the moment as well. Ladd put it correctly when he said:

> The doctrine of justification means that God has pronounced the eschatological verdict of acquittal over the man of faith in the present, in advance of the final judgment. The resulting righteousness is not ethical perfection; it is "sinlessness" in the sense that God no longer counts a man's sin against him (II Cor. 5:19).[53]

Therefore, it is correct to conclude that righteousness is a present experience with future aspects. In Galatians 3:8; Romans 3:24; and Acts 13:39, the present tense is used by the authors. The clear implication is justification becomes a beautiful present experience along with a significant eschatological element. It is "the invading and self-actualising present of salvation."[54] The eternal result is to experience God's full fellowship face-to-face.

Justification is at the very heart of the entire salvation experience.

Paul's doctrine of salvation has justification as its basic reference-point. His belief about justification is the source from which flows his view of Christianity as a world-religion of grace and faith, in which Gentiles and Jews stand on equal footing. . . . It is in terms of justification that he explains grace.[55]

Moreover, the justifying grace of God is justly meted out. When God graciously justifies sinners on the ground of Christ's obedience and death, God acts not only in grace; He acts justly. Paul declared, God is "righteous and that he justifies him who has faith in Jesus" (Rom. 3:26).

That is the theological core of the good news. It runs counter to the religious mind-set of the masses who attempt to justify themselves by works. Nevertheless it is the truth believers are to declare, for it is the message of life eternal. These truths lead to the next consideration.

Redemption

Another beautiful salvation idea that surfaces in the Scriptures is contained in a complex word already used many times in this book—*redemption*. Peter used the term, telling us: "You know that you were [redeemed] ransomed from the futile ways inherited from your fathers, not with perishable things such as silver or gold, but with the precious blood of Christ, like that of a lamb without blemish or spot" (1 Pet. 1:18-19).

Redemption is obviously very closely allied to the basic concept of salvation. At times it is used as a synonym for salvation, but it is actually more specific in scope in that it outlines the means by which salvation is possible.

The essential idea of redemption rests in the concept of the payment of a *ransom*. In the Old Testament the primary words employed are *padah* and *gaal*. In the LXX, the redemption is usually rendered by the Greek terms *lutrousthai* and, occasionally, by *hruesthai*. In a few instances the Bible employs the words *agorazein* and *exagorazein*, denoting the act of purchase in the marketplace, especially the slave market.

In the concept of paying a ransom, the thrust is to set someone or something free, for example, the purchasing of freedom of a soldier taken captive in war. In Israel both property and life could be "set free," redeemed through making the payment demanded. For example, the firstborn child was to be redeemed (Ex. 13:13-15). If persons sold themselves into slavery, they could be redeemed by a kinsman who would pay the price (Lev. 25:25-27,47-54).

Moreover, Yahweh was pictured as the great Deliverer of His people from Egypt. Thus He became the Redeemer (Ps. 78:35). The release of

Israel from their Babylonian captivity is described in redemptive language (Jer. 31:11; 50:33-34). Job personally expected the redeeming power of God to come to his rescue (19:25).

One of the rather surprising things about the concept of redemption in the Old Testament is the fact that it is not very often associated with being made free from sin. Some of the few exceptions are Psalm 130:8 where Israel will be redeemed from all their iniquities. Isaiah says much the same thing in 44:22. It has been suggested:

> It is possible that the scarcity of references to redemption from sin in the Old Testament is due to the ever-present proclamation of redemption through the sacrificial system, making formal statements along this line somewhat superfluous. Furthermore, redemption from the ills of life, such as the Babylonian captivity, would inevitably carry with it the thought that God redeems from sin, for it was sin which brought on the captivity.[56]

In the New Testament, the doctrine of redemption expands and is directly related to the person and work of Jesus Christ. *Lutroo* (Greek) in its various forms means "to free by ransom," "to let free for a ransom," "to buy back by a ransom," and "to purchase for a ransom."[57] It is used exclusively for the redeeming act of God in Jesus Christ. Thus the means of redemption is set forth. The thrust is on the self-offering of the Lord.

How does the redeeming Lord give Himself, and why? The emphasis in redemption rests on the idea of substitution on the cross; only by the cross is world redemption possible. Buchsel argued, "The ransom saying [e.g. Mark 10:45 and Matt. 26:28] undoubtedly implies substitution. . . . In these Gospels Jesus experiences death, not as one who is at least inwardly sustained by God's miraculous protection, but as one who is abandoned by God to the derison [sic] of His enemies, . . . He experiences death as one of the many who have fallen victim to corruption. *He has taken their place*. . . . All this is finally based on the fact that His life is a ransom for men, that *He offers Himself as a substitute*".[58] The Lord does not redeem His people with the ransom price of silver or gold as though they could be set free as a slave in the marketplace by the payment of money. Rather, believers are redeemed by the unbelievably high price of the precious blood of Christ who, as a lamb, poured out His life blood to buy them for God. Thereby He liberates believers from sin, death, and hell (1 Pet. 1:18-19). As C. E. B. Cranfield said, "The bearing of our sins means suffering the punishment of them in our place. . . . On the cross he bore not merely physical pain and sorrow . . . but, what was more dreadful, that separation from His Father . . . that was the due reward of our sins."[59]

The mention of a lamb in 1 Peter 1:18-19 moves into the imagery of sacrifice. Thus, the death of Jesus was both a ransom and a sacrifice as Jesus bore our sins. The basis of the idea rests in the sin-bearing motif of the Old Testament, but also the element of example is seen in the cross. As Leon Morris expressed it, "His sufferings were thus an example to the readers who were also liable to suffer for no wrongdoing but simply for their Christian profession."[60] Still, the primary emphasis is upon Christ bearing the penalty for believers' sins. Substitution is at the core of the concept. It is by substitution and satisfaction people are set free from their captivity.

The Lord's supper speaks of our redemption as well. Jesus declared His "body" was given for us, and in the shedding of His blood, the "new covenant" was established. Luke stressed this in 22:19-20 and again in Acts 20:28 when Paul spoke of "the church of God, which he hath purchased with his own blood" (KJV).

The question is never raised in the New Testament concerning *to whom* the ransom price was paid. The old patristic idea that Satan received the ransom is abhorrent to biblical concepts. The stress rests on the high price that was paid: the "precious blood of Christ." Thus believers now have full forgiveness of all their sins. As Buchsel has reminded us, "Full remission cannot be separated from the person of Jesus, it cannot be separated from His death. . . . Jesus' saying about His death is to be interpreted neither in terms of an example of punishment which serves as a deterrent, not in terms of man's need of a demonstration of the infinite love of God. . . . we appropriate His death as our ransom."[61] In Christ believers are set free and move into life at the full. People who live all their lives in bondage to sin, frustration, and fear of death, desperately need to hear the truth, so they can be redeemed by the precious blood of Christ, for that leads to eternal life.

Eternal Life

The concluding phrase of the well-known John 3:16 passage, actually reads *zoen aionion*: "life to the ages." This displays the more purely eschatological aspects of salvation. It raises the whole question of time. What is *everlasting*? This study begins by stating what it is not.

For the Greeks, especially Plato, eternity was not merely endless, extended time. *Everlasting* meant something quite different to the Greeks. They actually held to the concept of *timelessness*. In Platonic thought, time was only a *copy* of the real. Eternity is a timeless ultimate universal. So, "everlasting" is something not really commensurate with time as we know it. The fact that people in the West have been influenced by this Greek philosophy is evident. This is demonstrated in one of the hymns of Christian worship which reads: "When the trumpet of the Lord shall sound, / and *time shall be no more.*"[62] Oscar Cullmann declared, "How much the thinking of our days roots in Hellenism, and how little in biblical Christianity, becomes clear to us when we confirm the fact that far and wide the Christian church and Christian theology distinguish time and eternity in the Platonic-Greek manner."[63]

Cullmann rejected the idea that eternity is the eradication of time, and he is correct in so doing. Einstein taught us that God created time as He created space. In Einstein's words, humanity is bound up in a "time-space capsule." At the final judgment God is not going to eliminate space, the created universe. The Bible makes it clear He is going to purify it and make it as He originally intended it to be (2 Pet. 3:10-13). If this is true of space, then God is certainly not going to do away with time either, for the two are intrinsically interrelated. Eternity is not the end of time. It is the ushering in of time as God wants it to be, just as space will one day be as God desires.

This means eternity is not mere timelessness, nor is it an endless stretch of time as people know it. Of course, the Bible uses a "time word," *aeon* (age), to describe eternity (John 3:16); however, that does not mean the New Testament understands eternity as mere endless time. Paul probably would not make a statement like: "Eternity is a long, long time." The word *everlasting* means more than that. What does it imply?

Cullmann pointed out, "Eternity . . . is possible only as an attribute of God."[64] The Bible tells us God is the one "who is and who was and who is to come" (Rev. 1:4). This implies that eternity is a characteristic or attribute of God. Just as God's characteristics of love and holiness are real, and believers know something of these attributes in their experience, so with God's eternity. They do experience the eternity of God in their time. Thus time, like the other characteristics of God, are experienced, yet not in the full meaning of the terms. So eternity includes time because it is something God has manifested of Himself in creation (no pantheistic ideas are implied here), but eternity shall certainly see the transcendence of time as known in humanity's limited grasp of reality. Thus, time is not eliminated in eternity anymore than space; it is simply transcended. *Transcendence* is the key word.

This does not mean believers do not have and experience eternal life *now*. To the contrary! Everlasting life is not *all* eschatological in nature. Christians experience the reality of eternal life as certainly as they experience God's love and holiness in the present moment. Since they do not experience love and holiness in its final, full transcending character, so it is with eternity. Actually, eternal life has to do with a *quality* of life as well as a *quantity* of life because it is God's kind of life. Thus believers live in this limited world of time and space with eternity already in their hearts. As paradoxical as that sounds, such is surely the meaning of John 3:16 (and many other passages). This sort of principle is shot throughout the whole of Christian experience. As Cullmann put it, "The Christ-event signifies a revelation of the divine Lordship over time as a whole. Thus the Holy Spirit is nothing else than the anticipation of the end in the present."[65] Eternal life is life indeed.

Conclusion

Eternal life is something far more than timelessness or just the stretching out endlessly of earthly time. It is the moving into the transcendent realm of time and space as the transcendent God sees it. That is another aspect of the truth seen earlier in 1 John: "We shall be like him, for we shall see him as he is" (3:2).

Notice, finally, it is everlasting *life*, because it is sharing the eternity of God. "In him was life" (John 1:4). This is the salvation of God in Christ. What good news! That is what believers are to share: the good news of salvation.

Notes

1. See Werner Foerster and Georg Fohrer, "sozo, soteria, soter, soterios," in *Theological Dictionary of the New Testament*, 10 vols. 7:965.

2. Ibid., 966.

3. Ibid., 970.

4. Ibid., 973.

5. Ibid., 976.

6. A fine work in this area of study is in *The Interpreter's Dictionary of the Bible*, vol. 4, an article by Alan Richardson, 168-181. Also see, Claus Westermann, *Elements of Old Testament Theology* (Atlanta: John Knox Press, 1946).

7. Foerster and Fohrer, *Theological Dictionary*, 7:992.

8. Ibid., 998.

9. Sherman E. Johnson, *The Gospel According to St. Mark* (London: Adams and Charles Black, 1960), 83.

10. Henry E. Turlington, "Mark" in *The Broadman Bible Commentary*, vol. 8 (Nashville: Broadman Press, 1969). 294. Turlington followed Branscomb and Johnson in his final interpretation, but he was correct on the point quoted above.

11. Edward A. McDowell, "1-2-3 John" in *The Broadman Bible Commentary*, vol. 12 (Nashville: Broadman Press, 1972), 223.

12. Ibid.

13. Raymond E. Brown, *The Epistle of John* in *The Anchor Bible* (New York: Doubleday and Co., Inc., 1982), 618.

14. McDowell, *Broadman Bible Commentary*, 223 (author's italics).

15. *The Illustrated Bible Dictionary*, Part 2 (Wheaton: InterVaristy Press, 1980), 634.

16. R. H. Charles, *A Critical History of the Doctrine of a Future Life* (London: Adam and Charles Black, 1913), 367-368.

17. Ibid., 366.

18. Ibid., 431.

19. Rather strangely, John R. W. Stott as a well-known Evangelical thinker takes a similar stance in *Essentials: A Liberal/Evangelical Dialogue* (London: Hodder and Stoughton, 1988). This does not, however, mitigate his strong Evangelical stand on issues like the substitutionary atonement that is discussed in this book.

20. Clark Pinnock, *Christianity Today*, "Fire, then Nothing," 20 March 1987, 40. It has been contended by some, that annihilation is a worse punishment than everlasting punishment. To cease to exist is unthinkable torment.

21. Ibid. Pinnock wrote again on this argument in *Criswell Theological Review* 4 (Spring 1990):243-259.

22. Ibid., 40.

23. Paul Tillich, *Systematic Theology*, vol. II (Chicago: The University of Chicago Press, 1951), 67.

24. Rudolph Bultmann, *Theology of the New Testament* (London: SCM Press, Ltd., 1955), II, 19. The several quotations in this book from Bultmann are not meant to be exhaustive of his thought.

25. I. H. Leckie, *The World to Come and Final Destiny* (Edenburough: T. and T. Clark, 1922), 250.

26. David Wells, "Everlasting Punishment," *Christianity Today*, 20 March 1987, 42.

27. R. H. Charles, *A Critical History of the Doctrine of a Future Life* (New York: Schocken Books, 1963), 462. Charles does seem to hold that there are some who are finally unrepentant, for example, the angels of Satan, and they will be annihilated by self-execution. See 463.

28. Quoted by Alex R. Vidler, *Christian Belief* (London: SCM Press, Ltd., 1950) 109. This is not meant to imply C. H. Dodd is a universalist.

29. Roger Nicole, "Universalism: Will Everyone Be Saved?" *Christianity Today*, 20 March 1987, 36.

30. Ibid., 39.

31. Ibid., 37.

32. Ibid., 40.

33. Kenneth S. Kantzer, "Troublesome Questions," *Christianity Today*, 20 March 1987, 45.

34. There has also been debate over whether the streets of heaven are literally gold. But, to repeat, what makes heaven a blessed place is the Lord's presence whether the gold and precious stones of the New Jerusalem are known as precious materials in this life.

35. Nicole, "Universalism," 37-38.

36. Karl Barth, *The Epistle to the Romans* (London: Oxford University Press, 1933), 47 (Barth's italics).

37. Albert N. Arnold and D. B. Ford, "Commentary on the Epistle to the Romans, *An American Commentary on the New Testament* (Philadelphia: American Baptist Publication Society, 1989), 48.

38. R. C. H. Lenski, *The Interpretation of St. Paul's Epistle to the Romans* (Minneapolis: Augsburg Publishing House, 1936), 100.

39. William Sanday, "The Epistle to the Romans" in *The International Critical Commentary*, (New York: Charles Scribner's Sons, 1896), 44.

40. Nicole, "Universalism" in *Christianity Today*, 38.

41. Friedrich Buchsel and Johannes Herrmann, *"hileos, hilaskomai, hilasmos, hilas-terion"* in *Theological Dictionary of the New Testament*, 10 vols. (Grand Rapids: William B. Eerdmans Publishing Co., 1965), 3:318.

42. R. Abba, "Expiation," in *The Interpreter's Dictionary of the Bible*, 5 vols. (Nashville: Abingdon Press, 1962), 2:200.

43. Buchsel and Herrmann, *Theological Dictionary*, 3:317.

44. Ibid., 3:317.

45. Ibid.

46. George E. Ladd, *A Theology of the New Testament* (Grand Rapids: William B. Eerdmans Publishing Co., 1974), 448 (author's italics).

47. Donald G. Bloesch, "Expiation, Propitiation" in the *Holman Bible Dictionary* (Nashville: Holman Bible Publishers, 1991), 460.

48. Other important words, such as *reconciliation*, either have been or will be considered in other contexts.

49. Gottfried Quell and Gottlob Schrenk, *"dike, dikaios, dikaiosune, dikaioo, di-kaioma, dikaiosis, dikaiokrisia,"* *Theological Dictionary of the New Testament*, 10 vols. (Grand Rapids: William B. Eerdmans Publishing Co., 1964), 2:212.

50. Ibid., 2:216.

51. Ibid.

52. Ladd, *Theology of the New Testament*, 441.

53. Ibid., 446. I have followed George E. Ladd's presentation in this section. For a full discussion, see Ladd's *A Theology of the New Testament*, 437-450.

54. Quell and Schrenk, *Theological Dictionary*, 2:216.

55. *The Illustrated Bible Dictionary*, 2:843.

56. *Baker's Dictionary of Theology*, ed. Everett Harrison (Grand Rapids: Baker Book House, 1960), 438.

57. D. Procksch and F. Buchsel, *'luo, analuo, analusis, epiluo, epilusis, kataluo, kata-luma, akatalutos, lutron, antilutron, lutroo, lutrosis, lutrotes, apolutrosis,"* *Theological Dictionary of the New Testament*, 10 vols. (Grand Rapids: William B. Eerdmans Publishing Co., 1967), 4:349.

58. Ibid., 4:343-344 (Drummond's italics).

59. C. E. B. Cranfield, *The First Epistle of Peter* (London: SCM, 1950), 67-68.

60. Leon Morris, *New Testament Theology* (Grand Rapids: Zondervan Publishing House, 1986), 318.

61. Procksch and Buchsel, *Theological Dictionary*, 4:347-349.

62. *When the Roll Is Called Up Yonder* by James M. Black (Drummond's italics).

63. Oscar Cullmann, *Christ and Time*, trans. Floyd V. Filson (Philadelphia: Westminster Press, 1960), 61.

64. Ibid., 62. In all of Cullmann's arguments he seemed to view eternity too much as an endless succession of time. He took his cue from the expressions of the early church, but one wonders: Did he view time as a part of creation? He stated that time "is . . . not bound to creation" (Ibid., 63). This is rather hard to sustain, not only biblically, but in the light of science as Einstien pointed it out to us in his general theory of relativity.

65. Ibid., 72.

9

The Nature of God's Grace: *Basileus* The Kingdom of God

"He went about ... preaching the gospel of the kingdom"
(Matt. 4:23).

Introduction

There is little question in contemporary theological circles as to what constituted the central motif of Jesus' preaching; it was the announcement of the Synoptic Gospels. The experience of our Lord in Nazareth (Luke 4:16-30) certainly makes that clear. As George Beasley-Murray expressed it, "The teaching of Jesus on the kingdom of God ... pervades the entire proclamation of Jesus recorded in the gospels and appears largely to have determined the course of his ministry."[1] New Testament scholars have become vividly aware of this fact in recent years and have produced a wealth of writings as a consequence. And fittingly so, for Jesus is the Messiah who has ushered in the kingdom of God itself. The wonderful news is that anyone can enter that kingdom. Obviously, this has much to do with evangelism.

The first consideration in this admittedly far-too-brief study on the kingdom centers around the nature and purpose of the kingdom Jesus came to announce and personally bring in.

The Nature of God's Kingdom

The kingdom of God is a dynamic concept. It cannot be viewed biblically as static or special. Beasley-Murray stated, "Fundamentally, it means *God acting in sovereign power to judge and to save*—with accent on the latter. It becomes in the teaching of Jesus virtually a synonym for salvation."[2] Obviously, the kingdom, is the heart of what Christianity is all about. To study the concept is therefore vital. Yet, the idea is most complex, and one almost wonders where to begin. Perhaps terminology is again a good place to begin the study.

The Books of Mark, Luke, and Acts normally speak about the kingdom of God, as does John on occasion. Matthew, however, talked about the kingdom of heaven. He used that expression thirty-four times.

Some extreme dispensationalist approaches have seen significance here and have propounded the idea of two different kingdoms based on the terms employed, but this seems unwarranted. It is commonly agreed that Matthew was writing primarily to Jewish readers. Thus, he used the kingdom of *heaven* rather than the kingdom of *God* because of the Jewish tendency to avoid the direct use of God's name. "In any case," as one scholar put it, "no distinction in sense is to be assumed between the two expressions."[3] O. E. Evans agreed and called them "synonymous expressions."[4] This implies that the concept is deeply rooted in the Old Testament.

The Old Testament Meaning of the Kingdom

The kingdom of God, or God's kingly sovereign rule, is viewed biblically in a threefold manner: (1) as an eternal, universal fact; (2) as being made known on earth as people accept it; and (3) as a final consummation for all the created order.[5] This is true of the Old and New Testaments alike.

In the Old Testament the actual phrase "the kingdom of God" does not appear except on one occasion. The writer of Chronicles spoke of the "kingdom of the Lord" (1 Chron. 28:5). Yet, the term *kingdom* is employed in relationship to God numerous times. For example, "thy kingdom" (KJV) is seen in Psalm 45:6; "his kingdom" (KJV) occurs in Psalm 103:19; 145:12. "My kingdom" (KJV) is used as Yahweh speaks in 1 Chronicles 17:14. Phrases like "Thine is the kingdom, O Lord" are also found (see 1 Chron. 29:11, KJV). These types of usages occur frequently.

The theophanies of the Old Testament display God's kingly rule. The simplest and probably oldest form of theophany speaks of God's rule over nature. Amos 1:2 states:

> The Lord roars from Zion,
> and utters his voice from Jerusalem;
> the pastures of the shepherds mourn,
> and the top of Carmel withers.

Concerning this type of theophany, as Beasley-Murray pointed out, "Two ideas are expressed in them: *the coming of the Lord,* and the *reactions of nature at his coming.*"[6] This raises the question as to why God reveals Himself as He dies. His purpose is clear: to punish the wicked and reward His own people with deliverance from all oppression. This provides the link between the theophany and the holy war motif as illustrated in Judges 4:14. Yahweh comes for judgment and salvation. Nature reels in awe at the coming of the sovereign God.

Other theophanies strike different melodies, such as the "shepherd" note in Isaiah 40:11:

> He will feed his flock like a shepherd,
> he will gather the lambs in his arms,
> he will carry them in his bosom,
> and gently lead those that are with young.

The theology that lies back of this type of theophany demonstrates God as Master of creation and one who redeems His people. The exodus stands as the archetype. Therefore, the future is bright with hope. Future deliverance will surely come, because "Our God Reigns."

God's kingdom in the Old Testament is also portrayed in the well-known phrase, "the Day of the Lord." This expression is clearly not a date but an event. It was an event in which God acted in absolute sovereignty. The concept is most important, for it "forms the boundary between history and the kingdom of God."[7] Often, it came in the metaphor of battle: God was and is a mighty Warrior. The prophet asked, "Who can endure the day of his coming, and who can stand when he appears?" (Mal. 3:2).

The Book of Daniel displays the power of the coming of God. In Daniel 7, Yahweh came to subdue evil and deliver His people. "One like a son of man" (v. 13) came in the clouds, much like a theophany, to eliminate evil. The "one like a son of man" implies the messianic idea, even if only implicitly. At least it accords with the messianic traditions of Jesus. In Him, God will establish His rule.

It can thus be summarized by saying that the purpose of the coming of the Day of the Lord is to establish the kingdom of God on earth. The messianic reign will surely come. The whole idea emerges as central to Old Testament thought. As Koehler expressed it, "The one fundamental statement in the theology of the Old Testament is this: God is the ruling Lord."[8] This is seen in a political way and in a theological sense. Beasley-Murray brought it together in this description of the kingdom:

> 1. *The universality of the rule of Yahweh*. . . . The turning of the nations to God is integral to the hope of the kingdom. . . .
> 2. *The righteousness of the kingdom*. . . . [It is] the action of the Lord for the cleansing and renewal of the people. . . .
> 3. *The peace of the kingdom*. . . . This "peace" extends to the life of man in his relations with God and with others, for peace is an all-embracing synonym for salvation. . . .
> Thus, the goal of history is reached in the revelation and universal acknowledgment of Yahweh's sovereignty, the triumph of righteousness, and the establishment of peace and salvation in the world.[9]

All this means a time is coming when a kingdom will dawn on the earth in which people can share in the redemption of the sovereign Lord. The Lord of hosts is coming for the salvation of His creation. Thus the

Old Testament sets the stage for the glad New Testament announcement: "The time is fulfilled, and the kingdom of God is at hand; repent, and believe in the gospel" (Mark 1:15).

The Kingdom of God in the New Testament

There are a variety of approaches and views concerning what the kingdom of God means in the New Testament. For example, many scholars view the kingdom essentially on an individual basis. This thrusts the whole idea into the arena of personal religious experience. For example, Harnack's traditional liberal interpretation of the kingdom as "the Fatherhood of God, [and] the brotherhood of man" saw the eschatological elements of the New Testament teaching on the kingdom as "only the time-conditioned husk that contained the kernel of his [Jesus] real religious message."[10]

On the other hand, Johannes Weiss in his small book *The Preaching of Jesus About the Kingdom of God* set forth the idea that Jesus' teaching was in the spirit of Jewish apocalypses; therefore, all the kingdom passages are completely futuristic and eschatological.

Albert Schweitzer was in essential agreement with Weiss[11] and saw the ethical teaching of our Lord as designed for only a brief period before the kingdom comes. Schweitzer believed Jesus fully expected the kingdom to arrive in His own day. Therefore, when it did not, Jesus died a deeply disappointed, disillusioned man.

Rudolf Bultmann held to an imminent approach of the futuristic kingdom, but (as so often seen in Bultmann) it must be interpreted in existential terms. For Bultmann, the kingdom and salvation are virtually one and the same.

C. H. Dodd had much to say in this area of New Testament study. His "realized eschatology" has made a significant impact. Ladd summarized Dodd's grasp of the kingdom: "The Kingdom of God, which is described in apocalyptic language, is in reality the transcendent order beyond time and space that has broken into history in the mission of Jesus. In him, the 'wholly other' has entered into history."[12] Dodd can be criticized on two scores: (1) the "wholly other" transcendent concept as Dodd presented it is more platonic than biblical,[13] and (2) Dodd minimized the futuristic aspect of the kingdom. Jeremias made this sort of criticism concerning Professor Dodd. Later, however, Dodd did admit the kingdom yet awaits full consummation beyond temporal history.

Jeremias' view can be described as "eschatology in process of realization."[14] He views Jesus' entire ministry, the miracles, teaching, etc., as an event in which the kingdom of God is realized. However, there is the eschatological consummation that involves the resurrection and *parousia* of the Lord. In this climatic event, the triumph of God will be revealed.

Actually, there are several similarities between Jeremias and Dodd, albeit he criticized Dodd.

One final modern view to look at briefly is dispensationalism. This influential school holds that all Old Testament prophecy will be fulfilled literally. God will keep His "political" promises to Israel. Moreover, many dispensationalists distinguish between the kingdom of heaven and the kingdom of God. The kingdom of God speaks of the Lord's rule over all. The kingdom of heaven refers to God's promise to the sons of Abraham. It is the theocratic rule of God on earth. Jesus offered the Jews the kingdom, but they rejected it. Consequently, rather than establish the kingdom for the Jews, Jesus introduced a new message of peace for all who would believe, Jew and Gentile alike.

Dispensationalists hold that Matthew's Gospel reveals these realities. The mystery of the "kingdom of heaven" in Matthew 13 is the realm of professing Christians which is the present form of the kingdom until Jesus comes. The kingdom of heaven for the Jews will be realized at the *parousia* when Jesus comes and sets up the kingdom of David as promised in the Old Testament. The Messiah will then rule on earth for one thousand years. The basic presupposition of the entire scheme is two sets of God's people: Jews and Christians, that is, Israel and the church. This has been a very popular approach in many Evangelical circles, especially since the publication of the Scofield Reference Bible.[15]

Now what can be said about the Kingdom from the New Testament teachings on the subject? At the outset, it may help to look at the actual word *kingdom* itself.

Even though the theological implications of the term *kingdom* is rather controversial, there is no disagreement over the immediate lexical meaning of the term. In the Old Testament, it often simply meant "national or civic monarchy."[16] This usage was temporal and limited, but its root at times was used to denote the Redeemer King. Therefore, a timeless as well as a temporal element emerges implicitly as Yahweh rules and shall one day reign over all.

In the New Testament, "In relation to the general usage of *basileia*, . . . it is to be noted . . . that it signifies the 'being,' 'nature' and 'state' of the king. Since the reference is to a king, we do best to speak first of his 'dignity' or 'power.' . . . second . . . the dignity of the king is expressed in the territory ruled by him, i.e., his 'kingdom.' "[17] This is very straightforward; why then the theological controversy over ideas of the kingdom?

The disagreement over the nature of God's rule of dignity and power basically centers around the time element in the kingdom. That is, does the kingdom reveal itself as essentially eschatological or present? Many have defended the concept that the *basileia* is synonymous with the "eschaton," the final, futuristic order of God's rule over all. This approach, quite obviously, thrusts the kingdom *exclusively* into the future. The Hebrew word for kingdom as used by the Old Testament writers contains the idea of a reign or rule in the historical sense, and this concept became the foundation for the teaching of Jesus and the rest of the New Testament. God's people even pray for the coming of God's kingdom here on earth (Matt. 6:10). Yet, there are very clear eschatological elements in the kingdom of God.

Since the word used in the Scriptures is *both* eschatological and historical, there must be a present *and* a futuristic element in the very fabric of God's kingly rule. The messianic reign encompasses both. In other words, God is *now* the King of the universe and rules in the hearts of believers; and He must also *become* King of kings and Lord of lords for all in the eschaton. God's kingly rule *now* and *then* is the key to a full biblical understanding of the nature of the kingdom of God.

The Eschatological Kingdom

The futuristic aspect of God's kingdom means that, when the moment arrives, this age will end, and the "Age to Come" will be inaugurated in all its fullness. The kingdom, used in its "consummation aspect," means both the coming of God's kingly rule and the realm in which that rule is exercised. Therefore, inviting people to enter the kingdom means salvation, eternal life, and entering the glorious "Age to Come" where God rules over all.

Moreover, this coming of the kingdom of God denotes the final judgment of the devil and his angels (Matt. 25:41), the complete sanctification of God's people (Matt. 13:36-43), perfect union with Christ at the marriage feast of the Lamb (Luke 13:28-29), and the triumph of God. In other words, "The Kingdom of God is a synonym for the Age to Come."[18] It means *heaven*.

The New Testament produced a quite radical addition to the Old Testament eschatological concept. Israel saw the "Age to Come" with all its benefits as a purely Jewish experience, but Jesus came and invited all people into His kingdom (Matt. 28:18-20; compare 13:36-43). Jesus invited both Jews and Gentiles to enter the kingdom of God. Jewish particularism was eradicated. That will be a magnificent event when people come from both East and West and sit down at the marriage feast of the Lord, but there is more to the kingdom idea.

The Kingdom of God as Present Experience

Although C. H. Dodd probably went too far in his views on "realized eschatology," he can in principle help us. There is a definite sense in which the kingdom is already present. This aspect of God's kingly rule is not as central to Judaism as in the New Covenant. Jesus was the innovator here. He saw His own historical ministry as the fulfillment of the

Old Testament kingdom promise. In the synagogue at Nazareth (Luke 4:16-21), Jesus made it very clear: "Today this scripture has been fulfilled in your hearing" (v. 21). Jesus said, in essence, the kingdom is here and personified in Himself. One of the strongest statements Jesus made on this subject was: "If it is by the Spirit of God that I cast out demons, then the kingdom of God has come upon you" (Matt. 12:28). A debate has been going on for some time concerning the word *ephthasen*, "has come." However, the word surely means nothing less than "actual presence." As Beasley-Murray put it, "The final triumph, to be witnessed at the close of history, has therefore been decisively anticipated in the midst of history. That faith is at the heart of apostolic Christianity."[19] Satan is now a defeated, dethroned foe.

There are those, of course, who disagree. For example, Bultmann argued that Jesus reflected only the futuristic, Jewish concept of the kingdom. He believed the New Testament shift to a present aspect of the kingdom grew out of Paul's theology. Bultmann said, "For my part, the only interpretation I can give to the Pauline [view] . . . is a critical one."[20] He argued the Old-Testament-vintage Day of the Lord was essentially held by Jesus, and our Lord saw it arriving at the *parousia*. That is to say, Jesus did not essentially change the character of the Old Testament thrust; however, Bultmann viewed the *parousia* as a myth. He said, "We can no longer look for the return of the Son of Man on the clouds of heaven, or hope that the faithful will meet him in the air."[21] That, of course, decisively destroys the historicity of the Lord's return. For Bultmann, the kingdom in its present manifestation came from Paul, not Jesus.

Beasley-Murray has countered the Bultmannian line very convincingly in his work *Jesus and the Kingdom*. He declared, "The decisive shift of eschatology from the future alone to the future-in-the-present was the work of Jesus, not of Paul and John. *According to Jesus*, the coming of the kingdom of God is the *determinative factor* in his ministry of word and deed."[22] There is definitely a present-tense sense to God's rule.

This obviously implies that Jesus as Messiah is the "Revealer of the Kingdom."[23] Again, Beasley-Murray put it well:

> To recognize in Jesus the Revelation of the kingdom is to find the way into the kingdom, while to stumble over the truth of his person is to stumble into ruin.
> . . . Jesus portrays himself as Champion of the kingdom, Initiator of the kingdom, Instrument of the kingdom, Representative of the kingdom, Mediator of the kingdom, Bearer of the kingdom, Revealer of the kingdom.[24]

In a word, Jesus is the personification of the kingdom, the Ruler of that realm, the Door by which one enters, and thus the sovereign Lord of all. Jesus, in the days of His flesh, manifested the kingdom in His own person and in His words and deeds; it all culminated in His death and resurrection and the gift of the Spirit. The process will end in the *parousia*. Moreover, people can enter and enjoy its immediate fruit as they look forward to the consummation when the Lord comes again to rule over all creation, including Satan and his hosts of evil. No contemporary person can bring in the kingdom, but Christians can help people to enter that realm, and that is evangelism.

Of course, there abides an element of mystery in the kingdom: God's final and ultimate victory over all evil remains in the realm of the spiritual future. Yet there is a pragmatic victory over evil to be worked out in a historical setting because the kingdom has already come. The historical element is important because evil came into the human experience on a historical plane in the garden. Therefore, God desires to defeat Satan in a historical framework.

In other words, God is doing in history today through the "second Adam" what the "first Adam" failed to do. The historicity of all this is in some sense philosophically consistent. Moreover, this puts God right in the course of our human history. He does not stand aloof from our struggles. Even though the final deliverance comes at the Lord's second advent, believers can be victorious in Christ in the present moment by faith. In Luke 17:20, Jesus told His detractors the kingdom of God was already in their midst; therefore, when one receives Christ, the kingdom comes within, and is the beginning of final victory.

Thus, the kingdom is dynamically bound up in the history of the church and the history of the world alike. The church is the assembly of those who have already heard and submitted in faith to the gospel and have come to kingdom life in Christ. The church is thus a visible, tangible manifestation of the kingdom. The church is *not* the kingdom in totality, for Christ's kingship extends over all, but God's people demonstrate the kingdom in a contemporary dynamic fashion. Then the time will come when every knee shall bow, and all shall acknowledge Jesus as Lord (Phil. 2:9-11). That one divine moment is the destiny to which life is headed and, therefore, an "event whose significance is only finally comparable to the moment of creation at the beginning."[25] Then there shall be "a new heaven and a new earth" (Rev. 21:1), and, "the kingdom of the world has become the kingdom of our Lord and of his Christ, and he shall reign for ever and ever" (Rev. 11:15). This leads to the next consideration, the future kingdom.

The Future Kingdom

What about the future? What eschatological form will the kingdom of God take? Thinkers diverge greatly here. The theological battles between so-called premillennialist, postmillennialist, and amillennialist views go on interminably. It is not the purpose of this book to discuss this controversial issue; yet some things can be said quite confidently. First, and foundational, the kingdom has already come in the sense Christ came and opened the door to that eternal realm. The cross of our Lord and His glorious resurrection form the very core of establishing the kingdom of God on earth. Second, the church is now charged to proclaim that truth and lovingly call on people to press into the kingdom and become citizens of "heaven" (Phil. 3:20). That is the evangelistic task. Third, Jesus will surely come again to establish fully His reign on earth and bring to a consummation the complete victory of the cross and the empty tomb.

All Evangelicals can surely agree on the major points mentioned above. Furthermore, one's millennial views should in no manner affect one's commitment to evangelize and extend the kingly rule of Christ in the hearts of men and women. That is what matters the most.

At the same time, it is good to settle one's thinking on millennial concerns. One thing should be stressed on the issue: it appears important in the New Testament that the return of our Lord and the setting aright of all wrong takes place on a historical plane. It was in history, in time and space, that things went radically astray. Therefore, it appears Christ will certainly and historically rule on earth. Therefore, His church shall rule with Him until Satan and all evil are thrown in the eternal lake of fire. Philosophical consistency makes it difficult to "spiritualize" or "demythologize" all those realities and put the Lord's consummation out of a historical context. The immediate role of God's kingdom people is to help others join them in the kingdom and together evangelize the world. This must continue until He comes. Therefore, as presently in the kingdom, God's people look to the Day of Consummation when all creation bows before the King.

The Kingdom's Purpose

The above principles prepare the stage for a statement on the prime purpose of the setting up of the kingdom: *reconciliation*. The kingdom of God is a kingdom of reconciliation between God and an estranged creation. Paul told us two things about God's reconciling work in Christ. First, "God was in Christ, reconciling the world unto himself" (2 Cor. 5:19, KJV). Second, "The whole creation has been groaning in travail together until now; . . . as we wait for . . . the redemption of our bodies" (Rom. 8:22-23). Thus Paul presents a twofold unveiling of God's reconciling work in Christ, individual and cosmic.

Individual Reconciliation

Reconciliation (*katallasso*) means " to change," or "to exchange" or "re-store to favor," as in Romans 5:11 and 2 Corinthians 5:18-19.[26] The need of reconciliation is obvious. Human sin has driven several cleavages into life, shattering relationships; all need to be "restored to favor." Theologian Culbert G. Rutenber was correct when he said, "Sin and sinner are intertwined and cannot be separated. It is this fact which gives life its pathos and tragic aspect, both for us and for God. I cannot be abstracted from my sin."[27] The reality of universal, personal sin estranges people from God, from their fellows, even from themselves, and the cleavages are most serious. Sinful people are doomed to live out their lives alienated from God, others, and their own selves. This is what Paul meant when he stated, "The wages of sin is death" (Rom. 6:23).

As implied, the consequences of sin's wages are devastating, for it strikes right at the heart of life's essential relationships. Human life is human because of relationships. First, human beings are related to God because of the fact of creation (Gen. 1—3). They are His creatures, fashioned in His image. That means they have freedom of will, rational minds, and capacities to enter into relationship with their Creator. Second, people are related to their fellows. All are dynamically intertwined with other humans. The Bible says, He has "made of one blood all nations of men for to dwell on all the face of the earth" (Acts 17:26, KJV). Finally, human beings are related to themselves. *I* can talk to *me. I* can dialogue with *myself.* An animal cannot do that. God has given His human creatures the gracious gift of self-consciousness.

Now what is so devastating about personal sin is that it bludgeons and twists and warps all essential human relationships and one is reduced to less than human. In relationship to God, sin breeds guilt and remorse. This robs one of joy and peace and contentment. Regarding relationships with others who have been sinned against, lovelessness is the outcome. Love cements society and human relationships. Sin makes shambles of cohesive factors, destroying what God created humankind for: fellowship. Finally, evil even cuts one off from oneself. Inwardly, people are fragmented, frustrated, fearful, and frantic. They live off their nerves and feed on their fingernails. They are unhappy with themselves, they cannot accept themselves, and, consequently, they cannot accept God and others. There it is: people in sin are guilty, loveless, and in bondage. *If only one's sins were forgiven, and reconciliation with God, others, and oneself were effected!*

Right at the point of that heartfelt cry, the Holy Spirit brings the good news of Christ to the needy life. In Jesus of Nazareth, there is reconciliation. Brunner put it well when he declared, "But one thing there is not in Indian religion or in any religion outside Christianity: a man who came on earth to reconcile to God by the sacrifice of His life those who had become separated from God by their guilt and sin."[28]

We have seen earlier the meaning of the propitiation (*hilasmos*) as accomplished by the life, death, and resurrection of our Lord. In Christ, God and the estranged self meet, and a beautiful reconciliation takes place. That is good news. Peace with God is found.

The nature of God's reconciling grace is all encompassing, for it is reconciliation in and for *agape* love, that is, God's quality of love. Sinners are reconciled to God in and for Christlikeness. The results are most profound and wide sweeping. The barrier is broken; the veil in the temple is rent. Now one can come into God's holy presence through the blood of Christ, thus entering into full fellowship with the living, omnipotent God. Sins are fully and freely forgiven. Reconciliation means forgiveness. Guilt dissipates and the flow of forgiveness fills the life. "In [Christ], we have redemption through his blood, the forgiveness of our sins" (Eph. 1:7).

Moreover, the forgiveness of God is a moral forgiveness. The moral safeguards of the universe are preserved in the reconciling, atoning work of Christ on the cross. God's forgiveness, therefore, never "embarrasses" the forgiven. The cross makes it possible for God to forgive without making God's righteousness a minor matter. P. T. Forsyth described God's love: "It is the love for sinners of a God above all things *holy*, whose holiness makes sin damnable as sin and love active as grace. It can only act in a way that shall do justice to holiness, and restore it."[29] Forgiveness is infused with a moral quality in the atonement. Believers are reconciled by the great love of God, and with that comes peace, joy, and meaning in life. In Christ, they are related to Reality, and that is life indeed.

In the reconciling work of Christ, one is also reconciled in love to one's fellows. Lovelessness due to sin fades away. The middle wall of partition is broken down; he "has made us both one" (Eph. 2:14). Interpersonal peace ensues. In reconciliation, our Lord sheds the love of God "abroad in our hearts by the Holy Ghost" (Rom. 5:5, KJV). Believers are set free to love, even as Christ Himself loved. Now they truly can love one another as they are commanded to do. The Holy Spirit bears His fruit of *agape* in the lives of the reconciled, and they actually become Christlike. That is wholeness, and that is one aspect of what it means to be "filled with the Spirit" (Eph. 5:18). Reconciliation means love and acceptance into the family of God.

Finally, estranged sinners are reconciled to themselves. They know release. They walk in the "glorious liberty of the children of God" (Rom. 8:21). That means freedom from fear and frustration. Knowing they are accepted by God and by their fellows, they can now begin to accept themselves. They know they are not perfect, but they do know they are forgiven and accepted. That brings wholeness and inner peace. As psychiatry would express it, they become a well-integrated personality. The reconciled ones respect and value themselves in love for Christ's sake because of what He has done. Thus slavery to a perverted self and poor self-image are ended. They are reconciled in love. Such is human life in the full, divine sense.

Now all these realities come about solely because of God's reconciling love in Christ. As Rutenber put it: "Evangelism is the persistent effort to get people to take their blinders off and see where they are as the inheritors of the great possessions left them in the last will and testament of the Crucified One. Salvation is possessing one's possessions."[30] That is reconciliation, and this is the nature of the kingdom of God. However, there is more in the biblical truth of reconciliation. It has a cosmic theme.

Cosmic Reconciliation

"The whole creation has been groaning in travail . . . as we wait" (Rom. 8:23). Nature is in turmoil. Evil and suffering abound. Can this be God's world? Is He truly sovereign? The theodicy questions must be faced, especially as one attempts to evangelize. What can be said?

First of all, despite all the problems encountered, it must be emphatically declared that this is God's world. He not only created it, but also He rules it. "His Kingdom rules over all" (Ps. 103:19). The Bible even goes so far as to say God created *all* things, and "it was good" (Gen. 1:25). True, aspects of God's creation went astray and fell into sin. That tragedy precipitated evil and suffering. Yet God's gracious gift of freedom was worth the risk. It was better for God to grant freedom and run the perilous risk of a fall, than to make all His creatures mere robots. The present world with all its problems is still, in the words of the philosophers, the "best of all possible worlds." But why all the evil and suffering? How is the Christian to react to this dilemma?

There are several concepts to help the Christian witness in sharing Christ in the face of evil and suffering. For example, suffering can produce character. Also, some evil is fully deserved because of sin. Moreover, God aids the suffering, even suffering with us as He did in His Son on the cross. Several apologetic answers can be given, as many writers have pointed out; but in the final analysis, the answer is found in the universal reconciliation of the entire universe to the rule of God at the consummation of the age. The real answer to the problem of evil and suffering lies in the fact that one day, the Lord will come and put "all enemies under his feet" (1 Cor. 15:25). Righteousness, peace, and the glory of God will pervade the entire created order as evil, death, and decay vanish. This is beyond immediate human grasp, as all ultimate concepts are, but several things, at least in seminal form, can be known.

First, sin and evil will be completely done away in the "coming forth of the Lord." This truth is clearly seen throughout the Scriptures. Kingdom culmination and setting of what is wrong to what is right finds emphasis in the Book of Revelation. Werner Kümmel outlined the impact of apocalyptic writing generally, stating:

> Apocalypticism is controlled by a historical, ethical dualism. The present aeon is evil, standing under the lordship of demons; God has turned away from the earth; His will was formerly manifested in the history of the fathers; in the time of the end he will again reveal himself mightily and will finally prevail. The world lies in wickedness, but God will help. This aeon of the godless, earthly kingdom is coming to an end; the new aeon of God's transcendental kingdom stands at the door.[31]

Kümmel said that the Book of Revelation is the "total transformation of the Jewish into Christian apocalypticism of history."[32] This means, "God's victory in heaven guarantees His coming victory on earth."[33] The final coming of the Kingdom of God is a day of Judgment. All that is contrary to the will of the sovereign God is cast from His presence (Rev. 20:14—21:8). Righteousness will prevail.

Second, the full reconciliation of the redeemed takes place (1 Cor. 15:51-57). This manifests itself in the resurrection of the body.

Third, a universal reign of peace will commence that will last for all eternity. All sorrow and tears are past (Rev. 20:4; 22:3). The Prince of peace will reign.

Fourth, the whole created order will settle down into the thing of beauty God intended it to be when He first created it.

Fifth, God will dwell with His people in face-to-face fullness (Rev. 22:4).

Sixth, God's redeemed will rule with their sovereign Lord (Rev. 22:5).

Seventh, all creation will obey, worship, and adore "him who is seated on the throne" (Rev. 4:10; 11:15-19).

Eighth, God's full glory will be revealed (Rev. 11:19).

Finally, our reigning, sovereign God will be glorified by all reality (Rev. 7:11-12).

The conclusion of the matter is that all creation will one day be caught up in God's great reconciling work. That will be a glorious day to be sure. Reconciliation in the kingdom is truly cosmic. This is no doubt why Paul wrote, "I consider that the sufferings of this present time are not worth comparing with the glory that is to be revealed to us" (Rom. 8:18). That is the final biblical answer to the problem of evil and suffering.

There is one more significant truth about the consummation of the kingdom that needs emphasizing, God's reconciled creation will *serve* Him forever. John in the Revelation (7:13-15) wrote:

> Then one of the elders addressed me, saying, "Who are these, clothed in white robes, and whence have they come?" I said to him, "Sir, you know." And he said to me, "These are they who have come out of the great tribulation; they have washed their robes and made them white in the blood of the Lamb." Therefore are they before the throne of God, / and serve him day and night within his temple; / and he who sits upon the throne / will shelter them with his presence.

This leads to a very important kingdom principle directly related to contemporary evangelism, declaring the kingdom of God and urging people to enter it is to be the Christian's constant task. Especially in Acts believers discover a direct connection between evangelistic declaration and the kingdom of God. In Acts 8:12 the content of Philip's preaching in Samaria is presented as "good news about the kingdom of God and the name of Jesus Christ." Paul's message to Rome was "preaching the kingdom of God" (Acts 28:31). In the synagogue at Ephesus, Paul "for three months spoke boldly, arguing and pleading about the kingdom of God" (Acts 19:8).

Therefore, God's reconciled people are to testify and persuade others to the end result of convincing them to enter the kingdom and thus be reconciled to God. As Paul put it: "So we are ambassadors for Christ, God making His appeal through us. We beseech you on behalf of Christ, be reconciled to God" (2 Cor. 5:20). The gospel, the *kerygma*, is God's reconciling kingdom truth.

The implications are clear; those who enter the kingdom come to Christ through the door of repentance and faith (Acts 20:21). Each of those terms deserve a careful analysis, because confusion here not only muddles the gospel, it can divert people from entering the messianic kingdom and thus sharing in its glorious consummation.

The Conditions for Entering the Kingdom of God

The first condition to experiencing salvation centers in the repenting process.

Repentance

If any mistake is made in kingdom proclamation by segments of contemporary Evangelicals, it revolves around minimizing the call to repentance. However, if there is no repentance, there is no life (Luke 13:3).

Repentance is clearly an Old Testament emphasis as well as a New Testament truth. To the prophets repentance meant essentially "to turn back," as in Jeremiah 8:4 and Ezekiel 33:19. It is a constant prophetic theme. The Old Testament visualizes fellowship with God as personal. It also views sin as personal and destructive of one's personal fellowship with God. Therefore, repentance which restores fellowship must likewise be personal and deeply sincere. Repentance thus becomes a renewal of life and a new heart in commitment to Yahweh (Ezek. 18:31).

In the New Testament the verb *metanoeo* (to repent) occurs thirty-two times and the noun form *metanoia* twenty-two times. In everyday usage, it meant merely to change one's mind about an object or consideration, but the Holy Spirit by inspiration filled it full of rich theological content in the hands of those responsible for the Scriptures. It evolved to mean not just a change of mind, but a change of attitude, a change of feeling, a change in one's entire direction of life. *Metanoeo*, as used by biblical writers, Michel said, means a "change of heart either generally or in respect of a specific sin." *Metanoein* "implies that one has later arrived at a different view of something."[34] It involves the whole person: mind, emotions, and will. Above all, it engages the volitional aspect of one's personhood. It means, in the spiritual sense, to turn back or to be converted by the exercise of one's will. Those who enter the kingdom must exercise "repentance *to God*" (Acts 20:21, author's italics). One *decides* for God. It is a shift in one's entire orientation of life and moves a person toward God. Repentance is a total change that causes one to turn absolutely from sin and self, wholly to Christ and righteousness. Anything short of that indepth, radical commitment falls short of what the Bible means by repentance. Such is the essence of making Christ Lord.

Repentance is the heart of what is commonly called *conversion*. Conversion comes from the *epistrephein* word group and means to change, or to turn around. A truly repentant person is a converted person. At times the best translation of *metanoeo* is "to convert." The concept is used in the Bible both actively and passively. At times one is seen as converted by God (passive). Other times one is required to convert oneself (active). That paradox will be discussed later.

All of this gives reason to John the Baptist's demand to bring forth "fruit that befits repentance" (Matt. 3:8). Moreover, the preaching of our Lord was in essence the same. Jesus viewed repentance as vital if one is to live as a kingdom citizen (Mark 1:15; Luke 13:1-3). Jesus declared repentance involves the total person: the tree is "known by its fruit" (Matt. 12:33). Jesus even went beyond the prophets on this point. As one writer observed:

He [Jesus] deepens the prophetic demand in his interpretation of the inwardness of sin (Matt. 5:28), by his insistence on the second mile (v. 41) and love to enemies (v. 44); and by the radical rejection of everything that hinders return to God (Matt. 5:29; 6:19; 7:13; Mark 3:31-35; 10:21). . . .

> Repentance means becoming another person. . . . Entrance to the kingdom
> is for the poor in spirit, the receptive, the small and helpless.[35]

The preaching of Jesus on repentance ushered in a fresh, demanding note. The Old Testament proclaimers realized that only God could give a new heart and thus precipitate repentance. To make such a decision of depth lies beyond mere human attainment. They looked forward to the time when God in grace should perform the miracles of raising people from the "valley" of dry bones (Ezek. 37). Such a time would come when the Messiah arrived. So when Jesus announced: "The time is fulfilled, and the kingdom of God is at hand, repent, and believe in the gospel" (Mark 1:15), repentance became not only a possibility, it was demanded of those who would enter the kingdom. Now, in a way, what is "impossible" with people becomes "possible" with God (Mark 10:27). Thus the passive and active aspects of repentance are seen.

Therefore, in the preaching of the apostolic church, repentance was basic (Acts 2:38; 3:19; 5:31; 8:22; 2 Cor. 7:9; Heb. 6:15; Rev. 2:21). The early church saw it all quite simply: the Father's wish is "that all should reach repentance" (2 Pet. 3:9). They proclaimed that message in the power of the Spirit.

Furthermore, repentance is dynamically related to baptism in the New Testament (Acts 2:38). That connection provides further insight as to what repentance really means. For example, in Romans 10:9, Paul stated that one must confess with the mouth "Jesus is Lord." Most New Testament scholars view this primitive verbal confession as a baptismal confession. That is, one makes an open confession of Christ's lordship before the watching world in the dramatic act of baptism. Commentator Charles Vaughan stated that the passage is probably a "reference to the confession of faith in Baptism."[36] Dale Moody agreed and stated, "Many commentators believe that this is an early baptismal confession of faith, since baptism was often administered 'in the name of the Lord Jesus.' "[37] Rudolf Schnackenburg also agreed:

> The baptismal *confession* could well be in mind in Romans 10:9, since the
> passage possesses an almost liturgical style. The formula, "Jesus is Kurios"
> (cf. Philippians 2:11; I Corinthians 12:3), the terms "believe" and "con-
> fess," echoes baptismal terminology.[38]

The baptismal scene is charged with emotion. In the Roman world it was the custom to declare verbally "Caesar is Lord." To stand before the eyes of the world and declare "Jesus is Lord" was no small matter. It was an open, clear-cut repudiation of the lordship of Caesar and the exalting of Jesus as Lord. That could be extremely costly. As Hobbs stated in his commentary:

"Lord Jesus" is not just so many words to be repeated glibly. Since the Greek has no definite article, it may read "Jesus as Lord," or "Jesus is Lord." Those who worshiped Roman emperors said "Lord Caesar," or *Kurios Kaisaros*. Refusing to say this, Christians said, *Kurios Jesous*. Christians were persecuted, some even to death, because of this. To confess "Lord Jesus" involved more than simply uttering words. It came to be a matter of life and death.[39]

The connection between baptism and repentance thus begins to become clear. People would not submit to baptism making such verbal statements of Christ's lordship unless they had so completely turned to God that they were willing to lay down their very lives for Jesus' sake. In other words, no one would confess the Lord Jesus unless he or she had *truly repented*. Thus it becomes obvious what repentance is in its positive character. It is nothing less than a complete abandonment to the unequivocal lordship of Christ in one's life. Repentance is a turning from sin's dominion to God's mastery. It becomes a life-style. One does not repent just once; real repentance is a life of continual turning. Repentance thus produces the fruit of discipleship. Actually, the call of Christ is a call to discipleship. The repentant life is a deep, absolute, personal, inward developing relationship to Christ. It is no external religious form. It goes far beyond emotions or words. Sorrow for sin may be there, but sorrow (*metamelomai*) is *not* repentance (*metanoia*). In fact, the sorrow of this world can lead to death (2 Cor. 7:10). Godly sorrow can lead to or produce repentance (2 Cor. 7:10), but it can only lead—it is not repentance in itself. It is not our tears but our *turning* that effects salvation.[40] As Nygren expressed it, "To be a Christian is to have Christ as one's Lord, and thereby be freed from all other lords and powers. That is certainly nothing external."[41] Simply put, when one repents, one gives Christ complete control of life for time and eternity, and "except ye repent, ye shall all likewise perish" (Luke 13:3, KJV). Repentance is the first step into the kingdom of God.

Often it seems that preaching, witnessing, and sharing the message of Christ is rather bereft of the stress on the necessity of repentance. That situation must be changed. Minimizing repentance not only presents a truncated gospel, it may well lead people astray into false hopes of being Kingdom citizens when they really are not. How tragic it will be for some who thought they were truly converted only to hear the Lord say on that final day, "Depart from me, you cursed, into the eternal fire" (Matt. 25:41). Their blood may be on the hands of those who did not call them to true, biblical repentance.

Repentance is only the first step, although an important step. A repentant person must also exercise faith.

Faith

In Paul's declaration of Romans 10:9-10, he said one must not only confess the lordship of Christ, but also one is to "believe in the heart." Faith becomes the other vital ingredient to reconciliation with God and entrance into the kingdom. What does it mean to "believe in the Lord Jesus, and . . . be saved"? (Acts 16:31).

Repentance and faith are not in any sense in opposition to each other. To the contrary, they are intrinsically united. One cannot repent one day and exercise faith the next, or *visa versa*. As it has been put, "Repentance and faith are two sides of the same coin."[42] That must be kept clear. Repentance and faith are one act in which redemption is effected. Of course, that is speaking in an experiential, pragmatic manner. Thinkers have debated for centuries which comes first in the order of salvation, the *ordo salutis,* faith or repentance. For example, R. T. Kendall argued that John Calvin saw faith as the first gift of God in salvation, and then the regenerate person could repent. The next generation of Calvinists, termed "hyper-Calvinists" or "high-Calvinists," Theodore Beza, William Perkins, and the Puritans, reversed the order of salvation, as did Jacobus Arminius.[43] The point to be made in this context is that faith forms the other side of the coin to repentance in responding to the Spirit's call. In pragmatic evangelization, the call to the unconverted is simply to repent and believe the gospel (Acts 20:21). Such an act makes one a disciple of Jesus Christ, for salvation and discipleship are essentially one and the same.

The root words for faith in the Scriptures are packed with meaning. The linguistic usage of the terms are quite varied. The Old Testament root signifies "firmness" or "stability." The verb, *he'emin*, used in the *hiphil* means "to believe," "to trust," or "to say amen to." Implied is a relationship, ultimately a personal relationship, as is true with repentance. God is the primary object of personal faith; hence, faith points to a personal, saving, helping relationship with Yahweh. At times the concept of "faithfulness" is the prominent idea. At other times the sense is "true religion," often associated with "grace," "steadfast love," and "righteousness."

In classical Greek the verb meant "to trust," "have confidence in," whether of persons or of things. The noun connotes the idea of "trust," "reliance," and "be confident that." It can be used in the concrete sense of "pledge," "guarantee," or "proof."

In New Testament *koine* Greek, faith (*pistis*, noun, *pisteuo* verb)[44] can connote belief in God as almighty, self-revealing, and benevolent. In the Synoptics it can be translated *"trust,"* or "give credence to." The noun form, in the Synoptics, "mostly carries the meaning of confidence in

God and trust in his power to heal and save."[45] Jesus constantly used the word in this manner: "Your faith has made you well" (Mark 5:34).

For Paul, faith was the basic Christian attitude, the core of the divine-human encounter. The Pauline corpus presents no radical development of the basic ideas outlined above. For Paul *pistis* meant "utter dependence on God and belief in his power, as seen in Romans 4:16-20 and Colossians 2:12."[46] The idea of faith as "power" in Paul was, however, something of a development and meant to show true faith as not being mere words or a shallow, intellectual grasp of some Christian ideas. Faith has power to change life profoundly. As seen so often in Paul, true faith justifies one before God (Rom. 3:1-4). As Michael Green put it, "Faith is the hand, the empty hand, by which we receive the divine gift of justification, redemption and reconciliation."[47] Faith is absolute. Faith, flowing out of grace, precipitates power to be a disciple.

John at times uses the word in a rather distinctive manner. John speaks of the belief that Jesus is the Messiah sent by the Father, and by believing one receives life. In that context, *pisteuo* and *ginosko* (knowing experience) are virtually synonyms (John 8:24; 11:27; 20:31; 1 John 5:1,5).[48] John has something of an identification of believing with knowing, emphasizing the intellectual or theological content of faith. Of course, this does not mean John is opposed to the idea of personal training or believing as other New Testament writers display. Actually, John stands as an important thread in the whole fabric of faith. In the Bible, faith is a personal trust in God, but in a God believers theologically and intellectually know something about. *Pistis* is not a mere existential leap in the dark, it is a leap into Jesus Christ and all the Bible declares Him to be.

Vital truths flow from various biblical constructions using the word *faith*. For example, it is often connected to *epi*, "upon" (Acts 9:42). At other times it is followed by *eis*, "into." This implies that faith has a firm basis. Saving faith is *upon* or *into* God's work in Christ. It is personal, dynamic, and knowledgeable.

Different verbal tenses are used as well. For example, the aorist tense points to a single act in the past, which implied the determinative character of faith. That is to say, when one comes to believe in Jesus Christ, he or she commits the total self to Christ. "Faith is not [merely] accepting certain things as true, but trusting a Person, and [that] Person [is] Christ."[49] The present tense usage of *pistis* implies the idea of continuity. Faith is not a mere act in the past, it has a continuing impact in one's experience. The perfect tense carries both ideas, a post commitment with continuing positive results. The one who truly believes enters into a permanent position of trust, committal, reliance, and surrender. It thus demands a moral, cognitive response. This concept is true in the Old and New Testaments.

In substantive form, *pistis* is at times coupled with the definite article: "the faith." This, quite clearly designates the whole of the Christian religion.

Faith can also carry the connotation of "correction." Especially is this true in Paul (Rom. 14:1,22-23).

Several conclusions are therefore to be drawn. First, as Bultmann put it, "In primitive Christianity *pistis* became the leading term for the relation of man to God."[50] Faith is the means of coming to know God in a personal, saving way (Eph. 2:8-9).

Second, faith in God has a theological, cognitive content. Again, as Bultmann has said, "*Pistis* often means to believe God's words. Belief is thus put in Scripture (Jn. 2:22), in what is written in the Law and the prophets (Ac. 24:14), . . . also in what God is saying at the moment, e.g., through an angel (Lk. 1:20,45; Ac. 27:25)."[51]

Third, the moral element surfaces in true faith. To have faith in God is to obey God.[52] This is particularly emphasized in Hebrews 11. To refuse to believe in Christ is to be disobedient to God's righteousness as revealed in the gospel (Rom. 10:3).

Fourth, faith means *trust*. This is true in both Testaments. Intellectual content is necessary to save one from a baseless existentialism. However, real faith is absolute commitment, reliance, and rest in God through Jesus Christ for forgiveness and salvation. Hence, the person-to-person element of faith shines forth as central. In Martin Buber's well-known phrase, saving faith is an "I-Thou" relationship, never an "I-it" encounter with God. This is obviously at the heart of the whole idea in the challenge of the *kerygma*.

Fifth, faith is directly related to hope (Rom. 4:18). Faith points to the future as well as to the past and present. This is the prominent idea of Hebrews 11. Therefore, Christians are "strangers and pilgrims" on earth, Peter told us (1 Pet. 2:11, KJV); our "faith and hope are in God" (1:21).

In the sixth place, faith implies faithfulness. Rooted in the Old Testament idea of faith, this is the meaning of 2 Timothy 4:7 when Paul said, "I have fought the good fight, I have finished the race, I have kept the faith." True faith precipitates keeping the faith. This fruit of the Spirit (Gal. 5:22) is the natural outgrowth of Spirit inspired faith. God's people are faithful to the end.

Finally, the relationship of faith to *kerygma* is intrinsic and central. Bultmann's thoughts about the subject:

    a. . . . The specifically Christian use of *pistis* . . . is to be seen most clearly in the formula *pistis eis*. . . . *Pistis* is understood here as acceptance of the

Christian kerygma. It is thus the saving faith which recognizes and appropriates God's saving work in Christ. . . . *Pistis* contains the element of believing. Obedience, trust, hope and faithfulness are also implied. . . . Nevertheless, the primary sense of *pisteuein* in specifically Christian usage is acceptance of the kerygma about Christ.

. . . .

    b. . . . Paul in R[omans] 10:9 . . . states the content of Christian faith in a sentence in which he does not simply give his own view but is saying what is obviously self-evident to every Christian preacher: . . . that acknowledgment of Jesus as Lord is intrinsic to Christian faith along with acknowledgment of the miracle of His resurrection, i.e., acceptance of this miracle as true.

. . . .

    c. Faith [is] a Personal Relation to Christ. . . . the way to salvation. [Romans 10:9] proves clearly that to believe in Jesus Christ is to acknowledge Him as Lord. . . . [and] leads to calling upon Him, so that *pisteuein*, being followed by baptism, brings into a personal relation to Christ.

. . . .

    d. . . . *Pistis* also means "to be believing," "standing in faith."[53]

For evangelism, the call to faith must be done in such a fashion that people are led to *believe* in the manner that *pistis* implies in all its various shades of meaning.

As in the case of calling people to repentance, the presenting of the challenge of Christ to faith has been clouded. At times the *kerygma* seems to come over as merely a set of theological propositions one is urged to "believe" and give mere intellectual assent to the statements. This is a danger when one presents to a lost person a so-called plan of salvation. Those who would evangelize must make it very clear that when the *kerygma* is presented, the *person* of Jesus Christ is being presented. Granted, it is done in the context of declaring truth *about* Jesus, but in so doing, the *Lord Himself* must be presented and people must be called to encounter Him personally and dynamically in deep, profound repentance and faith. If Christians do not exercise extreme caution and be sure to do just that, they have not evangelized in the New Testament sense of the word.

To evangelize in the sense outlined above is utterly beyond human ability. The evangelizer can never confront a person with Christ apart from the power of God in the person of the Holy Spirit. Once again believers are face-to-face with the necessity of being Spirit-filled if they aspire to evangelize effectively.

Moreover, lost people themselves can never exercise faith and repentance and thus enter the kingdom apart from the operation of the Holy Spirit on their lives. Faith and repentance are a gift of grace from God: "For by grace you have been saved through faith; and this is not your own doing, it is a gift of God—not because of works, lest any man should boast" (Eph. 2:8-9).

This leads to the last important issue to address on the kingdom of God. Who is it that actually populates that kingdom? If repentance and faith are a gift of God, given to those whom He calls to His kingdom, who are those "called ones"?

The Citizens of the Kingdom: The Elect of God

"The Elect!" A term filled with emotion—and controversy! Cognate terms like "the predestined," "the foreknown," and "the called" are even more loaded with theological implications, especially for evangelism.

Let it be said first of all that the Bible abounds with the basic idea of key words like *predestination* and *election*. The Scriptures clearly have something to say on the subject. Here is but a sample:

Election:
He will send out his angels with a loud trumpet call, and they will gather his elect from the four winds, from one end of heaven to the other (Matt. 24:31).

Will not God vindicate his elect, who cry to him day and night? (Luke 18:7).

They were not yet born and had done nothing either good or bad, in order that God's purpose of election might continue, not because of works but because of his call (Rom. 9:11).

To the exiles . . . chosen and destined by God the Father and sanctified by the Spirit for obedience to Jesus Christ and for sprinkling with his blood (1 Pet. 1:2).

Predestination:
For those whom he foreknew he also predestined to be conformed to the image of his Son, in order that he might be the first-born among many brethren. And those whom he predestined he also called; and those whom he called he also justified; and those whom he justified he also glorified (Rom. 8:29-30).

He predestined us to be adopted as his sons through Jesus Christ, in accordance with his pleasure and will (Eph. 1:5, NIV).

In him, according to the purpose of him who accomplishes all things according to the counsel of his will, we who first hoped in Christ have been destined and appointed to live for the praise of his glory (Eph. 1:11).

Our task is to discover what these words mean and how they impact the evangelistic task.

The simple definition of the key words are quite straightforward. Election is seen as: "The act of choice whereby God picks an individual or group out of a larger company for a purpose or destiny of his own appointment."[54] Predestination can be defined as "a view of historical events which attributes their cause to a previously established plan or decision of God."[55] Other similar terms such as "chosen," "set apart," and "called" are also quite clear in their scriptural usages. The nuances of differences are not essential to this brief discussion.

All these words are used in a variety of ways in the Scriptures. God chooses or elects or predetermines events, nations, objects, and people for His divine purpose. The entire gambit of God's dealings emerge in some sense out of His electing, predetermined plans. For example, God elected Abraham to be a blessing to all the nations. Therefore, Israel became the elect, a chosen people to effect the promise. This idea was central to Jewish faith. God called Moses out of the wilderness for a specific task. He chose the prophets to be His voice to a needy people. He elected Mary to be the bearer of the Messiah. Jesus chose His twelve. Why God chooses whom He does, or what He does, when He does, is left to His wisdom. He acts in concordance to His own divine will and purpose and pleasure (Phil. 2:13).

The Hebrew word *bachar* (election) and the Greek equivalent *eklegomai* (used in the LXX) simply means "to choose out for oneself." God is building a benevolent kingdom, and in that divine work He elects and predestines. In this broad sense of the terms, four things can be said: (1) Election is a gracious choice on God's part. It is an act of undeserved favor or grace shown towards people, events, and nations. God is love, and He acts in that context. As Paul put it, "He destined us *in love*" (Eph. 1:5, author's italics). (2) Election is a sovereign choice, prompted by God's own good pleasure (Eph. 1:5,9). It is not earned by human effort. (3) Election is an eternal choice, a part of God's eternal purpose. (4) It results in the greatest good for the greatest amount of people for God's glory. Predestination and election in this broad, benevolent sense grows out of the very attributes of God Himself, that is, His grace, love, compassion, wisdom, holy sovereignty, and glory.

The concept in the sense discussed above presents very little problem. Christians are usually willing to grant God His attributes and purposeful actions, at least in the broad dimensions of those acts. They are glad to see God work out gracious redemptive ends in their world. However, when it comes to God electing, predestinating, choosing, and calling certain individuals to personal redemption—and seeing that as the only hope for salvation—then trouble begins. Rebellion against the thought is quite widespread. The idea appears to infringe on human freedom; it seems to present God as arbitrary; it apparently precipitates determination; it makes God a tyrant in the eyes of some, saving some and damning others. A host of hostile thoughts arise. Consequently, there are many that simply reject the whole idea. Others dilute the concept to the point that it loses all its potency. Some declare it is impossible to believe in predestination and election on a personal, individual salvation level and still be evangelistic. They feel it kills the entire evangelistic, worldwide mission of the church. The argument is made that, if the elect will surely be saved, why go out to seek and evangelize them? What is the answer to these things?

First, there is a substantial history behind the doctrine of personal election. The immediate historical focal point centers in the Reformation. John Calvin and Martin Luther propounded, taught, and preached the concept as did their disciples. They received much of their lead from Augustine of Hippo (354-430) who firmly believed in absolute predestination of individuals to salvation, but more important, the Reformers believed it to be thoroughly biblical. Since the Reformation days, the doctrine dominated large sections of the Evangelical church for many years. The English Puritans, Evangelical Lutherans, Presbyterians, Baptists, and Congregationalists all embraced the basic Reformed view.

Moreover, to say the doctrine attenuates fervent evangelism is difficult to substantiate historically. In recent centuries, George Whitefield, Jonathan Edwards, Charles H. Spurgeon, and a host of other fervent evangelists were thorough-going adherents of the concept. The Baptists with their fervent evangelism have deep roots in the doctrine, at least up to recent years. Of course, John Wesley and the Methodists and Pentecostals have rejected the idea and have, by and large, been very evangelistic. Accepting the doctrine does not necessarily negate commitment to evangelism and missions. On the contrary, most great revival movements, such as America's First Great Awakening, have grown out of theological Reformed thought, and it is true to the contemporary movement. Believers search the Scriptures to see what they have to say. The issue is not whether one argues as a "Calvinist" or an "Arminian"; rather, what the Bible states is that which essentially matters.

The biblical concept of personal election to salvation is predicated on the sovereignty of God. God's absolute sovereignty is at the very core of biblical religion. As T. W. Manson stated:

> The eternal and absolute sovereignty of God was an integral part of the religious heritage of the people among whom our Lord lived and worked. It was in their sacred Scriptures; it was in their synagogue discoveries; it was implied in their daily prayers. . . . In all these the essential idea is the same, that the sovereignty of God is universal and absolute.[56]

Manson argued that Jesus was in complete agreement with His Jewish background. Manson said:

> We may sum up the whole matter by saying that, as it appears in the life and teaching of Jesus, the sovereignty of God is essentially a working out,

to a predetermined and inevitable end, of God's holy purpose. This purpose embraces in its scope both the natural world and the world of self-
conscious beings.[57]

However, considerable resistance to aspects of the concept of God's sovereignty is quite clear. Especially is this true since the rise of rationalism
and existentialism. Often, the resistance to the doctrine, as James Boyce
pointed out:

> arises from an unwillingness on the part of man to recognize the sover-
> eignty of God, and to ascribe salvation entirely to grace. . . . Let the Scrip-
> tures be read with reference to this doctrine and every passage marked
> which indicates God's dealing with men as an absolute sovereign, and also
> every declaration which ascribes Election or the fruits of it to his choice
> and not to the will or acts of men, and every illustration afforded that this
> is God's usual method, and it will appear that scarcely any book of Scrip-
> ture will fail to furnish testimony to the fact that in the acts of grace, no
> less than those of providence, God "doeth according to his will in the
> army of heaven and among the inhabitants of the earth." [sic] (Dan.
> 4:35).[58]

As Strong expressed it, "God has a sovereign right to bestow more grace
upon one subject as another—grace being unmerited favor to sinners."[59]
That surely seems uncontestable. If we do not deserve God's favor, God
can give grace as He sees fit. If God is sovereign in the sense the Bible
declares, He is surely sovereign in all things, including personal
salvation.

Moreover, one must take human personal sin most seriously. The
blight of personal sin has so darkened the mind, people cannot be saved
unless they are mightily moved upon by God. Paul said, "The unspiritual man does not receive the gifts of the Spirit of God, for they are folly to
him, and he is not able to understand them because they are spiritually
discerned" (1 Cor. 2:14). Unless God acts, there is no hope for anyone.
Salvation has its birth in the activity of God the Spirit.

Furthermore, whatever the Bible means by predestination, it is God's
way of saving the most people possible. We must never forget: the Father's will is that none "perish, but that all should come to repentance"
(2 Pet. 3:9, KJV). That basic truth must be kept in the forefront.

Boyce suggested six major points in delineating God's sovereign action in seeing people redeemed. This theory, therefore, teaches that
election is:

1. An act of God, and not the result of the choice of the elect.
2. That this choice is one of individuals, and not classes.
3. That it was made without respect to the action of the persons elected.
4. By the good pleasure of God.

5. According to an eternal purpose.
6. That it is an election to salvation and not to outward privileges.[60]

Is this what the Bible actually teaches? Yes. Each of Boyce's points in order are:

1. The Scriptural basis for election as *an act of sovereign God:*

Paul was a "chosen instrument" (Acts 9:15).

Christ chose the "twelve" (Luke 6:13).

"I am not speaking of you all; I know whom I have chosen; it is that the scripture may be fulfilled, 'He who ate my bread has lifted his heel against me' " (John 13:18).

"You did not choose me, but I chose you and appointed you that you should go and bear fruit and that your fruit should abide; so that whatever you ask the Father in my name, he may give it to you" (John 15:16).

Who shall bring any charge against God's elect? It is God who justifies (Rom. 8:33).

He destined us in love to be his sons through Jesus Christ, according to the purpose of his will (Eph. 1:5).

In him, according to the purpose of him who accomplishes all things according to the counsel of his will (Eph. 1:11).

We are bound to give thanks to God always for you, brethren beloved by the Lord, because God chose you from the beginning to be saved, through sanctification by the Spirit and belief in the truth (2 Thess. 2:13).

2. The *choice is of individuals*:

When the Gentiles heard this, they were glad and glorified the word of God; and as many as were ordained to eternal life believed (Acts 13:48).

Even as he chose us in him before the foundation of the world, that we should be holy and blameless before him. He destined us in love to be his sons through Jesus Christ, according to the purpose of his will (Eph. 1:4-5).

For those whom he foreknew he also predestined to be conformed to the image of his Son, in order that he might be the first-born among many brethren (Rom. 8:29).

3. This point, *persons are not elected* because of their own merit, is merely a negative form of the next point.

4. Election is made through *the good pleasure of God*:

He came to his own home, and his own people received him not. But to all who received him, who believed in his name, he gave power to become children of God; who were born not of blood nor of the will of the flesh nor of the will of man, but of God (John 1:11-13).

"All that the Father gives me will come to me; and him who comes to me I will not cast out" (John 6:37).

"This is the will of him who sent me, that I should lose nothing of all that he has given me, but raise it up at the last day" (v. 39).

"No one can come to me unless the Father who sent me draws him; and I will raise him up at the last day" (v. 44).

"There are some of you that do not believe." For Jesus knew from the first who those were that did not believe, and who it was that would betray him. And he said, "This is why I told you that no one can come to me unless it is granted him by the Father" (John 6:64-65).

"Thou hast given him power over all flesh, to give eternal life to all whom thou hast given him" (John 17:2).

Of his own will he brought us forth by the word of truth that we should be a kind of first fruits of his creatures (Jas. 1:18).

Though they were not yet born and had done nothing either good or bad, in order that God's purpose of election might continue, not because of works but because of his call, she was told, "The elder will serve the younger." As it is written, "Jacob I loved, but Esau I hated."

What shall we say then? Is there injustice on God's part? By no means! For he says to Moses, "I will have mercy on whom I have mercy, and I will have compassion on whom I have compassion." So it depends not upon man's will or exertion, but upon God's mercy (Rom. 9:11-16).

So too at the present time there is a remnant, chosen by grace. But if it is by grace, it is no longer on the basis of works; otherwise grace would no longer be grace (Rom. 11:5-6).

When he who had set me apart before I was born, and had called me through his grace, was pleased to reveal his Son to me, in order that I might preach him among the Gentiles, I did not confer with flesh and blood (Gal. 1:15-16).

5. *Election is according to an eternal purpose,* before time began:

"Before I formed you in the womb I knew you,/ and before you were born I consecrated you;/ I appointed you a prophet to the nations" (Jer. 1:5).

"Then the King will say to those at his right hand, 'Come, O blessed of my Father, inherit the kingdom prepared for you from the foundation of the world' " (Matt. 25:34).

Even as he chose us in him before the foundation of the world, that we should be holy and blameless before him (Eph. 1:4).

Who saved us and called us with a holy calling, not in virtue of our works but in virtue of his own purpose and the grace which he gave us in Christ Jesus ages ago (2 Tim. 1:9).

All who dwell on earth will worship [the beast], every one whose name has not been written before the foundation of the world in the book of life of the Lamb that was slain (Rev. 13:8).

"The beast that you saw was, and is not, and is to ascend from the bottomless pit and go to perdition; and the dwellers on earth whose names have not been written in the book of life from the foundation of the world, will marvel to behold the beast, because it was and is not and is to come" (Rev. 17:8).

6. *Election is to salvation*:

"I have other sheep, that are not of this fold; I must bring them also, and they will heed my voice. So there shall be one flock, one shepherd" (John 10:16).

"My sheep hear my voice, and I know them, and they follow me" (John 10:27).

We know that in everything God works for good with those who love him, who are called according to this purpose. For those whom he foreknew he also predestined to be conformed to the image of his Son, in order that he might be the first-born among many brethren. And those whom he predestined he also called; and those whom he called he also justified; and those whom he justified he also glorified (Rom. 8:28-30).

After you have suffered a little while, the God of all grace, who has called you to his eternal glory in Christ, will Himself restore, establish, and strengthen you (1 Pet. 5:10).[61]

Now surely, this wealth of Scripture should once and for all settle the matter that the Bible does teach personal election. The mountain of texts is just too high to ignore or sidestep. One must courageously face it. This is why the Reformers were brave enough to come to grips with the issue. Yet, why the resistance to accept the plain scriptural teaching?

The reason most either ignore, explain away, or refuse to submit to the truth of election and predestination usually centers in the idea that it precludes freedom of will in one's *choosing* to repent and believe. It is obviously true that the Bible speaks volumes on "whosoever will" may come. Actually, all are even *commanded* to repent and believe. The list of passages on this score is far too long to record here, but they are well known. They too raise a mountain of truth. Freedom of will in coming to Christ is clearly and forthrightly taught in the Scriptures. There can be no dispute of that fact. Not only that, if human freedom is not a genuine reality, the entire idea of moral responsibility and judgment collapses. Years ago Basil Manly, Sr., a predestinarian, pointed this out, saying, "Unless it is admitted the Divine efficiency is consistent with human freedom and activity, it is obvious that there can be no holiness in the good actions of man, and no sinfulness in their evil actions; but the whole ground-work and foundation or morality will be overturned."[62] We must consistently maintain and earnestly contend for the concept of human freedom, but that obviously thrusts one into a real dilemma.

Several rational explanations for the quandary have been proposed throughout the course of the history of theology. Barth believed that God elects everyone to be saved, but that comes perilously close to universalism which is untenable. Others retreat into an "Arminian" stance and just explain away election. Others, from a "high-Calvinist" viewpoint, deny freedom. Then there are those who place all the emphasis on God "foreknowing" who will accept Christ, but that denies election all together. Anyone could elect individuals if they knew who would come to Christ. Not only that, the word *foreknowledge* in the biblical context implies far more than merely foretelling the future. It connotes determination in what will happen. The process theologians simply miss it all. Actually, every rational attempt seems to lack a satisfactory answer that does justice to the whole Bible.

What is the problem? The quandary usually arises because one demands a rational answer. Election and predestination are not purely rational human situations. In the profound truths of God, paradox is constantly encountered. The doctrine of election is a classic case, and this study has shown that in such situations the best thing to do is to rest in faith and trust God to do all things well.

Furthermore, it is wise to recognize the Bible has no room whatsoever for so-called double-predestination, or supralapsarianism, that is, God predestining some to eternal perdition. The Scriptures simply do not teach that. Of course, it is argued rationally that, if God elects some to eternal life, it follows those who are not elected are predestined to perdition, but the Bible never approaches such a concept. It is a deductive move never to be made.

Not only that, it should not be minimized that the purpose of election is to "the praise of of his glorious grace" (Eph. 1:6). God's purpose is to make people holy and blameless in His sight for His glory. All His purposes are benevolent and loving, whether rationally understood or not. Furthermore, the Bible makes it clear that predestination and election is God's way of seeing people saved. Because God loves all and wants all to be saved, it is His way of getting the largest number to receive Christ. Again, let it be understood, "He destined us in *love*" (Eph. 1:5, author's italics).

There is another vitally important fact: according to the Bible, predestination simply does not eradicate freedom to choose Christ, or people's responsibility so to do. Human beings do have real freedom, even if it is limited.

What does this truth call on people to do? First, people ought to submit humbly to God's truth and rest in His revelation, since they do not have all the answers. God is suprarational, but Christians do believe what He has revealed, and lovingly declare it. Charles H. Spurgeon from a pragmatic pastoral perspective on the subject had a good answer. He is reported to have prayed, "Lord, save your elect, and then elect some more!" That is not as trite as it may sound. The pastor recognized that God elects, but also "whosoever will" may come. Spurgeon preached and prayed in that dynamic tension, realizing both truths are clearly taught in the Scriptures. As Richard Fuller expressed it: "How do you reconcile these two doctrines? Reconcile! I do not reconcile them. Who made me a judge and reconciler of God's acts and attributes and clearly revealed testimonies? . . . let us rather with Job exclaim, . . . 'I will lay my hand upon my mouth.' "[63]

Professor D. A. Carson, quoting Packer, said, "God's control is absolute in the sense that men do only that which he has ordained that they should; yet they are truly free agents in the sense that their decisions are their own, and they are morally responsible for them."[64] Carson argued such an approach is a working model even if it is not a final rational solution. A purely rational answer will evade one's grasp. Since this is a suprarational truth, people must wait for eternity to resolve it. In the meantime, believers evangelize on the basis of this "working model." The sovereignty of God does not preclude human instrumentality in effecting His sovereign will. God does not simply act upon a person without means; sovereignty does not mean that. God uses people in effecting His purpose. So believers call people to Christ's kingdom. One day they will understand it all. In the meantime, in their theology of evangelism, believers realize the truth that salvation is of God, and they herald to the unbeliever the wonderful truth that "whosoever will" can be saved. The lost really can come to Christ.

Conclusion

Thus people hear the gospel of grace, repent and believe, and enter the glorious kingdom of God. One day those who have been reconciled shall see their Savior face-to-face to be parted from Him no more. That is the goal of all evangelism and the heart of the theology of evangelism. For an excellent, contemporary summary of the entire discipline of the theology of evangelism, see Appendix B: The Lausanne Covenant. However, to share that good message demands a measure of expertise. This study will now turn to that pragmatic ministry of evangelism.

Notes

1. George R. Beasley-Murray, *Jesus and the Kingdom of God* (Grand Rapids: William B. Eerdmans Publishing Co., 1986), X.

2. From personal correspondence, (Beasley-Murray's italics).

3. H. N. Ridderbos, "Kingdom of God, Kingdom of Heaven" in *The Illustrated Bible Dictionary*, (Wheaton, Ill.: Tyndale House Publishers, 1980), 2:853.

4. O. E. Evans, "Kingdom of God, of Heaven" in *The Interpreter's Dictionary of the Bible*, 5 vols. (Nashville: Abingdon Press, 1962-76), 3:17.

5. Ibid.

6. Beasley-Murray, *Jesus and the Kingdom of God*, 4.

7. Ibid., 11. This discussion of the kingdom of God is indebted to Beasley-Murray.

8. L. Koehler, *Old Testament Theology*, trans. A. S. Todd (Philadelphia: Westminster Press, 1957), 30.

9. Beasley-Murray, *Jesus and the Kingdom of God*, 20.

10. Ladd, *A Theology of the New Testament*, 58.

11. See Albert Schweitzer, *The Quest of the Historical Jesus*, trans. W. Montgomery (New York: Macmillan, 1961) and Johannes Weiss, *Die Predigt Jesu vom Reiche Gottes* (Goettingen: Vandenhoeck and Ruprecht, 1892).

12. Ibid., 58-59.

13. I have no quarrel with God being "wholly other." It is Dodd's platonic approach to the idea that constitutes the problem.

14. Ladd, *A Theology of the New Testament*, 59.

15. For a helpful discussion on dispensationalism and eschatology, see George E. Ladd's *Crucial Questions about the Kingdom of God*, and *The Blessed Hope*. Ladd took what is commonly called the "historical premillennialist" approach.

16. Hermann Kleinknecht, *"basileus, basileia, basilissa, basileuo, sumbasileuo, basileios, basilikos,"* in *Theological Dictionary of the New Testament*, 10 vols. (Grand Rapids: William B. Eerdmans Publishing Co., 1964), 1:566.

17. Ibid., 579.

18. Ladd, *Theology of the New Testament*, 64.

19. Beasley-Murray, *Jesus and the Kingdom of God*, 110.

20. Rudolf Bultmann in *Kerygma and Myth: A Theological Debate*, ed. H. W. Bartsch, trans. R. H. Fuller (London: SPCK, 1953), 116.

21. Ibid., 4.

22. Beasley-Murray, *Jesus and the Kingdom of God*, 338 (author's italics).

23. Ibid., 146.

24. Ibid.

25. Bruce Milne, *The End of the World* (Eastbourne: Kingway Publications, 1979), 34.

26. *The Analytical Greek Lexicon* (New York: Harper and Brothers, n.d.), 217.

27. Culbert G. Rutenber, *The Reconciling Gospel* (Philadelphia: The Judson Press, 1960), 35.

28. Emil Brunner, *The Great Invitation* (Philadelphia: The Westminster Press, 1955), 108.

29. P. T. Forsyth, *Positive Preaching and Modern Mind* (New York: Hodder and Stoughton, 1907), 353.

30. Rutenber, *The Reconciling Gospel*, 82.

31. Werner Georg Kümmel, *Introduction to the New Testament* (Nashville: Abingdon Press, 1966), 318.

32. Ibid., 323.

33. Ibid., 322.

34. Otto Michel, *"metamelomai, ametameletos,"* in *Theological Dictionary of the New Testament*, 4:626.

35. W. A. Quanbeck, "Repentance" in *The Interpreter's Dictionary of the Bible*, 5 vols. (Nashville: Abingdon Press, 1962-76), 4:34.

36. Charles John Vaughan, *St. Paul's Epistle to the Romans* (London: MacMillan and Co., 1859), 92.

37. Dale Moody, "Romans," in *The Broadman Bible Commentary*, 12 vols. (Nashville: Broadman Press, 1970), 10:236.

38. Rudolf Schnackenburg, *Baptism in the Thought of St. Paul*, trans. G. R. Beasley-Murray (Oxford: Basil Blackwell, 1964), 82. These few words just scratch the surface of the thinker's entire theology.

39. Herschel H. Hobbs, *Romans: A Verse-by-Verse Study* (Waco: Word Books Publishers, 1977), 134-135.

40. In the Old Testament *nicham* (sorrow) is at times translated "repentance." In the New Testament *metamelomai* (sorrow) is also rendered "repentance." The point being made here is that *metamelomai* can be different from *metanoia*, and in life experience often is. The play on these words and their impact is seen in 2 Corinthians 7:7-10.

41. Anders Nygren, *Commentary on Romans* (London: SCM Press, Ltd., 1952), 383.

42. *The Interpreter's Dictionary of the Bible*, 4:34.

43. For a full discussion of this particular issue, see R. T. Kendall, *Calvinism and English Puritanism to 1649* (Oxford: Oxford University Press, 1979).

44. It is unfortunate there is in English no verbal form of "faith." English must rely on the verb *believe*. This tends to weaken the verb *pisteuo* in translation.

45. *The Interpreter's Dictionary of the Bible*, 2:223-224.

46. Ibid., 224.

47. E. M. B. Green, *The Meaning of Salvation* (London: Hodder and Stoughton, 1965), 169.

48. *The Illustrated Bible Dictionary*, Part I, 496.

49. Ibid., 497.

50. Rudolf Bultmann, *"pisteuo, pistis, pistos, pistoo, apistos, apisteo, apistia, oligopistos, oligopistia"* in *Theological Dictionary of the New Testament*, 10 vols., 6:205.

51. Ibid.

52. For a full discussion of this basic principle, see John F. McArthur, *The Gospel According to Jesus*, (Grand Rapids: Zondervan Publishing House, 1988). Even if McArthur somewhat overstated the case, he has an important point to make. McArthur's work has spawned some debate of late. Lane Hodges and Charles Ryrie have entered this discussion.

53. Bultmann, 6:208-212.

54. *The Illustrated Bible Dictionary*, Part 1, 435.

55. *The Interpreter's Dictionary of the Bible*, 3:869.

56. T. W. Manson, *The Teachings of Jesus* (Cambridge: University Press, 1943), 142.

57. Ibid., 170.

58. James Petegru Boyce, *Abstract of Systematic Theology* (Pompano Beach, Florida, Reprint by Christian Gospel Foundation, 1887), 353. Much of this discussion depends on Boyce.

59. Augustus H. Strong, *Systematic Theology*, 779.

60. Boyce, *Abstract of Systematic Theology*, 348.

61. Ibid., 348-356.

62. Basil Manly, Sr., *Southern Baptist Sermons on* Sovereignty and Responsibility (Harrisburg: Gono Books, 1984), 21.

63. Richard Fuller quoted in Manly, *Sermons on Sovereignty and Responsibility*, 115.

64. D. A. Carson, *Divine Sovereignty and Human Responsibility* (Atlanta: John Knox Press, 1981), 207.

Part IV

The Practical Ministry of Evangelism:
A Pragmatic Theological Study

Introduction

The theology of evangelism becomes one of the chief cornerstones in laying the foundation of a practical outreach ministry. That follows because we act on the basis of what we conceive to be true and meaningful. Therefore, how we understand the meaning and implications of the gospel determines how we serve Jesus Christ on a pragmatic basis. Hopefully, the essence of evangelistic truth has been clearly set forth in this book. If that has been accomplished, it should motivate us to minister and evangelize with commitment and zeal in the real world where needs abound.

God Himself is on mission, the so-called *misseo-dei,* and He calls His people into a covenant of mutual labor. Therefore, the church must learn and implement the practical scriptural methods God honors in this grand enterprise. Ministry that succeeds flows in the stream of applying practical biblical methods to ministry.

The purpose of this final section is to discover those pragmatic, workable principles and methodologies that the Holy Spirit reveals in the Bible and thus uses to bring the alienated world to the foot of the cross. Not only that, but it is important to grasp what kind of people God uses in the grand scheme of evangelization. Those personal, spiritual principles shall also be sought, for God anoints people, not programs. Therefore, this section is admittedly practical and devotional. The rationale for such an approach is obvious: those who would evangelize effectively must not only know something of the theology of evangelism, they must be able to *do* something with skill and also *be* somewhat effective in their own spiritual lives. Moreover, this study shall essentially be a biblical study. We must learn to do and be what God discloses in His Word. In this way alone, one's evangelistic service to Christ will be effective to lead others to the salvation of the Lord. That is what ministry is all about; actually, such is the culmination of a theology of evangelism.

10

Church-Centered Evangelism:
A Practical Approach

*"The Lord added to their number day by day
those who were being saved" (Acts 2:47).*

Introduction

The entire church of Jesus Christ is called to mission (Matt. 28:19-20). All God's people are servants of their Lord (Eph. 4:11-12). It surely follows, therefore, that all believers are to follow their Lord in world evangelization. No one is exempt; no one is excused from being Christ's witness (Acts 1:8). All are to evangelize. Yet, it is also clear that multitudes of professing Christians rarely if ever engage in any concerted effort to lead others to faith in Jesus Christ.

Why do so many believers appear apathetic in introducing people to Jesus Christ? There are probably many reasons. For example, it is possible some embrace faulty theological views and thus see no real reason to evangelize. More often, however, the Lord's people simply do not grasp the biblical principles of how to engage pragmatically in God's scheme of world outreach and through fear or ignorance (or both) fail as a witness. The purpose of this chapter is to set out those Spirit-inspired principles as recorded in the Word of God which will hopefully inform, inspire, motivate, encourage, and prepare believers to engage in world evangelization.

Moving into a practical study concerning God's people in ministry, calls for grasping something of the biblical nature of the church, the body of Christ. The basic scriptural concept of the church must become deeply ingrained in the Christian's basic theological makeup if they are to meet the evangelistic challenge of the hour. In the New Testament, the church is presented on a two-tier level.

The Universal Church as Body of Christ

Christ loved the church and gave himself up for her, that he might sanctify her, having cleansed her by the washing of water with the word, that

289

he might present the church to himself in splendor, without spot or wrinkle or any such thing, that she might be holy and without blemish (Eph. 5:25-27).

In this important passage Paul presented the church in its eternal, all inclusive, worldwide perspective. He viewed it as composed of all true believers of all ages. Many graphic, biblical metaphors describe the various aspects of the universal church: "a royal priesthood" (1 Pet. 2:9), "a holy nation" (1 Pet. 2:9), "the Bride" of Christ (Rev. 21:9), "the body of Christ" (1 Cor. 12:12-27), and "God's building" (1 Cor. 3:9).

Several significant truths emerge from these metaphors and similar scriptural passages. In the first place, the church is apprehended as made up of a distinct, "peculiar" people (Titus 2:14, KJV). That is to say, believers in Christ are "a people for God's own possession" (1 Pet. 2:9, NASB). They hold that unique position because they have been bought by God at the tremendous price of the "precious blood of Christ" (1 Pet. 1:18-19). Belonging to God, they are thus expected to do His will, follow His lead, faithfully serve Him, and bring glory to His name. That truth forms the basic motivation for all ministry (Rom. 12:1).

Moreover, being God's own personal people, Christians should stand in bold contrast to the world. The Bible declares they are to be a "holy nation" (1 Pet. 2:9). The church is ultimately becoming through the sanctifying work of the Holy Spirit a people without "spot or wrinkle or any such thing" (Eph. 5:27). Consequently, God's people do not conform to this world, its standards, goals, ambitions, or sins. Christians are not to permit the world to cram them into its mold (Rom. 12:1-2). The church is set apart, *from* evil, *to* God and *for* God. True believers thus stand as a rebuke and judgment on the sinful world. At the same time, however, they are the "light of the world" (Matt. 5:14) and the "salt of the earth" (Matt. 5:13). The church is the world's only real hope. Consequently, the church fills its paradoxical role as the world's "enemy" and at the same time its only true help.

Third, the church in its universal configuration stands as something of a mediator: a "royal priesthood" (1 Pet. 2:9). In this priestly role the church offers up sacrifices to God (Heb. 8:3), officiates in worship (Lev. 23), and comes before God to intercede for needy people. That fact implies the church's worldwide mission, which is the real meaning of the "priesthood of all believers."

Finally, the church, as the "fellowship" of the saints (1 John 1:3), stands as God's model of what the ideal society should be. God's ideal for humanity has been warped and perverted, but God's love in Christ stepped in to redeem the wayward world (John 3:16). God intends to exalt His new, redeemed people as a pattern of what the world was before the "fall," and what it can become through redemption in Jesus

Christ. Thus, the church draws the world by word, example, and service to Christ. This forms the essence of covenant life. God designed the church as a living organism of new covenant life to bring glory to Jesus Christ and thus inspire people to faith in our Lord.

The Universal Church as New Covenant Life in Christ

God works among, and through, His people on the basis of *covenant.* Adam lived in covenant with God in Eden (Gen. 2:8-17). God called Abraham into covenant relationship with Himself while Abraham was still in Ur of the Chaldees (Gen. 12:1-2). The significant covenant of the Law was delivered to Israel at the foot of Mount Sinai (Ex. 19—20). The greatest and most glorious of all the covenants, however, and the one to which all others pointed, is the New Covenant of God in Jesus Christ.

The term *covenant* was defined in chapter 3 as "a gracious undertaking entered into by God for the benefit and blessing of man, and specifically of those men who by faith receive the promise and commit themselves to the obligations which this undertaking involves."[1] Therefore, when one responds to God's sovereign call and becomes a Christian through "repentance to God and of faith in our Lord Jesus Christ" (Acts 20:21), one enters into a living, dynamic, covenant fellowship with the living God, and in that relationship one loves and serves the Lord. One becomes a member in the community of the "towel and basin," a servant of Christ and others.

There is another very important implication of the covenant idea. By covenant commitment, believers are merged into a dynamic fellowship with all who share in it. Not only are Christ's covenant people vertically related to God, they are horizontally related to others who share in the same relationship (1 John 1:3). All who share in the covenant family are vitally connected to each other. The truth of the individual "priesthood of believers" is not meant to isolate Christians from one another. To the contrary, God's people are to minister to one another as priests of God in covenant fellowship. This is to be understood in a broad, universal sense. All believers become one in Christ regardless of age, country, culture, denomination, sex, time, or any human category. All who are "born again" (John 3:3, KJV) participate in the covenant and thus become brothers and sisters who together receive the grace of God.

The covenant principle actually constitutes the heart of what is implied in the biblical word *laos,* the people of God. The term is often misunderstood, such as setting the "laity" over against the "clergy." *Laos* simply means "people." The *laos* of God is comprised of *all* the redeemed men and women, regardless of their role in the church. It includes the professional, ordained leaders as well as those who hold no leadership positions whatsoever. In the New Covenant, all are one in Christ (Gal. 3:28).

These realities delineate the essential meaning of the church in its universal sense. There is, however, the practical outworking of the principles which are effected in the second New Testament aspect of the church—its local, limited manifestation.

The Local Aspect of the Church

The church in its local setting is where all the principles of the church's universal nature are pragmatically realized. The reason for that fact is obvious; a local congregation of like-minded believers can be seen, can worship, and can minister in and through. True, intimate fellowship is realized on the practical, local level. This does not mean the universal church does not really exist. It surely does, and in heaven believers will experience it in fullness. In the meantime, however, if Christians wish to minister in fellowship with God's covenant people, it must be done primarily in a local church. Hence, it is vitally necessary to be involved in a local congregation in the evangelistic enterprise. When people are reached for Jesus Christ, it is because a group of dedicated believers band themselves together in covenant fellowship to accomplish the task. This is what a local church is all about.

Therefore, a local church stands at the fountainhead of proclamation and makes its impact with the gospel. This does not mean witnessing the good news of God goes on only inside the four walls of a church building. To the contrary, the true Christian church carries its witness to the marketplaces of daily life. The local church becomes the place where believers meet together to worship, to be inspired and informed, to devise programs, to preach the gospel, and then go out into the world to minister. A church scattered in the world and ministering in Christ's name is just as much the church as when it is gathered together in worship.

Therefore, ministry is a central aspect of the local church life. This means the church is open to all needs of all people. It is not to be equated with nationalism or any particular political ideology. The church is to minister to all the needs of a needy world. Wherever there is any kind of problem, the church is to step in regardless of race, economic background, or other distinction and attempt to meet the needs of real people to the best of its ability and resources. Let it be made clear again that there is no conflict between evangelism and social involvement. The blending of the two is often the secret of cross-cultural evangelism—all kinds of evangelism for that matter.

The general nature and purpose of the church of Jesus Christ in evangelism is now evident. The church is God's covenant people involved in worship, proclamation, and ministry. It has a mission and message, and that in a unified whole. This is true in principle on a universal level and pragmatically workable on the local level. Because the divine commission is given to the entire church, the whole church (the *laos*) is to engage in it. No division is allowed in the *laos* nor any levels of responsibility; all are called to witness and minister, and all are responsible to do so because all have been brought into covenant life by the free grace of God. That is the nature of the covenant, and the nature of the church and its ministry. The *laos* of God possesses a most profound evangelistic calling.

The Church's Ministry to an Alienated World: Evangelism

> Jesus said, "All authority in heaven and on earth has been given to me. Go therefore and make disciples of all nations, baptizing them in the name of the Father and of the Son and of the Holy Spirit, teaching them to observe all that I have commanded you; and lo, I am with you always, to the close of the age" (Matt. 28:18-20).

At the heart of the Great Commission stands the church's primary task. Although there is much in that commission which encompasses the entire spectrum of the church's life and ministry, central to the call of Christ is the fact that believers are to become witnesses (Acts 1:8) and make disciples of all nations.

Churches must be crystal clear about its task and message. Covenant people must realize God has given them a clear message (kerygma) and places a premium stamp on the winning of the lost. Actually, one cannot be a balanced biblical believer and come to any other conclusion. This entire volume has hopefully made that clear. Of course, there have been shallow, superficial evangelistic activities, but that does not excuse anyone from giving evangelism first place in individual and covenant church life. This is true of the entire *laos* of God, not just the "professional" evangelist or preacher.

Social Dimensions of the Gospels

Giving evangelism priority does not mean there is no other ministry to perform in the covenant life of the local church. There are many worthy and needed social and family ministries in which to engage. To these the church should give itself. It is a tragedy to sever evangelism from social concern and action. The evangelism-social action cleavage, seen in some churches, is a twentieth-century aberration. Our evangelical forefathers knew nothing of it. For example, Charles G. Finney, the great American evangelist, was also a fervent abolitionist and social activist. Spurgeon will be remembered as a great gospel preacher; yet, at the same time, he built orphan homes and alms houses. So did Philipp Jacob Spener and a host of fellow German pietistic giants in the past. Social action is vital to ministry. This means getting down into the pain, agony, and hurt of people in their need, right out in the sin, suffering, and tragedy of the real world. God's people must invade the secular, needy, and suffering world. The love of Christ demands that. The apostle John said, "If any one has the world's goods and sees his brother in need, yet closes his heart against him, how does God's love abide in him? Little children, let us not love in word or speech but in deed and in truth" (1 John 3:17-18).

In the high hours of the church, God's covenant people have risen to the social needs of the world as well as to meet its spiritual poverty. A classic case in point is the great Puritan-Pietism movement. That thrust gave birth to much contemporary evangelicalism; still, social dimensions in ministry were far from neglected. For example, August Hermann Francke, the German Pietist, insisted that a concern for meeting social needs is the indispensable fruit of conversion. Francke was instrumental in the establishment of a home for unmarried women, an orphanage, a home for itinerant beggars, a hospital and dispensary, a widows' house, and a home for needy students. He also organized services to the blind, the deaf, and the mentally ill. Philipp Spener, a great gospel preacher in the movement, held believers should "prove in such service their obedience to God and their love to their fellow men." As an example of his concern, he influenced the founding of workhouses for the poor in Frankfort, Nuremberg, Augsburg, Leipzig, Halle, and Berlin, as well as schooling for orphans. It was out of German and Swiss Reformed Pietism that a whole host of new social movements germinated, grew, and flowered.

Further, the Pietists and their English counterparts, the Puritans, were overtly political in that they sought to bring direct pressure on the state to safeguard public morality, justice, and human rights. Yoder, a noted Mennonite scholar, observed:

> It is certainly not the case that pietism whether we think now of the eighteenth century movement or of its more recent spiritual heirs, was uninterested in social or political ethics. Few movements in church history . . . have been . . . so productive of institutional inventiveness and cultural creativity.[2]

William Wilberforce, a parliamentarian and a product of the Wesley-Whitefield English pietistic revival of the eighteenth century, kept slavery out of Britain. John Wesley, strong for abolition, also instituted medical clinics and even financial credit unions for the poor. George Whitefield founded orphanages. Degrellit, a Quaker, was instrumental in prison reform in several European countries. John Woolman was chiefly responsible for the eradication of slavery in Quaker communities in America. Charles G. Finney was seriously involved in the American abolition movement. Oberlin College in Ohio where Finney served as professor of theology and president in the nineteenth century was accused by the "old-school" Presbyterians of being a "hotbed of revivalism, fanaticism, and social reform." Oberlin became the northern "railhead" of the "underground railroad," thus effecting the freedom of many slaves.

Time fails to tell of the social work of men like William Booth, Robert Raikes, Lord Shaftesbury, and a multitude of others. Even the modern labor party of Britain grew out of evangelical concern. God's mature people understand, as one writer has put it, "a hungry man has no ears."

To say that the Evangelical church in its high hours was a mere evangelistic thrust with little social concern is a perversion of historical fact. Nevertheless, evangelism was seen as the priority; it comes first because it meets the deepest need—salvation. May God revive His churches and put them on the trail of needy people. May the Holy Spirit lay a true burden for a lost and broken world on all hearts. The godly young missionary David Brainerd had the right spirit when he said:

> I cared not where or how I lived or what hardships I went through so that I could but gain souls for Christ. While I was asleep I dreamed of these things, and when I awoke the first thing I thought of was this great work. All of my desire was for the conversion of the heathen and my hope was in God.

That attitude wins the world to Jesus Christ, and that is the church's goal.

Reaching the Goal

The church obviously has a great responsibility that demands every resource the church can muster, and that primarily means the resource of the people themselves. The task can never be accomplished unless all the people of God get involved and live out the implications of their covenant lives of ministry.

Sir John Lawrence posed the quandary the church faces in mobilizing all its forces for ministry and evangelism by stating that what most members want is "a building which looks like a church, a clergyman dressed in a way they approve, services of the kind they are accustomed to, and to be left alone." The prevailing attitude on the part of many seems to be that they pay the bill while the clergy does the ministry.

For many years, most churches have struggled with the so-called clergy-laity dualism. The ordained clergyman as a highly intellectualized professional leader has assumed more and more command of the ministry. This approach has so hardened through the years that the English word *lay* has become a synonym for "amateur" as over against "professional." The tragic result has been a loss of identity by the average church member. The so-called clergy has become overburdened by the enormity of its task. Neither the "ordained" nor the "nonordained" are happy. Moreover, many contemporary churches have obviously been inept in coping with the demands of a needy and lost world on the basis of its present structures for ministry. For some time, perceptive Christians have recognized the need of radical change and role defining. They generally agree the entire approach to ministry needs a fresh approach. This can be seen from two perspectives.

Ministry "Inside" the Church Body

Paul declared a most important ministry principle to the Ephesians:

> There is one body and one Spirit, just as you were called to the one hope that belongs to your call, . . . And his gifts were that some should be apostles, some prophets, some evangelists, some pastors and teachers, to equip the saints for the work of ministry, for building up the body of Christ, until we all attain to the unity of the faith and of the knowledge of the Son of God, to mature manhood, to the measure of the stature of the fulness of Christ; . . . speaking the truth in love, we are to grow up in every way into him who is the head, into Christ, from whom the whole body, joined and knit together by every joint with which it is supplied, when each part is working properly, makes bodily growth and upbuilds itself in love (Eph. 4:4,11-13,15-16).

This Ephesian passage makes it clear that a vital aspect of ministry in the local church is to be performed for the church itself. The church must minister to itself. God's intention for the body of Christ is to be healthy, robust, and full functioning. A church should reflect the love, power, grace, and compassion of Christ as it lives and ministers in the world as His "bodily" presence today. A congregation is to grow up into its Lord so that all the fullness of Christ can be manifest in the fellowship (Gal. 4:19). Christ Himself thus becomes the actual life of the church. For a local congregation to be all that, it must build up itself in faith; hence, internal ministry is essential. If the body of Christ fails on the internal level, it will never minister effectively in the world.

Therefore, God's people need those within its membership who can minister the Word of God: teachers and prophets. Further, the call is for administrators: those who can lead and organize. It needs pastors: those who can comfort and help. Thus, the church ministers to itself. That is not selfish. It is God's plan. It honors Christ because it forms Christ in the body, but it certainly does not encompass the sum of church-life service. There is much to do "outside" the Body. A local congregation must avoid the peril of ministering *only* to itself. It must not exist for itself and its own self-aggrandizement. People must not enjoy their own fellowship to the point they do not want it threatened by the bringing in of new members. This attitude soon degenerates into crass institutionalism, and that is but one step away from death. The church is to grow and mature, so it can engage in evangelism and ministry outside of its own organizational life. This leads to the second consideration.

Ministry "Outside" the Church

The local church is to impact the whole world. After all, that is where people in need are found. That is where God desires to establish His kingdom. Therefore, as the "salt of the earth" and "light of the world" the church ministers the gospel of Christ. In reality, if the church neglects its evangelistic task here, it profoundly fails. Through faith we can look for victory (2 Cor. 2:14). God is sovereign. The "gates of hell" will not prevail against the advancing armies of Christ (Matt. 16:18, KJV). The world can be reached for Christ through the message and the ministry of the church in covenant with the living God.

Why are churches rather inept in fulfilling their evangelistic role? Probably the reason for this issue is that the church has never really fully completed the Reformation of the sixteenth century relative to the priesthood of *all* believers. As one perceptive writer put it:

> Today, our current practices in the Church come uncomfortably close to a pre-Reformation understanding of "call" and "Christian ministry." We have a three-tiered understanding of Christian vocation in which believers think of clergy and missionaries as having the highest call, dedicated lay church leaders and officers are on the middle rung of this ladder, and then all other non-ordained Christians on the bottom rung. The compelling issue for Christian discipleship is: how can the church recover a New Testament understanding of *call* which applies to all persons and which empowers believers to incarnate the rule of the kingdom in all areas of their common life?[3]

There is still, it seems, a subtle hanging-on to the pre-Reformation idea of the priesthood of special people, those who have a "special call" from God. So we ordain them and elevate them to superior roles as Christian servants while the rest retain an inferior status. However, God has no such status levels. The salvation experience in Christ eliminates *all* levels of status. The "priesthood of all believers" means *all*, and that implies more than the principle that all can come to God without the intervention of a "professional" priest. The fact that all can come to God through Christ alone is a wonderful truth, but the priesthood of all believers means much more. Priestly *service* is the primary point in the concept. Such a reality cannot be stated strongly enough in the light of the present weakness in evangelism. The principle must be taken seriously without hanging on to an old medieval view that the "clergy" enjoys superior rank as Christians while the "laity" see themselves as inferior citizens in kingdom service. The full implications of the Reformation should be completed: all who are called in Christ should work for their Lord as priestly evangelists.

Not only does the laity need to understand their role, but also the clergy should be aware of it. If many of the nonordained in our churches have failed to grasp their exalted position in Christ, and have thus never seen themselves as ministers, some of the clergy have given themselves too high a position which is also foreign to the spirit of the New Testament. Peter said to the first-century "clergy" not to be "domineering over those in your charge but being examples to the flock" (1 Pet. 5:2).

This does not mean that all ministry roles are one and the same. They obviously are not. Just as the body is one with many different members, so also is Christ's body, the church (1 Cor. 12:12). Roles do differ, but all are *called* in Christ. Every Christian, therefore, has a distinct calling from the Lord of the harvest. In a very real sense, all are called to be "full-time Christian ministers." Some are called to be full-time Christian farmers, businessmen, mothers, physicians, congressional leaders, office workers, or laborers, serving Christ in their respective callings. All believers are to seek God's will for their lives and serve Christ in that context.

Of course, this does not mean there are no leaders in the life of the body. Paul acknowledged that those who labor as teachers and preachers and leaders are to receive special honor for their work (1 Tim. 5:17). All organizations, including the church, must have leaders who are to be followed. Nonetheless, God expects as much of followers as leaders. All are to "fit" in the body. In that sense the "clergy-laity dualism" is eliminated, and if we can solve that problem, kingdom progress will be greatly enhanced. Therefore, a prime need of the hour is to help the local church organize itself so as to utilize every church member. The call of God commands it; the needs of the world require it.

Utilizing every church member would be quite revolutionary in most congregations. It may well mean divesting the leaders (pastors, evangelists, and prophets, [Eph. 4:11]) of some of their responsibility. In most instances, they are far too burdened anyway. Most would welcome help. Actually, to develop church structures where the leaders "do it all" does not make sense—let alone conform to the New Testament pattern. Even the secular world knows that delegated responsibility is vital to any enterprise. Since the Holy Spirit can certainly raise up those who are able to fill various positions of ministry where there is need, all believers should be led to assume their own responsible roles.

Because church members are in the marketplaces of the secular world in their everyday pursuits, they are exactly where they need to be to evangelize effectively. There is a vital ministry to perform "in the church"; however, there is much more to do among the millions in the marketplace who do not know Christ. The clergy obviously has a difficult time penetrating that secular world, but the average church member is already penetrating it for hours every working day. To fail to lead all the people of God into ministry through the normal pursuits of daily life on the job is to miss not only a great opportunity for a far-reaching ministry, but also it thwarts God's plan.

When a local church is sensitized to the biblical approach to ministry and begins to challenge, mobilize, train, and send out the whole *laos* into the world to evangelize and serve, then the local church begins to become a New Testament church. Michael Green, British New Testament scholar, pointed out:

> Christianity was from its inception a "lay" movement, and so it continued for a remarkably long time. . . . It was an unselfconscious effort. . . . They went everywhere gossiping the gospel; they did it naturally, enthusiastically, and with the conviction of those who are not paid to say that sort of thing. Consequently, they were taken seriously, and the movement spread, notably among the lower classes.[4]

Simply put, through the ministry of all believers, the masses can be effectively reached with the gospel. As Goyder put it, there are to be "no passengers in the church. All are called." How can all these sound biblical principles be actualized to become a ministry?

We can be encouraged, for there are churches which have experienced good success. An excellent example of what can be done is found in a congregation on the West Coast of the United States: The Peninsula Bible Church, Palo Alto, California. This local church has taken great strides in implementing a ministry involving a surprising percentage of their church members. It is not a clergy-oriented church; the laity assume their roles. As a result, the church has experienced significant growth in numbers and ministry. The whole spirit of the congregation is quite fascinating and captivating. There is such an atmosphere of warmth and acceptance that all types and classes of people are drawn to the fellowship. The depth of the dedication to ministry among the people is significant. As a case in point, when the offering is received in the worship services, anyone who has a need is encouraged to take money out to meet their needs. Such is the level of commitment and ministry in the shared body. Needless to say, many are reached for Christ when they see that degree of concern for people's needs. The wall between the "ordained" and "nonordained" has virtually collapsed. The difficult and debilitating dualism has all but dissolved, and the church members see themselves as called ministers of Christ.

Of course, the practical outworking of the principle is not easy to effect. Long-standing prejudices which find comfort in the old way of doing things must be overcome, but perhaps a beginning can be effected by asking two key questions. First, what really is the basic role and responsibility of the "ordained" clergy leadership of the local congregation? Second, what is the place and service of the "nonordained" persons and the relationship between these two "groups" of believers?

The Roles of Church Members

We can find answers to the central questions above—at least in an elementary way—by first investigating what the New Testament presents as the position of the ordained leaders in a local congregation. Then a look at ordination itself followed by delving into the ministry role of all believers can be undertaken.

It should be recognized that many contemporary churches are probably not duplicating the New Testament pattern concerning the "ordained ministry." For example, there was most likely a plurality of elders or pastors in the first-century churches who arose within the church itself. Large congregations with multistaffs exemplify in some sense the principle today as do some Baptists and Presbyterians, for example. Further, the bishop no doubt had a somewhat different role than the present-day bishop in those communions that still keep the formal office, such as the Methodists, Anglicans, and others. Nonetheless, the New Testament words that describe the various offices and leaders in the early church can still present something of an insight into the function of today's clergy roles and responsibilities.

The biblical word *presbuteros,* usually translated "elder," is essentially a title of dignity. The early church, no doubt, borrowed it from the Jewish community. Members of the honored Sanhedrin, for example, were often called elders. It seems the Greeks used the term in a similar fashion before the Jews brought it into their vocabulary. It became a designation of honor for certain leaders. The actual *function* of the dignified office of the elder in the Christian church is found in the word *episkopos* or bishop, which literally means overseer. In other words, *elder* and *bishop* described the same essential office, "elder" being the term of dignity, "bishop" the function.

Thayer pointed this out clearly in his Lexicon when he stated, "They [the elders] did not differ at all from the (Greek) bishops or overseers (as is acknowledged also by Jerome and Tit. i.5) . . . is evident from the fact that the two words are used indiscriminately . . . . The title *episkopos* [bishop] denotes the function, *presbuteros* [elder] the dignity."[5] Moreover, Paul said that they had significant authority in the local church "for building you up and not for destroying you" (2 Cor. 10:8). Strong leadership does not imply "dictatorship" in a church.[6]

These leaders were, as the terms imply, the spiritually governing body of the local church. They were charged with the task of leading the congregation in its life, worship, and ministry. Paul told these bishops they had been made overseers by the Holy Spirit (Acts 20:28), and they were to "shepherd" *(poimainein)* the church of God. They were highly regarded persons in the New Testament churches (1 Tim. 5:17).

The office of the elder was not only one of spiritual leadership, but also these officers visited and prayed for the sick (Jas. 5:13-15). Further, 1 Timothy 5:17 (KJV) states the elders are to "labour in the word and doctrine." The writer of the Book of Hebrews revealed that those who rule (He used a different word here, but the reference is the same.) are also those who "have spoken unto you the word of God" (KJV) and, for the sake of the readers, keep "watch over your souls" (13:7,17,24). This combination of oversight, preaching, teaching, and pastoral responsibility clearly lines up with the entire New Testament concept of the spiritual leadership ministry. These ministers keenly felt their responsibility to God for the welfare of the flock under their charge. The Bible implies that elders or bishops were set apart, or "ordained" to this position (1 Tim. 5:22).

Another aspect of the "ordained" ministry is found in the Greek word *diakonos* ("deacon"). There seems to have been a special group of persons in the New Testament churches who were appointed to this particular office of ministry (see Acts 6:1-6). They were appointed with a particular ministry in mind. It should be made clear that the word is used at times interchangeably with the position of elder, evangelist, or even apostle (see 1 Cor. 3:5). Often the word is simply employed to designate any "servant" of Christ. In that sense, all Christians are "deacons." Still, it many times denotes a position in the life of the local church of a specific person called and set apart for a specific ministry (1 Tim. 3:8-10).

Thayer says that *diakonos* is used in connection with those who, by God's command, promote and proclaim religion among people. This position was seemingly a special role that boasted some sort of "setting aside" (1 Tim. 3:8-13). There are those who feel this office was held by women in New Testament times as well as men (1 Tim. 3:11; Rom. 16:1). Others disagree.

One of the most interesting passages concerning the so-called ordained ministry in the New Testament church is found in Ephesians 4:11-12: "These were his gifts: some to be apostles, some prophets, some evangelists, some pastors and teachers, to equip God's people for work in his service, to the building up the body of Christ" (NEB). These verses clearly present the basic leadership of the New Testament church, at least in the Ephesian congregation. It is of special interest because it gives insight into the organization and administrative structure of the early church. Although it would perhaps be incorrect to say that every New Testament congregation had such a structure, a general principle certainly can be found in the Ephesian model. Scottish New Testament commentator William Barclay pointed out that this Ephesian passage presents three kinds of leadership offices in Paul's time. One, there were those whose authority was universal to the entire church. Two, there were others whose service was not restricted to one place; they had a wandering, itinerant ministry. Three, there were those who served essentially one congregation in one place.

The first category is the *apostles*. The word means "one sent" by God to minister. This encompassed more than just the twelve. For instance, Barnabas (Acts 14:14), Andronicus and Junias (Rom. 16:7), and Paul were called apostles in the sense that the term is used in Ephesians 4. Apostleship required that these had seen the Lord and had been a witness to His resurrection. In the historical sense this specific office was thus destined to pass away. Yet, as the term implies, all true servants of Christ are apostles in spirit, for they are the "ones sent" *(apostolos)* by God to bear witness to the resurrection. Moreover, every age has seen ministries that have touched the whole church.

The second group of leaders, the wanderers, is called *prophets* and *evangelists*. The prophet, as the forthteller (more than a foreteller) of God's truth, went about preaching in the power of the Spirit and was a leader of great influence. Before long, this office seemed to fade away from the life of the early church. Perhaps there were those who abused the office so that it fell into disrepute. Some commentators suggest this. The evangelists were probably what today are called "missionaries." They were bringers of good news. They did not exercise the prestige or authority of the apostles, nor did they have the early influence of the Spirit-inspired prophets. They were, more or less, the rank-and-file missionaries of the church who went about proclaiming the gospel. Again, in spirit, all are to exemplify these principles.

Finally, there were the *pastors* and *teachers*. This group comprised the more settled and permanent leaders in a local church. This office title seems to be a double phrase to describe one essential ministry, probably the same office as elder or bishop. Their task is found in their title; they were to teach and preach, and the content of their message was the Christian faith. These were more than teachers and preachers, they were also pastors *(poimenos)* or shepherds. They were to feed the flock of God (1 Pet. 5:2) and to care for and protect the sheep (Acts 20:28). Jesus

Christ Himself is the supreme example, for He is called the chief Shepherd (1 Pet. 5:4) and the Shepherd of all people's souls (1 Pet. 2:25). As Barclay said, "The shepherd of the flock of God is the man who bears God's people on his heart, who feeds them with the truth, who seeks them when they stray away, and who defends them from all that would hurt or distort their faith."[7] As pointed out, there was probably a plurality of them in most local churches. Moreover, because all God's people are ministers, they must therefore have something of the shepherd's heart.

The primary impact of the Ephesian passage is to be understood in the fact that God gave gifted leaders as His gift to the churches so all believers might be equipped to do the work of ministry. This is most important to grasp because therein is seen the role of the "ordained" leaders. Further, they all apparently had some sort of special call and gift and ordination for that specific task, but that raises the question as to what their "ordination" actually was.

What Is Ordination?

The practice of ordination calls for a fresh approach in many segments of the professing church today. This is true for several reasons. It must be said immediately that the New Testament has no technical term that describes any sort of admission to a "professional" ministerial position. Actually, the New Testament says very little about ordination at all. The ministerial office and the attending serviceable function so often run together in the biblical passages that little distinction between the two is found. Function and office simply blend. At the same time, however, the Bible does seem to present some sort of "setting apart" or "ordination." For example, Paul and Barnabas had hands laid on them setting them apart for their missionary journey (Acts 13:1-3). Furthermore, Paul told Timothy, "Do not neglect the gift you have, which was given you by prophetic utterance when the council of elders laid their hands upon you" (1 Tim. 4:14). Other references to the "laying on of hands" are Acts 6:6 in the setting aside of the first deacons, as well as Hebrews 6:2, 1 Timothy 5:22, and 2 Timothy 1:6. What can be said in the light of Scripture concerning ordination?

First, ordination concepts seems to have developed as the early church grew and expanded. Second, ordination in the first century was obviously quite "informal." There appears to be very little ceremony involved. All that can be discovered in the New Testament is prayer, fasting, and laying on of hands (Acts 13:3). To make too much of ordination, as some do today, may be another instance of not completing the Reformation. We must never forget that the quest should be to develop biblical practices, not to rely on mere traditions. In the Bible, ordination was seemingly no more than laying hands on people and praying for the task to which God had called them. The implication is: ordination could occur more then once in a person's life as God called to new ministry, such as Paul and Barnabas (Acts 13:1-2).

Now this does not mean the Bible fails to denote responsibility and its attending authority as bestowed by the local church on certain leaders, as in the case of the seven (Acts 6:1-6). Nor does it deny the symbolic impartation of spiritual power, as in Timothy's case (1 Tim. 4:14). Nevertheless, ordination was not an elaborate ceremony; rather than sacramental, it was installational. It set apart—installed—to ministry. Thus, it did not set aside certain believers as "first-class" Christians while the "nonordained," in contemporary understanding of ordination, were reduced to "second-class" status.

It should be emphasized that the attending responsibility to which one is set aside did grant authority to build up the church on the basis of the role. Leadership authority was taken seriously in the New Testament. For example, Hebrews 13:17 states, "Obey your leaders and submit to them; for they are keeping watch over your souls, as men who will have to give account." This does not mean the leadership had *legal* authority over the rest of the congregation. Such authority is a delegated authority—delegated by God in view of His call—yet it does imply that the church was to submit to their leadership in the Spirit of Christ. Therefore, although the authority was to be taken seriously, it was not to be viewed in any sense as an autocratic rule. The authority is bestowed by the Spirit to serve the church (Acts 20:28). Lohse holds that the key to understanding ordination in the New Testament lies in its Jewish prototype, the ordination of scribes by their teachers. New Testament practice emphasized, however, the Spirit's work, according to Lohse. It may well be that the rite was merely taken over by the new Christian community to denote the same basic ideas.

One thing does seem certain, however, the first-century rite was informal, yet consistently practiced by the church. Later developments such as formal ceremonies and the concept of "apostolic succession" were just that—later developments. The New Testament puts the whole rite on a simple basis in its observance and in its theology.

The Ephesian passage under consideration has a second vital issue: the responsibility of the "nonordained." Paul told the Ephesians that the entire body of Christ is involved in the ministry of the kingdom. The so-called ordained leaders are merely God's gift to the whole congregation to aid and equip them all in their gifted roles of ministry. They are to "equip the saints for the work of ministry" (Eph. 4:12).

History is not without examples to reinforce the validity of this practical principle. Compare the marvelous ministry of Charles Haddon Spurgeon in the last century. He devoted a large part of his ministry to the training of young men to go out and share their faith in Christ. Spurgeon once said, "He who converts a soul draws water from a fountain, but he who trains a soul winner digs a well, from which thousands may drink to eternal life." Incidentally, Spurgeon was never formally ordained in the nineteenth-century patterns of ordination; he felt it was unscriptural.

When we come to the contemporary moment, we also find clear examples of the principle at work. I have a friend who excelled in his responsibility in this field. He started the work with two concerned laymen. He taught and encouraged them in the area of personal evangelistic ministry. These two men began to lead people to faith in Christ. Soon they recruited two more to join them in the work. Four men were thus engaged. Soon there were eight as the work multiplied. Along with several young people, they gave themselves to the task. Soon a host of trained and zealous Christians were constantly witnessing for Christ.

Christian Initiation

Furthermore, it is very important to point out that Christian initiation into the local church has much to say in respect to ordination. The patterns of how new believers were brought into the fellowship of a local congregation were established very early in church history. Actually, it may have been the New Testament pattern itself. Although the New Testament does not explicitly state it, many biblical scholars believe it was so. The early church apparently quite consistently followed the following sequence:

1. A declaration of desire on the part of the lost person to become a believer.
2. Full instruction on how to be saved. Here the full gospel was communicated.
3. Baptism in water with the verbal confession "Jesus is Lord" (Rom. 10:9). This constituted the public confession of faith.
4. The putting on of a white robe after baptism as a symbol of the receiving of the righteousness of Christ.
5. The laying on of hands, symbolic of receiving the Holy Spirit and being set aside to serve Christ and minister in the Holy Spirit's power.
6. The observance of the Lord's Supper by all the church.
7. Full welcome into the Body.

In this rite, *everyone* had hands laid on them. Therefore, in that sense, every believer became an ordained believer. The laying on of hands implies a "setting apart" and a receiving of the Spirit for ministry. Perhaps Martin Luther was right when he said, "All Christians are ordained to ministry at their baptism." British New Testament scholar George Beas-ley-Murray said he believed all true Christians are ordained to ministry in this New Testament initiation sense.

What was the meaning of the laying on of hands when Paul and Barnabas were "set apart" for their first missionary journey (Acts 13:1-3)? This obviously came after baptism. It was probably a special setting apart for a special service. Perhaps it was more of a "commissioning" type of exercise rather than a formal ordination as we think of it today. Thus, Paul's experience should not have too much weight placed on it to justify a view of ordination about which the New Testament reveals little or nothing. Spurgeon may well have been right in refusing ordination as it is commonly understood.

If the practice of Christian initiation and the commissioning of all by the laying on of hands were a common practice in contemporary churches, the knotty problems of the "ordained" and the "nonor-dained," the "clergy-laity dualism," and ordination of women—all of which have been such disturbing issues—would perhaps find some res-olution. Why not see all believers as being ordained in Christian initia-tion? Furthermore, why not then "set apart," in a "commissioning ser-vice" or "ordination service," all those who discover their "call" in ministry just like churches do for pastors? This is far reaching because, in principle, *all* who are in Christ have a call and, therefore, should be commissioned or "ordained" to it. Why not, as just one example, com-mission the church's Sunday School workers? Or, why not "set apart" a church member to fill *any role* the Holy Spirit has called that one to do, be it in the formal structures of the local church or in the world? Could the problem be that Christians have been more conditioned by tradition than by the New Testament?

Now all of this, as revolutionary as it appears, does not depreciate the leadership roles of pastors, teachers, or evangelists. Leaders, such as pas-tors, have a very real touch of God on their lives; but that does not mean God does not touch others also, and if He does, why not set them aside in a commissioning service? This is what the Bible seems to say. By practicing the scriptural pattern in all things, much good in practical ministry would quite naturally ensue, and the evangelistic life of the church would be deepened.

The Question

What does "nonordained" church members actually do? What is their role? If they, in God's sight, are ordained to ministry, how do they fit in the overall scheme of ministry and evangelism? Obviously, this is the essential, practical question a local church must answer if it truly desires to be a ministering body of Christ in today's world. Again we turn to Paul's key Ephesian passage (ch. 4).

This passage has been studied for years, but a few decades ago a New Testament scholar read it with more insight. He eliminated a "troublesome comma" separating verse 11 from verse 12 in most versions, and the answer to the questions burst forth. With the comma eliminated the verse reads: "His gifts were that some should be apostles, some prophets, some evangelists, some pastors and teachers to equip the saints for the work of ministry, for building up the body of Christ" (Eph. 4:11-12). He discovered that the so-called clergyman is the "equipper" of saints; it is the whole body of believers who do the work of ministry. At last interpreters can see that everyone is in the ministry, and that is the way to reach the whole world. Everyone could not only get involved, but also were commissioned to do so as they were equipped by their leaders.

This concept has been stressed over and again through countless books, sermons, and articles—and in this chapter more than once. With every Christian mobilized as a minister and coached by the clergy (Elton Trueblood's metaphor of clergyman as "coach" and all Christians as the "team" was very appropriate.), the whole world would soon feel the impact of the entire ministering, servant church. All thrilled at the new possibilities that these sound, scriptural concepts held. Consequently, many congregations went about to implement them in their local ministering church life. They taught and exhorted people to get educated and motivated to mission. This went on for years, but nothing of real consequence seemed to happen—at least in most congregations. The so-called faithful few were taken with the idea. The weary clergyman saw relief in sight. Yet after years of effort, the faithful few still bear the large burden of the work, and the average minister is still seen by most as the grossly overworked "professional." As important as the principle is, it did not captivate the large majority of church members. To be honest, the majority of church members have not been motivated or enlisted in ministry. The purpose of these statements is not to lament our failures but, rather, to suggest where there may be a breakthrough.

It has been something of a puzzle why Paul and his companions could go into a community, totally pagan, and in a very short time—often only weeks—leave a completely healthy, indigenous, growing, effective church. Pioneer mission work in the U.S.A. does not seem this effective. It appears Paul must have labored on the basis of a principle that is at the core of the New Testament. In Romans 12:3-8, 1 Corinthians 12—14, and the favorite Ephesians 4:4-13 passage, Paul's vital principle clearly emerges. In these passages Paul presented the church primarily as the ministering body of Christ. The metaphor of a body is most relevant and insightful to the theme. A body speaks of action, work, movement, and ministry. Thus, Paul's metaphor about the church as a serving, ministering people is perfect. The body can work and serve the world. Moreover, the perfect harmony of unity in diversity is met by the metaphor. But how does a local church become a real ministering body of Christ?

The Church Becoming a Ministering Body of Christ

In the passages listed above, Paul contended that a congregation becomes a vibrant, ministering body on the basis of the *charismata:* the "gifts of the Spirit." This becomes obvious when one comes to grips with the entire paragraph of the Ephesians passage along with the Romans and Corinthian passages. Paul held that a church becomes a full functioning, growing, ministering body when it is "gifted" by the Holy Spirit. It was the employment of this basic concept of the *charismata* in the local church that made Paul's missionary ministry so effective.

Several points need to be made concerning these ministering "gifts of the Spirit." If this is what it takes to develop a fully functioning body of Christ that ministers effectively in the world, their centrality is obvious.

The Nature of the Gifts

First, what are these gifts? The New Testament declares when Christ ascended to the Father, He "led a host of captives,/ and he gave gifts to men" (Eph. 4:8). The "gifts" are the consequence of the presence of the "Spirit of promise" (Eph. 1:13, KJV) who indwells all believers. Further, 1 Corinthians 12:4-6 makes it evident that "gifts" are ministering abilities enabling one to serve Christ effectively. Paul said, "Now there are varieties of gifts, but the same Spirit; and there are varieties of service, but the same Lord; and there are varieties of working, but it is the same God who inspires them all in every one." The gifts of the Spirit are equipping abilities of service. They are ministering enablements given to all laborers through the grace of God by the Holy Spirit. (See also Rom. 12:3-8.) In other words, the gifts *(charismata)* are abilities given by our Lord for the purpose of equipping believers for the work of the ministry. Moreover, it is important to distinguish these gifts of the Spirit from the fruits of the Spirit presented in Galatians 5:22-24. The fruits are the manifestation of the Spirit in daily life to develop Christlike character. The gifts are the manifestation of the Spirit through the believer to make service and ministry for Christ effectual.

Further, these "grace gifts" are not to be confused with natural talents. Though all have natural abilities—abilities that God will surely use in His service—the spiritual gifts are not human talents *per se.* The gifts stemmed solely from the Spirit. They were the result of His divine inner work. They were supernatural endowments. Yet, the distinction between natural talents and gifts should not be pressed too far. In actual practice, the gifts may very well blend in with one's natural talents in the service of Christ.

The Scope of the Gifts

Second, notice the scope of these gifts. In the three primary New Testament passages listed above, the spiritual gifts are enumerated:

Romans 12:3-8:

1. Prophecy
2. Ministration
3. Teacher
4. Exhortation
5. Giver
6. Ruler
7. He who shows mercy

1 Corinthians 12:8-10:

1. Utterance of wisdom
2. Utterance of Knowledge
3. Faith
4. Healing
5. Miracles
6. Prophecy
7. Discernment of spirits
8. Interpretation of tongues

1 Corinthians 12:28:

1. Apostles
2. Prophets
3. Teachers
4. Workers of miracles
5. The healing of sick
6. Serviceable ministries (helps)
7. Government (oversight)
8. Varieties of tongues

Ephesians 4:11:

1. Apostles
2. Prophets
3. Evangelists
4. Pastors and teachers

This list of the gifts of the Spirit makes it quite clear they cover the entire work of the ministry. Therefore, they are to be taken seriously. As Paul said, "It is important, brethren, that you should have clear knowledge on the subject of spiritual gifts" (1 Cor. 12:1, author's translation).

In listing the gifts, Paul stressed the Christians themselves with particular ministries, for example, apostles, prophets, and teachers. At other times, the emphasis rested upon the gift itself rather than the individual who was gifted, that is, faith or varieties of tongues. Perhaps the simplest thing to say is that a gift apart from a believer to exercise the gift is an abstraction, and a believer who is not exercising his or her gift is a relatively ineffectual Christian servant.

The lists in these biblical passages are probably not meant to be exhaustive. Perhaps they should be viewed as "categories" of gifts to which there are many different manifestations. John R. W. Stott said in an unpublished lecture at Spurgeon's College, London, that there are probably "thousands of gifts." Every age, culture, generation, and situation has its specific needs. Surely, the Spirit will step in to meet those needs by "gifting" His people to meet them. At any rate, the idea of the gifts of the Spirit makes it clear that God has provided in full measure for all needs of the church in its growth, worship, and ministry. The organization of the local church, its government, its instruction and equipping, its worship, its ministry of witness, and its entire corporate life are fully cared for. *The Interpreter's Bible* makes a valid point: "Let there be among the Corinthian Christians, and in every Christian church in any age, clear recognition of the simple truth that in such a divinely appointed organism as the body of Christ, for its vitality and its effective witness, a variety of functions is required."[8] Surely, the Spirit will see to it that no part of His work suffers for lack of a gift.

Who Possesses the Gifts?

Third, it must be stressed that the Holy Spirit distributes gifts to every believer. Lenski declared that the emphasis rests primarily on the dative in 1 Corinthians 12:7, thus highlighting that "to each one . . . each believer has his gifts, and every bestowal of a gift is for the common good." This is certainly reasonable. If all in the body are to serve Christ, all need gifts to do so. Therefore, all have gifts, bestowed by the Holy Spirit, so each one can effectively minister in Christ's name. To say one does not have a gift is tantamount to saying he or she is not even in the Body. The Holy Spirit creates the ministering body of Christ by the bestowal of these gifts (1 Cor. 12). All believers, whether they recognize it or not, have gifts to serve Christ. Ordination, in the sense of laying on of hands, is a symbol of receiving the Holy Spirit, of being set apart for ministry, and of receiving spiritual gifts.

Moreover, the gifted believer is to be correctly motivated in the exercise of his or her gift in ministry. The gifts must be employed only under the control of the Holy Spirit. They are not to be used simply when and how the believer wishes, let alone enjoyed selfishly. The gifts are exercised for ministry to others, and love is to be the highest aim in their use. Love makes for harmony and unity. Love outlasts all the gifts. To make this clear Paul wrote the great "love chapter" (1 Cor. 13).

To summarize, then, each gift must be understood as a Holy Spirit-imparted grace-gift, a supernatural endowment, and a God-ordained ability to minister for the enrichment of the body, to the end of ministry in Christian service.

The Revolutionary Implications of the Principle

Several conclusions concerning spiritual gifts are important. First, the local church in its organizational life should be structured so the members of the church can exercise the gifts committed to them by the Holy Spirit. In other words, the church's programs should be set up in such a manner that the Holy Spirit can manifest Himself in and through all His people as He wills. The church should "commission" people when they find God's ministering gift. The body of Christ "ordains" people to function in ministry because they are gifted so to do. The Spirit issues the call and imparts the gift; the congregation recognizes and affirms the gift. That obviously calls for a number of revolutionary approaches.

This may mean there will be significant change in the present structures of most local church programs. The entire church organizes on the basis of what spiritual gifts are manifest in the corporate life of the congregation. As Gordon Cosby said about the gifts of the Spirit, "If we take them seriously, they will set off a revolution in the churches that will bring in a whole new age of the Spirit." In other words, the church should start with gifted people—not programs. Church structures should be built around people so there can be a channel through which the gifted ones can exercise their ministry. This was surely Paul's methodology.

Thus the old administrative principle of developing an elaborate church program—usually through a "nominating committee" or a "church council"—and then cramming people into the structures will have to give way. Of course, this traditional approach has never proved truly satisfying anyway. How often the wrong person seems to get in the wrong job. The consequence is that both the person and the job suffer until next year's committee can appoint a new person—only to have the same problems over again. Is it not more in keeping with scriptural principles to approach the ministry from a "people perspective" than from a "program viewpoint"?

Can a church pragmatically structure itself on this principle? That is the question! It can if it will. Two cases in point can be cited. Ray C. Stedman, pastor of the Peninsula Bible Church in Palo Alto, California, says emphatically, "Yes!"[9] If all Stedman relates in his fascinating little volume *Body Life* is true, his church is a beautiful picture of a gifted, ministering body of Christ in a community. Further, a church in Chicago was organized on this concept. The pastor admitted to some painful days. Yet, the church saw real growth and significant involvement in ministry. And this church takes the principle right to its logical conclusion. The pastor said, "If we do not have people who are significantly gifted to meet the needs of a given program, then we drop the program."

Now these are new ideas to many and the issue faced is changing the older churches who have held to the status quo for decades. In such cases, it is probably not best to move too fast. However, the church can begin to turn in the right direction; and, when a person discovers his or her gift, the church can create a structure around that person so he or she can exercise it. As the congregation is educated in this principle, and it begins to take hold, it will spread as leaven in the lump. If the Holy Spirit is in control, it can be sanely and sensibly implemented.

When one actually discovers his or her gift, it is highly encouraging and motivating. On one occasion, while making a presentation to a group on this theme, a lady of about sixty-five burst out, "I've got the gift of helps!" She was excited. She had suddenly realized that what she had been doing in her ministry of helping people was actually the exercising of a spiritual gift. The pastor said later she now goes about her work with new zest and assurance of God honoring her labors.

Moreover, the principle liberates. While once speaking to a group in a large church, I remarked that all members of the congregation were to be witnesses, but not all possessed the same ministering gift. A lady came to me afterward and related how relieved she was. She had felt guilty for years for not doing certain things in ministry, even though she tried. She was now free to discover and exercise her gift. She no longer felt guilty for not having some other gift she believed she should have to be a "spiritual Christian."

All the above does not mean any believer is excused from witnessing. To the contrary, all are to witness; just not all will be gifted in all ministering areas. Actually, a witness is best in the context of exercising unique personal gifts. That is the point of it all for evangelization. Our words take on more acceptance when done in the context of personal ministry. Believers both serve and speak. Thus it is imperative for them to discover their gifts as well as understand the gospel. Elizabeth O'Connor wrote in *The Eighth Day of Creation,* "Almost from the time a person comes in touch with The Church of The Savior [Washington, D.C.] he hears about gifts and is confronted with the question, 'What are your gifts?' "[10] Such is the atmosphere a church should develop. That will make ministry and evangelism effective.

How does a person actually discover one's gift? Ray Stedman set out three questions in the attempt to help people discover their gifts: (1) What are your desires? What do you do well and like to do? (2) What ability is improving and developing? This is probably the work of the Holy Spirit; He "matures" people. (3) Do others recognize a gift in you? Spiritually minded people often have keen discernment.

Here are what can be called the "Ten Commandments of Discovering Your Gift." They can be personalized as follows:

1. Have faith that you have one or more gifts of the Spirit. The Bible says you do.
2. Study the Scriptures and what they say about the gifts: (1) Come to understand from the Bible the nature of the *missio Dei*—God's mission in the world. What does He actually want His people to do to cooperate in the *missio Dei?* (2) Attempt to understand the actual nature of the gifts as recorded in the Scriptures.
3. Ask: How has God truly used me in the past, not just what jobs have I done in the church?
4. Ask: What do spiritual people say (personal testimony, group fellowship)? Often others can help you discover your ministry.

5. Ask: What do I like to do? I like to exercise my abilities. That may well be your "gift," as Stedman pointed out.

6. Ask: What needs burden me? True burdens are placed by the Spirit of God. The Holy Spirit may have equipped you to meet those needs.

7. Ask: What challenges me, that is, what does the Holy Spirit lay on my heart? How do I feel led? What does God seem to be saying?

8. Ask: What open doors are before me? What opportunities to ministry are actually open? God may move you to enter that door of ministry, and if He does, He will surely equip you to do it.

9. Rest in Christ. Be open. (1) Do something—keep moving—be disciplined, (2) but be open to change.

10. Prayer and trust is the final exercise. God will reveal His will if you are sincere in seeking His purpose for your life.

Furthermore, it is not incidental that, when one discovers one's gift, one senses a strong obligation to exercise it. Elizabeth O'Connor correctly stated, "The identifying of gifts brings to the fore another large issue in our lives—the issue of commitment. Somehow if I name my gift and it is confirmed, I cannot 'hang loose' in the same way."[11]

Another very important principle surfaces in O'Connor's statement: "The church should be very affirming about the gifts." The local Body should authenticate and affirm its members' gifts. If all God's people are called to ministry, it is obligated so to do. Here a "commissioning" or "ordination" service can prove so helpful.

Not only that, the gifts of the Spirit, though given by God, must be developed and nurtured in the church. Paul told Timothy to "stir up the gift of God" in him (2 Tim. 1:6). One of the major roles of the clergy is not only to help members discover their gifts, but to be the "stirrer" of the gifts and to see to it that doors are open to minister the gifts. Again from O'Connor: "As the patron of gifts, the church must provide an abundance of unthreatening situations in which . . . [believers] . . . have an opportunity to . . . consider for themselves all manner of . . . adventures."[12] The leader and administrator should see to that.

How are these gifts to be exercised? Permit another set of "ten commandments" on "how to" exercise your gifts:

1. Thou shalt not be too rigid or restrictive as to the nature of the gifts.

2. Thou shalt not wait to minister until you discover your gift.

3. Thou shalt not get too subjective or existential.

4. Thou shalt not forget godliness and holiness in a disciplined life.

5. Thou shalt not forget responsibility to the body, the whole church.

6. Thou shalt not forget thy leader's role.

7. Thou shalt not forget the power of the Holy Spirit.

8. Thou shalt not forget others.

9. Thou shalt not forget the church and its need of revival.

10. Thou shalt not forget to witness and share Christ with the lost.

Finally, there is the need of motivation: to stir the whole people of God from their apathy. This task the Spirit of God alone can do. The believer must be informed, but the Spirit inspires. Perhaps, in the final analysis, the greatest contribution each can make is to pray God will pour out His Spirit to awaken, revive, and enliven His people.

Conclusion

No doubt many more practical things should be said at this point, such as how to train the people in personal evangelism, how to preach the gospel, and how to develop evangelistic outreach programs in the church, but these areas of study must be left to other pragmatic works. Moreover, a vast array of material has been produced on these subjects in the form of books and denominational and parachurch programs. The purpose of this chapter is to present the workable principle from the biblical perspective on how a local church can gear itself for an effective evangelistic ministry. When it becomes so geared, then it can implement the practical programs it sees as needful. For a useful guide on how to get a church organized for world evangelization, see Appendix C. What is important to realize is the evangelistic task is for the whole church, the called out body of Christ. The church must minister and evangelize on the basis of the gifts of the Spirit if it is to fulfill the challenge. That demands aiding believers in discovering their gifts, then leading God's gifted people in the development of their gifts for ministry, and providing the opportunity for the exercise thereof. This will fulfill the mandate of Ephesians 4:11-12, and the whole people of God will take their proper place and begin to minister. Such is the foundational principle. Thus it becomes the basis of the renewal, growth, and, most importantly, world evangelization which to this point has seemingly eluded our grasp.

Notes

1. *Baker's Dictionary of Theology,* 142.

2. Donald Bloesch, *The Evangelical Renaissance* (London: E. J. Brill, 1971), 124.

3. *Laos: All the People of God,* edited by Fisher Humphreys and Thomas A. Kindren (New Orleans: Convocation on the Laity 1984), 63.

4. Michael Green, *Evangelism in the Early Church,* 173.

5. Joseph Henry Thayer, *A Greek-English Lexicon of the New Testament* (New York: American Book Co., 1886), 531.

6. It is important to realize from a practical perspective that the larger a local church becomes, the stronger the leadership role becomes. A large congregation demands more decision making on the part of the leaders, but all should be done in love and helpfulness.

7. William Barclay, *Letters to the Galatians and Ephesians* (Philadelphia: The Westminster Press, 1954), 175.

8. John Short, "The First Epistle to the Corinthians," *The Interpreter's Bible,* 12 vols. (New York: Abingdon Press, 1953), 10:164.

9. See Ray C. Stedman, *Body Life* (Glendale: Regal Books, 1972).

10. Elizabeth O'Connor, *Eighth Day of Creation: Gifts and Creativity* (Waco: Word Books, 1971), 25.

11. Ibid., 42.

12. Ibid., 47.

11

Spiritual Power for the Task: A Devotional Study

"Stay in the city, until you are clothed with power from on high" (Luke 24:49).

Introduction

World evangelization is an all but impossible task. It staggers the imagination. To conceive of taking the gospel of Jesus Christ to the entire world seems presumptuous, if not somewhat arrogant. Yet, our Lord said, "Ye shall be my witnesses . . . unto the uttermost part of the earth" (Acts 1:8, KJV). If this truly be the commission for the church, then power must be had, and that power must come "from on high" (Luke 24:49). No mere human ability or ingenuity will see the task accomplished. If the Christian witness would be effective in evangelistic activities, the individual witness must be "clothed with power from on high." Right there God has stepped in. Our Lord has given His own power for the work.

It may seem that a full chapter on one's personal spiritual experience is somewhat a deviation from the more purely theological issues with which this volume has attempted to deal. Such is not the case, however. Evangelism is to be done, and the doing of evangelism requires a vital experience with Jesus Christ. To divorce one's own experience of Christ from evangelistic understandings ends in perverting both. A theology of evangelism (any theology for that matter) must result in Christlike action and character. True theology is a "theology of the road," a theology to be practiced. Effective evangelism, therefore, mandates a profound walk with Jesus Christ. This chapter deals with these vital devotional evangelistic issues. Moreover, the needed power of God manifests itself in a variety of ways requiring investigation. It begins in one's own Christian ethical and moral life-style.

The Power of a Holy Life

The service and ministry which makes the most lasting and vital impression on the world is a Christlike life. As a young minister I once had the opportunity of serving as associate pastor to a genuine "man of God." This minister was not the pastor of a large, influential church. He was not an outstanding or eloquent preacher, nor were his intellectual achievements extraordinary. Yet, his ministry was felt over a large area. Many came to faith in Christ through his witness. The one fact of his ministry which was so outstanding, and that which gave him such influence, was the profound godliness of his life. Although he died some years ago, the man's impact still remains. This simple illustration implies a number of important principles.

In the first place, the image of the Christian witness is most relevant to effectiveness in evangelism. Gavin Reid pointed out, "Image communication can have an important supporting role to play." This is true for any Christian. Recognizing this important fact, Paul said, "Brethren, join in imitating me, and mark those who so live as you have an example in us" (Phil. 3:17). Such a person will prove powerful in the mission.

Further, one's native ability is not necessarily the determining factor in a significant evangelistic ministry. God obviously uses what people possess in gifts and talents, but as long as one's life is totally committed to Christ, God will make that life useful whether one's abilities are few or many.

All who would aspire to be instrumental in evangelism must learn the principles of godly living. These principles are few and elemental, yet quite profound. The concept as a whole can be summarized as simply knowing God in the daily fellowship of Jesus Christ:

> That which we have seen and heard we proclaim also to you, so that you may have fellowship with us; and our fellowship is with the Father and with his Son Jesus Christ. And we are writing this that our joy may be complete.
> This is the message we have heard from him and proclaim to you, that God is light and in him is no darkness at all (1 John 1:3-5).

If life is to be effective, one must come to know the vital and dynamic fellowship of God, which constitutes a holy life. Fellowship with God is the core of Christianity. As Lenski said, "The sum and substance of true religion is fellowship with God."[1] Several things need to be said concerning the possibility of knowing God in the sense of living daily in His presence.

To begin with, John viewed fellowship with God as a marvel. This is true because of the fact that "God is light and in him is no darkness at all" (v. 5). The metaphor concerning the character of God as "light" is used in various places in the New Testament. This figure of light seems to refer to God's "otherness," His holiness. Various New Testament passages picture something of the wonder of what it means to walk with a holy God in the light.

First, God is complete light: "In him is no darkness at all" (v. 5). God is completely and unequivocally morally perfect. His righteousness is infinite and ultimate. He is absolute holiness.

Not only is the light which surrounds the Godhead infinite and morally perfect, it is also unchangeable light (Jas. 1:17). God's holiness is utterly unchanging, immutable. He can always be experienced as "the same yesterday and today and for ever" (Heb. 13:8). He is always perfect, reliable, unchangeable light.

Paul stated in 1 Timothy 6:15-16 that God's holiness is unapproachable light: "The Kings of kings and Lord of lords, . . . alone has immortality and dwells in unapproachable light, whom no man has ever seen or can see. To him be honor and eternal dominion. Amen." An appreciation of the holiness, sovereignty, and majesty of the God of light is a needed contemporary concept. He is so unequivocably holy, no person in mere humanity dares approach Him. The current humanistic overtones and sentimentalism about God tries to bring the Lord of utter holiness down to a level that is not found in the Scriptures. A fresh vision of the glory, holiness, and otherness of God is needed.

All this is what makes the possibility of fellowship with God the wonder and marvel it is. God is light, but human beings are darkness (sinful), the very antithesis of light (1 John 1:8,10). Nonetheless, humankind are invited actually to walk through their days with this holy God of infinite, unchanging, unapproachable light. How can it be?

Fellowship Through Confession

Fellowship with God is a glorious possibility; a holy life is conceivable. Yet, it must obviously be worked out in the practical sphere of everyday living if it is to have any dynamic in one's experience. Foundational to the pragmatic implementation of walking with God is the realization that fellowship begins with confession:

> If we say we have fellowship with him while we walk in darkness, we lie and do not live according to the truth; but if we walk in the light, as he is in the light, we have fellowship with one another, and the blood of Jesus his Son cleanses us from all sin. If we say we have no sin, we deceive ourselves, and the truth is not in us. If we confess our sins, he is faithful and just, and will forgive our sins and cleanse us from all unrighteousness (1 John 1:6-9).

John dealt with the early Gnostic error that human flesh was sinful in itself. This Hellenistic philosophy erroneously taught that since flesh is sinful, God is interested only in the spirit. This precipitated moral laxity, antinomianism, and a host of other errors. This approach as a philo-sophical-religious system has largely passed away, but the condoning of sin has not. Even for Christians, sin (walking in darkness) is an ever-present quandary. Sin invades the believer's experience and vital fel-lowship with God is just as unreal a dream for many today as it was for the early Gnostics. Lenski stated, "To think that we can remain in dark-ness and yet be in fellowship with him in whom there is no darkness whatever is the height of delusion, the saddest contradiction."[2] Chris-tians must never forget that God is light and cannot sanction the dark-ness of our personal sins.

How then can believers deal with sin so as to affect holy living? This is the basic issue. Sin disrupts communion with God, which is the es-sence of holiness of life, and blunts one's evangelistic effectiveness. The fundamental truth is found in 1 John 1:7: "If we walk in the light, as he is in the light, we have fellowship with one another, and the blood of Jesus his Son cleanses us from all sin." The key phrase is where John told us the blood of Jesus, God's Son, continually cleanses us (present tense) from all sin. This simply means that to walk in the light, believers must be constantly cleansed by the power of Christ's forgiveness. Could it be that our evangelistic proclamation of the death and resurrection of Christ as the remedy for the sinful life has been restricted too much to the conversion experience alone? John told us that believers are to be constantly, continually cleansed by the blood of Christ. The death of our Lord was efficacious not only on the day of redemption, but also every day. John referred to sanctification, not justification, *per se*. None-theless, a Christian's holiness depends on the sanctifying work of the Holy Spirit in personal experience and the daily cleansing from sin by Christ.

It seems, however, too few have actually grasped the biblical concept of how the believer is to deal with sin in order that the blood of Christ may be efficacious in cleansing and keeping one in fellowship with God. This in turn may well be the reason so little powerful evangelism takes place. The concept must be investigated in a little more depth.

The initial step in experiencing the cleansing of sins centers in a proper understanding and evaluation of how sin manifests itself in life's basic relationships. First of all, there is sin that primarily involves the believer and God alone. Second, some transgressions impact not only the Christian's walk with God but also touches one's relationship to another individual. Although every sin is basically and essentially an affront to God, at times other individuals are involved. Third, there is sin which at times invades the Christian as an individual in relationships with a group of people, like the church.

Moreover, such sins are specific, definable, and individual. When Christians see their daily sins as a nebulous, indefinite whole, they are not normally moved to deal with them in God's prescribed manner. Christians must see their sins specifically and individually, and deal with them from a biblical basis.

The Pragmatics of the Issue

In approaching the problem of sin as it involves just the believer and his or her personal relationship with God, the Bible says, "If we confess our sins, he is faithful and just, and will forgive our sins and cleanse us from all unrighteousness" (1 John 1:9). The word *confess* is obviously the key term in this verse. In the language of the New Testament, it is a most interesting word. It is a compound term meaning "to say the same as" or "to assent to" (*homologeo*). This implies that to confess sins is agree with the convicting Spirit of God that a particular thing in one's life actually is a sin. In other words, to confess sins scripturally is "to concede to" or "to agree with" the voice of God the Spirit as He convicts of some *particular* act of rebellion. This precludes a confession of sins like, "Lord, forgive me of all my sins!" Such a prayer may be acceptable for public worship, but this is not the way the Scriptures state a Christian is to confess privately. To confess sins according to 1 John is to name them individually, one by one, agreeing with the Spirit of God that the particular act truly is a sin. Then the promise comes: "He is faithful and just, and will forgive our sins and cleanse us from all unrighteousness" (1 John 1:9). Believers should also confess the secret sins of which they are not conscious.

Second, some sins may manifest themselves in relation to others as well as to God. In such cases, merely to confess the sin to God alone is insufficient to experience the full liberty of Christ's forgiveness. They should be confessed not only to God, but also Jesus further stated that if believers have sinned against another and at the same time "are offering your gift at the altar, and there remember that your brother has something against you, leave your gift before the altar and go; first be reconciled to your brother, and then come and offer your gift" (Matt. 5:23-24). If Christians sin against another person, and their fellowship is thus marred, restitution must be made to that person as well as to God. If believers fail to acknowledge sins against individuals, as much as is possible under present circumstances and as God leads, then they cannot really expect deep fellowship with God or with one another.

Fellowship with others is vital to fellowship with God. Christians must seek forgiveness from those against whom they have sinned and lost fellowship in order to walk in harmony with them. John said, "That which we have seen and heard we proclaim also to you, so that you may have fellowship *with us*" (1 John 1:3, author's italics). If God expects us to confess our sins to Him to have fellowship with Himself, certainly the principle applies to our human, interpersonal relationships as well.

Finally, we find at times sin can manifest itself not simply against God alone or just against a single individual, but it can be open, flagrant, and others know of it. How is this issue to be dealt with? James said there are times when believers should confess certain sins to someone or perhaps even to a group as well as to God (Jas. 5:16). They need some person or group in the fellowship of believers to whom they can be quite open, honest, and candid about themselves. Is not this the *koinonia* of love which the New Testament talks about? The local church should be such a fellowship of love and understanding that members feel unthreatened when they open their real selves to their fellow believers in Christ. Moreover, if a member's sins are well known so that reproach is brought upon the entire church, breaking the fellowship, then forgiveness should be sought from the entire church. This is what lies behind the principle of church discipline.

Now all of this must be seen in the most positive light, for it should be a liberating experience. As one becomes increasingly sensitive to the Holy Spirit, He will lead in this area of confession. It is important to become open with God and others and strip off the facade. But one must stay positive and not get too introspective. Morbid introspection is not spiritual health; it is psychological sickness. The Holy Spirit will point out true sin and what should be dealt with, and how. Sin is to be confessed in the realm of the real offense. True forgiveness and fellowship with God are found in true confession. The discipline of the holy life is vital in work for Christ. As Robert Murray McCheyne said, "A holy man is an awesome weapon in God's hands." But there is more to powerful evangelism.

The Power of the Holy Spirit

The Holy Spirit imparts power in evangelism in a threefold sense. First, God imparts the person and power of the Holy Spirit to believers to make their life holy. A Christian simply cannot live a holy life apart from the Holy Spirit. Second, the Holy Spirit fills believers personally with power (Acts 2:1-4). Third, the Holy Spirit falls on the whole church from time to time and mightily revives and awakens God's people (Ps. 85:6-7). The personal principles of a Spirit-filled life are next.

The Power of the Spirit-filled Life

The Holy Spirit demonstrates His own power through the believer. It is the Spirit that makes service and evangelistic witness effective and fruitful. R. A. Torrey correctly pointed out:

The Holy Spirit is the person who imparts to the individual believer the power that belongs to God. This is the Holy Spirit's work in the believer, to take what belongs to God and make it ours. All the manifold power of God belongs to the children of God as their birthright in Christ and becomes ours in actual and experimental possession through the Holy Spirit's work in us as individuals. To the extent that we understand and claim for ourselves the Holy Spirit's work, to that extent do we obtain for ourselves the fullness of power in Christian life and service that God has provided for us in Christ.[3]

If Christians are to be useful in the mission of God, the Scriptures make it abundantly clear that they are to be filled with the Holy Spirit (Eph. 5:18). Believers are not merely possessors of the Spirit, but they are to be filled with the Spirit as well. Powerful service is forcefully set out in the following passages of Scriptures:

> "Behold, I send the promise of my Father upon you; but stay in the city, until you are clothed with power from on high" (Luke 24:49).
> "You shall receive power when the Holy Spirit has come upon you; and you shall be my witnesses in Jerusalem and in all Judea and Samaria and to the end of the earth" (Acts 1:8).
> They were all filled with the Holy Spirit and began to speak in other tongues, as the Spirit gave them utterance (Acts 2:4).
> When they had prayed, the place in which they were gathered together was shaken; and they were filled with the Holy Spirit and spoke the word of God with boldness (Acts 4:31).
> Do not get drunk with wine, for that is debauchery; but be filled with the Spirit (Eph. 5:18).

Believers who are evangelistically effective also give testimony to the validity of the concept of the Spirit-filled life. For example, R. A. Torrey said, "I was led to seek the baptism [filling] with the Holy Spirit, because I became convinced from the study of the Acts of the Apostles that no one had a right to preach the gospel until he had."[4] Charles G. Finney wrote: "I was powerfully converted on the morning of the 10th of October, 1821. In the evening of the same day I received overwhelming baptisms [infillings] of the Holy Ghost."[5] Concerning his ministry after having been filled with the Spirit, A. T. Pierson said, "I have seen more conversion and accomplished more in eighteen months since I received that blessing than in the eighteen years previous."[6]

Dwight Lyman Moody was one of God's great evangelists. His effective ministry spanned two continents. It has been said of Moody that he put one foot in America, one in England, and shook the Western hemisphere for Jesus Christ. Moody was a tireless worker. In the earlier days of his Christian service, he toiled incessantly in the city of Chicago. Yet, he lacked a true anointing of the Holy Spirit to make his life and ministry mighty. The day came, however, when Moody met God in a powerful way. The journey to God's fullness was difficult for the zealous young man. The account of his spiritual pilgrimage to the Spirit's touch is quite fascinating.

During the Civil War days in America, Moody did a significant work holding evangelistic meetings and distributing Gospels and tracts among the soldiers and prisoners of war. He ministered on many battlefields in the Southern states. Later he returned to Chicago. There he went to work in the Sunday School movement. Through his efforts, the International Sunday School lessons were started. This method of Bible study is used by many churches to the present day.

Moody also became prominent in the Young Men's Christian Association in America. In 1870, at a YMCA convention, he first met Ira David Sankey, who became his well-known singing partner.

In 1867, Moody traveled to Great Britain. He intended to study the methods of Christian work employed in England. He was especially anxious to hear pastor Charles Haddon Spurgeon. He also wanted to meet George Muller who had founded on faith a large orphanage at Bristol. Moody was at that time unknown in England.

During that first visit to Britain, Moody met Henry Varley, a well-known nineteenth-century evangelist. As they sat together on a bench in a public park in Dublin, Varley said to the American evangelist, "The world has yet to see what God will do with and for and through and in and by the man who is fully consecrated to him." Moody thought, *I am a man, and it lies with the man himself whether he will or will not make that entire and full consecration. I will try my utmost to be that man.*

Moody's hunger for a deeper experience of God was aided by the preaching of Henry Moorehouse, another well-known English preacher. Moorehouse came to the Chicago church where Moody pastored soon after his return to America. Every night for a week, Moorehouse spoke from the text John 3:16; "For God so loved the world, that he gave his only begotten Son, that whosoever believeth in him should not perish, but have everlasting life." Moorehouse's preaching on the love of God transformed Moody's whole approach to evangelism.

A critical year for Moody was 1871. He realized how little he was humanly fitted for his work, and how much he therefore needed the Holy Spirit's power. This realization was heightened by two ladies in his church membership. They deeply impressed young Moody. In relating the incident, Moody stated:

> I thought I had the power. I had the largest congregation in Chicago, and there were many conversions. I was in a sense satisfied. But right along those two godly women kept praying for me, and their earnest talk about

anointing for special service set me thinking. I asked them to come and talk with me, and they poured out their hearts in prayer that I might receive the filling of the Holy Spirit. There came a great hunger into my soul. I did not know what it was. I began to cry out as I never did before. I really felt that I did not want to live if I could not have this power for service.[7]

At that stage, the Chicago fire wiped out both Farwell Hall and the Illinois Street church sanctuary, D. L. Moody's church buildings. He journeyed to New York city to collect funds for the sufferers of the Chicago fire, but inwardly he was seeking power from on high. He said:

My heart was not in the work of begging. I could not appeal. I was crying all the time that God would fill me with his Spirit. Well, one day, in the city of New York—oh, what a day!—I cannot describe it, I seldom refer to it; it is almost too sacred an experience to name. Paul had an experience of which he never spoke for fourteen years. I can only say that God revealed himself to me, and I had such an experience of his love that I had to ask him to stay his hand. I went to preaching again. The sermons were not different; I did not present any new truths, and yet hundreds were converted. I would not now be placed back where I was before that blessed experience if you should give me all the world.[8]

Moody had a life-changing experience. In principle it sounds much like that of John Wesley, Charles G. Finney, and others whom God has used significantly. Is such an encounter legitimate? Perhaps the question can be best answered by looking at the example of our Lord.

The Example of Jesus

Jesus lived out His entire ministry in the power and fullness of the Holy Spirit. This is reiterated constantly in the Gospels: "For the one whom God sent speaks authentic words of God—and there can be no measuring of the Spirit given to *him*!" (John 3:34, Phillips). Jesus was full of the Holy Spirit (Luke 4:1). Christians should attempt to emulate Christ in His relationship to the Spirit of God.

Space forbids delving into the numerous New Testament passages that teach this essential truth. Suffice it to say, the Bible sets forth Jesus as the prime example of the Spirit-filled life, and the overwhelming weight of the Word of God fully supports the theme that being filled with the Holy Spirit is a valid experience. There is little or no power in evangelism apart from the Spirit's anointing.

More Historical Accounts

Since the Spirit-filled life is a biblically based concept, it should be expected to surface constantly in the course of history, especially in the lives of those whom God uses in significant ways. Church history repeatedly attests to the reality of being "filled with all the fulness of God" (Eph. 3:19).

The early church fathers, Origen, Jerome, Ambrose, and others, talked much about the work of the Holy Spirit in the believer's life. As the years of God's dealings with His people unfolded, giants of the Christian faith were constantly found emphasizing the theme. Leaders like Savonarola, Fenelon, George Fox, Madam Guyon, John Bunyan, and a multitude of others give testimony to the necessity of being dynamically related to the Holy Spirit of God.

The eighteenth century witnessed a fresh emphasis on the theme. No one in those days was more godly or significantly used by the Spirit than young David Brainerd. His biographer Lawson described those encounters:

> Brainerd, the consecrated missionary, endured almost incredible hardships while laboring among the American Indians; but he lived so close to God that his life has been an inspiration to many. . . .
>
> Such intense longings and prayers after holiness as we read of in the journals of Brainerd are scarcely recorded anywhere else. "*I long for God,* and a conformity to His will, an inward holiness, ten thousand times more than for anything here below," says he. On Oct. 19, 1740, he wrote: "In the morning, I felt my soul *hungering and thirsting* after *righteousness.* In the forenoon, while I was looking on the sacramental elements, and thinking that Jesus Christ would soon be 'Set forth crucified' before me, my soul was filled with light and love, so that I was almost in an ecstasy; my body was so weak I could hardly stand. I felt at the same time an exceeding tenderness, and most fervent love towards all mankind; so that my soul, and all the powers of it seemed, as it were, to melt into softness and sweetness. . . . This love and joy cast out fear, and my soul longed for perfect grace and glory."[9]

During the nineteenth century, another surge of interest in the Spirit-filled life emerged. Charles H. Spurgeon, no doubt the greatest of all Victorian preachers, during one of his sermons quoted Luke 11:13: "If you then, who are evil, know how to give good gifts to your children, how much more will the heavenly Father give the Holy Spirit to those who ask him!" Spurgeon then cried out to the eager congregation:

> O, let us ask Him at once with all our hearts. Am I not so happy as to have in this audience some who will immediately ask? You that are the children of God to you is this promise specially made. Ask God to make you all the Spirit of God can make you, not only a satisfied believer who has drunk from self, but a useful believer who overflows his neighborhood with blessing.

The Spirit-filled life did not end with the closing of the nineteenth century. Many contemporary Christians seek God's fullness. Only the fullness of the Holy Spirit of God can move one to a level of Christian experience and effectiveness that makes evangelism possible. Even the "signs and wonders" of Acts 4:29-30 emerge by the Spirit's power. Right at the core of every great evangelical awakening is found the out-pouring of the Holy Spirit on believers.

Therefore, in the light of all that has been said biblically, historically, and experientially, it is evident that God fully expects all believers to be filled with the Holy Spirit. One issue thus remains to be addressed: how to maintain that level of Christian experience.

How Is One to Be Filled with the Spirit?

Five simple principles form the spiritual disciplines to experience the Spirit-filled life:

Acknowledge.—First, there must be an acknowledgment of need. If Christians are satisfied with their present spiritual state, little progress will be made in the things of God. The Lord Jesus Christ said, "Blessed are those who hunger and thirst for righteousness, for they shall be sat-isfied" (Matt. 5:6).

Abandon.—After God creates something of a genuine hunger and thirst for His best, and having acknowledged one's need, the next im-perative step is to abandon all sins. The confession of all known iniqui-ties is essential. Paul said, "I always take pains to have a clear conscience toward God and toward men" (Acts 24:16).

Abdicate.—The next exercise is to abdicate the throne of one's life to Christ's kingship. The one basic issue is: Will I control my own life, or will I truly make Jesus Lord of all? A decision must be made. God's Word is very plain on this point. The Holy Spirit is given to "those who obey him" (Acts 5:32). Jesus must be Lord.

Ask.—After acknowledging need, abandoning sin, and abdicating control of their lives, believers simply ask God to fill them with His Spirit. Jesus said, "If you then, who are evil, know how to give good gifts to your children, how much more will the heavenly Father give the Holy Spirit to those who ask him!" (Luke 11:13). God deeply desires His people to come into His presence by prayer and ask Him for the fullness of the Spirit. The admonition of Paul to the Ephesians to be "filled with the Spirit" (5:18) is instructive here. The verb "filled" is a second person present, imperative. It literally means, "You are constantly to be filled with the Spirit." Likewise, Luke's promise in 11:13 is present tense, meaning "keep on asking." Seeking the Spirit's fullness is a continuing daily discipline. It is not a "once for all" experience as is the receiving of the Spirit at conversion. Christians need to be daily "filled with all the fulness of God" (Eph. 3:19). Actually, it is a "state" of relationship with

God[10] the Father as He waits for cleansed, yielded, Christians to seek Him daily for the Spirit's fullness.

Accept.—Finally, having asked, believers now accept the gift of fullness by faith, and thank God for His goodness. They need not necessarily pray long and agonizingly. God honors acceptance by faith. Christians accept salvation by faith and do not ask for any sign or particular feeling, so also they claim by faith the infilling of the Holy Spirit. That brings power to evangelism and service.[11]

Moreover, there are times evangelization comes with such Holy Spirit unction and power on the whole church that multitudes are swept into the kingdom. Those events are *spiritual awakenings.* Apathy among believers brings the need of a new spiritual awakening. In a true awakening or revival, complacency is dissipated, and evangelism reaches great heights during these refreshing times. America has been especially touched by such thrilling movements.

The First Great Awakening

No event in early American life is of more spiritual significance than what is called the First Great Awakening. It reversed the course of history, sacred and secular. The Colonies were never quite the same again. Jonathan Edwards, of Northampton, Massachusetts, the personification of the revival, was a remarkable character. Intellectually, he had few peers; philosophers consider him the first scintillating thinker in American thought. Being an ardent student, he had a brilliant mind, ending his career as president of Princeton University.

Although Edwards' preaching proceeded out of his thoroughgoing Calvinism, he preached with great persuasion to win people to Christ. Here is an excerpt from his most famous sermon, "Sinners in the Hands of an Angry God":

O sinner! consider the fearful danger you are in. Tis a great furnace of wrath, a wide and bottomless pit, full of fire of wrath, that you are held over in the hand of God whose wrath is provoked and incensed as much against you as many of the damned in hell. You hang by a slender thread, with the flames of divine wrath flashing about it, and ready every moment to singe it and burn it asunder; and you have no interest in any Mediator, and nothing to lay hold of to save yourself, nothing to keep off the flames of wrath, nothing of your own, nothing that you ever have done, nothing that you can do, to induce God to spare you one moment. Therefore let every one that is out of Christ now awake and fly from the wrath to come. The wrath of Almighty God is now undoubtedly hanging over a great part of this congregation. Let every one fly out of Sodom. Haste and escape for your lives, look not behind you, escape to the mountain, lest ye be consumed.[12]

People were deeply convicted by the power of the Holy Spirit in Edwards's preaching.

Edwards was not the only revival preacher in the Great Awakening, however. Many pulpits shook under the proclamation of men like Gilbert Tennent, James Davenport, John Rowland, Shubal Stearns, and no less a personage than George Whitefield. Whitefield sailed the Atlantic to the New World many times, profoundly influencing people as diverse as the staunch Puritans and Benjamin Franklin. He died on his seventh preaching tour of America and is buried in a little crypt under the pulpit of the Presbyterian Church in Newburyport, Massachusetts.

Through these outstanding personalities and scores of others, tens of thousands were converted. The church returned to apostolic simplicity. The whole moral and political atmosphere of the Colonies was radically purified. Even secular historians eulogize those days. It was God's great hour of power for early America.

Great Britain simultaneously experienced revival in the ministry of Wesley and Whitefield, but the movement subsided like the ebb and flow of the ocean tide. The Revolution came, and spiritual life once more deteriorated. Then quite suddenly God again poured out His Spirit. Beginning once more in New England, God also visited the South as the Second Great Awakening erupted like an exploding volcano.

The Second Great Awakening

In the late 1780s, a surge of revival power swept the newly formed United States. As the First Awakening had its beginnings among Congregationalists and Presbyterians, the Second Awakening broke out in Methodist and Baptist circles, especially in Virginia and the Carolinas. Although it began essentially as a Baptist and Methodist movement, the Presbyterians and others were not exempt. Caught up in the awakening were two Carolina Presbyterian ministers, James McGready and Barton Stone.

McGready and Stone were destined to be significantly used by God. Trekking through the Cumberland Gap (The American westward movement was well underway.), they took up their ministries in Kentucky. James McGready, after two or three years in Tennessee, settled in Logan County, Kentucky, and began preaching at the Red River Meeting House. McGready was an "impassioned preacher, diligent pastor, and fervent man of prayer."[13] In June of 1800, he called on the people of south-central Kentucky to gather for an extended four-day observance of the Lord's Supper. People came in expectation of blessings, and God met their faith. The Holy Spirit fell on them powerfully. Friday and

Saturday saw floods of repentant tears and then times of exuberant re-
joicing. The Spirit moved even deeper on Sunday when the Lord's Supper was served. The climax came on the final day when John McGee, a
Methodist minister, gave the closing exhortation. His own words described the scene:

> I . . . exhorted them to let the Lord omnipotent reign in their hearts, and
> submit to him, and their souls should live . . . I turned again and losing
> sight of fear of man, I went through the house shouting and exhorting
> with all possible ecstasy and energy, and the floor was soon covered by
> the slain.[14]

People had come in unprecedented numbers from a hundred-mile ra-
dius of Red River. Because the multitudes could not be housed in the
existing buildings in the community, they brought bed rolls and tents,
and the first camp meeting was born. It was all quite unplanned, but a
new movement and methodology emerged.

The experience was quite incredible. McGready said:

> No person seemed to wish to go home—hunger and sleep seemed to affect
> nobody—eternal things were the vast concern. Here awakening and con-
> verting work was to be found in every part of the multitude. . . . Sober
> professors who had been communicants for many years, now lying pros-
> trate on the ground, crying out in such language as this: "O! how I would
> have despised any person a few days ago, who would have acted as I am
> doing now! But I cannot help it!" . . . persons of every description, white
> and black, were to be found in every part of the multitude . . . crying out
> for mercy in the most extreme distress.[15]

The Cane Ridge Revival

Of the people gathered at Red River, none was singled out by God's
Spirit for more usefulness than Barton Stone. He had been preaching at
the Cane Ridge Meeting House in Bourbon County, Kentucky, invited
and urged to serve there by frontiersman Daniel Boone. Stone was so
overwhelmed with the Red River revival that he went home and in May
of 1801 called for a similar meeting at Cane Ridge. The work began, and
many were blessed. He called for another meeting in August, and to the
utter astonishment of all, over 20,000 people arrived for the six day
camp meeting. It was an unbelievable event, for this was the sparsely
populated frontier.

Among the thousands converted was James B. Finley, who later became a Methodist circuit rider. He wrote of the Cane Ridge meeting:

> The noise was like the roar of Niagara. The vast sea of human beings
> seemed to be agitated as if by a storm. I counted seven ministers, all

preaching at one time, some on stumps, others in wagons, and one was standing on a tree which had, in falling, lodged against another. . . . Some of the people were singing, others praying, some crying for mercy in the most piteous accents, while other were shouting most vociferously. While witnessing these scenes, a peculiarly strange sensation, such as I had never felt before, came over me. My heart beat tumultuously, my knees trembled, my lips quivered, and I felt as though I must fall to the ground. A strange supernatural power seemed to pervade the entire mass of mind there collected. . . . I stepped up on to a log, where I could have a better view of the surging sea of humanity. The scene that then presented itself to my mind was indescribable. At one time I saw at least five hundred swept down in a moment, as if a battery of a thousand guns had been opened upon them and then immediately followed shrieks and shouts that rent the very heavens.[16]

The American frontier was set ablaze. The Presbyterians and Methodists immediately caught fire, and the flame soon broke out among the Baptists in Carroll County, Kentucky, on the Ohio River. Great personalities emerged from the awakening such as Peter Cartwright and the Methodist circuit riders. Southern revivalism, which continues to this day, had its birth in this movement. The camp meeting motif of evangelism spread all over eastern America. The entire frontier was radically transformed. The so-called Bible Belt emerged in the South. Instead of gambling, cursing, and vice, spirituality and genuine Christianity characterized the early westward movement. It became God's great hour.

Yet, like the First Great Awakening, the second also waned. The War of 1811 came and went, and spiritual stagnation settled in. In all such movements, it seems that spiritual deadness inevitably creeps in like a grim reaper cutting down the blessed results of revival. Then the Prayer Revival of 1858 dawned and impacted America and Britain, but it has now been many years since such a movement has occurred, at least in America and Western Europe.

Few in Europe and North America today have ever seen a widespread spiritual awakening. Still, many long for an awakening that would bring the masses to the cross and radically revitalize the churches and nations. The church needs it; society as a whole needs it. During such times God revives His people, and multitudes are won to Christ. Evangelistic ministries produce an impact that is phenomenal, including social revolution.

Is there any hope? Are there any harbingers of an awakening on the horizon? The answer is simple but profound; revival will come if God's people pray (2 Chron. 7:14). If individual believers and churches will join in seeking the power of God at their disposal for revival and world evangelism, it will surely come. The psalmist prayed correctly when he cried:

Lord, thou wast favorable to thy land;
thou didst restore the fortunes of Jacob.
Thou didst forgive the iniquity of thy people;
thou didst pardon all their sin.

Thou didst withdraw all thy wrath;
thou didst turn from thy hot anger.

Restore us again, O God of our salvation,
and put away thy indignation toward us!
Wilt thou be angry with us for ever?
Wilt thou prolong thy anger to all generations?
Wilt thou revive us again,
that thy people may rejoice in thee?
Show us thy steadfast love, O Lord,
and grant us thy salvation (Ps. 85:1-7).

May all join in that fervent prayer, *for prayer alone brings revival.* In that context, evangelization emerges in the power of the Spirit on a level hardly imaginable. When the Holy Spirit falls and a spiritual awakening dawns, it creates passion in God's people. This, too, is a tremendous source of power for evangelism.

The Power of a Holy Passion

Thomas Chalmers prayed, "Recall the twenty-one years of my service; give me back its shipwreck, give me its standings in the face of death, give me it surrounded by fierce savages with spears and clubs, give it back to me with clubs knocking me down, give all this back to me, and I will be your missionary still."

This is the attitude God honors. This is the kind of passion which communicates the gospel to people. A shallow emotional, approach to spirituality is not desired. God desires His witnesses to be burdened, concerned, enthusiastic, and zealous to spread the good news to the millions who desperately need to hear the message. The Holy Spirit will instill this attitude in believers as they seek His strength, wisdom, and compassion. It is my hope that all Christians would become so committed to the evangelistic task that such a passion would grip the entire church.

The Power of Prayer

Prayer is probably the final answer to effective evangelism. It is a tremendous resource of power. Little will be said here on the theme, however. It is not that the subject is in any manner secondary. On the contrary, it is primary. The reason for saying little here is that so much fine material has already been produced on the subject. Prayer is essential to spiritual power in one's life and ministry, not to mention its centrality in revival. Believers get what they claim by faith in prayer. Every great spiritual movement has been conceived, born, and matured in intercession. Prayer has been the key to open the treasure house of God's bounty. Probably one of our basic problems today is that "ye have not, because ye ask not" (Jas. 4:2, KJV). Renewal and effective evangelism wait on the power of prayer.

The Power of the Word of God

The "good seed" that falls in the ground and brings forth fruit is the Word of God. It is a word of power: "Is not my word like fire, says the Lord, and like a hammer which breaks the rock in pieces?" (Jer. 23:29).

The Bible itself has much to say about the power of the Word in the hands of the Holy Spirit:

It is the instrument of the Holy Spirit in conversion (Jas. 1:18).

It produces faith (Rom. 10:17).

It is the means of cleansing (Eph. 5:25-26).

It is that which builds one up in Christ (Acts 20:32).

It is a source of wisdom (Ps. 119:130).

It gives the assurance of eternal life (1 John 5:13).

The Christian who desires to win others to Christ should realize that the "sword of the Spirit" (Eph. 6:17) is a most powerful weapon in this warfare. Thus the good news can be shared in the full assurance that God will honor His Word of power and speak it to the hearts of the hearers (Rom. 1:16-17). The proclaimer honors God by declaring God's Word forthrightly in faith (see chap. 3).

In the final analysis, it is probably correct to sum it all up by emphasizing the resource that is found in one's life of surrender to Jesus Christ.

The Power of a Committed Life

God's action through the life of the Christian waits for that life to be surrendered *totally* to His will and purpose. Knowledge comes through committal (John 7:17); prayer is dependent upon a surrendered will (1 John 3:22); one's joy and winsome testimony is based on a yieldedness to God's authority (John 15:10-11), and the Holy Spirit empowers only those who present themselves unreservedly to God's desire (Acts 5:32).

Even the secular psychologists tell us of the unifying influence and powerful impact of being committed to a great cause. The world longs to see those who are committed to Christ and the evangelization of the world. Moreover, the mission task God lays upon His people is such that only the resource and power of a deep committal will see it accomplished. The world needs to hear the gospel from committed people. This alone will bring the revival all Christians long to experience. May God deeply "revive us again" (Ps. 85:6), and may there be profound prayer and intercession to that end.

Conclusion

Christians and church leaders need to implement and actualize personally all the principles outlined above. Moreover, the truths should be shared in practical programs of discipleship training in the churches. Today there are ample resources for every level of training in discipleship and evangelism. These sources should be utilized and God's people trained. The world waits to hear the gospel communicated in power. If all the church can be mobilized, empowered, and equipped, it could be that this generation will really see "the evangelization of the world."

Notes

1. R. C. H. Lenski, *The Interpretation of the Epistles of St. Peter, St. John, and St. Jude* (Minneapolis: Augsburg Publishing House, 1945), 382.

2. Ibid., 383.

3. R. A. Torrey, *How to Obtain Fullness of Power* (London: Lakeland Paperbacks, 1955), 31.

4. Lewis A. Drummond, *Leading Your Church in Evangelism* (Nashville: Broadman Press, 1975), 153-154.

5. Ibid., 154.

6. Ibid.

7. Lewis A. Drummond, *The Revived Life* (Nashville: Broadman Press, 1982), 89.

8. Ibid., 90.

9. James Gilchrist Lawson, *Deeper Experiences of Famous Christians* (Anderson, Ind.: The Warner Press, 1911), 374 (author's italics).

10. Francis W. Beare, "The Epistle to the Ephesians," *The Interpreter's Bible*, 12 vols. (Nashville: Abingdon Press, 1953), 10:714. This is an instructive word on the passage.

11. The Bible also speaks about the "anointing" of the Holy Spirit. This may be seen as primarily the same as being filled with the Spirit; yet, there seems to be times when the Holy Spirit comes upon believers with unusual power to perform a certain task in Kingdom service.

12. Jonathan Edwards, found in *American Poetry and Prose,* ed. Norman Foerster (Boston: Houghton Mifflin Co., 1947), 104.

13. Mendell Taylor, *Exploring Evangelism* (Kansas City: Beacon Hill Press, 1964), 409.

14. Ibid., 410.

15. Ibid.

16. Ibid., 412.

12

A Worldwide Vision: An Epilogue

"Forgiveness of sins should be preached in his name TO ALL NATIONS" (Luke 24:47, author's emphasis).

Introduction

It is redundant to say all the world needs Jesus Christ. The plethora of arguments presented concerning Christ as the only hope of all peoples make that obvious. The nature of God and the human predicament testify to it. Our Lord Himself emphasized this essential truth in commission passages. All Scripture and history attest to the fact that the early church took the call seriously, setting out to evangelize their known world. Such a vision of a worldwide mission guided and motivated the first-century believers, leading them into a commitment still followed for missionary advance to this day. The apostles and first-century Christians recognized if the gospel is all believers claim it to be, love demands the sharing of it with everyone everywhere. This implies several motivating realities and presents a summary of all that has been said in this theology of evangelism.

All People Are Alienated

The Bible clearly states, "All have sinned and come short of the glory of God" (Rom. 3:23). From Eden to the present moment, everyone rebels and disobeys God, the rightful Lord of all. Moreover, "the wages of sin is death" (Rom. 6:23). Judgment for human sin is inevitable. Already people are alienated from God (Eph. 2:12), strangers to the covenant (2:12), without hope (2:12), and dead in trespasses and sins (2:2). That is not to speak of the horror of the future when God judges the world by Jesus Christ and the lost hear the fateful, fearful words of the Lord, "Depart from me, you cursed, into the eternal fire prepared for the devil and his angels" (Matt. 25:41). It is sadly true, people everywhere really are *lost*. It is a worldwide problem, demanding a universal answer, and there is a solution.

Christ Is the Only Hope

There is hope in Christ. Through the life, death, and resurrection of our Lord Jesus Christ, forgiveness and newness of life is available for all. A full and meaningful life with God is possible. Jesus said, "I came that they may have life, and have it abundantly" (John 10:10). All the world reaches out for that level of life, whether they recognize it or not.

Furthermore, everlasting life is found only in Jesus Christ. Such is true for all people wherever they may be found. Peter made it clear when he said, "There is salvation in no one else, for there is no other name under heaven given among men by which we must be saved" (Acts 4:12). Universalism, syncretism, Pelagianism, or any other departure from biblical teaching on the uniqueness of Christ, must be discarded. The Scriptures declare Christ to be the world's only hope: "I am the way, and the truth, and the life; no one comes to the Father, but by me" (John 14:6). Not only is Christ the only hope, but also the message of Christ has innate power to convince people of that fact.

The Power of the Gospel

"I am not ashamed of the gospel: it is the power of God for salvation to everyone who has faith" (Rom. 1:16). From Damascus to Rome, Paul saw first hand what the gospel can accomplish. Be it on the island of Crete, in the Philippian jail, at the areopagus in sophisticated Athens, or in Rome itself, the gospel proved to be the power of God to salvation. It communicates to all peoples of all cultures of all times. It is good news for everyone. The "wisdom of God" (1 Cor. 1:21) in the gospel may seem "foolishness" to some, but it is powerful truth that convicts, convinces, and converts. It can thus be shared with confidence. That leads to another essential reality.

God's Plan for World Redemption

God brings Christ to the lost world through the agency of His church. The conversion of Cornelius clearly shows this (Acts 10—11).

Cornelius was a religious man, but lost. An angel appeared to him while he was praying and said, "Send to Joppa and bring Simon called Peter; he will declare to you a message by which you will be saved" (11:13-14). Now surely the angel knew the message of the gospel. He could have shared it with Cornelius. However, he did not do so. Rather, he said to send for Peter, a believer; Peter would tell them the story of salvation. God planned to bring the gospel to the whole lost world through His redeemed people. That truth is constantly and consistently held forth in the New Testament. What a privilege! What a responsibility! Through the dedicated ministry of the entire church, the world is to hear the redemption story.[1] It demands deep and profound commitment.

Commitment to the Task

The initiatory confession, "Jesus is Lord" (Rom. 10:9), is not a statement to be made at one's baptism alone. The statement speaks of a life commitment to the lordship of Jesus Christ—regardless of the cost. That alone will please God and see the task of world evangelization accomplished. A proper theology of evangelism and a deep personal commitment to Jesus Christ will result in profound zeal to win the lost world. The old cliche has it right: people behave as they believe. Therefore, if all that has been set forth in this work fails to motivate you to share Christ with a dying world, something is radically wrong.

I trust the truth and challenge of the gospel has been put forth plainly and convincingly enough that all shall say with Isaiah, "Here am I! Send me" (Isa. 6:8). If that be our earnest heart cry, God will unquestionably respond and say, "Go, . . . Until cities lie waste/ without inhabitant,/ and houses without men,/ and the land is utterly desolate" (Isa. 6:9-11). That kind of commitment will reach the entire world with the "word of the cross" (1 Cor. 1:18) May every believer in Christ, therefore, pray for that commitment and go in the Spirit of God.

Note
1. See Appendix D for a statement on "evangelical affirmations." It emphasizes the essential doctrines of evangelicalism and stresses the need for world missions.

Appendix A
The Chicago Statement
on Biblical Inerrancy

Introduction

In October 1978 an international conference of nearly 300 theological scholars and church leaders from all Protestant denominations met at Chicago under the auspices of the International Council on Biblical Inerrancy and produced the following statement:

The Statement

The authority of Scripture is a key issue for the Christian church in this and every age. Those who profess faith in Jesus Christ as Lord and Savior are called to show the reality of their discipleship by humbly and faithfully obeying God's written Word. To stray from Scripture in faith or conduct is disloyalty to our Master. Recognition of the total truth and trustworthiness of Holy Scripture is essential to a full grasp and adequate confession of its authority.

The following statement affirms this inerrancy of Scripture afresh, making clear our understanding of it and warning against it's denial. We are persuaded that to deny it is to set aside the witness of Jesus Christ and of the Holy Spirit and to refuse that submission to the claims of God's own Word which marks true Christian faith. We see it as our timely duty to make this affirmation in the face of current lapses from the truth of inerrancy among our fellow Christians and misunderstanding of this doctrine in the world at large.

This statement consists of three parts: a Summary Statement, Articles of Affirmation and Denial, and an accompanying exposition. It has been prepared in the course of a three-day consultation in Chicago. Those who have signed the summary statement and the articles wish to affirm their own conviction as to the inerrancy of Scripture and to encourage and challenge one another and all Christians to a growing appreciation and understanding of this doctrine. We acknowledge the limitations of a document prepared in a brief, intensive conference and do not propose that this Statement be given creedal weight. Yet we rejoice in the deepening of our own convictions through our discussions together, and we pray that the Statement we have signed may be used to the glory of our God toward a new reformation of the church in its faith, life, and mission.

We offer this Statement in a spirit, not of contention, but of humility and love, which we purpose by God's grace to maintain in any future dialogue arising out of what we have said. We gladly acknowledge that many who deny the inerrancy of Scripture do not display the consequences of this denial in the rest of their belief and behavior, and we are conscious that we who confess this doctrine often deny it in life by failing to bring our thoughts and deeds, our traditions and habits, into true subjection to the divine Word.

We invite response to this statement from any who see reason to amend its affirmations about Scripture by the light of Scripture itself, under whose infallible authority we stand as we speak. We claim no personal infallibility for the witness we bear, and for any help which enables us to strengthen this testimony to God's Word we shall be grateful.

A Summary Statement

1. God, who is Himself Truth and speaks truth only, has inspired Holy Scripture in order thereby to reveal Himself to lost mankind through Jesus Christ as Creator and Lord, Redeemer and Judge. Holy Scripture is God's witness to Himself.
2. Holy Scripture, being God's own Word, written by men prepared and superintended by His Spirit, is of infallible divine authority in all matters upon which it touches: it is to be believed, as God's instruction, in all that it affirms; obeyed, as God's command, in all that it requires; embraced, as God's pledge, in all that it promises.
3. The Holy Spirit, its divine Author, both authenticates it to us by His inward witness and opens our minds to understand its meaning.
4. Being wholly and verbally God-given, Scripture is without error or fault in all its teaching, no less in what it states about God's acts in creation, about the events of world history, and about its own literary origins under God, than in its witness to God's saving grace in individual lives.
5. The authority of Scripture is inescapably impaired if this total divine inerrancy is in any way limited or disregarded, or made relative to a view of truth contrary to the Bible's own; and such lapses bring serious loss to both the individual and the church.

Articles of Affirmation and Denial

Article I. WE AFFIRM that the Holy Scriptures are to be received as the authoritative Word of God. We deny that the Scriptures receive their authority from the church, tradition, or any other human resource.

Article II. WE AFFIRM that the Scriptures are the supreme written norm by which God binds the conscience, and that the authority of the church is subordinate to that of Scripture. We deny that church creeds, councils, or declarations have authority greater than or equal to the authority of the Bible.

Article III. WE AFFIRM that the written Word in its entirety is revelation given by God. We deny that the Bible is merely a witness to revelation, or only becomes revelation in encounter, or depends on the responses of men for its validity.

Article IV. WE AFFIRM that God who made mankind in His image has used language as a means of revelation. We deny that human language is so limited by our creatureliness that it is rendered inadequate as a vehicle for divine revelation. We further deny that the corruption of human culture and language through sin has thwarted God's work of inspiration.

Article V. WE AFFIRM that God's revelation with the Holy Scripture was progressive. We deny that later revelation, which may fulfil [sic] earlier revelation, ever corrects or contradicts it. We further deny that any normative revelation has been given since the completion of the New Testament writings.

Article VI. WE AFFIRM that the whole of Scripture and all of its parts, down to the very words of the original, were given by divine inspiration. We deny that the inspiration of Scripture can rightly be affirmed of the whole without the parts, or of some parts but not the whole.

Article VII. WE AFFIRM that inspiration was the work in which God by His Spirit, through human writers, gave us His Word. The origin of Scripture is divine. The mode of divine inspiration remains largely a mystery to us. We deny that inspiration can be reduced to human insight, or to heightened states of consciousness of any kind.

Article VIII. WE AFFIRM that God in His work of inspiration utilized the distinctive personalities and literary styles of the writers whom He had chosen and prepared. We deny that God, in causing these writers to use the very words that He chose, overrode their personalities.

Article IX. WE AFFIRM that inspiration, though not conferring omniscience, guaranteed true and trustworthy utterance on all matters of which the biblical authors were moved to speak and write. We deny that the finitude or fallenness of these writers, by necessity or otherwise, introduced distortion or falsehood into God's Word.

Article X. WE AFFIRM that inspiration, strictly speaking, applies only to the autographic text of Scripture, which in the providence of God can be ascertained from available manuscripts with great accuracy. We further affirm that copies and translations of Scripture are the Word of God to the extent that they faithfully represent the original. We deny that any essential element of the Christian faith is affected by the absence of the autographs. We further deny that this absence renders the assertion of biblical inerrancy invalid or irrelevant.

Article XI. WE AFFIRM that Scripture, having been given by divine inspiration, is infallible, so that, far from misleading us, it is true and reliable in all the matters it addresses. We deny that it is possible for the Bible to be at the same time infallible and errant in its assertions. Infallibility and inerrancy may be distinguished, but not separated.

Article XII. WE AFFIRM that Scripture in its entirety is inerrant, being free from all falsehood, fraud, or deceit. We deny that biblical infallibility and inerrancy are limited to spiritual, religious, or redemptive themes, exclusive of assertions in the fields of history and science. We further deny that scientific hypotheses about earth history may properly be used to overturn the teaching of Scripture on creation and the flood.

Article XIII. WE AFFIRM the propriety of using inerrancy as a theological term with reference to the complete truthfulness of Scripture. We deny that it is proper to evaluate Scripture according to standards of truth and error that are alien to its usage or purpose. We further deny that inerrancy is negated by biblical phenomena such as a lack of modern technical precision, irregularities of grammar or spelling, observational descriptions of nature, the reporting of falsehoods (e.g., the lies of Satan), the use of hyperbole and round members, the topical arrangement of material, variant selections of material in parallel accounts, or the use of free citations.

Article XIV. WE AFFIRM the unity and internal consistency of Scripture. We deny that alleged errors and discrepancies that have not yet been resolved vitiate the truth claims of the Bible.

Article XV. WE AFFIRM that the doctrine of inerrancy is grounded in the teaching of the Bible about inspiration. We deny that Jesus' teaching about Scripture may be dismissed by appeals to accommodation or to any natural limitation of His humanity.

Article XVI. WE AFFIRM that the doctrine of inerrancy has been integral to the church's faith throughout its history. We deny that inerrancy is a doctrine invented by scholastic Protestantism, or is a reactionary position postulated in response to negative higher criticism.

Article XVII. WE AFFIRM that the Holy Spirit bears witness to the Scriptures, assuring believers of the truthfulness of God's written Word. We deny that this witness of the Holy Spirit operates in isolation from or against Scripture.

Article XVIII. WE AFFIRM that the text of Scripture is to be interpreted by grammatico-historical exegesis, taking account of its literary forms and devices, and that Scripture is to interpret Scripture. We deny the legitimacy of any treatment of the text or quest for sources lying behind it that leads to relativizing, dehistoricizing, or discounting its teaching, or rejecting its claims to authorship.

Article XIX.   WE AFFIRM that a confession of the full authority, infallibility, and inerrancy of Scripture is vital to a sound understanding of the whole of the Christian faith. We further affirm that such confession should lead to increasing conformity to the image of Christ. We deny that such confession is necessary for salvation. However, we further deny that inerrancy can be rejected without grave consequences, both to the individual and to the church.

Exposition

Our understanding of the doctrine of inerrancy must be set in the context of the broader teachings of the Scripture concerning itself. This exposition gives an account of the outline of doctrine from which our summary statement and articles are drawn.

Creation, Revelation, and Inspiration

The Triune God, who formed all things by His creative utterances and governs all things by His Word of decree, made mankind in His own image for a life of communion with Himself, on the model of the eternal fellowship of loving communication within the Godhead. As God's image-bearer, man was to hear God's Word addressed to him and to respond in the joy of adoring obedience. Over and above God's self-disclosure in the created order and the sequence of events within it, human beings from Adam on have received verbal messages from Him, either directly, as stated in Scripture, or indirectly in the form of part or all of Scripture itself.

When Adam fell, the Creator did not abandon mankind to final judgment but promised salvation and began to reveal Himself as Redeemer in a sequence of historical events centering on Abraham's family and culminating in the life, death, resurrection, present heavenly ministry, and promised return of Jesus Christ. Within this frame God has from time to time spoken specific words of judgment and mercy, promise and command, to sinful human beings, so drawing them into a covenant relation of mutual commitment between Him and them in which He blesses them with gifts of grace and they bless Him in responsive adoration. Moses, whom God used as mediator to carry His words to His people at the time of the exodus, stands at the head of a long line of prophets into whose mouths and writings God put His words for delivery to Israel. God's purpose in this succession of messages was to maintain His covenant by causing His people to know His Name—that is, His nature—and His will both of precept and purpose in the present and for the future. This line of prophetic spokesmen from God came to completion in Jesus Christ, God's incarnate Word, who was Himself a prophet—more than a prophet, but not less—and in the apostles and prophets of the first Christian generation. When God's final and climactic message, His word to the world concerning Jesus Christ, had been spoken and elucidated by those in the apostolic circle, the sequence of revealed messages ceased. Henceforth, the church was to live and know God by what He had already said, and said for all time.

At Sinai, God wrote the terms of His covenant on tables of stone, as His enduring witness and for lasting accessibility, and throughout the period of prophetic and apostolic revelation He prompted men to write the messages given to and through them, along with celebratory records of His dealings with His people, plus moral reflections on covenant life and forms of praise and prayer for covenant mercy. The theological reality of inspiration in the producing of biblical documents corresponds to that of spoken prophecies; although the human writers' personalities were expressed in what they wrote, the words were divinely constituted. Thus, what Scripture says, God says; its authority is His authority, for He is its ultimate Author, having given it through the minds and words of chosen and prepared men who in freedom and faithfulness spoke from God as they were carried along by the Holy Spirit (1 Pet. 1:12). Holy Scripture must be acknowledged as the Word of God by virtue of its divine origin.

Authority: Christ and the Bible

Jesus Christ, the Son of God who is the Word made flesh, our Prophet, Priest, and King, is the ultimate Mediator of God's communication to man, as He is of all God's gifts of grace. The revelation He gave was more than verbal; He revealed the Father by His presence and His deeds as well. Yet His words were crucially important; for He was God, He spoke from the Father, and His words will judge all men at the last day.

As the prophesied Messiah, Jesus Christ is the central theme of Scripture. The Old Testament looked ahead to Him; the New Testament looks back to His first coming and on to His second. Canonical Scripture is the divinely inspired and, therefore, normative witness to Christ. No hermeneutic, therefore, of which the historical Christ is not the focal point is acceptable. Holy Scripture must be treated as what it essentially is—the witness of the Father to the incarnate Son.

It appears that the Old Testament canon had been fixed by the time of Jesus. The New Testament canon is likewise now closed inasmuch as no new apostolic witness to the historical Christ can now be borne. No new revelation (as distinct from Spirit-given understanding of existing revelation) will be given until Christ comes again. The canon was created in principle by divine inspiration. The church's part was to discern the canon which God had created, not to devise one of its own.

The word *canon*, signifying a rule or standard, is a pointer to authority, which means the right to rule and control. Authority in Christianity belongs to God in His revelation, which means, on the one hand, Jesus Christ, the living Word, and, on the other hand, Holy Scripture, the written Word. But the authority of Christ and that of Scripture are one. As our Priest, Christ testified that Scripture cannot be broken. As our Priest and King, He devoted His earthly life to fulfilling the law and the prophets, even dying in obedience to the words of messianic prophecy. Thus, as He saw Scripture attesting Him and His authority, so by His own submission to Scripture He attested its authority. As He bowed to His Father's instruction given in His Bible (our Old Testament), so He requires His disciples to do—not, however, in isolation but in conjunction with the apostolic witness to Himself which He undertook to inspire by His gift of the Holy Spirit. So Christians show themselves faithful servants of their Lord by bowing to the divine instruction given in the prophetic and apostolic writings which together make up our Bible.

By authenticating each other's authority, Christ and Scripture coalesce into a single fount of authority. The biblically interpreted Christ and the Christ-centered, Christ-proclaiming Bible are from this standpoint one. As from the fact of inspiration we infer that what Scripture says, God says, so from the revealed relation between Jesus Christ and Scripture we may equally declare that what Scripture says, Christ says.

Infallibility, Inerrancy, Interpretation

Holy Scripture, as the inspired Word of God witnessing authoritatively to Jesus Christ, may properly be called *infallible* and *inerrant*. These negative terms have a special value, for they explicitly safeguard crucial positive truths.

Infallible signifies the quality of neither misleading nor being misled and so safeguards in categorical terms the truth that Holy Scripture is a sure, safe, and reliable rule and guide in all matters.

Similarly, *inerrant* signifies the quality of being free from all falsehood or mistake and so safeguards the truth that Holy Scripture is entirely true and trustworthy in all its assertions.

We affirm that canonical Scripture should always be interpreted on the basis that it is infallible and inerrant. However, in determining what the God-taught writer is asserting in each passage, we must pay the most careful attention to its claim and character as a human production. In inspiration, God utilized the culture and conventions of his penman's milieu, a milieu that God controls in His sovereign providence; it is misinterpretation to imagine otherwise.

So history must be treated as history, poetry as poetry, hyperbole and metaphor as hyperbole and metaphor, generalization and approximation as what they are, and so forth. Differences between literary conventions in Bible times and in ours must also be observed; since, for instance, nonchronological narration and imprecise citation were conventional and acceptable and violated no expectations in those days, we must not regard these things as faults when we find them in Bible writers. When total precision of a particular kind was not expected nor aimed at, it is no error not to have achieved it. Scripture is inerrant, not in the sense of being absolutely precise by modern standards, but in the sense of making good its claims and achieving that measure of focused truth at which its authors aimed.

The truthfulness of Scripture is not negated by the appearance in it of irregularities of grammar or spelling, phenomenal descriptions of nature, reports of false statements (e.g. the lies of Satan), or seeming discrepancies between one passage and another. It is not right to set the so-called "phenomena" of Scripture against the teaching of Scripture about itself. Apparent inconsistencies should not be ignored. Solution of them, where this can be convincingly achieved, will encourage our faith, and where for the present no convincing solution is at hand we shall significantly honor God by trusting His assurance that His Word is true, despite these appearances, and by maintaining our confidence that one day they will be seen to have been illusions.

Inasmuch as all Scripture is the product of a single divine mind, interpretation must stay within the bounds of the analogy of Scripture and eschew hypotheses that would correct one biblical passage by another, whether in the name of progressive revelation or of the imperfect enlightenment of the inspired writer's mind.

Although Holy Scripture is nowhere culture-bound in the sense that its teaching lacks universal validity, it is sometimes culturally conditioned by the customs and conventional views of a particular period, so that the application of its principles today may call for a different sort of action.

Skepticism and Criticism

Since the Renaissance, and more particularly since the Enlightenment, worldviews have been developed which involve skepticism about basic Christian tenets. Such are the agnosticism which denies that God is knowable, the rationalism which denies that He is incomprehensible, the idealism which denies that He is transcendent, and the existentialism which denies rationality in His relationships with us. When these un- and antibiblical principles seep into men's theologies at presuppositional level, as today they frequently do, faithful interpretation of Holy Scripture becomes impossible.

Transmission and Translation

Since God has nowhere promised an inerrant transmission of Scripture, it is necessary to affirm that only the autographic text of the original documents was inspired and to maintain the need of textual criticism as a means of detecting any slips that may have crept into the text in the course of its transmission. The verdict of this science, however, is that the Hebrew and Greek text appear to be amazingly well preserved, so that we are amply justified in affirming, with the Westminster Confession, a singular providence of God in this matter and in declaring that the authority of Scripture is in no way jeopardized by the fact that the copies we possess are not entirely error free.

Similarly, no translation is or can be perfect, and all translations are an additional step away from the *autographs*. Yet the verdict of linguistic science is that English-speaking Christians, at least, are exceedingly well served in these days with a host of excellent translations and have no cause for hesitating to conclude that the true Word of God is within their reach. Indeed in view of the frequent repetition in Scripture of the main matters with which it deals and also of the Holy Spirit's constant witness to and through the Word, no serious translation of Holy Scripture will so destroy its meaning as to render it unable to make its reader wise "for salvation through faith in Christ Jesus" (2 Tim. 3:15).

Inerrancy and Authority

In our affirmation of the authority of Scripture as involving its total truth, we are consciously standing with Christ and His apostles, indeed with the whole Bible and with the mainstream of church history from the first days until very recently. We are concerned at the casual, inadvertent, and seemingly thoughtless way in which a belief of such far-reaching importance has been given up by so many in our day.

We are conscious, too, that great and grave confusion results from ceasing to

maintain the total truth of the Bible whose authority one professes to acknowledge. The result of taking this step is that the Bible which God gave loses its
authority, and what has authority instead is a Bible reduced in content according to the demands of one's critical reasonings and in principle reducible still
further once one has started. This means that at bottom independent reason
now has authority, as opposed to scriptural teaching. If this is not seen and if for
the time being basic evangelical doctrines are still held, persons denying the full
truth of Scripture may claim an evangelical identity while methodologically
they have moved away from the evangelical principle of knowledge to an unstable subjectivism, and will find it hard not to move further.

We affirm that what Scripture says, God says. May He be glorified. Amen and
Amen.

Addendum to Appendix A

The Chicago Statement on Biblical Hermeneutics

Summit I of the International Council on Biblical Inerrancy took place in Chicago on October 26-28, 1978, for the purpose of affirming afresh the doctrine of
the inerrancy of Scripture, making clear the understanding of it and warning
against its denial. In the four years since Summit I, God has blessed that effort in
ways surpassing most anticipations. A gratifying flow of helpful literature on
the doctrine of inerrancy as well as a growing commitment to its value give
cause to pour forth praise to our great God.

The work of Summit I had hardly been completed when it became evident
that there was yet another major task to be tackled. While we recognize that
belief in the inerrancy of Scripture is basic to maintaining its authority, the values of that commitment are only as real as one's understanding of the meaning
of Scripture. Thus the need for Summit II. For two years plans were laid and
papers were written on themes relating to hermeneutical principles and practices. The culmination of this effort has been a meeting in Chicago on November
10-13, 1982, at which we have participated.

In similar fashion to the Chicago Statement of 1978, we herewith present
these affirmations and denials as an expression of the results of our labors to
clarify hermeneutical issues and principles. We do not claim completeness or
systematic treatment of the entire subject, but these affirmation and denials
represent a consensus of the approximately one hundred participants and observers gathered at this conference. It has been a broadening experience to engage in dialogue, and it is our prayer that God will use the product of our diligent efforts to enable us and others to more correctly handle the word of truth (2
Tim. 2:15).

Articles of Affirmation and Denial

Article I.   WE AFFIRM that the normative authority of Holy Scrip-
                    ture is the authority of God Himself and is attested by
                    Jesus Christ, the Lord of the church.
                    WE DENY the legitimacy of separating the authority of

Christ from the authority of Scripture or of opposing the one to the other.

Article II. WE AFFIRM that as Christ is God and Man in one Person, so Scripture is, indivisibly, God's Word in human language.

WE DENY that the humble, human form of Scripture entails errancy any more than the humanity of Christ, even in His humiliation, entails sin.

Article III. WE AFFIRM that the Person and work of Jesus Christ are the central focus of the entire Bible.

WE DENY that any method of interpretation which rejects or obscures the Christ-centeredness of Scripture is correct.

Article IV. WE AFFIRM that the Holy Spirit who inspired Scripture acts through it today to work faith in its message.

WE DENY that the Holy Spirit ever teaches to anyone anything which is contrary to the teaching of Scripture.

Article V. WE AFFIRM that the Holy Spirit enables believers to appropriate and apply Scripture to their lives.

WE DENY that the natural man is able to discern spiritually the Biblical message apart from the Holy Spirit.

Article VI. WE AFFIRM that the Bible expresses God's truth in propositional statements, and we declare that Biblical truth is both objective and absolute. We further affirm that a statement is true if it represents matters as they actually are but is an error if it misrepresents the facts.

WE DENY that, while Scripture is able to make us wise unto salvation, Biblical truth should be defined in terms of this function. We further deny that error should be defined as that which willfully deceives.

Article VII. WE AFFIRM that the meaning expressed in each Biblical text is single, definite and fixed.

WE DENY that the recognition of this single meaning eliminates the variety of its application.

Article VIII. WE AFFIRM that the Bible contains teachings and mandates which apply to all cultural and situational contexts and other mandates which the Bible itself shows apply only to particular situations.

WE DENY that the distinction between the universal and particular mandates of Scripture can be determined by cultural and situational factors. We further deny that universal mandates may ever be treated as culturally or situationally relative.

Article IX.   WE AFFIRM that the term hermeneutics, which historically signified the rules of exegesis, may properly be extended to cover all that is involved in the process of perceiving what the Biblical revelation means and how it bears on our lives.

WE DENY that the message of Scripture derives from, or is dictated by, the interpreter's understanding. Thus we deny that the "horizons" of the Biblical writer and the interpreter may rightly "fuse" in such a way that what the text communicates to the interpreter is not ultimately controlled by the expressed meaning of Scripture.

Article X.   WE AFFIRM that Scripture communicates God's truth to us verbally through a wide variety of literary forms.

WE DENY that any of the limits of human language render Scripture inadequate to convey God's message.

Article XI.   WE AFFIRM that translation of the text of Scripture can communicate knowledge of God across all temporal and cultural boundaries.

WE DENY that the meaning of Biblical texts is so tied to the culture out of which they came that understanding of the same meaning in other cultures is impossible.

Article XII. WE AFFIRM that in the task of translating the Bible and teaching it in the context of each culture, only those functional equivalents which are faithful to the content of Biblical teaching should be employed.

WE DENY the legitimacy of methods which either are insensitive to the demands of cross-cultural communication or distort Biblical meaning in the process.

Article XIII. WE AFFIRM that awareness of the literary categories, formal and stylistic, of the various parts of Scripture is essential for proper exegesis, and hence we value genre criticism as one of the many disciplines of Biblical study.

WE DENY that generic categories which negate historicity may rightly be imposed on Biblical narratives which present themselves as factual.

Article XIV. WE AFFIRM that the Biblical record of events, discourses and sayings, though presented in a variety of appropriate literary forms, corresponds to historical fact.

WE DENY that any event, discourse or saying reported in Scripture was invented by the Biblical writers or by the traditions they incorporated.

Article XV.   WE AFFIRM the necessity of interpreting the Bible according to its literal, or normal sense. The literal sense is the grammatical-historical sense—that is, the meaning which the writer expressed. Interpretation according to the literal sense will take account of all figures of speech and literary forms found in the text.

WE DENY the legitimacy of any approach to Scripture that attributes to its meaning which the literal sense does not support.

Article XVI. WE AFFIRM that legitimate critical techniques should be used in determining the canonical text and its meaning.

WE DENY the legitimacy of allowing any method of Biblical criticism to question the truth or integrity of the writer's expressed meaning or of any other scriptural teaching.

Article XVII. WE AFFIRM the unity, harmony and consistency of Scripture and declare that it is its own best interpreter.

WE DENY that Scripture may be interpreted in such a way as to suggest that one passage corrects or militates against another. We deny that later writers of Scripture misinterpreted earlier passages of Scripture when quoting from or referring to them.

Article XVIII.WE AFFIRM that the Bible's own interpretation of itself is always correct, never deviating from, but rather elucidating, the single meaning of the inspired text. The single meaning of a prophet's words includes, but is not restricted to, the understanding of those words by the prophet and necessarily involves the intention of God evidenced in the fulfillment of those words.

WE DENY that the writers of Scripture always understood the full implications of their own words.

Article XIX. WE AFFIRM that any preunderstandings which the interpreter brings to Scripture should be in harmony with scriptural teaching and subject to correction by it.

WE DENY that Scripture should be required to fit alien preunderstandings inconsistent with itself, such as naturalism, evolutionism, scientism, secular humanism, and relativism.

Article XX. WE AFFIRM that since God is the author of all truth, all truths, Biblical and extra-Biblical, are consistent and cohere, and that the Bible speaks truth when it touches on matters pertaining to nature, history or anything else. We further affirm that in some cases extra-Biblical data have value for clarifying what Scripture teaches and for prompting correction of faulty interpretations.

WE DENY that extra-Biblical views ever disprove of Scripture or hold priority over it.

Article XXI.   WE AFFIRM the harmony of special with general revelation and therefore of Biblical teaching with the facts of nature.

WE DENY that any genuine scientific facts are inconsistent with the true meaning of any passage of Scripture.

Article XXII.   WE AFFIRM that Genesis 1—11 is factual, as is the rest of the book.

WE DENY that the teachings of Genesis 1—11 are mythical and that scientific hypotheses about earth history or the origin of humanity may be invoked to overthrow what Scripture teaches about creation.

Article XXIII. WE AFFIRM the clarity of Scripture and specifically of its message about salvation from sin.

WE DENY that all passages of Scripture are equally clear or have equal bearing on the message of redemption.

Article XXIV. WE AFFIRM that a person is not dependent for understanding of Scripture on the expertise of Biblical scholars.

WE DENY that a person should ignore the fruits of the technical study of Scripture by Biblical scholars.

Article XXV.   WE AFFIRM that the only type of preaching which sufficiently conveys the divine revelation and its proper application to life is that which faithfully expounds the text of Scripture as the Word of God.

WE DENY that the preacher has any message from God apart from the text of Scripture.

Appendix B
The Lausanne Covenant[1]

Introduction

We members of the Church of Jesus Christ, from more than 150 nations, participants in the International Congress on World Evangelization at Lausanne, praise God for His great salvation and rejoice in the fellowship He has given us with Himself and with each other. We are deeply stirred by what God is doing in our day, moved to penitence by our failures and challenged by the unfinished task of evangelization. We believe the gospel is God's good news for the whole world, and we are determined by His grace to obey Christ's commission to proclaim it to all mankind and to make disciples of every nation. We desire, therefore, to affirm our faith and our resolve, and to make public our covenant.

1. The Purpose of God

We affirm our belief in the one eternal God, Creator and Lord of the world, Father, Son and Holy Spirit, who governs all things according to the purpose of His will. He has been calling out from the world a people for Himself, and sending His people back into the world to be His servants and His witnesses, for the extension of His Kingdom, the building up of Christ's body, and the glory of His name. We confess with shame that we have often denied our calling and failed in our mission, by becoming conformed to the world or by withdrawing from it. Yet we rejoice that even when borne by earthen vessels the gospel is still a precious treasure. To the task of making that treasure known in the power of the Holy Spirit we desire to dedicate ourselves anew (Isa. 40:28; Matt. 28:19; Eph. 1:11; Acts 15:14; John 17:6,18; Eph. 4:12; 1 Cor. 5:10; Rom. 12:2; 2 Cor. 4:7).

2. The Authority and Power of the Bible

We affirm the divine inspiration, truthfulness and authority of both the Old and New Testament Scriptures in their entirety as the only written word of God, without error in all that it affirms, and the only infallible rule of faith and practice. We also affirm the power of God's word to accomplish His purpose of salvation. The message of the Bible is addressed to all mankind. For God's revelation in Christ and in Scriptures is unchangeable. Through it the Holy Spirit still speaks today. He illumines the minds of God's people in every culture to perceive its truth freshly through their own eyes and thus discloses to the whole church ever more of the many-colored wisdom of God (2 Tim. 3:16; 2 Pet. 1:21; John 10:35; Isa. 55:11; 1 Cor. 1:21; Rom. 1:16; Matt. 5:17-18; Jude 3; Eph. 1:17-18; 3:10,18).

3. The Uniqueness and Universality of Christ

We affirm that there is only one Saviour and only one gospel, although there is a wide diversity of evangelistic approaches. We recognize that all men have some knowledge of God through His general revelation in nature. But we deny that this can save, for men suppress the truth by their unrighteousness. We also reject as derogatory to Christ and the gospel every kind of syncretism and dialogue which implies that Christ speaks equally through all religions and ideologies. Jesus Christ, being Himself the only God-man, who gave Himself as the only ransom for sinners, is the only mediator between God and man. There is no other name by which we must be saved. All men are perishing because of sin, but God loves all men not wishing that any should perish but that all should repent. Yet those who reject Christ repudiate the joy of salvation and condemn themselves to eternal separation from God. To proclaim Jesus as "the Saviour of the world" is not to affirm that all men are either automatically or ultimately saved, still less to affirm that all religions offer salvation in Christ. Rather it is to proclaim God's love for a world of sinners and to invite all men to respond to Him as Saviour and Lord in the wholehearted personal commitment of repentance and that Jesus Christ has been exalted above every other name; we long for the day when every knee shall bow to Him and every tongue shall confess Him Lord (Gal. 1:6-9; Rom. 1:18-32; 1 Tim. 2:5-6; Acts 4:12; John 3:16-19; 2 Pet. 3:9; 2 Thess. 1:7-9; John 4:42; Matt. 11:28; Eph. 1:20-21; Phil. 2:9-11).

4. The Nature of Evangelism

To evangelize is to spread the good news that Jesus Christ died for our sins and was raised from the dead according to the Scriptures, and that as the reigning Lord He now offers the forgiveness of sins and the liberating gift of the Spirit to all who repent and believe. Our Christian presence in the world is indispensable to evangelism, and so is that kind of dialogue whose purpose is to listen sensitively in order to understand. But evangelism itself is the proclamation of the historical, biblical Christ as Saviour and Lord, with a view to persuading people to come to Him personally and so be reconciled to God. In issuing the gospel invitation we have no liberty to conceal the cost of discipleship. Jesus still calls all who would follow Him to deny themselves, take up their cross, and identify themselves with this new community. The results of evangelism include obedience to Christ, incorporation into His church and responsible service in the world (1 Cor. 15:3-4; Acts 2:32-39; John 20:21; 1 Cor. 1:23; 2 Cor. 4:5; 5:11,20; Luke 14:25-33; Mark 8:34; Acts 2:40,47; Mark 10:43-45).

5. Christian Social Responsibility

We affirm that God is both the Creator and the Judge of all men. We therefore should share His concern for justice and reconciliation through human society and for the liberation of men from every kind of oppression. Because mankind is made in the image of God, every person, regardless of race, religion, color, culture, class, sex or age, has an intrinsic dignity because of which he should be respected and served, not exploited. Here too we express penitence both for our neglect and for having sometimes regarded evangelism and social concern as mutually exclusive. Although reconciliation with man is not reconciliation with

God, nor is social action evangelism, nor is political liberation salvation, never-theless we affirm that evangelism and socio-political involvement are both part of our Christian duty. For both are necessary expressions of our doctrines of God and man, our love of our neighbour and our obedience to Jesus Christ. The message of salvation implies also a message of judgment upon every form of alienation, oppression and discrimination, and we should not be afraid to de-nounce evil and injustice wherever they exist. When people receive Christ they are born again into His kingdom and must seek not only to exhibit but also to spread its righteousness in the midst of an unrighteous world. The salvation we claim should be transforming us in the totality of our personal and social re-sponsibilities. Faith without works is dead (Acts 17:26,31; Gen. 18:25; Isa. 1:17; Ps. 45:7; Gen. 1:26-27; Jas. 3:9; Lev. 19:18; Luke 6:27,35; Jas. 2:14-26; John 3:3,5; Matt. 5:20; 6:33; 2 Cor. 3:18; Jas. 2:20).

6. The Church and Evangelism

We affirm that Christ sends His redeemed people into the world as the Father sent Him, and that this calls for a similar deep and costly penetration of the world. We need to break out of our ecclesiastical ghettos and permeate non-Christian society. In the church's mission of sacrificial service, evangelism is primary. World evangelization requires the whole church to take the whole gos-pel to the whole world. The church is at the very center of God's cosmic purpose and is His appointed means of spreading the gospel. But a church which preaches the cross must itself be marked by the cross. It becomes a stumbling block to evangelism when it betrays the gospel or lacks a living faith in God, a genuine love for people, or scrupulous honesty in all things including promotion and finance. The church is the community of God's people rather than an insti-tution, and must not be identified with any particular culture, social and politi-cal system, or human ideology (John 17:18; 20:21; Matt. 28:19-20; Acts 1:8; 20:27; Eph. 1:9-10; 3:9-11; Gal. 6:14,17; 2 Cor. 6:3-4; 2 Tim. 2:19-21; Phil. 1:27).

7. Cooperation in Evangelism

We affirm that the church's visible unity in truth is God's purpose. Evange-lism also summons us to unity, because our oneness strengthens our witness, just as our disunity undermines our gospel of reconciliation. We recognize, however, that organizational unity may take many forms and does not neces-sarily forward evangelism. Yet we who share the same biblical faith should be closely united in fellowship, work and witness. We confess that our testimony has sometimes been marred by sinful individualism and needless duplication. We pledge ourselves to seek a deeper unity in truth, worship, holiness and mis-sion. We urge the development of regional and functional cooperation for the furtherance of the church's mission, for strategic planning, for mutual encour-agement, and for the sharing of resources and experience (John 17:21,23: Eph. 4:3-4; John 13:35; Phil. 1:27; John 17:11-23).

8. Churches in Evangelistic Partnership

We rejoice that a new missionary era has dawned. The dominant role of Western missions is fast disappearing. God is raising up from the younger churches a great new resource for world evangelization, and is thus demonstrating that the responsibility to evangelize belongs to the whole body of Christ. All churches should therefore be asking God and themselves what they should be doing both to reach their own area and to send missionaries to other parts of the world. A reevaluation of our missionary responsibility and role should be continuous. Thus a growing partnership of churches will develop, and the universal character of Christ's church will be more clearly exhibited. We also thank God for agencies which labour in Bible translation, theological education, missions, church renewal and other specialist fields. They too should engage in constant self-examination to evaluate their effectiveness as part of the church's mission (Rom. 1:8; Phil. 1:5; 4:15; Acts 13:1-3; 1 Thess. 1:6-8).

9. The Urgency of the Evangelistic Task

More than 2,700 million people,[2] which is more than two-thirds of mankind, have yet to be evangelized. We are ashamed that so many have been neglected; it is a standing rebuke to us and to the whole church. There is now, however, in many parts of the world an unprecedented receptivity to the Lord Jesus Christ. We are convinced that this is the time for churches and parachurch agencies to pray earnestly for the salvation of the unreached and to launch new efforts to achieve world evangelization. A reduction of foreign missionaries and money in an evangelized country may sometimes be necessary to facilitate the national church's growth in self-reliance and to release resources for unevangelized areas. Missionaries should flow ever more freely from and to all six continents in a spirit of humble service. The goal should be, by all available means and at the earliest possible time, that every person will have the opportunity to hear, understand, and receive the good news. We cannot hope to attain this goal without sacrifice. All of us are shocked by the poverty of millions and disturbed by the injustices which cause it. Those of us who live in affluent circumstances accept our duty to develop a simple life-style in order to contribute more generously to both relief and evangelism (John 9:4; Matt. 9:35-38; Rom. 9:1-3; 1 Cor. 9:19-23; Mark 16:15; Isa. 58:6-7; Jas. 1:27; 2:1-9; Matt. 25:31-46; Acts 2:44-45; 4:34-35).

10. Evangelism and Culture

The development of strategies for world evangelization call for imaginative pioneering methods. Under God, the result will be the rise of churches deeply rooted in Christ and closely related to their culture. Culture must always be tested and judged by Scripture. Because man is God's creature, some of his culture is rich in beauty and goodness. Because he has fallen, all of it is tainted with sin and some of it is demonic. The gospel does not presuppose the superiority of any culture to another, but evaluates all cultures according to its own criteria of truth and righteousness and insists on moral absolutes in every culture. Missions have all too frequently exported with the gospel an alien culture, and churches have sometimes been in bondage to culture rather than to the Scripture. Christ's evangelists must humbly seek to empty themselves of all but their personal authenticity in order to become the servants of others, and churches must seek to transform and enrich culture, all for the glory of God (Mark 7:8-9,13; Gen. 4:21-22; 1 Cor. 9:19-23; Phil. 2:5-7; 2 Cor. 4:5).

11. Education and Leadership

We confess that we have sometimes pursued church growth at the expense of church depth, and divorced evangelism from Christian nurture. We also acknowledge that some of our missions have been too slow to equip and encourage national leaders to assume their rightful responsibilities. Yet we are committed to indigenous principles, and long that every church will have national leaders who manifest a Christian style of leadership in terms not of domination but of service. We recognize that there is a great need to improve theological education, especially for church leaders. In every nation and culture, there should be an effective training programme for pastors and laymen in doctrine, discipleship, evangelism, nurture and service. Such training programmes should not rely on any stereotyped methodology but should be developed by creative local initiatives according to biblical standards (Col. 1:27-28; Acts 14:23; Titus 1:5,9; Mark 10:42-45; Eph. 4:11-12).

12. Spiritual Conflict

We believe that we are engaged in constant spiritual warfare with the principalities and powers of evil, who are seeking to overthrow the church and frustrate its task of world evangelization. We know our need to equip ourselves with God's armor and to fight this battle with the spiritual weapons of truth and prayer. For we detect the activity of our enemy, not only in false ideologies outside the church, but also inside it in false gospels which twist Scripture and put man in the place of God. We need both watchfulness and discernment to safeguard the biblical gospel. We acknowledge that we ourselves are not immune to worldliness of thought and action, that is, to a surrender to secularism. For example, although careful studies of church growth, both numerical and spiritual, are right and valuable, we have sometimes neglected them. At other times, desirous to ensure a response to the gospel, we have compromised our message, manipulated our hearts through pressure techniques, and become unduly preoccupied with statistics or even dishonest in our use of them. All this is worldly. The church must be in the world; the world must not be in the church (Eph. 6:12; 2 Cor. 4:3-4; Eph. 6:11; 13:18; 2 Cor. 19:35; 1 John 2:18-24; 4:18; Gal. 1:6-9; 2 Cor. 2:17; 4:22; John 17:15).

13. Freedom and Persecution

It is the God-appointed duty of every government to secure conditions of peace, justice and liberty in which the church may obey God, serve the Lord Christ, and preach the gospel without interference. We therefore pray for the leaders of the nations and call upon them to guarantee freedom of thought and conscience, and freedom of practice and propagate religion in accordance with the will of God and set forth in the Universal Declaration of Human Rights. We also express our deep concern for all who have been unjustly imprisoned, and especially for our brethren who are suffering for their testimony of the Lord

Jesus. We promise to pray and work for their freedom. At the same time we refuse to be intimidated by their fate. God helping us, we too will seek to stand against injustice and to remain faithful to the gospel, whatever the cost. We do not forget the warnings of Jesus that persecution is inevitable (1 Tim. 1:1-4; Acts 4:19; 5:29; Col. 3:24; Heb. 13:1-3; Luke 4:18; Gal. 5:11; 6:12; Matt. 5:10-12; John 15:18-21).

14. The Power of the Holy Spirit

We believe in the power of the Holy Spirit. The Father sent His Spirit to bear witness to His Son; without His witness ours is futile. Conviction of sin, faith in Christ, new birth and Christian growth are all His work. Further, the Holy Spirit is a missionary spirit; thus evangelism should arise spontaneously from a Spirit-filled church. A church that is not a missionary church is contradicting itself and quenching the Spirit. Worldwide evangelization will become a realistic possibility only when the Spirit renews the church in truth and wisdom, faith, holiness, love and power. We therefore call upon all Christians to pray for such a visitation of the sovereign Spirit of God that all His fruit may appear in all His people and that all His gifts may enrich the body of Christ. Only then will the whole church become a fit instrument in His hands, that the whole earth may hear His voice (1 Cor. 2:4; John 15:26-27; 16:8-11; 1 Cor. 12:1; John 8:6-8; 2 Cor. 3:18; John 7:37-39; 1 Thess. 5:19; Acts 1:8; Pss. 85:4-7; 67:1-3; Gal. 5:22-23; 1 Cor. 12:4-31; Rom. 12:3-8).

15. The Return of Christ

We believe that Jesus Christ will return personally and visibly in power and glory, to consummate His salvation and His judgment. This promise of His coming is a further spur to our evangelism, for we remember His words that the gospel must first be preached to all nations. We believe that the interim period between Christ's ascension and return is to be filled with the mission of the people of God, who have no liberty to stop before the End. We also remember His warning that false Christs and false prophets will arise as precursors of the final Antichrist. We therefore reject as a proud, self-confident dream the notion that man can ever build a utopia on earth. Our Christian confidence is that God will perfect His kingdom, and we look forward with eager anticipation to that day, and to the new heaven and earth in which righteousness will dwell, and God will reign for ever. Meanwhile, we rededicate ourselves to the service of Christ and of men in joyful submission to His authority over the whole of our lives (Mark 14:62; Heb. 9:28; Mark 13:10; Acts 1:8-11; Matt. 28:20; Mark 13:21-23; John 2:18; 4:1-3; Luke 12:32; Rev. 21:1-5; 2 Pet. 3:13; Matt. 28:18).

Conclusion

Therefore, in the light of this our faith and our resolve, we enter into a solemn covenant with God and with each other, to pray, to plan and to work together for the evangelization of the whole world. We call upon others to join us. May God help us by His grace and for His glory to be faithful to this our covenant! Amen, Alleluia!

Addendum to Appendix B

In July of 1989, Lausanne II met in Manila, the Philippines. The "Manila Manifesto" was written and adopted by the conference. It shows the development of thought and emphasis relative to world evangelization since the formulation of the Lausanne Covenant of 1974. It is as follows:

The Manila Manifesto

Calling the whole church to take the whole gospel to the whole world.

Introduction

In July 1974 the International Congress on World Evangelization was held in Lausanne, Switzerland, and issued the Lausanne Covenant. Now in July 1989 [sic] over 3,000 of us from about 170 countries have met in Manila for the same purpose, and have issued the Manila Manifesto. We are grateful for the welcome we have received from our Filipino brothers and sisters.

During the 15 years which have elapsed between the two congresses some smaller consultations have been held on topics like Gospel and Culture, Evangelism and Social Responsibility, Simple Life-style, the Holy Spirit, and Conversion. These meetings and their reports have helped to develop the thinking of the Lausanne movement.

A "manifesto" is defined as a public declaration of convictions, intentions and motives. The Manila Manifesto takes up the two congress themes, "Proclaim Christ until He comes" and "Calling the Whole Church to take the Whole Gospel to the Whole World." Its first part is a series of 21 succinct affirmations. Its second part elaborates these in 12 sections, which are commended to churches, alongside the Lausanne Covenant, for study and action.

Twenty-One Affirmations

1. We affirm our continuing commitment to the Lausanne Covenant as the basis of our cooperation in the Lausanne movement.
2. We affirm that in the Scriptures of the Old and New Testaments God has given us an authoritative disclosure of his character and will, his redemptive acts and their meaning, and his mandate for mission.
3. We affirm that the biblical gospel is God's enduring message to our world, and we determine to defend, proclaim and embody it.
4. We affirm that human beings, though created in the image of God, are sinful and guilty, and lost without Christ, and that this truth is a necessary preliminary to the gospel.
5. We affirm that the Jesus of history and the Christ of glory are the same person, and that this Jesus Christ is absolutely unique, for He alone is God incarnate, our sin-bearer, the conqueror of death and the coming judge.
6. We affirm that on the cross Jesus Christ took our place, bore our sins and died our death; and that for this reason alone God freely forgives those who are brought to repentance and faith.
7. We affirm that other religions and ideologies are not alternative paths to

God, and that human spirituality, if unredeemed by Christ, leads not to God but to judgment, for Christ is the only way.

8. We affirm that we must demonstrate God's love visibly by caring for those who are deprived of justice, dignity, food and shelter.

9. We affirm that the proclamation of God's kingdom of justice and peace demands the denunciation of all injustice and oppression, both personal and structural; we will not shrink from this prophetic witness.

10. We affirm that the Holy Spirit's witness to Christ is indispensable to evangelism, and that without his supernatural work neither new birth nor new life is possible.

11. We affirm that spiritual warfare demands spiritual weapons, and that we must both preach the word in the power of the Spirit, and pray constantly that we may enter into Christ's victory over the principalities and powers of evil.

12. We affirm that God has committed to the whole church and every member of it the task of making Christ known throughout the world; we long to see all lay and ordained persons mobilized and trained for this task.

13. We affirm that we who claim to be members of the Body of Christ must transcend within our fellowship the barriers of race, gender and class.

14. We affirm that the gifts of the Spirit are distributed to all God's people, women and men, and that their partnership in evangelization must be welcomed for the common good.

15. We affirm that we who proclaim the gospel must exemplify it in a life of holiness and love; otherwise our testimony loses its credibility.

16. We affirm that every Christian congregation must turn itself outward to its local community in evangelistic witness and compassionate service.

17. We affirm the urgent need for churches, mission agencies and other Christian organizations to cooperate in evangelism and social action, repudiating competition and avoiding duplication.

18. We affirm our duty to study the society in which we live, in order to understand its structures, values and needs, and so develop an appropriate strategy of mission.

19. We affirm that world evangelization is urgent and that the reaching of unreached peoples is possible. So we resolve during the last decade of the twentieth century to give ourselves to these tasks with fresh determination.

20. We affirm our solidarity with those who suffer for the gospel, and will seek to prepare ourselves for the same possibility. We will also work for religious and political freedom everywhere.

21. We affirm that God is calling the whole church to take the whole gospel to the whole world. So we determine to proclaim it faithfully, urgently and sacrificially, until he comes.

A. The Whole Gospel

The gospel is the good news of God's salvation from the powers of evil, the establishment of His eternal kingdom and His final victory over everything which defies His purpose. In His love God purposed to do this before the world began and effected His liberating plan over sin, death and judgment through the death of our Lord Jesus Christ. It is Christ who makes us free, and unites us in his redeemed fellowship.

(1) Our Human Predicament

We are committed to preaching the whole gospel, that is, the biblical gospel in its fulness. In order to do so, we have to understand why human beings need it.

Men and women have an intrinsic dignity and worth, because they were created in God's likeness to know, love and serve Him. But now through sin every part of their humanness has been distorted. Human beings have become self-centered, self-serving rebels, who do not love God or their neighbor as they should. In consequence, they are alienated both from their Creator and from the rest of His creation, which is the basic cause of the pain, disorientation and loneliness which so many people suffer today. Sin also frequently erupts in anti-social behavior, in violent exploitation of others, and in a depletion of the earth's resources of which God has made men and women his stewards. Humanity is guilty, without excuse, and on the broad road which leads to destruction.

Although God's image in human beings has been corrupted, they are still capable of loving relationships, noble deeds and beautiful art. Yet even the finest human achievement is fatally flawed and cannot possibly fit anybody to enter God's presence. Men and women are also spiritual beings, but spiritual practices and self-help techniques can at the most alleviate felt needs; they cannot address the solemn realities of sin, guilt and judgment. Neither human religion, nor human righteousness, nor socio-political programs can save people. Self-salvation of every kind is impossible. Left to themselves, human beings are lost forever.

So we repudiate false gospels which deny human sin, divine judgment, the deity and incarnation of Jesus Christ, and the necessity of the cross and the resurrection. We also reject half-gospels, which minimize sin and confuse God's grace with human self-effort. We confess that we ourselves have sometimes trivialized the gospel. But we determine in our evangelism to remember God's radical diagnosis and his equally radical remedy.

(2) Good News for Today

We rejoice that the living God did not abandon us to our lostness and despair. In His love He came after us in Jesus Christ to rescue and remake us. So the good news focuses on the historic person of Jesus, who came proclaiming the kingdom of God and living a life of humble service, who died for us, becoming sin and a curse in our place, and whom God vindicated by raising Him from the dead. To those who repent and believe in Christ God grants a share in the new creation. He gives us new life, which includes the forgiveness of our sins and the indwelling, transforming power of his Spirit. He welcomes us into His new community, which consists of people of all races, nations and cultures. And He promises that one day we will enter His new world, in which evil will be abolished, nature will be redeemed, and God will reign for ever.

This good news must be boldly proclaimed, wherever possible, in church and public hall, on radio and television, and in the open air, because it is God's power for salvation and we are under obligation to make it known. In our preaching we must faithfully declare the truth which God has revealed in the Bible and struggle to relate it to our own context.

We also affirm that apologetics, namely "the defence and confirmation of the gospel" (Phil. 1:7), [KJV] is integral to the biblical understanding of mission and essential for effective witness in the modern world. Paul "reasoned" with people out of the Scriptures, with a view to "persuading" them of the truth of the gospel. So must we. In fact, all Christians should be ready to give a reason for the hope that is in them (1 Pet. 3:15).

We have again been confronted with Luke's emphasis that the gospel is good news for the poor (Luke 4:18, 6:20, 7:22) and have asked ourselves what this means to the majority of the world's population who are destitute, suffering or oppressed. We have been reminded that the law, the prophets and the wisdom books, and the teaching and ministry of Jesus, all stress God's concern for the materially poor and our consequent duty to defend and care for them. Scripture also refers to the spiritually poor who look to God alone for mercy. The gospel comes as good news to both. The spiritually poor, who, whatever their economic circumstances, humble themselves before God, receive by faith the free gift of salvation. There is no other way for anybody to enter the Kingdom of God. The materially poor and powerless find in addition a new dignity as God's children, and the love of brothers and sisters who will struggle with them for their liberation from everything which demeans or oppresses them.

We repent of any neglect of God's truth in Scripture and determine both to proclaim and to defend it. We also repent where we have been indifferent to the plight of the poor, and where we have shown preference for the rich, and we determine to follow Jesus in preaching good news to all people by both word and deed.

(3) The Uniqueness of Jesus Christ

We are called to proclaim Christ in an increasingly pluralistic world. There is a resurgence of old faiths and a rise of new ones. In the first century too there were "many 'gods' and many 'lords' " (1 Cor. 8:5). Yet the apostles boldly affirmed the uniqueness, indispensability and centrality of Christ. We must do the same.

Because men and women are made in God's image and see in the creation traces of its Creator, the religions which have arisen do sometimes contain elements of truth and beauty. They are not, however, alternative gospels. Because human beings are sinful, and because 'the whole world is under the control of the evil one' (1 Jn. 5:19), even religious people are in need of Christ's redemption. We, therefore, have no warrant for saying that salvation can be found outside Christ or apart from an explicit acceptance of his work through faith.

It is sometimes held that in virtue of God's covenant with Abraham, Jewish people do not need to acknowledge Jesus as their Messiah. We affirm that they need him as much as anyone else, that it would be a form of anti-Semitism, as well as being disloyal to Christ, to depart from the New Testament pattern of taking the gospel to "the Jew first. . . ." We therefore reject the thesis that Jews have their own covenant which renders faith in Jesus unnecessary.

What unites us is our common convictions about Jesus Christ. We confess him as the eternal Son of God who became fully human while remaining fully divine, who was our substitute on the cross, bearing our sins and dying our death, exchanging His righteousness for our unrighteousness, who rose victorious in a transformed body, and who will return in glory to judge the world. He alone is the incarnate Son, the Saviour, the Lord and the Judge, and He alone, with the Father and the Spirit, is worthy of the worship, faith and obedience of all people. There is only one gospel because there is only one Christ, who because of his death and resurrection is himself the only way of salvation. We therefore reject both the relativism which regards all religions and spiritualities as equally valid approaches to God, and the syncretism which tries to mix faith in Christ with other faiths.

Moreover, since God has exalted Jesus to the highest place, in order that everybody should acknowledge him, this also is our desire. Compelled by Christ's love, we must obey Christ's Great Commission and love his lost sheep, but we are especially motivated by "jealousy" for his holy name, and we long to see him receive the honor and glory which are due to him.

In the past we have sometimes been guilty of adopting towards adherents of other faiths attitudes of ignorance, arrogance, disrespect and even hostility. We repent of this. We nevertheless are determined to bear a positive and uncompromising witness to the uniqueness of our Lord, in his life, death and resurrection, in all aspects of our evangelistic work including inter-faith dialogue.

(4) The Gospel and Social Responsibility

The authentic gospel must become visible in the transformed lives of men and women. As we proclaim the love of God we must be involved in loving service, and as we preach the Kingdom of God we must be committed to its demands of justice and peace.

Evangelism is primary because our chief concern is with the gospel, that all people may have the opportunity to accept Jesus Christ as Lord and Savior. Yet Jesus not only proclaimed the Kingdom of God, he also demonstrated its arrival by works of mercy and power. We are called today to a similar integration of words and deeds. In a spirit of humility we are to preach and teach, minister to the sick, feed the hungry, care for prisoners, help the disadvantaged and handicapped, and deliver the oppressed. While we acknowledge the diversity of spiritual gifts, callings and contexts, we also affirm that good news and good works are inseparable.

The proclamation of God's kingdom necessarily demands the prophetic denunciation of all that is incompatible with it. Among the evils we deplore are destructive violence, including institutionalized violence, political corruption, all forms of exploitation of people and of the earth, the undermining of the family, abortion on demand, the drug traffic, and the abuse of human rights. In our concern for the poor, we are distressed by the burden of debt in the two-thirds world. We are also outraged by the inhuman conditions in which millions live, who bear God's image as we do.

Our continuing commitment to social action is not a confusion of the Kingdom of God with a Christianized society. It is, rather, a recognition that the biblical gospel has inescapable social implications. True mission should always be incarnational. It necessitates entering humbly into other people's worlds, identifying with their social reality, their sorrow and suffering, and their struggles for justice against oppressive powers. This cannot be done without personal sacrifices.

We repent that the narrowness of our concerns and vision has often kept us from proclaiming the lordship of Jesus Christ over all of life, private and public, local and global. We determine to obey his command to seek 'first the kingdom of God, and his righteousness' (Mt. 6:33).

B. The Whole Church

The whole gospel has to be proclaimed by the whole church. All the people of God are called to share in the evangelistic task. Yet without the Holy Spirit of God all their endeavors will be fruitless.

(5) God the Evangelist

The Scriptures declare that God himself is the chief evangelist. For the Spirit of God is the Spirit of truth, love, holiness and power, and evangelism is impossible without him. It is he who anoints the messenger, confirms the word, prepares the hearer, convicts the sinful, enlightens the blind, gives life to the dead, enables us to repent and believe, unites us to the Body of Christ, assures us that we are God's children, leads us into Christlike character and service, and sends us out in our turn to be Christ's witnesses. In all this the Holy Spirit's main preoccupation is to glorify Jesus Christ by showing him to us and forming him in us.

All evangelism involves spiritual warfare with the principalities and powers of evil, in which only spiritual weapons can prevail, especially the Word and the Spirit, with prayer. We therefore call on all Christian people to be diligent in their prayers both for the renewal of the church and for the evangelization of the world.

Every true conversion involves a power encounter, in which the superior authority of Jesus Christ is demonstrated. There is no greater miracle than this, in which the believer is set free from the bondage of Satan and sin, fear and futility, darkness and death.

Although the miracles of Jesus were special, being signs of his Messiahship and anticipations of his perfect kingdom when all nature will be subject to him, we have no liberty to place limits on the power of the living Creator today. We reject both the skepticism which denies miracles and the presumption which demands them, both the timidity which shrinks from the fullness of the Spirit and the triumphalism which shrinks from the weakness in which Christ's power is made perfect.

We repent of all self-confident attempts either to evangelize in our own strength or to dictate to the Holy Spirit. We determine in future not to "grieve" or "quench" the Spirit, but rather to spread the good news 'with power, with the Holy Spirit and with deep conviction' (1 Thess. 1:5).

(6) The Human Witnesses

God the evangelist gives his people the privilege of being his 'fellow workers' (2 Cor. 6:1). For, although we cannot witness without him, he normally chooses to witness through us. He calls only some to be evangelists, missionaries or pastors, but he calls his whole church and every member of it to be his witnesses.

The privileged task of pastors and teachers is to lead God's people (laos) into maturity (Col. 1:28) and to equip them for ministry (Eph. 4:11-12). Pastors are not to monopolize ministries, but rather to multiply them, by encouraging others to use their gifts and by training disciples to make disciples. The domination of the laity by the clergy has been a great evil in the history of the church. It robs both laity and clergy of their God-intended roles, causes clergy breakdowns, weakens the church and hinders the spread of the gospel. More than that, it is fundamentally unbiblical. We therefore, who have for centuries insisted on "the priesthood of all believers" now also insist on the ministry of all believers.

We gratefully recognize that children and young people enrich the church's worship and outreach by their enthusiasm and faith. We need to train them in discipleship and evangelism, so that they may reach their own generation for Christ.

God created men and women as equal bearers of his image (Gen. 1:26-27), accepts them equally in Christ (Gal. 3:28) and poured out His Spirit on all flesh, sons and daughters alike (Acts 2:17-18). In addition, because the Holy Spirit distributes his gifts to women as well as to men, they must be given opportunities to exercise their gifts. We celebrate their distinguished record in the history of missions and are convinced that God calls women to similar roles today. Even though we are not fully agreed what forms their leadership should take, we do agree about the partnership in world evangelization which God intends men and women to enjoy. Suitable training must therefore be made available to both.

Lay witness takes place, by women and men, not only through the local church (see Section 8), but through friendships, in the home and at work. Even those who are homeless or unemployed share in the calling to be witnesses.

Our first responsibility is to witness to those who are already our friends, relatives, neighbors, and colleagues. Home evangelism is also natural, both for married and for single people. Not only should a Christian home commend God's standards of marriage, sex and family, and provide a haven of love and peace to people who are hurting, but neighbors who would not enter a church usually feel comfortable in a home, even when the gospel is discussed.

Another context for lay witness is the workplace, for it is here that most Christians spend half their waking hours, and work is a divine calling. Christians can commend Christ by word of mouth, by their consistent industry, honesty and thoughtfulness, by their concern for justice in the workplace, and especially if others can see from the quality of their daily work that it is done to the glory of God.

We repent of our share in discouraging the ministry of the laity, especially of women and young people. We determine in [sic] future to encourage all Christ's followers to take their place, rightfully and naturally, as his witnesses. For true evangelism comes from the overflow of a heart in love with Christ. That is why it belongs to all his people without exception.

(7) The Integrity of the Witnesses

Nothing commends the gospel more eloquently than a transformed life, and nothing brings it into disrepute so much as personal inconsistency. We are charged to behave in a manner that is worthy of the gospel of Christ, and even to 'adorn' it, enhancing its beauty by holy lives. For the watching world rightly seeks evidence to substantiate the claims which Christ's disciples make for him. A strong evidence is our integrity.

Our proclamation that Christ died to bring us to God appeals to people who are spiritually thirsty, but they will not believe us if we give no evidence of knowing the living God ourselves, or if our public worship lacks reality and relevance.

Our message that Christ reconciles alienated people to each other rings true only if we are seen to love and forgive one another, to serve others in humility, and to reach out beyond our own community in compassionate, costly ministry to the needy.

Our challenge to others to deny themselves, take up their cross and follow Christ will be plausible only if we ourselves have evidently died to selfish ambition, dishonesty and covetousness, and are living a life of simplicity, contentment and generosity.

We deplore the failures in Christian consistency which we see in both Christians and churches: material greed, professional pride and rivalry, competition in Christian service, jealousy of younger leaders, missionary paternalism, the lack of mutual accountability, the loss of Christian standards of sexuality, and racial, social and sexual discrimination. All this is worldliness, allowing the prevailing culture to subvert the church instead of the church challenging and changing the culture. We are deeply ashamed of the times when, both as individuals and in our Christian communities, we have affirmed Christ in word and denied him in deed. Our inconsistency deprives our witness of credibility. We acknowledge our continuing struggles and failures. But we also determine by God's grace to develop integrity in ourselves and in the church.

(8) The Local Church

Every Christian congregation is a local expression of the Body of Christ and has the same responsibilities. It is both 'a holy priesthood' to offer God the spiritual sacrifices of worship and 'a holy nation' to spread abroad his excellences in witness (1 Pet. 2:5,9). The church is thus both a worshipping and a witnessing community, gathered and scattered, called and sent. Worship and witness are inseparable.

We believe that the local church bears a primary responsibility for the spread of the gospel. Scripture suggests this in the progression that 'our gospel came to you' and then "rang out from you' (1 Thess. 1:5,8). In this way, the gospel creates the church which spreads the gospel which creates more churches in a continuous chain-reaction. Moreover, what Scripture teaches, strategy confirms. Each local church must evangelize the district in which it is situated, and has the resources to do so.

We recommend every congregation to carry out regular studies not only of its own membership and program but of its local community in all its particularity, in order to develop appropriate strategies for mission. Its members might decide to organize a visitation of their whole area, to penetrate for Christ a particular place where people assemble, to arrange a series of evangelistic meetings, lectures or concerts, to work with the poor to transform a local slum, or to plant a new church in a neighboring district or village. At the same time, they must not forget the church's global task. A church which sends our missionaries must not neglect its own locality, and a church which evangelizes its neighborhood must not ignore the rest of the world.

In all this each congregation and denomination should, where possible, work with others, seeking to turn any spirit of competition into one of cooperation. Churches should also work with para-church organizations, especially in evangelism, discipling and community service, for such agencies are part of the Body of Christ, and have valuable, specialist expertise from which the church can greatly benefit.

The church is intended by God to be a sign of his kingdom, that is, an indication of what human community looks like when it comes under his rule of righteousness and peace. As with individuals, so with churches, the gospel has to be embodied if it is to be communicated effectively. It is through our love for one another that the invisible God reveals himself today (1 Jn. 4:12), especially when our fellowship is expressed in small groups, and when it transcends the barriers of race, rank, sex and age which divide other communities.

We deeply regret that many of our congregations are inward-looking, organized for maintenance rather than mission, or preoccupied with church-based activities at the expense of witness. We determine to turn our churches inside out, so that they may engage in continuous outreach, until the Lord adds to them daily those who are being saved (Acts 2:47).

(9) Cooperation in Evangelism

Evangelism and unity are closely related in the New Testament. Jesus prayed that his people's oneness might reflect his own oneness with the Father, in order that the world might believe in him (Jn. 17:20,21), and Paul exhorted the Philippians to 'contend as one person for the faith of the gospel' (Phil. 1:27). In contrast to this biblical vision, we are ashamed of the suspicions and rivalries, the dogmatism over non-essentials, the power-struggles and empire-building which spoil our evangelistic witness. We affirm that cooperation in evangelism is indispensable, first because it is the will of God, but also because the gospel of reconciliation is discredited by our disunity, and because, if the task of world evangelization is ever to be accomplished, we must engage in it together.

'Cooperation' means finding unity in diversity. It involves people of different temperaments, gifts, callings and cultures, national churches and mission agencies, all ages and both sexes working together.

We are determined to put behind us once and for all, as a hangover from the colonial past, the simplistic distinction First World sending and Two-Thirds World receiving countries. For the great new fact of our era is the internationalization of missions. Not only are a large majority of all evangelical Christians now non-western, but the number of Two-Thirds World missionaries will soon exceed those from the West. We believe that mission teams, which are diverse in composition but united in heart and mind, constitute a dramatic witness to the grace of God.

Our reference to 'the whole church' is not a presumptuous claim that the universal church and the evangelical community are synonymous. For we recognize that there are many churches which are not part of the evangelical movement. Evangelical attitudes to the Roman Catholic and Orthodox Churches differ widely. Some evangelicals are praying, talking, studying Scripture and working with these churches. Others are strongly opposed to any form of dialogue or cooperation with them. All evangelicals are aware that serious theological differences between us remain. Where appropriate, and so long as biblical truth is not compromised, cooperation may be possible in such areas as Bible translation, the study of contemporary theological and ethical issues, social work and political action. We wish to make it clear, however, that common evangelism demands a common commitment to the biblical gospel.

Some of us are members of churches which belong to the World Council of Churches and believe that a positive yet critical participation in its work is our Christian duty. Others among us have no link with the World Council. All of us urge the World Council of Churches to adopt a consistent biblical understanding of evangelism.

We confess our own share of responsibility for the brokenness of the Body of Christ, which is a major stumbling-block to world evangelization. We determine to go on seeking that unity in truth for which Christ prayed. We are persuaded that the right way forward towards closer cooperation is frank and patient dialogue on the basis of the Bible, with all who share our concerns. To this we gladly commit ourselves.

C. The Whole World

The whole gospel has been entrusted to the whole church, in order that it may be made known to the whole world. It is necessary, therefore, for us to understand the world into which we are sent.

(10) The Modern World

Evangelism takes place in a context, not in a vacuum. The balance between gospel and context must be carefully maintained. We must understand the context in order to address it, but the context must not be allowed to distort the gospel.

In this connection we have become concerned about the impact of "modernity," which is an emerging world culture produced by industrialization with its technology and urbanization with its economic order. These factors combine to create an environment, which significantly shapes the way in which we see our world. In addition, secularism has devastated faith by making God and the supernatural meaningless; urbanization has dehumanized life for many; and the mass media have contributed to the devaluation of truth and authority, by replacing word with image. In combination, these consequences of modernity pervert the message which many preach and undermine their motivation for mission.

In AD 1900 only 9% of the world's population lived in cities; in AD 2000 it is thought that more than 50% will do so. This worldwide move into the cities has been called "the greatest migration in human history"; it constitutes a major challenge to Christian mission. On the one hand, city populations are extremely cosmopolitan, so that the nations come to our doorstep in the city. Can we develop global churches in which the gospel abolishes the barriers of ethnicity? On the other hand, many city dwellers are migrant poor who are also receptive to the gospel. Can the people of God be persuaded to relocate into such urban poor communities, in order to serve the people and share in the transformation of the city?

Modernization brings blessings as well as dangers. By creating links of communication and commerce around the globe, it makes unprecedented openings for the gospel, crossing old frontiers and penetrating closed societies, whether traditional or totalitarian. The Christian media have a powerful influence both in sowing the seed of the gospel and in preparing the soil. The major missionary broadcasters are committed to a gospel witness by radio in every major language by the year AD 2000.

We confess that we have not struggled as we should to understand modernization. We have used its methods and techniques uncritically and so exposed ourselves to worldliness. But we determine in the future to take these challenges and opportunities seriously, to resist the secular pressures of modernity, to relate the lordship of Christ to the whole of modern culture, and thus to engage in mission in the modern world without worldliness in modern mission.

(11) The Challenge of AD 2000 and Beyond

The world population today is approaching 6 billion. One third of them nominally confess Christ. Of the remaining four billion half have heard of him, and the other half have not. In the light of these figures, we evaluate our evangelistic task by considering four categories of people.

First, there is the potential missionary work force, *the committed*. In this century this category of Christian believers has grown from about 40 million in 1900 to about 500 million today, and at this moment is growing over twice as fast as any other major religious group.

Secondly, there are *the uncommitted*. They make a Christian profession (they have been baptized, attend church occasionally and even call themselves Christians), but the notion of a personal commitment to Christ is foreign to them. They are found in all churches throughout the world. They urgently need to be re-evangelized.

Thirdly, there are *the unevangelized*. These are people who have a minimal knowledge of the gospel, but have had no valid opportunity to respond to it. They are probably within reach of Christian people if only these will go to the next street, road, village or town to find them.

Fourthly, there are *the unreached*. These are the two billion who may never have heard of Jesus as Savior, and are not within reach of Christians of their own people. There are, in fact, some 2,000 peoples or nationalities in which there is not yet a vital, indigenous church movement. We find it helpful to think of them as belonging to smaller "people groups" which perceive themselves as having an affinity with each other (e.g. a common culture, language, home or occupation). The most effective messengers to reach them will be those believers who already belong to their culture and know their language. Otherwise, cross-cultural messengers of the gospel will need to go, leaving behind their own culture and sacrificially identifying with the people they long to reach for Christ.

There are now about 12,000 such unreached people groups within the 2,000 larger peoples, so that the task is not impossible. Yet a present only 7% of all missionaries are engaged in this kind of outreach, while the remaining 93% are working in the already evangelized half of the world. If this imbalance is to be redressed, a strategic redeployment of personnel will be necessary.

A distressing factor that affects each of the above categories is that of inaccessibility. Many countries do not grant visas to self-styled missionaries, who have no other qualification or contribution to offer. Such areas are not absolutely inaccessible, however. For our prayers can pass through every curtain, door and barrier. And Christian radio and television, audio and video cassettes, films and literature can also reach the otherwise unreachable. So can so-called "tent-makers" who like Paul earn their own living. They travel in the course of their profession (e.g. business people, university lecturers, technical specialists and language teachers), and use every opportunity to speak of Jesus Christ. They do not enter a country under false pretenses, for their work genuinely takes them there; it is simply that witness is an essential component of their Christian life-style, wherever they may happen to be.

We are deeply ashamed that nearly two millennia have passed since the death and resurrection of Jesus, and still two-thirds of the world's population have not yet acknowledged Him. On the other hand, we are amazed at the mounting evidence of God's power even in the most unlikely places of the globe.

Now the year 2000 has become for many a challenging milestone. Can we commit ourselves to evangelize the world during the last decade of this millennium? There is nothing magical about the date, yet should we not do our best to reach this goal? Christ commands us to take the gospel to all peoples. The task is urgent. We are determined to obey him with joy and hope.

(12) Difficult Situations

Jesus plainly told his followers to expect opposition. "If they persecuted me," he said, "they will persecute you" (Jn. 15:20). He even told them to rejoice over persecution (Mt. 5:12), and reminded them that the condition of fruitfulness was death (Jn. 12:24).

These predictions, that Christian suffering is inevitable and productive, have come true in every age, including our own. There have been many thousands of martyrs. Today the situation is much the same. We earnestly hope that *glasnost* and *perestroika* will lead to complete religious freedom in the Soviet Union and other Eastern bloc nations, and that Islamic and Hindu countries will become more open to the gospel. We deplore the recent brutal suppression of China's democratic movement, and we pray that it will not bring further suffering to the Christians. On the whole, however, it seems that ancient religions are becoming less tolerant, expatriates less welcome, and the world less friendly to the gospel.

In this situation we wish to make 3 statements to governments which are reconsidering their attitude to Christian believers.

First, Christians are loyal citizens, who seek the welfare of their nation. They pray for its leaders and pay their taxes. Of course, those who have confessed Jesus as Lord cannot also call other authorities Lord, and if commanded to do so, or to do anything which God forbids, must disobey. But they are conscientious citizens. They also contribute to their country's well-being by the stability of their marriages and homes, their honesty in business, their hard work and their voluntary activity in the service of the handicapped and needy. Just governments have nothing to fear from Christians.

Secondly, Christians renounce unworthy methods of evangelism. Though the nature of our faith requires us to share the gospel with others, our practice is to make an open and honest statement of it, which leaves the hearers entirely free to make up their own minds about it. We wish to be sensitive to those of other faiths, and we reject any approach that seeks to force conversion on them.

Thirdly, Christians earnestly desire freedom of religion for all people, not just freedom for Christianity. In predominantly Christian countries, Christians are at the forefront of those who demand freedom for religious minorities. In predominantly non-Christian countries, therefore, Christians are asking for themselves no more than they demand for others in similar circumstances. The freedom to 'profess, practise and propagate' religion, as defined in the Universal Declaration of Human Rights, could and should surely be a reciprocally granted right.

We greatly regret any unworthy witness of which followers of Jesus may have been guilty. We determine to give no unnecessary offense in anything, lest the name of Christ be dishonored. However, the offence of the cross we cannot avoid. For the sake of Christ crucified we pray that we may be ready, by His grace, to suffer and even to die. Martyrdom is a form of witness which Christ has promised especially to honor.

Conclusion: Proclaim Christ Until He Comes

'Proclaim Christ until he comes.' That has been the theme of Lausanne II. Of course we believe that Christ has come; he came when Augustus was Emperor of Rome. But one day, as we know from his promises, he will come again in unimaginable splendor to perfect his kingdom. We are commanded to watch and be ready. Meanwhile, the gap between his two comings is to be filled with the Christian missionary enterprise. We have been told to go to the ends of the earth with the gospel, and we have been promised that the end of the age will come only when we have done so. The two ends (of earth space and time) will coincide. Until then he has pledged to be with us.

So the Christian mission is an urgent task. We do not know how long we have. We certainly have no time to waste. And in order to get on urgently with our responsibility, other qualities will be necessary, especially unity (we must evangelize together) and sacrifice (we must count and accept the cost). Our covenant at Lausanne was 'to pray, to plan and to work together for the evangelization of the whole world.' Our manifesto at Manila is that the whole church is called to take the whole gospel to the whole world, proclaiming Christ until he comes, with all necessary urgency, unity and sacrifice.

Notes

1. The *Lausanne Covenant* and *Manila Manifesto* are reprinted here by permission of Leighton Ford, Leighton Ford Ministries.

2. This number has increased significantly since the framing of the Covenant.

Appendix C
Building an Evangelistic Church

Introduction

Perhaps as never before, the church needs to take a fresh look at itself. The virtual tidal wave of urbanization, secularism, and humanism sweeping over the scene especially in Europe and North America, demands the demise of old, irrelevant structures and the development of approaches to ministry which meet contemporary needs and presents the gospel in a communicative, relevant manner. These dynamics should motivate a local church to conduct a "diagnostic survey" of itself. The purpose of such a survey is to evaluate objectively the life of a local congregation so that its ministry and witness may become more effective in current society. All sincere Christians surely desire to see the evangelistic life and total ministry of their church enhanced, but before this happens it may be essential to "overhaul" aspects of the present local church outreach ministry program. Such an undertaking calls for objectivity, honesty, and not a little bravery. The outline following will provide in broad terms some guidelines for conducting such a survey and developing a strategy to meet real needs of real people in the marketplaces of life, and thus see the church grow. It seems clear, if we can come to understand just where we are in local church life in the light of today's world, we can see more clearly where we need to go to reach people for Christ. A congregation must look to the future, decide what it wants to accomplish, and set goals to that end.

I. The Setting of Goals or Aims

In setting goals, ask these questions:

1. What is the essential mission of the church, and how does it relate to our congregation? Remember, above all, the local church is to minister in the world, the marketplace, and reach people for Christ. A congregation that focuses on itself unduly, spells its own ultimate death.
2. How should this mission affect the aims and plans of our local church, and does it actually do so?
3. Therefore, what should be, the aims of our congregation?
4. Are the church members conscious of these aims? If not, why not?
5. Do these aims govern the development of the church program and the organizations and their functions? If not, why?
6. Set definite growth goals: long-, mid-, and short-range goals. These goals are to cover all aspects of church life.
7. Are the goals measurable and attainable, that is, are they concrete?
8. Are the goals and aims a true challenge?

II. Surveying the Community

1. Prepare a map of the community, indicating by a colored line the area surrounding the church, assuming the church ministers to a definite area or parish. (Show church location.)

2. Prepare a description of the church's area of responsibility: location, type of housing, age, industrial or residential, racial patterns, subcultural groups, institutions, income level, general culture, problems related to its environment, etc. The demographics of the field are vital to have in hand. This will take some study. Discover the future of the community as well as the present. This affects goal setting and, hence, programming.

3. Describe the community needs that should be met by the church.

4. Evaluate the effectiveness of the church in meeting the needs of its community. What can and should be done to meet these needs? Anticipate future needs and prepare for these also.

III. Surveying the Organizational Life of the Church

The General Life of the Church

1. Summarize briefly the history of the local church and how this relates (if it does) to the present congregational life.

2. Evaluate and criticize the church's constitution and/or bylaws if it has any.

3. Study the church property and buildings. What long-, mid-, and short-range plans should be made by the church concerning its growth, location and future building needs, finances, resources, etc.? How adequate are the present buildings and resources to meet the needs of the community? What repairs or changes or building plans are vital for the present and future? Are the present buildings used to the best advantage in accordance with the church's message and ministry? What other building resources are available?

The Worship Life of the Church

1. What is the program of church music? Is this vital aspect of church life given proper interest and work? Does it aid real praise and worship, that is, is it vital and dynamic on the people's level?

2. Study the church services of worship. Are they relevant? Is the language used communicable? Are the church ordinances meaningfully observed? What is being done to educate in worship? Are the services "alive"? Is real worship happening—if not, why not? What can be done? What should be kept? Do we understand the relationship between worship and mission?

The Evangelism and World Missions Life of the Church

Describe the outreach ministry of the church. What is actually being done now? Is there a responsible evangelistic committee? What is the record of successful outreach over the past ten years? Are the church organizations involved in evangelism? How conscious are the church members of the need and centrality of evangelism? Are the worship services effectively evangelistic? How can the church reach outsiders? What training in evangelism is given members? What challenges are being presented? How can we be more relevant to different groups of people in the community? How can the lost be found and reached? What is being done in worldwide evangelization?

The Pastoral Care Life of the Church

1. How are members received into the church? What does the church do to integrate new members into the total church programs? What plans are there for conserving and discipleship training of new members in the Christian life and church life? How adequate and useful are the membership rolls? What action is taken concerning inactive members? Are there discipleship training programs functioning that reach all age groups?

2. Evaluate church ministries. What services are rendered to family life—before and after marriage? What about the church's "crisis" ministry in times of death, serious illness, birth, divorce, etc.? What about the problems of broken families, delinquency, crime, drugs, AIDS, etc. when these occur in the life of the church members and in the community? To what extent is the whole church involved in pastoral care?

3. Are special subcultures being ministered to, for example, singles, language groups, homeless, ethnics, poor, etc.

The Christian Education Life of the Church

Evaluate the overall effectiveness of the church's educational program. This should include the work of the Sunday School, women's organizations, men's organizations, youth ministries, geriatrics, "lay" training in evangelism, discipleship programs, etc. These questions must be asked: Is our church truly educating people in the Bible? Is there any segment of the membership not receiving teaching in the Scriptures? If so, what can be done? Are organizations in line with the mission? Is there a leadership training program? Are all God's people given an opportunity to exercise their gifts of the Spirit and serve? Are the gifts being developed?

The Stewardship Life of the Church

Study the church plan for promoting and practicing Christian stewardship. Describe and evaluate the plan of church finance. What emphasis is placed on this important aspect of dedication? What portion of the membership gives regularly? What is done to increase this number? How seriously hindered is the life and ministry of the church because of poor stewardship? Is there a reluctance to emphasize stewardship? How about a stewardship campaign? Does the church spend its monies in such a way as to encourage giving? Is the whole world in the vision?

The Recreational and Social Ministry Life of the Church

Evaluate church recreation, for old and young, and other specialized activities, for example, drama, camps, youth clubs, holiday clubs, etc. What sort of impact is the church making on the community? What social needs exist? How can the church help to meet these needs? Does the church really care and thus seek to meet real needs of real people? The outside world really sets the agenda here, that is, the "market place" needs determine the program.

The Leadership Life of the Church

Evaluate leadership participation. What proportion of church members have some definite place of service in the church program? In the light of the study of the church organizations, how adequate is the church leadership? How are leaders discovered? What training, if any, do they receive to do their job effectively?

The Administrative Life of the Church

1. Study the problem of coordination and correlation. Is the church well integrated? How do the organizations relate to one another and help one another? Is the leadership of the church's total program unified and harmonious? Are there "churches within the church"? Are there too many overlappings and duplications of activities and functions? Do all the organizations live, minister, develop, function, and serve in the light of the overall mission of the church? Is there any general group coordinating the entire church life? Is too much power vested in a few?

2. Study the administrative facilities of the church. Is there adequate equipment, for example, duplicators, typewriters, computers, etc.? Does the pastor do an unfair amount of this work? Could the load be shared by others? Are good records kept? Are they used and found helpful to a better church life? Is the latest technology utilized as much as possible?

3. Is there a need for new paid staff workers? What are the anticipated needs in the future? Are plans now being laid?

4. Study and evaluate the promotional and publicity plans of the church. Are the monies used wisely and effectively? Do these plans "grab" people in their interests, that is, do they truly communicate?

IV. Surveying the Church Leadership

In surveying the church leaders be sure to maintain a spirit of understanding and patience; people are often sensitive here.

Interviewing the Pastor

How does the minister see his role? How does he face the problem of getting new programs started in the church? How does he cope with the problems of relationships with staff and church members? How does he feel about the need of church administration? How does he feel about the evangelistic enterprise? Is he biblically oriented? What does the pastor consider his primary function in the life of the church? Does he preach in a communicative way? Is he able to fulfill that role? If not, why not? What plan does he have to find time for leisure and for his family? What would he like to see changed in the church? Does he continue to grow in mind and spirit and how? Is he "growth oriented"? Does he have a vision—with practical approaches—to growth and development?

Interviewing the Official Body (Deacons, Stewards, Elders, etc.)

How do they see their role? What do they consider to be their relationship to the pastor and church? What are their particular problems? What do they feel hinders the life and effectiveness of the church? Are their attitudes in line with the New Testament? Are they "servant minded"? Do they look "outward" (to the world) or "inward" (to their own needs)? Are they "growth oriented"?

Interviewing the Church Lay Leaders

What do they feel is their role in the life of the church? Do they feel they were properly enlisted? Do they feel they are receiving proper training for their various tasks? Do they feel overworked with too many responsibilities?

It is well to interview at random a few representative lay members (such as a young person, an old person, and even children) to get something of the reaction of the average person who attends but takes no active part in leadership. Do they feel everything is done by the few? Is it so? Do they feel like mere spectators? What would they like changed? Are there ample opportunities for developing and utilizing their spiritual gifts of ministry? This is vital! Are they growing in biblical knowledge and in their relationship to Christ?

Summary and Suggestions

Much more needs to be done, but it is obvious that the purpose of such an extensive survey is the assessment of the total church life and its impact on the world with a view to growth and Kingdom extension. A *world vision* is vital.

All of the organizations will have to be looked at in depth and evaluated to that end. Perhaps an analogy could be found in an extensive physical examination that a doctor would carry out on a patient for the purpose of diagnosing ills so that the proper remedy may be found. This undertaking must be the work of several. Perhaps a group of the key leaders in the church would be the logical ones to do the work. As already emphasized, it must be done on biblical principles with objectivity, honesty, bravery, and above all, in the spirit of helpfulness, understanding, and love. Much discussion and prayer must go into venture. The whole idea is for a local church to understand itself in the light of the great mission of the church and to attempt to bring itself and all its activities in line with that mission on the basis of total lay involvement, serving on the principle of exercising their spiritual gifts. The goal is to reach every lost person for Christ.

Moreover, such a survey must not be just put on paper and laid to rest. *It should form a working plan to change and update the whole ministry life of the church.* This is the positive outcome of the survey. There are, by way of summary, four exercises that appear vital to a growing, evangelizing church:
1. Immerse God's people in the Word of God. Expository preaching, quality Bible teaching, memorization, training, etc., are essential.
2. Develop a viable and vital prayer ministry that can involve all the people.
3. Institute a program of lay training in evangelism and discipleship.
4. Experiment with "church growth" methods until you find what will work where you are.

Pastors and leaders should deeply devote themselves to implement these principles. Do not be deterred. Set these priorities constantly before the church.

Much education and promotion on the new plans and programs are called for. Moreover, it is an on-going, constant updating plan. Such a work must constantly go on. In the end, however, it would be hoped that God's Spirit will so lead in the matter that His blessings will result in a far more effective ministry for the church with many more thus won to Christ, Christians deepened, and God's kingdom furthered. As stated, the church survey must also be more than a mere diagnostic exercise; the church must build a great new program to meet total needs of people to the glory of God. The rewards are well worth the extensive effort.

Appendix D
Evangelical Affirmations[1]

Evangelical Christianity is engaged in a broad conflict on many fronts. Internally, it is struggling over moral improprieties, doctrinal lapses, and problems of self-identity. Externally, it is carrying on a lingering battle with liberal Christianity and seeking to plug leaks in its doctrinal structure that still come from that source. Moreover, new pressures are rising from the occult and from various syncretistic movements combining elements of paganism, Islam, Buddhism or other historic religions with Christianity. In Western Europe and North America (and increasingly in other parts of the world as well), modern secularism has become a major foe of evangelical Christianity.

Each of these religious movements presents its own conception of reality, and all differ from evangelical faith in doctrines that lie at the very core of biblical Christianity.

Modern secularism sees the world without God; or if it formally acknowledges the existence of some ill-defined "god," it squeezes God and all religion to the periphery of life. Either way, a theoretical atheism or a practical, functioning atheism views the universe as controlled merely by natural or human forces. Logically, the exclusion of God from the universe rules out the very possibility of miracle in any biblical sense and yields a worldview without incarnation, resurrection, and judgment. Unfortunately, it is possible to give lip allegiance to theistic or even Christian beliefs while choosing to live practically as though God does not exist.

By contrast, historic Christianity has always affirmed that God lives and acts in this world. Evangelical faith insists on the reality of divine action in creation, providence, revelation, and redemption. History is not a mindless process, but the unfolding events through which the Triune God works out His purposes in the universe. The God and Father of our Lord Jesus Christ, and the God of the Bible, is the sovereign Lord who controls the destiny of the nations and guides the intimate details of personal life. The hairs of our head are numbered, and God sees every sparrow that falls.

Both the existence and the nature of God, therefore, are fundamental questions. For atheism, whether it be theoretical or practical, the issue is settled negatively in advance: the supernatural intervening God who worked miracles, revealed Himself in Jesus Christ and the Bible, and is now active in and important to our daily lives, is impossible.

World religions and modern occultic concepts of reality introduce a strange and exotic dimension to this spiritual warfare. New manifestations of spiritism, Satanism, demonology, the New Age movement, various syncretistic cults, and other developments have set a much larger and more complicated agenda for evangelical witness.

Conflicts have sometimes escalated into cataclysmic confrontations between belief and unbelief and between good and evil. Such confrontations have increased in intensity due to a resurgent evangelicalism, now variously estimated to number between 30 million adherents (*Christianity Today* poll) and 66 million adherents (Gallup's poll) in the United States and 500 million worldwide (according to David Barret).

Neither evangelicalism nor its conflicts, both internal and external conflicts, are new in the history of Christianity. Evangelical faith has deep roots in the history of mainstream churches. It did not suddenly rise from eighteenth and nineteenth-century revivals. It can be traced back through the Reformation and the ancient church to find its base in New Testament Christianity.

Recently, however, some have declared that several evangelical doctrines are theologically innovative and do not represent the central traditions of the Christian church. Other observers have asked if the evangelical movement has become so fragmented theologically that it no longer has a coherent self-identity. In another vein, the moral failure of a number of prominent Evangelicals has been all too apparent. We are shamed by our inconsistencies in living out the ethical values we profess, and we recognize the need to confess our sins before God.

In the last decade of the twentieth century, a number of these troubling issues have come into sharper focus. We realize that our own house is not entirely in order. Many of our worst problems we have brought on ourselves. Not only on the outside, but even within our own ranks, some confusion exists as to exactly who are Evangelicals.

Evangelical Affirmations/89 seeks to clarify the character of the evangelical movement and to affirm certain truths critical to the advancement of the church of Christ. As we do so, we sadly confess that our own sinful failures have often discredited our proclamation of those great biblical truths. For our sinful lapses into sexual misconduct, neglect of the poor, lack of accountability on the part of our leaders, and self-seeking divisiveness, we repent before God and our neighbors.

The following affirmations do not constitute a complete doctrinal statement or a comprehensive confession of faith. Rather, they represent evangelical truths that specially need to be asserted and clarified in our day. We address these affirmations primarily to our fellow Evangelicals who, though confessing their personal commitment to these doctrines, have sometimes raised questions as to their importance and as to how essential they are to an authentic evangelical faith. Only secondarily have we addressed these affirmations to non-Evangelicals. In this latter case we are concerned to clarify differences between Evangelicals and non-Evangelicals within the Christian churches. We also wish to remove some of the caricatures of evangelicalism the general public often holds and to state what Evangelicals really believe on issues growing out of the interaction of Evangelicals with modern culture.

1. Jesus Christ and the Gospel

We affirm the good news that the Son of God became man to offer Himself for sinners and to give them everlasting life.

We affirm that Jesus Christ is fully God and fully man with two distinct natures united in one person. The incarnation, substitutionary death and bodily resurrection of Jesus Christ are essential to the gospel. Through these events a gracious God has acted in time and history to reach out to humanity and save all who believe in Him.

Without Christ and the biblical gospel, sinful humanity is without salvation and is left to create its own "gospels." These "gospels" take various forms, and many are set forth by so-called "Christian" sects that omit the heart of the biblical gospel. Any "gospel" without the Christ of the Bible cannot be the saving gospel, and leaves sinners estranged from God and under His wrath.

We affirm that the people of God are commanded to witness to the world concerning God's offer of redemption in Christ. The gospel, working by the Holy Spirit, is powerful to transform the lives of individuals lost in sin, provides believers with meaning for life on this earth, empowers the church to accomplish Christ's work in the world, serves as a leavening influence in society, and sustains the faithful in hope for the life to come.

2. Creation and Fall

We affirm that the Triune God created heaven and earth, and made human beings, both male and female, in His own image. In His providence God upholds all things and reveals Himself through creation and history.

Because of Adam's fall, all became sinners and stand under God's righteous judgment. Human rebellion against God shows itself today in many ways: such as in atheistic denials of God's existence, in functional atheism that concedes God's existence but denies His relevance to personal conduct, in oppression of the poor and helpless, in occult concepts of reality, in the abuse of earth's resources, in theories of an accidental naturalistic evolutionary origin of the universe and human life, and in many other ways.

As a result of the fall of the race into sin, human beings must be born again to new life in Christ. They can be pardoned and redeemed by faith in Christ alone.

3. God as Source and Ground of Truth

We affirm that God the Creator is the source of truth and the ground of the unity of all truth. By revelation God makes known the truth concerning Himself, the world, human sin, and redemption. God's revelation addresses the whole person—intellect, will, and emotion. The Holy Spirit accompanies His Word in convicting, instructing, nurturing, and empowering His people so they learn to live in fellowship with God and other persons in accordance with scriptural directives.

We reject irrationalistic theologies and philosophies that compromise or deny objective truth. We also reject rationalistic alternatives based on autonomous human reason.

We recognize that as finite and sinful creatures we do not have complete knowledge of God, and that "now we know in part." We rejoice, nonetheless, that God reveals Himself in creation and the Bible.

We encourage Christian churches and Christian schools to develop and implement disciplined instruction that relates the mind of Christ to all knowledge, that emphasizes the compatibility of scientific inquiry with biblical teachings about nature, and that challenges believers to understand and apply a Christian view of the world to all of life.

4. Holy Scripture

We affirm the complete truthfulness and the full and final authority of the Old and New Testament Scriptures as the Word of God written. The appropriate response to it is humble assent and obedience.

The Word of God becomes effective by the power of the Holy Spirit working in and through it. Through the Scriptures the Holy Spirit creates faith and provides a sufficient doctrinal and moral guide for the church. Just as God's self-giving love to us in the gospel provides the supreme motive for the Christian life, so the teaching of Holy Scripture informs us of what are truly acts of love.

Attempts to limit the truthfulness of inspired Scripture to "faith and practice," viewed as less than the whole of Scripture, or worse, to assert that it errs in such matters as history or the world of nature, depart not only from the Bible's representation of its own veracity, but also from the central tradition of the Christian churches.

The meaning of Scripture must neither be divorced from its words nor dictated by reader response. The inspired author's intention is essential to our understanding of the text.

No Scripture must be interpreted in isolation from other passages of Scripture. All Scripture is true and profitable, but Scripture must be interpreted by Scripture. The truth of any single passage must be understood in light of the truth of all passages of Scripture. Our Lord has been pleased to give us the whole corpus of Scripture to instruct and guide His church.

5. The Church

We affirm that the church is a worshiping and witnessing community of Christians who profess faith in Christ and submit to His authority. Christ is building His church where His Word is preached and His name confessed. He sustains His church by the power of the Holy Spirit.

We affirm that the church is to provide for corporate worship on the part of believers, the instruction of the faithful in the Word of God and its application, and the fellowship, comfort, exhortation, rebuke, and sharing in the needs of the entire body of Christ. In a day of lax doctrine and even more lax discipline, we specially affirm that Scripture requires the defense of sound doctrine, the practice of church discipline, and a call for renewal.

We affirm the mission of the church to be, primarily, that of evangelism of the lost through witness to the gospel by life and by word; and secondarily, to be salt and light to the whole world as we seek to alleviate the burdens and injustices of a suffering world. Though some are specially called to one ministry or another, no believer is exonerated from the duty of bearing witness to the gospel or of providing help to those in need.

We distance ourselves from any movement that seeks to establish a world church on the premise of a religious pluralism that denies normative Christian doctrines. Rather we encourage efforts that help believers and faithful churches move toward fellowship and unity with one another in the name of Christ, the Lord of the church.

6. Doctrine and Practice

We affirm the critical need to conjoin faith and practice. To profess conversion without a genuine change of heart and life violates biblical teaching and substitutes dead orthodoxy for a living faith. Christian leaders bear a heavy responsibility to serve as spiritual role models and moral examples. Any disjunction between faith and practice generates hypocrisy.

We send forth an urgent call for the practice of holiness and righteousness. Justification by faith must issue in sanctification. By the power of the indwelling Holy Spirit, we are to deny such characteristics of a selfish nature as immorality, evil desire, and covetousness, to walk in righteousness and integrity, and to practice justice and love at all times. Purity of doctrine must be accompanied by purity of life.

7. Human Rights and Righteousness

We affirm that God commands us to seek justice in human affairs whether in the church or in society. In accord with the biblical call for righteousness, God's people should model justice in social relationships and should protest, confront, and strive to alleviate injustice. We must respond to the plight of the destitute, hungry, and homeless; of victims of political oppression and gender or race discrimination, including apartheid; and of all others deprived of rightful protection under the law. We confess our own persistent sin of racism, which ignores the divine image in humankind.

We affirm the integrity of marriage, the permanence of the wife-husband relationship, the importance of the family for the care and nourishment of children, and the primary responsibility of parents for the instruction of their children.

We affirm that Evangelicals living in democratic societies should be active in public affairs. We advocate a public philosophy that advances just government and protects the rights of all. In cooperation with like-minded persons, we should support and promote legislation reflecting consistent moral values. We condemn abortion-on-demand as a monstrous evil, deplore drug and alcohol abuse, and lament sexual hedonism, pornography, homosexual practices, and child abuse. We encourage Evangelicals to exercise responsible stewardship of their own personal wealth and the conservation of the earth's resources.

8. Religious Liberty

We affirm the duty of state and society to provide religious liberty as a basic human right. We deplore any oppression to maintain or elicit religious commitments. We hold that civil government should not arbitrate spiritual differences, and that neither church nor mosque nor temple nor synagogue should use political power to enforce its own sectarian doctrines or practices. We do not consider laws to protect individual rights, such as the right to life or the freedom of anyone to confess his or her faith openly in society, to be a sectarian position.

9. Second Coming and Judgment

We affirm that Christ will return in power and glory to bring full and eternal salvation to His people and to judge the world. This prospect of the Lord's return to vindicate His holiness and subjugate all evil should accelerate our witness and mission in the world.

We affirm that only through the work of Christ can any person be saved and resurrected to live with God forever. Unbelievers will be separated eternally from God. Concern for evangelism should not be compromised by any illusion that all will be finally saved (universalism).

We affirm the preaching of ultimate hope in and through Christ. In an age of anxiety and despair, the blessed hope of God's ultimate victory is not only a warning of divine judgment, but a wonderful hope that gives light and meaning to the human heart.

Conclusion: Evangelical Identity

Evangelicals believe, first of all, the gospel as it is set forth in the Bible. The word *evangelical* is derived from the biblical term *euangelion* meaning "good news." It is the Good News that God became man in Jesus Christ to live and die and rise again from the dead in order to save us from our sin and all its consequences. The Savior's benefits and His salvation are bestowed upon us freely and graciously and are received through personal faith in Christ. They are not conditioned on our merit or personal goodness but are based wholly on the mercy of God.

Evangelicals are also to be identified by what is sometimes called the material or content principle of evangelicalism. They hold to all of the most basic doctrines of the Bible: for example, the triuneness of God the Father, God the Son, and God the Holy Spirit; the preexistence, incarnation, full deity and humanity of Christ united in one person; His sinless life, His authoritative teaching; His substitutionary atonement; His bodily resurrection from the dead, His second coming to judge the living and the dead; the necessity of holy living; the imperative of witnessing to others about the gospel; the necessity of a life of service to God and humankind; and the hope in a life to come. These doctrines emerge from the Bible and are summarized in the Apostles' Creed and the historic confessions of evangelical churches.

Evangelicals have a third distinguishing mark. In accordance with the teaching of their Lord they believe the Bible to be the final and authoritative source of all doctrine. This is often called the formative or forming principle of evangelicalism. Evangelicals hold the Bible to be God's Word and, therefore, completely true and trustworthy (and this is what we mean by the words *infallible* and *inerrant*). It is the authority by which they seek to guide their thoughts and their lives.

These then are the three distinguishing marks of all Evangelicals. Without constant fidelity to all three marks, Evangelicals will be unable to meet the demands of the future and interact effectively with the internal and external challenges noted in these affirmations.

Evangelical churches also hold various distinctive doctrines that are important to them; but, nonetheless, they share this common evangelical faith.

We offer these Affirmations[2] to God, to Christians everywhere, and to our world. In sincere repentance and sorrow, we remind ourselves of our own sins and failures, and we pray that God would renew us in confessing Christ as our Lord and Savior in all that we say and do.

Soli Deo Gloria

Notes

1. Taken from the book EVANGELICAL AFFIRMATIONS edited by Kenneth S. Kantzer and Carl F. Henry. Copyright 1990 by Trinity Evangelical Divinity School. Used by permission of the Zondervan Publishing House.

2. The consultation on Evangelical Affirmations co-sponsored by the National Association of Evangelicals and Trinity Evangelical Divinity School, May 14 to 17, 1989.

Index